Brahman and Dao

Studies in Comparative Philosophy and Religion

Series Editor: Douglas Allen, University of Maine

This series is based on the view that significant and creative future studies in philosophy and religious studies will be informed by comparative research. These studies emphasize aspects of contemporary and classical Asian philosophy and religion, and their relationship to Western thought. This series features works of specialized scholarship by new and upcoming scholars in Asia and the West, as well as works by more established scholars and books with a wider readership. The editor welcomes a wide variety of manuscript submissions, especially works exhibiting highly focused research and theoretical innovation.

Mysticism and Morality: A New Look at Old Questions, by Richard H. Jones
Gandhi's Experiments with Truth: Essential Writings by and about Mahatma Gandhi, edited by Richard L. Johnson
To Broaden the Way: A Confucian-Jewish Dialogue, by Galia Patt-Shamir
Comparative Philosophy and Religion in Times of Terror, by Douglas Allen
Pyrrhonism: How the Ancient Greeks Reinvented Buddhism, by Adrian Kuzminski
Ethics of Compassion: Bridging Ethical Theory and Religious Moral Discourse, by Richard Reilly
Reality, Religion, and Passion: Indian and Western Approaches in Hans-Georg Gadamer and Rūpa Gosvāmi, by Jessica Frazier
Brahman and Dao: Comparative Studies of Indian and Chinese Philosophy and Religion, edited by Ithamar Theodor and Zhihua Yao

Brahman and Dao

Comparative Studies of Indian and Chinese Philosophy and Religion

Edited by Ithamar Theodor and Zhihua Yao

LEXINGTON BOOKS
Lanham • Boulder • New York • Toronto • Plymouth, UK

Published by Lexington Books
A wholly owned subsidiary of Rowman & Littlefield
4501 Forbes Boulevard, Suite 200, Lanham, Maryland 20706
www.rowman.com

10 Thornbury Road, Plymouth PL6 7PP, United Kingdom

British Library Cataloguing in Publication Information Available

Library of Congress Cataloging-in-Publication Data

Brahman and Dao : comparative studies of Indian and Chinese philosophy and religion / Edited by Ithamar Theodor and Zhihua Yao.
pages cm. — (Studies in comparative philosophy and religion)
Includes bibliographical references and index.
ISBN 978-0-7391-7172-1 (cloth : alk. paper) — ISBN 978-0-7391-8814-9 (electronic) 1. Philosophy, Indic. 2. Philosophy, Chinese. 3. Philosophy, Comparative. 4. India—Religion. 5. China—Religion. I. Theodor, Ithamar, 1959– II. Yao, Zhihua, 1968–

B121.B73 2014
181'.11—dc23

2013032223

∞™ The paper used in this publication meets the minimum requirements of American National Standard for Information Sciences—Permanence of Paper for Printed Library Materials, ANSI/NISO Z39.48-1992.

Printed in the United States of America

For Darshan and Kalpa Bhagat,

Dear Friends and Supporters

Contents

Acknowledgments

It is with great pleasure that we wish to acknowledge and thank all those who have helped and supported the publication of this volume in various ways. Keith Knapp had encouraged us right from the earlier stages and helped to gather together the editorial team, and similarly Kwong-loi Shun was offering continuing support and advice throughout the process of preparing this volume. The Professorship in Indian Religions and Culture, Department of Cultural and Religious Studies at The Chinese University of Hong Kong supported the publication in various ways, and so did the Department of Asian Studies, University of Haifa. We wish to thank the colleagues at The Chinese University of Hong Kong for their ongoing encouragement, friendship, and support. We are grateful to Steven Mathews for the style editing, to Alex Cherniack for the Sanskrit language editing, and to Xiaohong Wang for the Chinese language editing. Josephine Ng and Kwok Fai Au-Yeung encouraged this work through their friendship, and special thanks go to our families who bore the weight of this publication. At last, we wish to thank Darshan and Kalpa Bhagat for their friendship and support which had enabled the publication of this volume; it is to them that this book is dedicated.

Ithamar Theodor and Zhihua Yao
The Chinese University of Hong Kong
May 24, 2013

Introduction

The ancient Greeks, Indians, and Chinese have distinct, unique, and rich philosophical and religious traditions, which have greatly contributed to human civilization. There are various studies comparing Greek and Indian philosophies and religions, laying out parallels and exploring possible historical contacts. There are similar works comparing Chinese and Western philosophy and religion. However, so far there is no systemic comparative study of Chinese and Indian philosophies and religions. Therefore there is a need to fill this gap.

Through the efforts of many generations of Indian Buddhist missionaries to China, such as the legendary Bodhidharma, and Chinese Buddhist pilgrims to India, such as Faxian and Xuanzang, there has been a long and rich history of Buddhist transmission to China. Despite this fact, the indigenous Indian and Chinese philosophical and religious traditions did not encounter each other, except through the medium of Buddhism. However, is this actually the case? Do we have much evidence for pre-Buddhist Sino-Indian cultural exchange? Stated even more radically, can we speak of a pre-Aryan Indo-Chinese cultural continuum? What would these comparative studies lead to? Are these possible parallels simply coincidental similarities or a result of historical diffusion? Before we can address these challenging issues, we need to undertake a phenomenological study describing the similarities and differences as found between Indian and Chinese philosophy and religion. The scholarly essays in this volume are meant to make such an attempt. It is hoped that this can be a basis for further works that would take the

Indo-Chinese discourse a step forward, toward the gradual articulation of a unifying Indo-Chinese historical and cultural theory.

This book not only looks into the past, but also into the future. The twenty-first century is becoming "the Asian century"; as such it is characterized by the rise of Asia, specifically China and India. Naturally, this rise is not only economical and political, but also cultural and philosophical. This may possibly lead to the articulation of multicultural philosophies that absorb Indian and Chinese ideas, whilst intertwining them in new ways with other ideas. As befitting a global era, these new philosophies will aspire to be multicultural, multireligious, environmentally friendly, and further some general aspects of spirituality. As such it may be worth examining some ideas and themes these two great cultures share. The present book looks into four such themes: 1) metaphysics and soteriology, 2) ethics, 3) body, health, and spirituality, and 4) language and culture.

The first section of the book looks into metaphysics and soteriology. It is generally agreed that Indian and Chinese philosophies were developed within a framework of soteriology or practical wisdom, which has been loosely labeled as "religion." But how do the metaphysical discourses interact with their soteriological frameworks? Four essays in this section look into the subtlety of this relationship. Through careful comparison between the cosmogonies as presented in the newly excavated text *Taiyi sheng shui* and some hymns of the *Ṛgveda* Book X, especially X.129, one finds that they developed from similar mythological motifs of the primeval water and the pole star. Both texts share a tendency of demystifying or rationalizing this myth by proposing a philosophical or naturalized account of cosmogony. However, given the differences in the practical or soteriological usage underlining these texts, their philosophized cosmogonies have very different features. In the history of Indian and Chinese cultures it is found that similar religio-spiritual and philosophical developments have taken place around the so-called "Axial Era." The discovery of "spirit" or "Brahman" behind natural phenomena prepared the ground for the philosophy of a spiritual essence underlying the physical world. This is evident in some major Daoist writings in China and in some principal Upaniṣads in India also. How can we know this spiritual reality? The Advaita Vedānta and Neo-Confucian thinkers promoted a path of intellectual/spiritual realization characterized by both ineffability and rationality. On the one hand, ultimate knowledge is unreachable through intellectual speculation; it implies mystical directness that has to be accompanied by silence. On the other hand, the intellectual preparation of the aspirants by means of reading Hindu and Confucian scriptures was considered as necessary. Both traditions emphasized the importance of scriptures in the process of attaining ultimate knowledge. However, Advaitic and Confucian philosophical systems differed in their perceptions of selfhood and in their premises regarding the nature of reality. A similar contrast is found in the concept of the five aggregates in Buddhism and in Twofold Mystery Daoism. In its original Buddhist context, the concept of the temporary coming together of the five aggregates served as an explanation of the insubstantiality of self. Insight into this insubstantiality of self should bring release from suffering and liberation as cessation. Daoism co-opted the concept; yet in a different soteriological framework, changed its function. With the goal of immortality in mind, Daoists sought to retrace the steps of "becoming," back to the origin of all being, Dao. The concept of five aggregates offered a new explanation of this process of "becoming"; its details made it retraceable and thus an instruction for the way to immortality. Thus the function of this concept in the soteriological frameworks of Buddhism and Daoism underscores a major difference in philosophical outlook and soteriology: impermanence versus immortality.

The section concerned with ethics takes as its point of departure or perhaps its axis the *junzi*, the superior person or the gentleman who has his Indian equivalent in the dharmic person or the person in *sattva guṇa*. They undergo self-cultivation in order to transform themselves into ideal moral persons with ideal moral qualities. Both are acting within a larger set of social rules, and exercise rationality, empiricism, and reason judging what is right and proper in these given set of rules, *dharma* and *li*. This constant endeavor for refining one's actions and finding that which is appropriate under the circumstance (*yi*) is performed in relation to an external system of rules that is divinely inspired, as *li* represents heaven (*tian*), similar to *dharma* that is established by the divine descending to earth. However, the moral path is not only external rather it represents an inner law or the innate characteristics of the individual; this is designated as *svabhāva* defined by one's constitution of *prakṛti* or *xing*. The Confucian concept of *yi* acts as a personal appropriation of the norms of *li*, just like the *sattva guṇa* that appropriates the norms of *dharma* under the changing circumstances. The agents' attitude in paving the path of action determines their degree of spirituality, or to what extent their actions represent the Dao or *sattva*. As such, it is not only performing one's duties, rather it is the performance of duties for the right reasons and in the right state of mind. The metaphysical relations between both systems, Indian and Chinese, are even more far reaching. Similar to the Dao which balances the constant changing influences of *yin* and *yang*, the *sattva guṇa* balances the constant influence of *tamas* and *rajas*, thus paving the path of morality and spirituality for the dharmic person. The term *ren* that seems to connect Hinduism and Confucianism in a deep way, is also closely related to Indian Buddhism's sense of compassion (*karuṇā*). However, despite the similarities highlighted in the feeling of compassion for the suffering of others, it is apparent that the larger metaphysical framework is different; whereas Confucianism is humanistic and highlights family values such as caring for one's parents, Indian Buddhism highlights the forest or renouncer's tradition, in which the feeling of compassion is aimed at those who lack true wisdom and are thus entangled in family life. As such for Mencius, the feeling of compassion refers not only to concern for the suffering of others in general, but also to familial affection; affectionate feeling for one's parents begins early in life, and eventually is developed into full-fledged virtue. As opposed to that, the Buddha saw family life as an obstacle to that of the enlightened person, and taught that his students should leave their homes first if they wanted to embark on the path of compassionate life, as it is not easy, while living in a home, to lead the holy life utterly perfect and pure. The section ends with an epistemological discussion looking into the nature of moral knowledge in Confucianism and the Hindu school of Advaita Vedānta, arguing that the Confucian conception of moral knowledge is similar to the spiritual or liberating knowledge, which includes moral knowledge in the Advaita Vedānta tradition: they both represent knowledge that not merely informs but also transforms its possessors; as such this kind of knowledge represents both belief and desire, which are not two separate mental states, but rather form a single mental state of "besire." This category is unique in that it combines the dimensions of ontology and ethics. By arguing that this category is represented in at least two major schools of Indian and Chinese thought, the chapter opens the gate, so to speak, to consider characterizing Asian thought in a new way, or by articulating a specific Asian category that may be different than its Western counterparts.

Perhaps the unifying theme of the third section is the identification of health with spirituality, or the notion that a balanced bodily state represents a spiritual state or at least a point of departure for spirituality. The Yogic view of the body is dualistic, that is, considering the body to represent a combination of *prakṛti* and *puruṣa*. *Prakṛti* is composed of the three *guṇa*s whereas the *puruṣa* is of an entirely different nature. The working of the *guṇa*s manifests through the five gross elements and the three subtle ones. The Daoist understanding is somewhat similar in that the body represents an ongoing flux and interchange of *yin* and *yang* manifested through the five elements, although these elements slightly differ from the five Indian elements. According to the Yogic view, the healthy human body is said to have an appropriate mixture and right amount of the *doṣa*s and this sustains the physical vitality, adaptability, and immunity. On the contrary, the unhealthy person is said to "under-produce" or "over-produce" a certain *doṣa*, thus an impropriate mixture of the three *doṣa*s is generated. According the Daoist view, the notion of health is referred to as a state of dynamic balance, and as such the healthy person was called "man of balance." Stated differently, the body pervaded by the Dao represents both spirituality and health. As such, both systems, Yoga and Daoyin, aspire to bring the body into a harmonious spiritual state; the Yoga school considers this state to represent the *sattva guṇa* whereas the Daoist school considers this to represent the Dao. Daoyin practice, as much as other forms of Daoist body cultivation, aims at creating perfect harmony among these various forces and patterns, which guarantees health and long life. Yogic practice considers the lower *guṇa*s of *rajas* and *tamas* as obstacles to be overcome in order to reach the highest goal that is the separation of the *puruṣa* from *prakṛti*. The sattvic state, in which the body is balanced, healthy, and under mental and physical control represents the required point of departure for this separation to take place. Despite the central role that the negative view of the body plays in many Buddhist teachings, longevity and freedom from disease are ideals that are mentioned frequently in Buddhist scriptures as the body is important as a vehicle for Buddhist practice, and correct practice can extend longevity and prevent or treat the arising of disease.

The last section explores issues of language and culture. The arrival of Buddhism to China at the beginning of the Common Era generated a cultural confluence which not only united India and China in some significant ways, but furthered cultural innovations which were to influence and shape Asian culture in centuries to come. Buddhism adhered to an egalitarian ethos according to which the message of the Buddha was to be transmitted through the various local languages other than Sanskrit or Pali. The translators of Buddhist scriptures and culture had to invent and introduce many new words and terms in order to express the highly sophisticated Buddhist concepts. Due to this, new words and concepts have been gradually articulated and rhyme dictionaries compiled. Despite the translation of Buddhism into Chinese, Chinese people were fascinated by the Sanskrit language and its alphabet known as *siddhaṃ*. Through the study of the Sanskrit alphabet, the Chinese gained not only a general knowledge of phonetics, but also developed phonetic theories of the Chinese language. The Chinese took these phonetic and orthographic exercises very seriously, and this became an integral part of the traditional Sanskrit studies in East Asia. For centuries the Chinese tried to unpack all these meanings associated with the Sanskrit alphabet. In the course of their inquiry, some very surprising ideas about the Sanskrit alphabet and even the Sanskrit language emerged, becoming eventually part of the collective Chinese conception of the supernatural and the spiritual. Another related topic is *geyi*, a technique for rendering Buddhist terms into Chinese. While obviously a means for bridging Indian and Chinese cultures, much about *geyi* remains unclear. *Geyi* exemplifies the problems that arise when interpreting across cultural, historical, and religious boundaries.

In the context of culture the final two chapters single out two aspects: playfulness and non-dichotomy. The notion of play is a pivotal concept in the Daoist classic *Zhuangzi* and in the Gauḍīya Vaiṣṇava devotional tradition of India. The Sanskrit term *līlā* denotes play in the spiritual sense and play in the sense of game. In both traditions, play and experience of play have the following features: naturalness, transformative aspect, risky nature, freedom that it offers, being lost within it, its effortlessness, and its self-representative nature. As such, play embodies an irrational nature, suggesting that humans are more than rational creatures. It connects humans to the cosmic while simultaneously subsuming and transcending wisdom and folly. The Daoists and Hindus hold remarkably similar positions on the phenomenon of play, despite very different philosophical presuppositions about the nature of reality. The idea of non-duality (*advaita*) appears to shed light on the thoughts of two major modern intellectuals, Rabindranath Tagore and Qian Mu, both of whom assume a non-dichotomous approach as representing Indian and Chinese thought, while assigning a dichotomous approach to the West. Both thinkers associated the West with the pursuit of wealth, power, dependence on replacements, and the loss of internal moral guidance. India and China, however, were associated with authentic living, spirituality, and moral values, with both thinkers sharing an optimistic attitude with regard to the future of their own cultures.

I

METAPHYSICS AND SOTERIOLOGY

1

One, Water, and Cosmogony

Reflections on the Ṛgveda X.129 and the Taiyi sheng shui

Zhihua Yao

In recent decades, a series of previously unknown classical Chinese philosophical texts were found. They are dated from around the fourth century BCE and greatly enrich our understanding of Confucianism, Daoism, and other Chinese philosophical schools in their formative stages. These texts present some challenging issues with regard to the origin and nature of this intellectual corpus and its relationship with the received classics. One of the texts that attracted much attention since its discovery is the *Taiyi sheng shui* 太一生水 (hereafter TYSS). It is a short text that presents a rather sophisticated scheme of cosmogony that is not seen in the received Daoist or Confucian classics.

In the current chapter I attempt to analyze this cosmogony by comparing it with some hymns on cosmogony in the *Ṛgveda* Book X, especially X.129 (hereafter ṚV X.129). Through careful comparison between these two short but sophisticated texts I will conclude that they developed from similar mythological motifs of the primeval water and the pole star, and that they share a tendency of demystifying or rationalizing this myth by proposing a philosophical or naturalized account of cosmogony. However, given the enormous differences in Indian and Chinese culture, their philosophized cosmogonies have very different features. In ṚV X.129, we find a strong background of yogic practice, which adds to the dimensions of skepticism and epistemology to Vedic cosmogony. In contrast, we sense a strong background of divinatory practice in TYSS. This adds to the dimensions of purely calculative naturalism and ethical guidance that is found in Chinese cosmogony.

ONE AND WATER

The very beginning of TYSS presents a rather clear picture of cosmogony with a set of philosophical categories. These categories play important roles in the subsequent development of Chinese philosophy. It therein says:

> Grand One (*taiyi* 太一) gave birth to water. Water returned and assisted Grand One, thereby forming Heaven. Heaven returned and assisted Grand One, thereby forming Earth. Heaven and Earth [repeatedly assisted each other], thereby forming the numinous (*shen* 神) and the luminous (*ming* 明). The numinous and the luminous repeatedly assisted each other, thereby forming *yin* and *yang*. *Yin* and *yang* repeatedly assisted each other, thereby forming four seasons. Four seasons repeatedly assisted each other, thereby forming cold and hot. Cold and hot repeatedly assisted each other, thereby forming moist and dry. Moist and dry repeatedly assisted each other, forming the year, and the process came to an end.[1]

To better understand this passage we can draw a table to indicate the three different stages of the cosmogonical process and its key elements:

Primeval elements:	Grand One, water
Spatial elements:	Heaven, Earth
	the numinous, the luminous
	yin, yang
Temporal elements:	four seasons
	cold, hot
	moist, dry
	the year

Firstly, we have two primeval elements: Grand One and water. Although the text suggests that in the beginning Grand One was the only primeval element in the sense that it "gave birth to water," later in the text it says that "Grand One stored in water and moved with the seasons."[2] This suggests that water is more primeval than Grand One. The exact relationship between the two elements will be the main topic of the latter part of the chapter, but for now we treat both as primeval elements. We then have a group of spatial elements: Heaven and Earth, *yin* and *yang*, the numinous and the luminous, which, as I will argue later, refer to the moon and the sun respectively. Being the feminine and masculine principles, *yin* and *yang* can be borderline cases, because they connect the spatial elements with the temporal ones, with the temporal elements being closely related to each other. Among them, cold, hot, moist, and dry indicate the climates of the four seasons of winter, summer, spring, and autumn respectively. Collectively they form the yearly cycle.

We can apply Kuiper's (1970) distinction of the two stages of Vedic cosmogony to this Chinese cosmogony. The primeval elements of Grand One and water correspond to the first stage of the primordial state in Vedic cosmogony, while the spatial and temporal elements roughly correspond to the second stage of creation in Vedic cosmogony. We will primarily focus our discussion on the first stage of the primordial state. According to Holdrege (1996, 35), the following elements or creative principles are characteristic in the primordial state in various versions of Vedic cosmogony:

1. The unmanifest Absolute, which is the ultimate source of creation: That One (*tad ekam*) in ṚV X.129 and the unborn (*aja*) in ṚV X.82;
2. The personal creator god, who is the fashioner of the three worlds—earth, mid-regions, and heaven: Prajāpati in ṚV X.121, Viśvakarman in ṚV X.81 and X.82;
3. Water (*ap, ambhas, salila*), which serves as the primordial matrix of creation (ṚV X.129, X.121, X.82) and which is at times associated with Vāc, the goddess of speech (ṚV X.125, X.71);
4. The cosmic embryo or egg (*garbha*), which contains the totality of creation in yet an undifferentiated form (ṚV X.121, X.82);
5. Puruṣa, the cosmic Man out of whose body the different parts of the universe are formed (ṚV X.90, X.130).

Both primeval elements, Grand One and water, in TYSS are found among these creative principles of Vedic cosmogony. And interestingly, they appear together in only one hymn, the famous Nāsadīya Hymn of ṚV X.129. Attributed to the Vedic philosopher Parameṣṭhin, this hymn is one of the most important philosophical texts that mark the dawn of Indian philosophy. It reveals the primordial state of the world with a unique tone of philosophical inquiry:

> The nonexistent did not exist, nor did the existent
> exist at that time.
> There existed neither the midspace nor the heaven beyond.
> What moved (*āvarīvar*)? From where and in whose protection?
> Did water exist, a deep depth?
>
> Mortal did not exist nor immortal then.
> There existed no distinction of night nor of day.
> That One breathed without wind through its inherent force.
> There existed nothing else beyond that.

Darkness existed, hidden by darkness, in the beginning
All this was an undistinguished ocean (*salila*).
When the thing coming into being was concealed by voidness (*tuchya*)
then was That One born by the power of heat (*tapas*).[3]

These verses depict a primordial state in which there is no distinction of existent and nonexistent, heaven and midspace, mortal and immortal, day and night. Such a search for a beginning beyond existents and nonexistents can also be found from the Daoist philosopher Zhuangzi, who says: "There was a beginning. There was a not yet beginning to be a beginning. There was a not yet beginning to be a not yet beginning to be a beginning. There was the existent; there had been the nonexistent. There was a not yet beginning to be nonexistent. There was a not yet beginning to be a not yet beginning to be nonexistent. If suddenly there was the nonexistent, we do not know, when it came to the nonexistent, whether it was really anything existing, or really not existing."[4] Zhuangzi does not characterize the primordial state before "suddenly there was the nonexistent" in positive terms. In contrast, Parameṣṭhin presents a positive picture of the primordial state.

First there was an undistinguished ocean (*salila*) or a deep water (*ambhas*). There was also "That One," which strikingly parallels with Grand One in TYSS. At first sight, both terms indicate an abstract philosophical principle. But as I will discuss later, Grand One (*taiyi*) is much more complicated than the monistic Absolute One. So is That One, because it breathed, although windlessly. It sounds more like a living entity than an abstract Absolute. Beyond water and That One, we are told, all were hidden by darkness and concealed by voidness. Neither darkness nor voidness is mentioned in TYSS, but as we will see later, darkness is a correlative element of water and One in the Chinese cosmograph. In TYSS, Grand One stored in water, meanwhile it gave birth to water.[5] Now in ṚV X.129, That One could possibly store in water, but it did not give birth to water. Instead, it was born by the power of heat (*tapas*).

Elsewhere in the *Ṛgveda* X, That One is not mentioned. Instead it is frequently represented by the image of the cosmic egg that floats on the surface of the waters (ṚV X.82, 121), or by a personalized creator Prajāpati ("lord of created beings," ṚV X.121) or Viśvakarman ("maker of all," ṚV X.81, 82). So the first four creative principles in the *Ṛgveda* listed above can be summarized into two: water and creator. The fifth creative principle cosmic man seems not to be related to either of them and should be treated as a separate tradition.[6]

In the creation myths of many other cultures, we find water with or without creator(s) is depicted as the primordial state of the world. In Egyptian mythology, *nu* is water or celestial water, and it is the primordial state covered by darkness: "In the beginning there existed neither heaven nor earth, and nothing existed except the boundless mass of primeval water which was shrouded in darkness, and which contained within itself the germs and beginnings, male and female, of everything which was to be in the future world. The divine primeval spirit, which formed an essential part of the primeval matter, felt within itself the desire to begin the work of Creation . . ." (Van Over 1980, 278). In Babylonian mythology, the beginning of the world is described as follows: "Long since, when above the heaven had not been named, when the earth beneath still bore no name, when the ocean (*apsu*), the primeval, the generator of them, and the originator Tiamat, who brought forth them both—their waters were mingled together" (Van Over 1980, 175). Here Apsu and Tiamat are god and goddess of water, and they are both responsible for the creation of the heaven and the earth.

The familiar passage of the Genesis 1:1–2 describes the beginning of the world vividly: "In the beginning God created the heavens and the earth. Now the earth was formless and empty, darkness was over the surface of the deep, and the Spirit of God was hovering over the waters" (New International Version of the Bible). This Judeo-Christian myth shows striking similarities to ṚV X.129 and mentions all the key elements of the primordial state: water, creator and its spirit, darkness and voidness. A group of creation myths from the Native American tribes such as Diegueno, Eskimo, Garos, Huron, Hopi, and Maidu depict water as the primordial state of the world (see Van Over 1980, 67, 85, 61, 48, 68, 63). The Hopi myth mentions two goddesses dwelling in the water: "In the beginning there was nothing but water everywhere, and two goddesses, both named Huruing Wuhti, lived in houses in the ocean, one of them in the east, and the other in the west" (Van Over 1980, 63). Similarly, an African myth and a Siberian-Altaic myth describe the beginning of the world as water (Van Over 1980, 221, 128).

The *Hne wo te yy*, a collection of myths of the Yi people in Southwest China, describes the beginning of cosmos in this way: "Water derived from Chaos; this was One. Muddy waters became full; this was Two. The waters turned into golden color; this was Three."[7] This myth is interesting in that it agrees with TYSS and ṚV X.129 in depicting the primordial state as water and One. Meanwhile, its three-staged creation process is similar to what we see in Laozi's *Daodejing*, Chapter 42: "Dao gave birth to One; One gave birth to Two; Two gave birth to Three; Three gave birth to the myriad things."[8]

THE POLE STAR AND ASTROLOGY

If we understand "Grand One" in TYSS or "That One" in ṚV X.129 along the lines of these creation myths, both of them could be identified with a personal creator. But the actual situation is more complicated than this. As we will see in the latter verses of ṚV X.129, That One is closely related to mind (*manas*), while Grand One is much more subtle than a personal god. One way to understand Grand One or *taiyi* is indeed to associate it with a personal god, as it is said in the *Heguanzi*: "The center is the position of Grand One; the hundred spirits look up to it and are controlled by it."[9] Starting from Emperor Wu's reign (140–87 BCE) in the Han dynasty, the worship of Grand One or Taiyi as the chief god was officially promoted and remained important in the early Han state religion. This central deity was actually a personification of the pole star that is located in the center of the sky. Sima Qian informed us in his "Treatise on the Heavenly Offices" in the *Shiji*: "The brightest star of the pole star asterism in the Central Palace is the constant abode of Grand One."[10] Besides referring to the pole star and its spirit, Grand One seemed to more often refer to its literal meaning of "grand" (*tai/da* 太/大) or "one" (*yi* 一), both of which are interchangeable with the central philosophical concept Dao, designating the abstract cosmic principle. I will just give one example from the Liyun chapter of the *Book of Rites*: "Thus, the rites are always rooted in Grand One. Separating, it made Heaven and Earth; revolving, it made *yin* and *yang*; changing, it made four seasons; ordering, it made ghosts and spirits."[11]

Textual sources for the latter usage, for example, the *Book of Rites*, the *Zhuangzi*, and the *Lüshi Chunqiu*, are generally dated earlier. This fact leads Qian (1932) to conclude that Grand One was a philosophical concept that was not identified with the astral body of the pole star, the cult devoted to its god and various associated astrological methods until the Han dynasty. Based on some recent archaeological findings Li (1995–1996), however, argues that Grand One in the sense of the original creative principle, the pole star, and the supreme celestial spirit existed simultaneously during the Warring States period (475–221 BCE), when TYSS was possibly composed. These different senses of Grand One were also "interchangeable and mutually explanatory" (Li 1995–1996, 26). By bringing together a variety of evidence from archeology, the paleographic record, and the history of astronomy, Pankenier (2004) further argues that as early as the second millennium BCE there existed an astral-terrestrial correspondence between the archaic kingship in the Bronze age and the north pole. As Li (1995–1996, 25) admits, we still cannot know exactly when the worship of Grand One as a personal god began. Nevertheless, it is evident that the pole star's unique characteristics and powerful associations as the pivot of the sky made it the celestial archetype of the cosmically empowered Chinese monarch throughout history. Therefore, it is reasonable to assume that Grand One, in the sense of the abstract cosmic principle or the supreme cosmic deity, was derived from general knowledge of the pole star in ancient Chinese astronomy and astrology.

As I have argued extensively elsewhere (Yao 2002), the particular kind of astrology underlying TYSS is known as the Divination of Grand One and Nine Palaces (*taiyi jiugong zhan* 太一九宮占). This ancient technique of astrology features a central figure, Grand One or the pole star rotating around "Nine Palaces," nine numbers from one to nine that represent their correlative spatial and temporal elements respectively. Another better-known divinatory technique was recorded in the *Book of Change* and features an application of eight trigrams. Later Confucian philosophers developed their cosmological and metaphysical speculations mainly based upon the *Book of Change* and its associated divinatory techniques. Similarly, I think the author of TYSS, being most probably a Daoist or Yin-yangist philosopher, was proposing a cosmogony on the basis of the cosmograph as used in the Divination of Grand One and Nine Palaces.

Recall our distinction of the three-staged cosmogony in TYSS, among which, the third stage is comprised of temporal elements: four seasons, their respective climates (cold, hot, moist, and dry), and the year. TYSS emphasizes this final stage of cosmogony by stating again the cosmogonical process in a reversed order:

> The year was produced by moist and dry; moist and dry were produced by cold and hot. Cold and hot [were produced by four seasons]. Four seasons were produced by *yin* and *yang*. *Yin* and *yang* were produced by the numinous and the luminous. The numinous and the luminous were produced by Heaven and Earth. Heaven and Earth were produced by Grand One.[12]

It is a rather curious fact that this cosmogony does not end up with the creation of "the myriad things" as most other systems of cosmogony do. A possible reason is that the cosmogony as elaborated in TYSS is not really intended to explain the formation of the world. It is rather intended to rationalize a cosmograph, and therefore the temporal elements and their associated climates become its focus because, "the cosmograph was concerned primarily with time rather than space" (Allan 2003, 248). The following passage of TYSS shows even more clearly the trace of this astrological technique:

> Therefore, Grand One stored in water and moved with the seasons. Circling and [beginning again, it took itself] as the mother of the myriad things. Waning and waxing, it took itself as the guideline of the myriad things. This is what Heaven cannot destroy, what Earth cannot bury, what *yin* and *yang* cannot bring to closure. The gentleman who knows this is called (unreadable) . . .[13]

In this passage all the key elements of cosmogony are mentioned. The two primeval elements, Grand One and water, are brought to an intimate relationship with the former storing in the latter. The temporal elements are condensed into one term "seasons" (*shi* 時), through which Grand One moves. This movement, being manifested through the seasons, is in contradistinction to the various spatial elements: Heaven, Earth, *yin* and *yang*, which seem to contribute negatively to the movement of Grand One by means of "killing," "destroying," and "bringing to closure." It is interesting to note that the pair of spatial elements, the numinous (*shen* 神) and the luminous (*ming* 明), is not explicitly mentioned. Instead, it talks about something waning and waxing, and something circling and beginning again. Presumably, these characteristics are attributed to the moon and sun respectively. Therefore, the numinous and the luminous can be reasonably identified as the moon and the sun respectively. This identification is supported by Xun Shuang 荀爽, a commentator of the *Book of Change* from the Han dynasty. He says: "The numinous is that which resides in Heaven; the luminous is that which resides in Earth. The numinous is bright through the night; the luminous illuminates through the day."[14] The moon and the sun, are on the one hand celestial bodies, and on the other hand they are also basic units of time, as *yue* 月 in Chinese means both "the moon" and "month," and *ri* 日 "the sun" and "day." Through its movements through the seasons and its manifestation in the sun and the moon, Grand One functions as the "mother" and the "guideline" of the myriad things.

In the Divination of Grand One and Nine Palaces, the movement of Grand One through Nine Palaces, signifying their correlative temporal, spatial, celestial, and human factors respectively, is the key to the operation of this cosmograph. At least two methods have been passed down to us. In the first method, Grand One resides at Palace One in the north for one day, then moves to Palace Two in the southwest and stays there for another day. It then keeps moving through Palaces Three, Four, Five, Six, Seven, Eight, and Nine sequentially spending one day in each palace. Finally, it returns to Palace One before starting another cyclic movement of nine days. The second method has a different route of Palaces One, Eight, Three, Four, Nine, Two, and Six by bypassing Palace Five in the center. In each of these eight palaces, Grand One dwells for forty-five days and thus forms a cyclic movement of a lunar year.

In both methods, Grand One resides in Palace One and returns to the same palace after a journey of one round. In this cosmograph, which was also widely applied to other practices including Chinese medicine, Palace One is correlated to the elements of water, north, winter, and darkness, among others. This explains why TYSS says that "Grand One stored in water," which seems to mean that water is more primeval than

Grand One and conceals it in a watery state. This contradicts what is said in the beginning of TYSS: "Grand One gave birth to water." These contradictory statements with regard to the priority of the two elements have puzzled many scholars. Such a puzzle would naturally arise if we try to understand them in terms of a linear causal relation. However, if we keep in mind the correlative scheme of the cosmograph, then it would be reasonable to say either "Grand One stored in water" or "Grand One gave birth to water."

Some later textual sources explain the correlation between water and Grand One or simply "One" in more explicit terms. For instance, a lost passage of the *Lingsu jing* 靈樞經, a classic of Chinese medicine, says: "Grand One is the honorific style (*hao* 號) of water. It was first the mother of Heaven and Earth, and later the fount of the myriad things."[15] A commentary on the *Book of Rites* cites Zheng Xuan 鄭玄, a scholar of the Han dynasty: "[The sum of] the Heavenly and Earthly numbers is fifty-five. Heavenly One gives birth to water in the north; Earthly Two gives birth to fire in the south; Heavenly Three gives birth to wood in the east; Earthly Four gives birth to metal in the west; Heavenly Five gives birth to earth in the center."[16] The statements "Heavenly One gives birth to water" and "Heaven One gives birth to water" are almost identical to what is said in TYSS: "Grand One gave birth to water."

Having clarified the correlation between water and Grand One or Heavenly One, we should note that in the actual practice of the Divination of Grand One and Nine Palaces, Grand One (*taiyi*) "is often replaced at the center by Zhaoyao 招搖 (in Boötes), which was also regarded as the pivot of the Dipper by the ancient Chinese" (Li 1995–1996, 20). While Grand One corresponds to Kochab, Zhaoyao is another important star in the circumpolar Central Palace (the Purple Tenuity Palace). So Grand One's movement with seasons through the Nine Palaces does not contradict its role as the constant pivot in the sky.

In India, knowledge of the pole star can also be traced back very early to the Indus Valley Civilization (mature period 2600–1900 BCE). Parpola (1994, 2009) has deciphered a series of scripts that signify astral names, including the pole star, which indicated its popularity among the people in the Indus Valley. The *Ṛgveda*, the earliest known literature of India does not, however, explicitly speak of a fixed star in the northern sky. The early Vedic silence regarding stars and planets was probably due to "the prevalence of planetary worship among the rivals and enemies of the Vedic Aryans" (Parpola 1994, 201). The trace of this worship can be seen in the Vedic marriage ritual that is still followed by a section of Hindu society today. In this ritual the groom shows the star called *dhruva* to the bride. Literally meaning "steadfast, firm, fixed," *dhruva* refers to the unmoving pole star, which in turn symbolizes marital faithfulness. In the ritual, the groom is also advised to recite a mantra to the pole star. Parts of this mantra, according to Parpola, show the link between the pole star and Varuṇa, who is one of the primal gods of the Vedic Aryans:

> Firm dwelling, firm origin. The firm one art thou, standing on the side of firmness. Thou art the pillar of the stars; thus protect me against the adversary.
> I know thee as the nave of the universe. May I become the nave of this country.
> I know thee as the centre of the universe. May I become the centre of this country.
> I know thee as the string that holds the universe. May I become the string that holds this country.
> I know thee as the pillar of the universe. May I become the pillar of this country.
> I know thee as the navel of the universe. May I become the navel of this country. (Parpola 1994, 245)

Parpola (1994, 245–6) further points out that this connection between the pole star and Varuṇa is implied in ṚV VIII.41.9: "Fixed is Varuṇa's dwelling-place; [there] he rules the Seven as king."[17] Elsewhere in the *Ṛgveda*, it also implies the idea that the stars are bound to the pole star: "Those stars, which, being fixed from above, were to be seen in the night, have gone somewhere in daytime."[18]

In addition to the connection with the pole star, Varuṇa is also associated with water. In the *Ṛgveda*, among the various roles of this primal god, Varuṇa is "the lord (and husband) of waters" (*apāṃ patiḥ*) and he is identified with the ocean and waters. In post-Vedic mythology, Varuṇa is marginalized and becomes almost exclusively the god of waters, who possesses the rivers and has his abode in the ocean. Moreover, Varuṇa is often identified with the night, darkness, the black color, and the womb. These, along with the pole star and water, are a set of correlative elements similar to those found in the Chinese cosmograph. Only in India they are weaved into rich and colorful myths.

Varuṇa is not mentioned in ṚV X.129. Nevertheless, That One, being intimately connected to waters in the primordial state, could be identified with this personal god. In later Purāṇic literature, Viṣṇu emerged as a chief god and his place or foot (*viṣṇupada*) is believed to be in the north above the Seven Sages (*saptarṣi*), wherein the pole star Dhruva is located. In ancient Indian astronomy, the Seven Sages refers to the Big Dipper. By tracing these Purāṇic sources back to some Yajurvedic texts, Iyangar (2011) has argued forcefully that Dhruva can be identified as the star Thuban (α-Draconis) that was nearest to the north celestial pole during the period 3200–2400 BCE. The Purāṇic myths also depict the primordial state of the world as Viṣṇu, in the form of his incarnation Nārāyaṇa, lying in waters with a lotus growing out of his navel, upon which Lord Brahmā begins to create the world. Again we see a strong correlation between creator, water, and the pole star.

So far we do not see any element of astrology in the Vedic and Purānic philosophical or mythological accounts of the pole star and water. However, ṚV X.190, with its emphasis on "the year," seems to suggest a theme similar to that of TYSS and therefore a possible astrological implication. This hymn reads:

> From Fervor kindled to its height Eternal Law and Truth were born:
> Thence was Night produced, and thence the billowy flood of sea arose.
>
> From that same billowy flood of sea the Year was afterwards produced,
> Ordainer of the days nights, Lord over all who close the eye.
>
> Dhātar, the great Creator, then formed in due order Sun and Moon.
> He formed in order Heaven and Earth, the regions of the air, the light.[19]

These verses are attributed to Aghamarṣaṇa, who is regarded as the first philosopher of India and is credited with formulating "the doctrine of time" (*kālavāda*) (Barua 1921, 8). The priority that the temporal element, the Year (*saṃvatsara*), enjoys in this hymn is strikingly similar to the case of TYSS. Moreover, this cosmogony can also be analyzed into three main stages. First, heat (*tapas*), as the first creative principle, gave birth to Eternal Law and Truth. Recall in ṚV X.129, That One was also born from heat. These elements produced Night, and Night produced water. This stage can be understood as corresponding to the primordial state that is depicted in ṚV X.129 and TYSS, in which water, Night (= darkness), and the heat that gives rise to That One are functioning. In the second stage, water gave birth to the Year, who is the ordainer of the days and nights and the Lord of life and death. In this stage, the temporal elements the Year, days, and nights are produced directly from water. In contrast, the temporal elements in TYSS are produced by *yin* and *yang*. In the final stage, the Year as the creator Dhātar formed, in due order, the sun and the moon, Heaven and Earth, the firmament and light. All these correspond to the spatial elements in TYSS.

EPISTEMOLOGY AND ETHICS

The two elements unique to ṚV X.190 are Eternal Law and Truth. In TYSS there is no parallel to these epistemologically oriented concepts. ṚV X.129

has no exact parallel to these concepts either, but it turns quickly to epistemological issues in the following verses:

> Then, in the beginning, there arose desire,
> which was the primal seed of mind.
> Searching in their hearts through inspired thinking,
> sages found the connection of the existent in the nonexistent.
>
> Their line was stretched across:
> What was below it? What above it?
> There were placers of seed and there were powers.
> There was inherent force below, impulse above.[20]

The heat (*tapas*) that gives birth to That One in ṚV X.129 verse 3 has developed into desire (*kāma*). From the primal seed of desire there develops the mind (*manas*). In their minds and hearts, the sages found the connection of the existent and the nonexistent. In other words, the human mind or thought is the foundation of whatever exists or does not exist. The most fundamental ontological concepts "existent" and "nonexistent" are built on the epistemological foundation of the mind and its thought. From the same mind, there also stretched a line, which points to an image of sexual union: the masculine figure above and the feminine one below.

In China, the image of sexual union is often used to illustrate the origin of the world. In the *Daodejing*, especially, this image is frequently mentioned. For instance, it says in chapter 42: "The myriad things carry *yin* (the feminine) and embrace *yang* (the masculine)."[21] Actually, here it presents an even more feministic image: the feminine principle *yin* above and the masculine principle *yang* below. But ṚV X.129 is unique in placing this image of sexual union on the intelligent "line" of the human mind. This emphasis on the inner experience of the human mind was probably derived from the yogic practice that prevailed among various Indian religious and philosophical schools. A consequence of this is their careful study of inner experiences, therefore turning to epistemological inquiry and even leading to skepticism. This is evident in the final two verses of ṚV X.129:

> Who really knows, and who can here declare it,
> from where it was born, and from where comes this creation?
> The gods are later than the creation of this world.
> Who knows then from where it came into being?
>
> This creation—from where it came into being,
> whether it was produced or whether not—
> he who is the overseer of this world in the highest heaven
> surely knows. Or perhaps he does not know![22]

In these final verses of ṚV X.129 we sense a conflict between the theistic and naturalistic tendencies. On the one hand, the author thinks that the gods were born after this world and therefore could not know its origin. This naturalistic tendency is in conformity with the emphasis on the human mind and the abstract cosmic principle "That One." On the other hand he seems to believe in a supreme deity "who is the overseer of this world in the highest heaven." However, he also casts doubt on this deity's knowledge of the origin of the world. Nevertheless, the skeptical spirit runs through the whole passage. As we know, the skeptical question "How do you know?" is essential to any epistemological inquiry and has contributed historically to the epistemological turn in Indian philosophy as early as the sixth century.

In contrast, although TYSS has shown a strong and thorough naturalistic tendency, it does not end up with skeptical questions. Instead, like many other classical Chinese philosophical texts, after laying out often naturalistic and rationalistic metaphysical ideas about the Heavenly Way, it turns to the human way and urges humans to follow the Heavenly Way. This is evident in the final passage of TYSS:

> The Way of Heaven values weakness. It reduces that which completes, in order to benefit that which produces; it attacks the strong, and punishes the [high . . .] Below is soil; it is called Earth. Above is air; it is called Heaven. "The Way" is also its style name, while clear-musky is its name. To undertake affairs by means of the Way, one must be entrusted with the name. Thus, affairs are accomplished and the person long-lived. If a sage, in undertaking affairs is entrusted with its name, then merit is achieved and his person goes unharmed. Heaven and Earth, name and style name, both of them stand together. Hence, if they transgress their correct positions, they will not match up. [Heaven is deficient] in the northwest; what is below it is high and strong. Earth is deficient in the southeast; what is above it is [broad and thick. What is deficient above], has an excess below. And what is deficient below, has an excess above.[23]

Some parts of this passage are hardly intelligible in a context of cosmogony. But it is clear that this cosmogony results in serving as an ethical guideline. It reflects a rather general characteristic of Chinese philosophy that emphasizes ethics, or, more precisely, an ethics based on a naturalized cosmology. Skepticism was not a strong tradition in Chinese philosophy. This contributed, in part, to the fact that an epistemological turn did not really occur in the history of Chinese philosophy.

CONCLUSION

Through a careful analysis and comparison of ṚV X.129 and TYSS, two rather distinctively short and early philosophical texts in India and China, we found that they share similar mythological motifs of the primeval water and the pole star. Given their different backgrounds of astrological and yogic practices, the two texts end up with two different directions: an epistemological skepticism in ṚV X.129 and the ethical guidelines in TYSS. This in turn reflects the general characteristics of classical Indian and Chinese philosophies: an early development of epistemology versus an emphasis on ethics.

We can even infer that Indian philosophy is generally an intellectual by-product of yogic practice. It thus features an emphasis on the soteriology of achieving the ultimate liberation and the epistemology of recognizing inner experiences. Chinese philosophy, on the other hand, is by and large an intellectual by-product of divinatory practice and thus features an emphasis on the purely calculative naturalistic metaphysics and their application as ethical guidance.[24]

NOTES

1. TYSS: 太一生水，水反輔太一，是以成天。天地反輔太一，是以成地。天地[復相輔]也，是以成神明。神明復相輔也，是以成陰陽。陰陽復相輔也，是以成四時。四時復[相]輔也，是以成寒熱。寒熱復相輔也。是以成濕澡。濕澡復相輔也，成歲而止。

2. TYSS: 太一藏於水，行於時。

3. ṚV X.129.1–3: *nāsad āsīn no sad āsīt tadānīṃ nāsīd rajo no viomā paro yat* |
kim āvarīvaḥ kuha kasya śarmann ambhaḥ kim āsīd gahanaṃ gabhīram ||
na mṛtyur āsīd amṛtaṃ na tarhi na rātriyā ahna āsīt praketaḥ |
ānīd avātaṃ svadhayā tad ekaṃ tasmād dhānyan na paraḥ kiṃ canāsa ||
tama āsīt tamasā gūḷham agre apraketaṃ salilaṃ sarvam ā idam |
tuchyenābhu apihitaṃ yad āsīt tapasas tan mahinājāyataikam ||

My translation is influenced by Brereton (1999), but differs from his in some major points.

4. The Qiwulun chapter of the *Zhuangzi*: 有始也者，有未始有始也者，有未始有夫未始有始也者。有有也者，有無也者，有未始有無也者，有未始有夫未始有無也者。俄而有無矣，而未知有無之果孰有孰無也。

5. Note the contradiction between the two statements. We will discuss this later.

6. For a comprehensive study of cosmic man in Indo-European myths of creation, see Lincoln 1975.

7. *Hne wo te yy*, p. 1: 混沌演出水是一，渾水滿盈盈是二，水色變金黃是三。

8. Chapter 42 of the *Daodejing*: 道生一，一生二，二生三，三生萬物。

9. The Taihong chapter of the *Heguanzi*: 中央者，太一之位，百神仰制焉。

10. The "Treatise of Heavenly Offices" of the *Shiji*: 中宮天極星，其一明者，太一常居也。

11. The Liyun chapter of the *Book of Rites*: 是故夫禮，必本於大一，分而為天地，轉而為陰陽，變而為四時，列而為鬼神。

12. TYSS: 故歲者，濕燥之所生也。濕燥者，寒熱之所生也。寒熱者，[四時之所生也]。四時者，陰陽之所生也。陰陽者，神明之所生也。神明者，天地之所生也。天地者，太一之所生也。

13. TYSS: 是故太一藏于水，行于時，周而又[始，以己為]萬物母；一缺一盈，以己為萬物經。此天之所不能殺，地之所不能埋，陰陽之所不能成。君子知此之謂.

14. Xun Shuan's commentary to the *Book of Change* : 神者在天，明者在地。神以夜光，明以晝照。

15. 太一者，水之尊號，先天地之母，後萬物之源。This lost passage is recovered from a Daoist work of the Song dynasty. For more discussions, see Yao 2002.

16. 天地之數五十有五，天一生水於北，地二生火於南，天三生木於東，地四生金於西，天五生土於中。This commentary is by Kong Yingda 孔穎達 from the Tang dynasty. Another text from the "Treatises on Calendars" in the *Hanshu* explains the same idea with slightly different wordings: "Heaven One gives birth to water; Earth Two gives birth to fire; Heaven Three gives birth to wood; Earth Four gives birth to metal; Heaven Five gives birth to earth" (天以一生水，地以二生火，天以三生木，地以四生金，天以五生土). Quoted from Feng 2007, 514 n1.

17. ṚV VIII.41.9c: . . . *varuṇasya dhruvaṃ sadaḥ sa saptānām irajyati* . . . | |

18. ṚV I.24.10a: *amī ya ṛkṣā nihitāsa uccā naktaṃ dadṛśre kuha cid diveyuḥ* | Parpola's (1994) translation.

19. ṚV X.190: *ṛtaṃ ca satyaṃ cābhīddhāt tapaso adhy ajāyata* |
tato rātrī ajāyata tataḥ samudro arṇavaḥ | |
samudrād arṇavād adhi saṃvatsaro ajāyata |
ahorātrāṇi vidadhad viśvasya miṣato vaśī | |
sūryācandramasau dhātā yathāpūrvam akalpayat |
divaṃ ca pṛthivīṃ ca antarikṣam atho suvaḥ | | Griffith's (1896) translation.

20. ṚV X.129.4–5: *kāmas tad agre sam avartatādhi manaso retaḥ prathamaṃ yad āsīt* |
sato bandhum asati nir avindan hṛdi pratīṣyā kavayo manīṣā | |
tiraścīno vitato raśmir eṣām adhaḥ svid āsīd upari svid āsīt |
retodhā āsan mahimāna āsan svadhā avastāt prayatiḥ parastāt | |

21. Chapter 42 of the *Daodejing*: 萬物負陰而抱陽。

22. ṚV X.129.6–7: *ko addhā veda ka iha pra vocat kuta ājātā kuta iyaṃ visṛṣṭiḥ* |
arvāg devā asya visarjanena athā ko veda yata ābabhūva | |
iyaṃ visṛṣṭir yata ābabhūva yadi vā dadhe yadi vā na |
yo asyādhyakṣaḥ parame vioman so aṅga veda yadi vā na veda | |

23. TYSS: 天道貴弱，削成者以益生者，伐于強，責于[高 . . .] 下，土也，而謂之地；上，氣也，而謂之天。道亦其字也，青昏其名。以道從事者必托其名，故事成而身長。聖人之從事也，亦托其名，故功成而身不傷。天地名字並立，故訛其方，不思相[當。天不足]於西北，其下高以強。地不足于東南，其上[廣以厚。不足于上]者，有餘於下；不足于下者，有餘於上。With my emendations.

24. My thanks to Ithamar Theodor and Asko Parpola for their comments and to Steven Matthews for his editorial assistance.

BIBLIOGRAPHY

Allan, Sarah. 2003. "The Great One, Water, and the *Laozi*: New Light from Guodian." *T'oung Pao* 89: 237–285.

Barua, Benimadhab. 1921. *A History of Pre-Buddhistic Indian Philosophy*. Delhi: Motilal Banarsidass Publishers, 1998 reprint.

Brereton, Joel P. 1999. "Edifying Puzzlement: *Ṛgveda* 10.129 and the Uses of Enigma." *Journal of the American Oriental Society* 119.2: 248–260.

Feng, Shi 馮時. 2007. *Zhongguo tianwen kaogu xue* 中國天文考古學. Beijing: Zhongguo shehui kexue chubanshe.

Griffith, Ralph T. H., trans. 1896. *The Rig Veda*. New York: Quality Paperback Book Club, 1992 reprint.

Hne wo te yy 勒俄特衣, in *Liangshan Yiwen ziliao xuanyi* 涼山彝文資料選譯, vol.1, edited and translated by Qubi Shimei 曲比石美 et al. Chengdu: Xinan minzu xueyuan yinshuachang, 1978.

Holdrege, Barbara A. 1996. *Veda and Torah: Transcending the Textuality of Scripture*. Albany, NY: State University of New York Press.

Iyangar, R. N. 2011. "Dhruva the Ancient Indian Pole Star: Fixity, Rotation and Movement." *Indian Journal of History of Science* 46.1: 23–39.

Kuiper, F. B. J. 1970. "Cosmogony and Conception: A Query." *History of Religions* 10.2: 91–138.

Lincoln, Bruce. 1975. "The Indo-European Myth of Creation." *History of Religions* 15.2: 121–145.

Li, Ling. 1995–1996. "An Archaeological Study of Taiyi 太一 (Grand One) Worship," translated by Donald Harper. *Early Medieval China* 2: 1–39.

Pankenier David W. 2004. "A Brief History of Beiji 北極 (Northern Culmen), with an Excursus on the Origin of the Character *di* 帝." *Journal of the American Oriental Society* 124.2: 211–236.

Parpola, Asko. 1994. *Deciphering the Indus Script*. Cambridge: Cambridge University Press.

Parpola, Asko. 2009. "'Hind Leg' + 'Fish': Towards Further Understanding of the Indus Script." *Scripta* 1: 37–76.

Qian Baocong 錢寶琮. 1932. "Taiyi kao" 太一考. *Yanjing xuebao* 燕京學報 12: 2449–78.

ṚV = Rig Veda, A Metrically Restored Text, edited by Barend A. van Nooten and Gary B. Holland. Harvard Oriental Series, vol. 50. Cambridge, MA: Harvard University Press, 1994.

TYSS = *Taiyi sheng shui* 太一生水 from Jingmenshi Bowuguan 荊門市博物館, *Guodian Chu mu zhujian* 郭店楚墓竹簡. Beijing: Wenwu Press, 1998.

Van Over, Raymond, ed. 1980. *Sun Songs: Creation Myths from around the World*. New York: New American Library.

Yao, Zhihua 姚治華. 2002. "*Taiyi sheng shui* yu taiyi jiugong zhan" 太一生水與太乙九宮占, in Pang Pu 龐樸, ed., *Gumu xinzhi* 古墓新知 (Taipei: Taiwan Guji Publications), 47–67.

2

Exploring Parallels between the Philosophy of Upaniṣads and Daoism

Ram Nath Jha

A period from 2000 BC to 500 BC presents some common features in world history and especially in the area of spiritual philosophical development. Scholars brand it as an Axial Era. If we go through the history of Indian and Chinese culture we find that similar religio-spiritual philosophical developments were taking place around that period. It was being felt that every natural phenomenon was being presided over by some spiritual entity known as Dao, Spirit, or Brahman. As gravitational laws of Newton and relativity theory of Einstein revolutionize the scientific world and give a boost to the space sciences, likewise the discovery of Dao, Spirit, or Brahman behind natural forces prepared the ground for the philosophy of a spiritual essence behind the physical world; this is evident from the Dao's thought in China or the Upaniṣadic philosophy in India. Dao's thought or Daoism and the concept of an all-pervading Brahman are dealt with by the *Daodejing* and *Zhuangzi* in China and by the Principal Upaniṣads in India respectively.

We find that there are lots of similarities between Daoism and Upaniṣadic philosophy which can be explored and presented through metaphysics, epistemology, and axiology. Both of them believe in the spiritual essence of the world. Both of them believe that the world is an appearance of that something which because of not being visible is considered like null and void, because it cannot be pursued by empiric potentialities. Around 2000 BC the same thing was felt in the early philosophy in China. First, there was a feeling of individual spirits behind all the natural phenomena which ultimately paved the way to a pervading spiritual essence behind all the things of the physical world. That spiritual essence was branded by the name known as Way or Dao. In fact, this idea is old.[1] Dao came later—sometime around the sixth century BC—and preached it as a system. The idea, in some form or other, might have been found in the ideas of intellectuals from ancient China. The idea is prevalent in ancient Chinese intellectuals, and eventually a subsequent scholar will come along to systematize and popularize it as a system of philosophy. For example, "The ultimate truth is singular" has been mentioned time and again in different hymns of the *Ṛg Veda*. To clarify it more, the concept of singularity was refined by the concept of non-duality by Yājñavalkya in the *Bṛhadāraṇyaka Upaniṣad*. This concept of non-duality was philosophized and propagated by Śaṅkara as monism or Advaitavāda in the ninth century. Since that period Advaitavāda or monism is known as a separate philosophical system of Vedānta. In India whatever was preached by the propounders of orthodox philosophical systems was already prevalent in seed form in the Vedic literature,[2] likewise all that which was systematized, preached, and popularized by Laozi's Daoism had its elements in earlier thought of China (Reifler 1981, 19–26).

If we explore the parallels between the philosophy of the Upaniṣads and Daoism, it is quite clear that both of them emphasize the individual's spiritual upliftment.[3] Both of them are supposed to be intuitive and closely associated with nature.[4] Daoism opposed Confucian decorum and intellectual endeavor for leading day to day life,[5] whereas Upaniṣadic seers cautioned common people from getting involved *in* the ritualistic cycle of non-ending bondage.[6] Both of them showed the realizational depth viz. direct experience of reality in the area of spirituality and contributed the same to humanity at large.[7] The above common features between Daoism and Upaniṣadic philosophy provide a platform on which a comparison of the views of different philosophical aspects such as ontology, epistemology, and ethics give a clear-cut idea about the similarities of the two great cultures. To understand two cultures deeply is possible only when a comparative study of the thinkers from two major lands, thinking on the same intellectual level,[8] is taken up. It is also helpful in the sense that each side of them will serve as a perspective for the other through their understandings, because a great thought can only be thoroughly understood in the perspective of another great thought.

The Upaniṣadic text can be divided into two parts—non-sectarian and sectarian. The principal Upaniṣads such as Īśā, Kena, Kaṭha, Praśna, Muṇḍaka, Māṇḍūkya, Aitareya, Taittirīya, Bṛhadāraṇyaka, and Chāndogya are known as non-sectarian which Śaṅkara has commented upon. These Upaniṣads only deal with philosophical queries and are not related to any particular sect. Similarly the history of Daoism can be divided into four separate periods—Philosophical or Proto-Daoism, Classical Daoism, Modern Daoism, and Contemporary Daoism (Ball 2004, 52). The first period, philosophical Daoism, is so called simply because there is no evidence of any formal Daoist religious organization at this time—from antiquity up to the second century. The classic works of philosophy in this period are *Daodejing* and *Zhuangzi* (Ball 2004, 52). This chapter is based mainly on principal Upaniṣads, *Daodejing*, and *Zhuangzi*.

ONTOLOGY

Ontology is the study of the real and final nature of matter. If we go through the evolution of the world from the ultimate cause of the above philosophies, we find a similarity. In Daoism the ultimate base of world is considered as an indistinct, inexplicable spiritual background which at the time of the emergence of the world develops into *yin* and *yang* diversities which became responsible for the natural phenomena, forces, and things of the universe. Laozi says:

> The Dao generated one;
> One generated two;
> Two generated three;
> Three generated the ten thousand things.
> The ten thousand things,
> Carrying *yin* and embracing *yang*,
> Used the empty vapor to achieve harmony. (*Daodejing* 42)

The above-mentioned statement of Laozi has been elaborated by Huang (2000, 155) as: "In the first phase of non-being, the Dao generated *hun dun qi*, the vapor of chaos, also known as *chong xu qi*, the empty vapor which constituted one. One, being unable to generate things, split into two: *yin* and *yang* (the female vital force and male vital force), or heaven and earth, which constituted two. By using empty vapor as a medium, *yin* and *yang* blended with each other into harmony, and the three of them, *yin*, *yang*, and the empty vapor, generated the ten thousand things."

In the Upaniṣads also for the development of the universe, the Ultimate Cause (*brahman*) as the base of the universe is superimposed on himself as an ego-force (*puruṣavidha*[9] or *prajāpati* according to Śaṅkara's commentary) which did not enjoy the state of aloneness, hence divided itself into two dichotomies—*pati* (masculine principle) and *patnī* (feminine principle)—and hence was responsible thereafter for creating the polarities in the form of diverse forces and things of the world.[10] Here it is called "the deep and remote female," a phrase from the sixth chapter of *Daodejing*, which is very important in the context of the creation process because it stands for Dao, which is inexhaustible and which gives life to the ten thousand things (Huang 2000, 125). This concept will be explained later on.

In the Upaniṣads the five basic natural forces are known as earth, water, fire, air, and ether, which ultimately were responsible for the evolution of inanimate and animate things of the universe. In Daoism (not in philosophical Daoism but in the later period) we also find the five elements as metal, wood, fire, water, and earth.[11] Three of them—fire, water, and earth—are similar as in the Upaniṣadic philosophy while the rest of the five elements—metal and wood—differ. In fact, metal and wood in the Upaniṣadic philosophy are included in the earth.

Nevertheless, the three basic elements earth, water, and fire prevalent in Daoism can have a synchronization of thought in the three basic elements in the Chāndogya Upaniṣad as *ap*,[12] *tejas*, and *anna*. *Ap* stands for water, *tejas* for fire, and *anna* for earth. It was out of these three elements the whole world was evolved:

> Whatever red form fire has it is the form of heat, whatever (is) white (is the form) of water. Whatever (is) dark (it is the form of) earth. (*Chāndogya Upaniṣad* 6.4.1)

And it was for the later period in the *Taittirīya Upaniṣad* 2.1.1 that the five elements were recognized: "From this Self, verily, ether arose; from ether air; from air fire; from fire water; from water the earth."

Though five elements in Daoism are not directly related with the creation process, still, they symbolize natural elements such as seasons, colors, et cetera. The number of five elements here finds some similarity in Daoism and Upaniṣadic philosophy, though partially. It opens up an avenue for the scholar to do some research work in the context of evolutional phases of the universe. We are to find how and in what way the Upaniṣadic thinkers prompted for the discovery of the rest of the five elements—*vāyu* (air) and *ākāśa* (space)—and what prompted the Daoists to discover the other two elements—wood and metal. The researchers here in this context are also invited to explore the various possibilities which led to these two different modes of findings.

ESSENCE AND NON-ESSENCE: CONSTITUENTS OF INDIVIDUAL BEING

Like the evolution of the universe, the individual being is also formed by essence and non-essence (*ātman* and *anātman*, i.e., *māyā* in the Upaniṣads and *yin* and *yang* in Daoism). According to the Upaniṣads man is not an ordinary entity. He is internally a spiritual essence and externally a material covering.[13] Both these constituents are responsible for the individual's formation. The individual's essence aspect is eternal and non-essence aspect is transitory. In Daoism the passive *yin* and active *yang* are symbols of non-essence and Dao as essence. Something and nothing are also used in Daoism for non-essence and essence respectively.[14]

The highest essence of a human being and the universe is Brahman/ātman in the Upaniṣads and Dao in Daoism.[15] This highest essence cannot be named since it has neither form nor traits. Being without form and trait, it neither can be known nor can it be described by any available means. Hence it is nameless, unknowable, unperceivable, ungraspable, unthinkable, et cetera but still dimly visible to the trained eyes. This highest essence is not transformed into manifestations, but simply appears as manifestation. This manifestation is ever-changing, rolls on and on, and moves in the cyclic order of appearance and disappearance. It cannot support itself. If Brahman or Dao takes itself out, manifestations viz. world of name and form cannot exist.

Māyā is one of the foundational concepts of the Upaniṣads. It is the creative power of Brahman/ātman that causes plurality of this universe: "The Supreme Reality manifests itself into different forms through *māyā*."[16] As per accepted maxim (*siddhānta*) "Power is not different from its power holder" (*śakti-śaktimatorabhedaḥ*),[17] this *māyā* is not different from its substratum Brahman/ātman. There is a striking parallel in Laozi's *Daodejing* where we find the mention of "valley spirit" or "deep and remote female" or "mysterious female" which stands for the creative aspect of Dao that gives life to the ten thousand things or multiple entities:

> The valley spirit never dies;
> It is called the deep and remote female.
> The gate of the deep and remote female
> Is called the root of heaven and earth. (*Daodejing* 6)

As per my understanding, mysterious or deep and remote female is the functional and creative aspect of Dao. According to Huang (2000, 125), "the deep and remote female," "the gate of the deep and remote female," and "the root of heaven and earth" all stand for the Dao, which gives life to the ten thousand things. Some scholars, including Zhu Xi, read "the deep and remote female" as the female reproductive organ. This chapter reiterates the concept that the Dao is empty but its function is inexhaustible.

Māyā is looked upon in three different ways: (a) from the view point of Brahman/ātman, the Ultimate Reality, it is negligible; (b) from the view point of reasoning, it is indefinable; and (c) from the view point of common people, it is real. The mysterious female can also be looked upon in above-mentioned ways: (a) from the view point of Dao, it is negligible; (b) from the view point of reasoning, it is indefinable; and (c) from the view point of common people, it is real. According to Swami Vivekananda: "*Māyā* is not the theory for the explanation of this world; it is simply a statement of facts as they exist, that the very basis of our being is contradiction, that wherever there is good, there must also be evil, and wherever there is evil, there must be some good, wherever there is life, death must follow as its shadow, and everyone who smiles will have to weep, and vice versa" (Vivekananda 2007, 97). Similarly the mysterious female is the statement of contradictory duality such as heaven and earth, *yin* and *yang*, something and nothing, active and passive, et cetera.

There are two layers of Reality (*Brahman*) in the Upaniṣadic philosophy: transcendental reality (*para brahman*) and empirical reality (*avara brahman*) (*Muṇḍaka Upaniṣad* 2.2.9). Daoism also accepts the same. In the beginning when the Dao was an indistinguishable mass, heaven and earth had not separated from each other and the ten thousand things had not been generated yet, there were no living things in this universe, then "non-being" (*wu* 無), is the name for the first phase of Dao:

> There was something
> That into an indistinguishable mass had wrought itself,
> Born before heaven and earth.
> Desolate and formless,
> It stood alone, unchanging,
> And may be regarded as
> The mother of heaven of earth.
> Not knowing its name,
> I gave it the alias "Dao,"
> And reluctantly named it "vast." (*Daodejing* 25)

When heaven and earth separated from each other, and the ten thousand things were generated, myriads of living things emerged in the universe, then 'being' (*you* 有) is the name for the second phase of Dao.

There is one more striking parallel regarding the meaning of two opposite principles. In the *Yijing*, which predates the scriptures attributed to Laozi, the two terms *yin* and *yang* take their meanings from the slopes of a mountain—shaded (north) and sunny (south) respectively (Ball 2004, 111). The two opposite principles (Brahman and *māyā*) have the same meanings as shade and light in the *Kaṭha Upaniṣad* but with a slight difference: "The knowers of Brahman speak of them [i.e., individual self (*jīvātman*) and Brahman, or witness self and universal self (*paramātman*)] as shade and light" (*Kaṭha Upaniṣad* 1.3.1).

Brahman limited by *māyā* is known as individual self. This individual self, here, is symbolized by shade and Brahman or pure consciousness by light. Brahman and *māyā* are supposed to be the two aspects of the same reality with opposite nature (*Śvetāśvatara Upaniṣad* 4.10). Brahman is static but *māyā* is creative; Brahman is always singular but *māyā* projects it as plural; Brahman is conscious but *māyā* is non-conscious; Brahman is infinite but *māyā* is finite, so on and so forth.

EPISTEMOLOGY

Epistemology is the study of the interrelation of mind and matter in the processes of perception and knowledge. In the area of epistemology the Upaniṣadic seers and Daoists believe in direct experience of reality which transcends not only intellectual thinking but also sensory perception, inference, and verbal testimony. Though Daoists do not use these terms (perception, etc.) as such, but to philosophize Laozi's idea of knowledge for contemporary readers it is necessary to present it through these established terms. The Upaniṣads accept two types of knowledge—higher (*vidyā/parā*) and lower (*avidyā/aparā*)—and associates lower knowledge with disciplines based on intellectual practices related to empirical reality and behavior and higher with spiritual realization: "He who, knows these two *vidyā* and *avidyā* together, attains immortality through *vidyā*, by crossing over death through *avidyā*" (*Īśā Upaniṣad* 11, my translation).

Avidyā (lower Knowledge) includes textual, rational, and theoretical knowledge whereas *vidyā* (higher knowledge) is the realization of ultimate truth (*brahmasākṣātkāra*), direct and immediate knowledge:

> To him he said, two kinds of knowledge are to be known, as, indeed, the knowers of Brahman declare—the higher as well as the lower. Of these, the lower is the *Ṛg Veda*, the *Yajur Veda*, the *Sāma Veda*, the *Atharva Veda*. Phonetics, Ritual, Grammar, Etymology, Metrics, and Astrology. And the higher is that by which the Undecaying is apprehended. (*Muṇḍaka Upaniṣad* 1.1.4–5)

Chinese philosophy has also emphasized the distinction between the intuitive and rational and hence developed two complimentary philosophical traditions—Daoism and Confucianism. Daoism purely belongs to intuitive tradition. Here, intuitive means to merge individual mind into universal principle, that is, to become identified with Dao,[18] and lead day to day life accordingly. It clearly rejects knowledge governed by intellectual activity based on sense-object-contact, verbal testimony, and so on. It is based on the firm belief that the human intellect can never comprehend the Dao. In the words of Zhuangzi: "The most extensive knowledge does not necessarily know it; reasoning will not make men wise in it. The sages have decided against both these methods" (*Zhuangzi*, Chapter 22).

Upaniṣadic seers also reject reasoning as the means for realizing Ultimate Truth: "The Absolute Truth realizing wisdom cannot be achieved through reasoning" (*Kaṭha Upaniṣad* 1.2.9). The knowledge acquired through sense-organs or any cognitive faculty is not acceptable to the Upaniṣadic seers. They say that senses, mind, and other faculties are limited in their scope of perception. The senses can perceive only the worldly objects; even mind and intellect cannot go beyond the imaginary world. Their scope of activity remains in confinement of material kingdom. They cannot grasp the mysterious world which forms the Substratum or Essence of the physical world. The cognitive faculty cannot grasp that mysterious Essence:

> He who dwells in (the organ of) speech, yet is within speech, whom speech does not know, . . . He who dwells in the eye, yet is within the eye, whom the eye does not know, . . . He who dwells in the ear, yet is within the ear, whom the ear does not know, . . . He who dwells in the mind, yet is within the mind, whom the mind does not know, . . . He who dwells in the skin, yet is within the skin, whom the skin does not know. (*Bṛhadāraṇyaka Upaniṣad* 3.7.17–21)

Therefore the seer concludes that the senses, mind, intellect, and reasoning are good and valid in so far as the physical or the material world is concerned, but in order to observe the universal principle Brahman and in order to uplift himself to that state of truth, man has to switch off the ordinary tendencies or sensory perceptions and reasoning: "When the five (senses) knowledges together with the mind cease (from their normal activities) and the intellect itself does not stir, that, they say, is the highest state" (*Kaṭha Upaniṣad* 2.3.10).

The same view is expressed by Laozi. He says that the sense-organs and mind have got a limited scope. They can perceive this physical universe but cannot grasp the mysterious essence. Therefore, he advises that if a person wants to see the physical world, she/he must apply senses and mind. But if she/he wants to realize the mysterious world, she/he must close them. To quote:

> He who knows does not speak;
> He who speaks does not know.
> Stop your hole,
> Close your door,
> Soften your brightness,
> Mingle with the dust,
> File your sharpness,
> And unravel your entanglements.
> This is called deep and remote concord. (*Daodejing* 56)

Language as the instrument of providing exact knowledge of Supreme Reality or not, has been an important issue since the beginning of knowledge traditions. A group of knowledge systems such as Nyāya-Vaiśeṣika, Grammarians, Newtonian science, Confucianism, et cetera, accepts language as the perfect means to map reality as it is. On the contrary, Upaniṣadic philosophy, Advaita Vedānta, Śūnyavāda, Plato, Daoism, Modern Physics, et cetera, profess language as insufficient means to capture reality. According to lalter, language can capture only that reality which is cognized through senses and mind. Since senses and mind are capable only of grasping limited aspects of reality, hence language cannot map Absolute Reality which is unlimited, unchanging, non-dual, and pure consciousness. In the west, generally linguists and grammarians accept language as the perfect tool to know reality as it is. The semanticist Alfred Korzybski made exactly the same point with his powerful slogan "The map is not the territory" (Capra 1991, 36).[19] The Upaniṣadic seers clearly deny the efficacy of language in realizing Supreme Essence: "Whence words return along with the mind, not attaining it, he who knows that bliss of Brahman fears not at any time" (*Taittirīya Upaniṣad* 2.4.1).

Laozi has also the same opinion about language: "A dao that can be spoken about / Is not the constant Dao; / A name that can be named / Is not the constant name" (*Daodejing* 1). Śaṅkara, the propagator of non-dualism (monism or Advaitavāda) and great commentator of Upaniṣads, speaks in the same way: "Loud speech in a stream of words, the efficiency in expounding or commenting upon the śāstras, these bring only a little joyous, material satisfaction to the scholar; but they are insufficient to liberate him completely."[20]

What Upaniṣadic seers and Daoists are concerned with is a direct experience of reality which transcends not only intellectual thinking but also sensory perception. In the words of Upaniṣads: "What is soundless, touchless, formless, imperishable, tasteless, constant, odourless, without beginning, without end, higher than the great, and stable; by discerning That, one is liberated from the mouth of death" (*Katha Upaniṣad* 1.3.15, my translation).

In a nutshell, Upaniṣadic seers and Daoists do not believe in approximate knowledge. They believe in Absolute knowledge. Anyone who claims acquiring absolute knowledge through perception, reasoning, and verbal testimony is not acceptable to them. He only exhibits his superficial understanding of reality: "If you think that you have understood Brahman well, you know it but slightly" (*Kena Upaniṣad* 2.1); "To whomsoever it is not known, to him it is known: to whomsoever it is known, he does not know. It is not understood by those who understand it; it is understood by those who do not understand it" (*Kena Upaniṣad* 2.3). "Knowing as if not knowing / Is peerless; / Not knowing as if knowing / Is a sickness" (*Daodejing* 71); "Hence the sage man / Assumed the office of nonaction, / Conducted speechless instruction" (*Daodejing* 2).

The intention of the above-mentioned facts can be expressed through the words of Capra (1991, 367), a renowned modern physicist and the acknowledged author of the famous book *The Dao of Physics*: "Mystics (Upaniṣadic Seers and Daoists) are generally not interested in approximate knowledge. They are concerned with absolute knowledge involving an understanding of the totality of existence. Being well aware of the essential interrelationship of all aspects of the universe, they realize that to express something means, ultimately, to show how it is connected to everything else. As this is impossible, the mystics often insist that no single phenomenon can be fully explained. They are not generally interested in explaining things but rather in the direct and non-intellectual experience of the unity of all things."

Conclusively as per Upaniṣadic philosophy and Daoism all intellectual concepts and theories are limited and approximate. Intellectual activities can never provide any complete and definitive understanding. Truth is dimensionless and world thereof and the world evolved from thereof is an opportunity for upliftment. The life in the world of pleasure and miseries is for this experimentation until one feels oneness with the limitless.

ETHICS

Ethics is the study of ideal conduct; the highest knowledge, said Socrates, is the knowledge of good and evil, the knowledge of the wisdom of life. Knowledge prompts behavior. One's worldview decides her/his actions. The Upaniṣadic and Daoistic worldview is holistic; they do not believe in plurality as cognized by sense-organs, rather they believe in the essence of this multifarious universe which is non-dual and known as Brahman/ātman in the Upaniṣads and Dao in Daoism. Consequently they believe in consuming minimum for themselves and trying to give maximum to others by maintaining ecological balance. Both of them accept material things valuable so far as they fill the belly and sustain the life. Beyond this need, if they are amassed, they lead to greed, boastings, competitions, jealousy, and hatred. The actions of charity, compassion, sympathy, help of needy people, righteousness, performance of rites, et cetera, are good in so far as they are helpful to the beings all around. They all are good if they do not lead to boasting and ego-consciousness.

The above-mentioned ethical activities are, according to the Upaniṣadic seers and Daoists, supposed as the action of ordinary virtue. The highest value is the knowledge of the nature of Brahman/ātman or Dao and the highest virtue is that which leads to dissolution of ego. Brahman or Dao is supposed to be the highest truth regarding all aspects of reality where it is ontological object, knowledge, or ethical behavior. This is why the Upaniṣadic seer declares knowledge as Brahman itself.[21] Yājñavalkya in the *Bṛhadāraṇyaka Upaniṣad* says that a man, even if he performs austerity and sacrifices and gives gifts to poor people for thousands of years, without the knowledge of Brahman/ātman, all his actions are useless: "Whosoever, . . . without knowing this Imperishable performs sacrifices, worships, performs austerities for a thousand years, his work will have an end" (*Bṛhadāraṇyaka Upaniṣad* 3.8.10).

Laozi also professes the same thing. He says that the lower path of righteousness, morality, and rites are risky as there lies the possibility of being gripped by ego consciousness and attachment to impermanent things: "A man of the highest virtue does not keep to virtue and / That is why he has virtue. A man of the lowest virtue never / Strays from virtue and that is why he is without virtue. / The former never acts yet leaves nothing undone. / The latter acts but there are things left undone" (*Daodejing* 38).

The path of lower morality is not the *summum bonum* of an individual. One must rise to the highest morality of selfless action and behavior through the knowledge of Highest Essence which opens the gate of Heaven or so to reach an identity with the Highest Essence: "A person, who realizes Brahman, becomes Brahman" (*Muṇḍaka Upaniṣad* 3.2.9).

Laozi also professes the same thing. After having shown the hollowness of the lower path of morality, virtue, and righteousness, he also propounds that the highest value in life is to realize Dao, the ultimate Essence. He says that only the highest value, the realization of Dao, can transform an ordinary person to an accomplished one:

> A turbulent wind does last a whole morning;
> A torrential rain does not last a whole day.
> Who does these?
> Heaven and earth.
> Even heaven and earth cannot last long,
> How can man?
> Therefore, who pursues the Dao
> Identifies with the Dao. (*Daodejing* 23)

Upaniṣadic seers profess that the possibilities and stimulating agencies for achieving the highest value and highest morality are inherent in the nature of manifestations. The purpose of the manifestations is to train human beings in self development, through the interaction with multifarious worldly objects. Through this gradual process they achieve the highest state which culminates in realizing one's identity with the Highest Essence and their oneness with all the manifestations. Hence, as per Upaniṣadic seers and Laozi, the manifestations are considered as the means to realize ultimate truth:

> This eternal greatness of the knower of Brahman is not increased by work nor diminished. One should know the nature of that alone. Having found that, one is not tainted by evil action. Therefore he who knows it as such, having become calm, self-controlled, withdrawn, patient and collected sees the Self in his own self, sees all in the Self. Evil does not overcome him, he overcomes all evil. Evil does not burn (affect) him, he burns (consumes) all evil. Free from evil, free from taint, free from doubt he becomes knower of Brahm[an]. (*Bṛhadāraṇyaka Upaniṣad* 4.4.23)
>
> The functions of the sense-organs, mind and activities such as dying, sustaining, eating etc. prove their substratum viz. ātman/Brahman. A person of wisdom easily understands and realizes the ultimate Truth with the help of these instruments and activities, but not deluded one. (*Bhagavadgītā* 15.9–10)
>
> When it is known through every state of cognition, it is rightly known, for (by such knowledge) one attains life eternal. Through one's own self one gains power and through wisdom one gains immortality. If here (a person) knows it, then there is truth, and if here he knows it not, there is great loss. Hence, seeing or (seeking) (the Real) in all beings, wise men become immortal on departing from this world [by destroying ego consciousness]. (*Kena Upaniṣad* 2.4–5)

Laozi also has the same idea when he says: "The Dao generates them, / Virtue nurtures them, / Matter forms them, / And instruments complete them. / Hence, the ten thousand things / Honor the Dao and treasure virtue" (*Daodejing* 51).

There is striking parallel regarding the state of desireless-action or *niṣkāma karman* as propounded by the *Bhagavadgītā*,[22] a representative text of Vedic thought.[23] The actions of the Daoist sage arise out of his intuitive wisdom, spontaneously and in harmony with his environment. He does not need to force himself or anything around him, but merely adapts his action to the movements of the Dao. Such a way of acting is called *wuwei* 無為 literally meaning 'non-action' in Daoist philosophy. But non-action does not mean absence of action; rather it means action for the welfare of all beings without any personal desire: "The Dao generates them, / Nurtures them, / Grows them, / Raises them, / Shapes them, / Solidifies them, / Stores them, / Covers them. / It generates without possessing, / Assists without taking credit, / Leads without dominating. / This is called deep and remote virtue" (*Daodejing* 51). Zhuangzi also says: "Non-action does not mean doing nothing and keeping silent. Let everything be allowed to do what it naturally does, so that its nature will be satisfied" (cited from Capra 1991, 129–130).

The *Īśā Upaniṣad* 1–2 says in the same way: "All whatsoever exists in this universe is pervaded by the Supreme Reality. . . . Keeping this in mind or moreover realizing this state of existence if a person performs his duty that will not cling to him" (my translation). According to the *Bhagavadgītā* the action of a realized human being is not guided by limited mind, rather it is as per the dynamic process of universal law or so to say Brahman/ātman. Hence the action, which is not ego consciousness-oriented or result-oriented, is regarded as non-action or *niṣkāma-karman*: "But the man whose delight is in the Self alone, who is content with the Self, who is satisfied with the Self, for him there exists no work that needs to be done" (*Bhagavadgītā* 3.17); "Therefore, without attachment, perform always the work that has to be done, for man attains to the highest by doing work without attachment" (*Bhagavadgītā* 3.19).

CONCLUSION

Thus, with the above discussion, we find the parallels between the philosophy of Upaniṣads and Daoism, though in brief, but by touching almost all the aspects of philosophical issues such as ontological, epistemological, and ethical. It can be extended further. Finally, I end my chapter by the statement of the great quantum physicist Werner Heisenberg:

> It is probably true quite generally that in the history of human thinking the most fruitful developments frequently take place at those points where two different lines of thought meet. These lines may have their roots in quite different parts of human culture, in different times or different cultural environments or different religious traditions: hence if they actually meet, that is, if they are at least so much related to each other that a real interaction can take place, then one may hope that new and interesting developments may follow. (Capra 1991, 9)

I want to conclude by saying that more and more research on Laozi indicates the urge of the scholars to understand him more and more deeply. This type of urge can find a better answer when comparative study of two thinkers of two different cultures is taken up. The above-mentioned analysis is the attempt of reinterpreting Daoism from the Upaniṣadic point of view by exploring parallels from principal Upaniṣads, *Daodejing*, and *Zhuangzi*. As per my understanding a researcher well-versed in the Upaniṣads can understand Laozi better and *vice versa*. It was this necessity that prompted me to take up this study.

NOTES

1. As per my understanding, the concept of yin and yang diversities has been presented in the beginning of the *Yijing* as *qian* 乾 and *kun* 坤. This concept also suggests other opposite polarities such as Heaven and Earth, Light and Shadow, et cetera. The essence or the primary cause of this primordial duality is something which would have been named as Dao in *Daodejing*. See Reifler 1981, 19–26.

2. Vedic literature includes Saṃhitās, Brāhmaṇas, Āranyakas, and Upaniṣads.

3. *Bṛhadāraṇyaka Upaniṣad* 4.4.5 (unless otherwise indicated, all translations of the Upaniṣads are from Radhakrishnan 2010): "That self is, indeed, *Brahman* [Supreme Reality], consisting of (or identified with) the understanding, mind, life, sight, hearing . . . and all things. . . . As is his desire so is his will, as is his will, so is the deed he does, whatever deed he does, that he attains." *Daodejing* 4 (all translations of the *Daodejing* are from Huang 2000): "Therefore the sage keeps to the deed that consists in taking no action and practices the teaching that uses no words."

4. *Taittirīya Upaniṣad* 2.1.1: "From this Self, verily, ether arose; from ether air; from air fire; from fire water; from water the earth; from the earth herbs; from herbs food; from food the person." *Bhagavadgītā* 3.16 (all translations of *Gītā* are from Radhakrishnan 2009): "He—who does not follow this ever-changing natural cycle, leads a sinful life, gets involved in sensuous pleasure—lives in vain, O Arjuna!" In the words of *Huainanzi* quoted in Needham 1956, 88: "Those who follow the natural order flow in the current of the Dao."

5. *Zhuangzi*, chapter 22 (all translations of the *Zhuangzi* are from Legge 1971): "The most extensive knowledge does not necessarily know it; reasoning will not make men wise in it. The sages have decided against both these methods." *Zhuangzi*, chapter 24: "A dog is not reckoned good because it barks well; and a man is not reckoned wise because he speaks skillfully."

6. *Bṛhadāraṇyaka Upaniṣad* 3.8.10: "Whosoever, O Gārgi, in this world, without knowing this Imperishable performs sacrifices, worship, performs austerities for a thousand years, his work will have an end."

7. *Bṛhadāraṇyaka Upaniṣad* 3.5.1: "*Brahman* that is immediately present and directly perceived, who is the self in all things." *Kaṭha Upaniṣad* 2.1.1: "Some wise man, however, seeking life eternal, with his eyes turned inward, saw the self." *Daodejing* 23: "Therefore, he who pursues the Dao identifies with the Dao."

8. Similarities in above-mentioned issues prove the equality of thoughts between Upaniṣadic seers and Daoists.

9. *Bṛhadāraṇyaka Upaniṣad* 1.4.1 and also see commentary of Śaṅkarācārya on *Bṛhadāraṇyaka Upaniṣad*.

10. *Bṛhadāraṇyaka Upaniṣad* 1.4.1–3: "In the beginning this (world) was only the self in the shape of a person. . . . He, verily, had no delight. Therefore he who is alone has no delight. He desired a second. He became as large as a woman and a man in close embrace. He caused that self to fall into two parts. From that arose husband and wife. Therefore, as Yājñavalkya used to say, this (body) is one half of oneself, like one of the two halves of a split pea. Therefore this space is filled up by a wife. He became united with her. From that human beings were produced."

11. These principal cosmic forces or influences could, according to the Chinese, then further be classified according to the 'Five Elements' or 'Five Phases' (*wux-*

ing 五行) theory. This theory was put forward in the *Great Norm* (*hongfan* 洪範), a treatise inserted in the *Classic of History* (*shujing* 書經). See Ball 2004, 113.

12. *Ap* is the original word (*prātipādika*) and is always used as *āpaḥ* in plural.

13. *Īśā Upaniṣad* 1: "(Know that) all this, whatever moves in this moving world, is enveloped by God." *Bṛhadāraṇyaka Upaniṣad* 3.4.2: "This is your self that is within all things." *Bṛhadāraṇyaka Upaniṣad* 3.7.15: "He who dwells in all beings, yet is within all beings, whom no beings know, whose body is all beings, who controls all beings from within, he is your self, the inner controller, the immortal." *Māṇḍūkya Upaniṣad* 1: "This self is *Brahman*." *Daodejing* 32, 37: "Dao is constant and nameless."

14. *Daodejing* 40: "The myriad creatures in the world are born from Something, And Something from Nothing."

15. According to *Taittirīya Upaniṣad* 2.1, *Bṛhadāraṇyaka Upaniṣad* 3.9.28, and *Māṇḍūkya Upaniṣad* 7, Brahman is existence (non-changing), knowledge (consciousness), infinity, bliss, and nondual. According to Laozi, his Dao, the law of nature, is the unchanging and ultimate truth of the universe, which, being invisible, inaudible, and intangible (*Daodejing* 14), is too "deep and remote" to be made thoroughly clear in human language. See Huang 2000, 119.

16. *Ṛgveda* 6.47.18 and *Bṛhadāraṇyaka Upaniṣad* 2.5.19. There are two types of Upaniṣads: Upaniṣads as parts of Saṃhitā such as *Īśā Upaniṣad, Muṇḍaka Upaniṣad,* et cetera, and Upaniṣads as parts of Brāhmaṇa such as *Kena Upaniṣad, Māṇḍūkya Upaniṣad,* et cetera. Sometimes the same verse (*mantra*) is found in Saṃhita as well as in Upaniṣad. The above-mentioned verse falls under this category.

17. This is a popular maxim accepted in Indian intellectual tradition.

18. *Daodejing* 23: "Therefore, he who pursues the Dao / Identifies with the Dao. . . ."

19. A section of Indian grammarians do not accept language as the perfect means to capture reality as it is. For example, Bhatṛhari in his *Vākyapadīya* 2.238 says, "We desire to realize truth through unreal means, that is, language."

20. *Talks on Śaṅkara's Vivekacūḍāmani* 58.

21. "Brahman is Existence, Knowledge (Consciousness) and Infinity" (*satyaṃ jñānam anantam brahma*) (*Taittirīya Upaniṣad* 2.1.1.); *Daodejing* 78: "Every one in the world knows yet no one can put this *knowledge* into practice."

22. *Bhagavadgītā* 2.47: "To action alone hast thou a right and never at all to its fruits; let not the fruits of action be thy motive; neither let there be in thee any attachment to inaction."

23. *Bhagavadgītā Śaṅkarabhāṣya Upodghāṭa*, p. 2: "This Gītāśāstra is the compendium of the essence of all types of Vedic meanings and very difficult to be understood" (*idaṃ gītāśāstraṃ samastavedārthasārasaṅgrahabhūtaṃ durvijñeyārtham*).

BIBLIOGRAPHY

Ball, Pamela. 2004. *The Essence of Dao*. London: Arcuturus Publishing Limited.

Capra, Fritzof. 1991. *The Dao of Physics*. London: Flamingo an imprint of HarperCollins Publishers.

Capra, Fritzof. 1997. *The Web of Life*. London: Flamingo an imprint of HarperCollins Publishers.

Chinmayananda, Swami. 2009. *Talks on Śaṅkara's Vivekacūḍāmani*. Mumbai: Central Chinmaya Mission Trust.
Huang, Chichung. 2000. *Dao Te Ching. A Literal Translation with Notes and Commentary*. Fremont California: Asian Humanities Press.
James Legge, trans. 1971. *Chuang Tzu*, arranged by Clae Waltham. New York: Ace Books.
Lau, D. C., trans. 1963. *Lao Tzu: Tao Te Ching*. London: Penguin Books.
Needham, J. 1956. *Science and Civilization in China. Vol. 2*. London: Cambridge University Press.
Radhakrishnan, S. 2009. *The Bhagavadgītā*. New Delhi: HarperCollins publishers India.
Radhakrishnan, S. 2010. *The Principal Upaniṣads*. New Delhi: HarperCollins publishers India.
Reifler, Sam. 1981. *I Ching*. London: Bantam Books.
Śaṅkarācārya, Ādi. 2007. *Bhagavadgītā Śaṅkarabhāṣya*. Gorakhpur: Gītā Press.
Vivekananda. 2007. The Complete Works of Swami Vivekananda. Vol. 2. Kolkata: Advaita Ashram.

3

The Way of Silent Realization

Ineffability and Rationality in the Philosophical Mysticisms of Śaṅkara and Zhan Ruoshui

Sophia Katz

One of the perspectives from which the comparison between Brahman and Dao has been undertaken in research literature is that of philosophical mysticism.[1] Karl Albert in his *Einführung in die philosophische Mystik* characterized Ātman/Brahman and Dao as terms accepted by the Indian and Chinese traditions respectively in order to point out the ultimate reality, which albeit ineffable, can be approached through a mystical experience of unity (Albert 1996, 11–15, 71–102). Rudolf Bock attempted to compare the concept of Dao in the *Daodejing* with that of Ātman/Brahman in the Upaniṣads (Bock 2003, 185–196). He pointed out that both works ascribe to Ātman/Brahman and Dao similar attributes, such as being nameless, silent, all embracing, and ungraspable (Bock 2003, 195).

While the scholarly insights in these and other related research works are thought-provoking, it is noteworthy that in all examples known to me, the comparisons are made between the Hindu mystical traditions and the so-called "philosophical Daoism" as represented by the *Daodejing* and the *Zhuangzi*.[2] This implies that the Dao under discussion is a "Daoist Dao," usually understood as natural and non-moral, whereas the Confucian metaphysical and moral Dao (as well as the Confucian philosophical mysticism in general) remain largely outside of the framework of comparative research.[3]

This chapter focuses on the Confucian philosophical mysticism, comparing it to the mystical approaches found in Advaita Vedānta. To facilitate the study, I concentrate on the connection between mystical silence and attainment of the ultimate knowledge,[4] as expressed in the scholarship of two selected representatives of these respective traditions—the most important Advaitic philosopher, Ādi Śaṅkara (788–820), and a less known yet influential in his time Confucian scholar, Zhan Ruoshui 湛若水 (1466–1560). Since the nature of mystical experiences is closely connected to the mode of the mystic's self-perception (Trauzettel 1997, 6–9), I dedicate a special attention to understanding the meaning of "selfhood" in the writings of these scholars.

SILENT REALIZATION IN ADVAITA VEDĀNTA AS EXPRESSED IN THE SCHOLARSHIP OF ŚAṄKARA

The idea that knowledge of the ultimate reality can be approached through silence was well accepted by representatives of Advaita Vedānta. Silencing one's speech (*vāk-mauna*), controlling one's organs of perception (*karaṇa-mauna*), and stopping physical actions (*kaṣta-mauna*) were seen as a possible way to enter into "a silence of deep sleep" (*suṣupti-mauna*)—an Advaitic and mystical state of mind, in which the realization of unity of Ātman and Brahman is fully actualized (Venkatesananda 1993, 415). The most famous example of applying silence as a teaching method was that of Dakṣiṇāmūrti, a manifestation of Śiva, who, according to the tradition, was able to enlighten his disciples through silence. Śaṅkara's philosophical hymn, *Dakṣiṇāmūrti stotra*, elucidated the principles of Advaitic teaching, while the invocation verses to this hymn, attributed to one of Śaṅkara's followers, made a clear connection between Dakṣiṇāmūrti's silence and Advaitic realization/knowledge (*jñāna*). According to the text, "the teacher taught in silence, but the doubts of the students were all dispelled" (Yegnasubramanian 2004, 29–33).

The meaning of *jñāna* was the grasping that one's real Self, Ātman, is not associated with one's body or mental capacities, but rather is identical with the universal Self and the ultimate reality, Brahman. Attaining *jñāna* effectively implied the loss of one's personal identity and was accompanied by silence because realizing the unity and factual identity of Ātman/Brahman led to the disappearance of the subject-object distinction. According to the interpretation of Śrī Ramaṇa Maharṣi (1879–1850), the loss of personal identity was precisely the reason why the doubts of Dakṣiṇāmūrti's disciples could be dispelled in the silent presence of their teacher (Maharṣi 2006, 385). Yet silence could be helpful only for well-prepared disciples. Less experienced aspirants could not benefit from it. They needed teachers and words (Maharṣi 2006, 547). One of the most effective methods of intellectual preparation in Advaita Vedānta was considered to be reading and meditating over the Mahāvākyāni—the

"Great Sayings" of the Upaniṣads and especially on the statement "That thou art" (*tat tvam asi*).

Tat Tvam Asi (That Thou Art)

The expression "that thou art" (*tat tvam asi*) appeared nine times in the Chāndogya Upaniṣad (VI. 8–16), where it was employed by Uddālaka Āruṇi Gautama in order to instruct his son, Śvetaketu. Illustrating his argument with a series of examples from the world of nature and everyday life, Uddālaka encouraged his son to understand that the identity associated with the individual "I" as a particular person is an illusion. Concluding his examples with a refrain, containing the phrase "that thou art," Uddālaka seems to suggest that his son, Śvetaketu, is no other but the same "very finest that ensouls the world":

> It is this very fineness which ensouls all this world,
> it is the true one, it is the soul.
> You are that, Śvetaketu. (Deutsch & Dalvi 2004, 14)

The meaning of the phrase "that thou art" was widely debated by representatives of different Vedāntic schools, who, despite the differences in interpretations, agreed that "that" (*tat*) is Brahman.[5] Their efforts, therefore, concentrated on understanding the meaning of the word "thou" and its relationship to "that" in an attempt to resolve the question of whether or not Śvetaketu was indeed Brahman, and if he was, in which sense. Śaṅkara, who like other Advaitists, affirmed such an identity, explained that one should understand the "meaning of the word 'thou' as a pure 'I,' ever-liberated" (Śaṅkara, *Upadeśa Sāhasrī* (hereafter *U.S.*) 18.181; Alston 1990, 368). According to Śaṅkara, "the word 'that' comes to mean the inmost Self, and the word 'thou' comes to mean the same as the word 'that'" (*U.S.* 18.197; Alston 1990, 375).

Illuminating further the meaning of the sentence "that thou art," Śaṅkara employed the double negation "not thus, not thus" (*neti, neti*), which in his view, was "the only description of the Absolute."[6] He claimed that "the two terms 'that' and 'thou' taken together (as united by the word 'art') express the same meaning as the phrase 'not thus, not thus'" (*U.S.* 18.198; Alston 1990, 376). Śvetaketu, therefore, was indeed Brahman. Yet, in order to realize it, there was a need for him to shed all the illusory identities of Śvetaketu as a particular person. Like the Absolute which could not be described in words, but could only be intuitively "singled out" through negation "not thus, not thus," so the pure "I" of Śvetaketu had to be "singled out" and thus liberated from the illusion of associating it with one's body, mental capacities, or social ties.

The Way of Discernment: Face and Reflection

To explain the difference between one's pure "I" and one's empirical "I," Śaṅkara used the example of one's face and its reflection (*ābhāsa*) in a mirror. Even though "men take the reflection of the face in the mirror to be one with the face," (*U.S.* 18.63; Alston 1990, 300) the form reflected in a mirror is not the real face itself. In the same way, one's empirical and ego-self is a mere reflection of the supreme Self in the mirror of the intellect. Therefore, it should not be perceived as a reality in itself. However, the empirical self, like a reflection of the face in a mirror, is not a mere illusion. The face and its reflection, though not identical, are still connected through the agency of a mirror. In the same way, the supreme "I" and the empirical "I" of Śvetaketu were connected through the agency of an empirical knower (*pramātṛ*). It was no other than Śvetaketu, who had to realize that he is the supreme Self (Alston 1990, 326).

Since Brahman itself could not be considered as a subject or object of knowledge, the realization of one's pure Self was possible only through apprehension of its reflection in an intellect and by gradually moving from this reflection to the pure "I." Explaining this idea of Śaṅkara, a seventeenth century commentator, Rāma Tīrtha, suggested that the acceptance of a reflection theory makes the sentence "that thou art" useful for purposes of intellectual/spiritual enlightenment. The word "thou" referring to both a pure self of Śvetaketu and its reflection in an intellect, is a bridge allowing one to proceed from realizing the difference between one's pure self and its reflection, toward "that" (*tat*) pure Self, to which words and concepts cannot be applied (Alston 1990, 326–27).

Minimalizing and Expanding: The Nature of the Self

In the process of instructing his son, Uddālaka asked Śvetaketu to split the banyan fruit and tell what he sees inside of it. Receiving the boy's reply that inside the fruit there are a number of fine seeds, Uddālaka encouraged Śvetaketu to split these seeds as well. He then once again posed the question, "What do you see inside it?" Śvetaketu's answer, "Nothing, sir," became a pivot point of Uddālaka's guidance: he revealed to his son that the invisible fineness inside the seeds is that very fineness which allows the banyan tree to grow so big (Deutsch and Dalvi 2004, 14).

The example of the banyan fruit illustrated well the methodology of searching for one's self by breaking and removing the layers of familiar associations which affect one's self-perception. Intriguingly, proceeding from the bigger to the smaller, splitting the fruit and then the seeds, resulted in discovering not a solid substance which could be identified, but rather emptiness and nothingness. Similarly, disassociating oneself from false perceptions regarding one's selfhood (by means of a double negation "not thus, not thus") would gradually lead one on the road of "splitting" and minimalizing the realm associated with one's self only to discover that no identifiable self can be found. Yet, this very discovery was the essence of *jñāna,* since the nothingness at the very center of banyan seeds was that "very fineness which ensouls all the world." It was "that" (*tvam*). It was Śvetaketu. It was the realized unity of Ātman and Brahman.

The essence of such a discovery, on the one hand, consisted in an actual and immediate loss of one's private identity. On the other hand, however, it also led one to an extreme expansion of one's self. According to Śaṅkara, when the unity of Ātman and Brahman is realized, one "sees all as his own Self alone, which is the meaning of the whole sentence ('that thou art')" (*U.S.* 18.223; Alston 1990, 387).

The experience of realization, therefore, is characterized by a double dynamic: the realm of one's self is minimalized to the point of nothingness, which in turn leads to the all-embracing expansion of the self. This double dynamic can be understood with the help of a theory of introvertive and extrovertive mystical experiences, conceptualized by Stace (1960).[7] While the technique of applying a double negation "not thus, not thus" to all familiar definitions building one's individual identity was supposed to direct one's search inward, it surprisingly resulted in an understanding that "all is self," which was directed outward. The introvertive and extrovertive modes of mystical experiences were unified through silent realization, summarized by the Great Saying "that thou art."

SILENT REALIZATION IN CONFUCIANISM AS EXPRESSED IN THE SCHOLARSHIP OF ZHAN RUOSHUI

Although less noted by modern researchers, the possibility of approaching the ultimate reality through silence was discussed by Confucian scholars. The founder of the tradition, Confucius (551–479 BCE), openly expressed his wish to remain silent and thus resemble Heaven, which "does not speak" (*Lunyu* 17.19). Even more important was an idea of realizing/knowing in silence (*mo er shi zhi* 默而識之), expressed in the *Analects* of Confucius and paralleled by a statement from the commentarial part of the *Book of Changes*.[8] The question of the meaning of silence and its connection to one's intellectual transformation engaged numerous commentators. One of the most interesting examples of Confucian discourse on this issue was presented during the sixteenth century by the Ming dynasty scholar, Zhan Ruoshui.[9]

In the later years of his life Zhan undertook several trips to the sacred mountain Heng (Hengshan 衡山).[10] Accompanied by his disciples, he used the traveling time as an opportunity for reflecting, discussing philosophical issues, and instructing his students. It was during his first trip to Mt. Heng in 1544 at the age of seventy-nine *sui* that Zhan articulated philosophical insights significant for understanding his mystical quest. Zhan's discussions with his students not only emphasize the importance of silence in the process of attaining knowledge, but also reveal his particular vision of selfhood, which most likely was influenced by what he himself experienced while traveling.

A Teaching of Travelling to the Mountains: Zhan Ruoshui on Observation and Self-Perception

In 1544, while on route to Mt. Heng, Zhan explained to his followers what the proper way of encountering mountains should be. Referring to the statement of his teacher, Chen Xianzhang 陳獻章 (1428–1500),[11] Zhan reminded his students that one should not allow one's heart/mind to chase after any external objects, including extraordinary views and mountains. He further claimed that the world of nature can help one understand one's own selfhood and suggested that mountains should be observed with/through one's self (*yiwo guanshan* 以我觀山).[12]

Zhan's guidance, which his disciples would later dub the "Teaching of Travelling to the Mountains" (Zhan 1555, *juan* 33, 22) contradicted, at least at first glance, the method of "observing things with/through things" (*yiwu guanwu* 以物觀物), conceptualized by Shao Yong 邵雍 (1012–1077). The method of "observing things with/through things"[13] was well-accepted and praised by Confucian intellectuals: it was supposed to safeguard one from selfishness and thus from being affected by personal emotions, preferences, and biases. The oddness of Zhan's suggestion prompted his students to inquire about its meaning. Elaborating his ideas, Zhan challenged the understanding of one's "I" (*wo*) as an accumulator of selfish interests, promoting a mystical vision of one's self as united with all other beings:[14]

> [I, Zhan Ruoshui] said: "Among ten thousand things there is nothing that is not [my own] self (*wo* 我). If one's [emotions] are changed following the scenery, the self will be lost."[15] [The student] asked: "When one sees falcons dwelling in the mountains and singing birds,—what then?" [I] replied: "This is the flight of my essential nature (*xing* 性)." [Then I was] asked [again]: "when one sees fishes swimming and leaping in deep waters,—what then?" [I said]: "This is a [playful] hiding of my essential nature." The question [followed]: "when one sees monkeys and deer running and jumping,—what then?" [I] said: "This is the movement of my essential nature." "And when one sees grass and trees flourish?" [was the next question]; [I replied]: "This is the growth of my essential nature. There is no flight, [playful] hiding,

> movement or growth outside of my essential nature; there is nothing that is not [my own] self. This is why [if one] takes [all this as] one's self and observes, [he] will [find] benefit everywhere. But if [one] lets one's self to follow scenery, [he will enjoy] shaped stones and large trees and unavoidably lose determination. Not only that there will be no benefit, but there will be harm. (Zhan 1555, *juan* 33, 22)

Zhan's argumentation is interesting, because it reveals his sensitivity to different aspects of one's selfhood. On the one hand, Zhan claimed that one's self should be "autonomous" in a way that will allow the authenticity of one's selfhood to be preserved without being affected or changed by encounters with external things. On the other hand, Zhan repeatedly emphasized the importance of understanding that other things and beings should be perceived as if they were one's own self.

Zhan's conscious intellectual engagement with the question of one's selfhood received a special manifestation in laudatory scripts, written to accompany his portraits created on different occasions by several painters.[16] Intriguingly, these laudatory scripts present examples of an intellectual mindset that exhibits elements of both introvertive and extrovertive forms of mysticism.

In Search for the Genuine Self: "Reversed Observation"

While there is no doubt that Zhan willingly allowed his images to be portrayed (Bauer 1990, 423), his laudatory scripts emphasized again and again that the portraits did not represent his selfhood. Thus on one occasion he claimed that he had no form or voice and that it was the painter, Lu Xishang 盧希商, who "formed" him (Zhan 1555, *juan* 22, 25). In another piece, Zhan criticized the tendency of people to look for skillful and realistic representation of oneself in a portrait, claiming that the question of whether or not the painted image looks like the depicted person is altogether irrelevant, for one's selfhood should be perceived not according to one's appearances, but in unity with Heaven, Earth, and all other beings:

> When Mr. Ou had finished painting the [image] of an elderly Mr. [Zhan] Ganquan (Zhan Ruoshui) and left, someone asked: "This drawing of [yours] looks like [you] or not?" Then I answered to that: "What does it mean looks like [me] or not? [One would] rather ask 'Does this painting resemble me (*wo* 我)? Does [this] 'me' resemble my genuine 'I' (*zhenwo* 貞我)? Does my genuine 'I' resemble Heaven and Earth?'"[17] Heaven and Earth are not yet resembled [by me], thousand things are not yet "there [in me]," but rather "I" is searched for between reflections and echoes; how is it different from [the mistaken practice] of looking for a [superlative] horse according to the [external attributes, such as its] color or sex?[18] One only sees [the image of]

> oneself [reflected] in "one's soup or on the wall"[19] and tries to figure out whether it is similar or different! (Zhan 1555, *juan* 22, 24)

Zhan's articulation in this passage leaves no doubts that he perceived one's "genuine I" and one's image, captured in colors by a painter or appearing on the water-surface, as different entities. More importantly, Zhan insisted that in order to find one's genuine self, one had to reverse the direction of one's search: instead of looking for reflections of oneself in external objects, one had to seek first to reflect and contain in one's self Heaven, Earth, and the multitude of beings.

While the framework of references, used by Zhan to justify this "reversed" search, was clearly Confucian (it was connected to the proposition of Mencius "to return to oneself" (*fanshen* 反身), for "ten thousand things are there in me") (*Mengzi* 7A.4), there are indications that his perception of selfhood as a reflection of Heaven, Earth, and other beings was based not only on the intellectual understanding of Confucian scriptures, but also on his personal experience. Referring in one of the laudatory scripts to the episode of observing the sun together with Zhou Zizheng 周自正, the painter who accompanied him during the first trip to Mt. Heng, Zhan gave a rare testimony of his own experience of mystical absorbance:

> [. . .] At that moment I [felt] as in the state of oblivion, as if I have forgotten whether I was the sun or myself, whether I observed the sun or the sun observed me, or was it that I observed my own birth? My dream has been long. [If] I would like to know the span of my life by looking at my facial and bodily features [appearing] in the sun, what signs and omens would be there? People see [the sun] as a fire-like wheel, I see [it] as a water-like crystal. One's original essence (*benti* 本體) is revealed [in it]; how pure its clearness is! (Zhan 1555, *juan* 22, 22)[20]

Looking at one's features appearing in the sun differed from seeing one's face reflected in a mirror.[21] Unlike a mirror or still water which is cool and detached, the sun, with its brightness and warmth, penetrated into one's being and did not allow one's image to be generated on the surface. What Zhan observed then was not the reflection of his face, but rather his real face: in the mystical experience of unity, the sun was Zhan's genuine "I" and the genuine "I" of the sun was no other than he, Zhan Ruoshui.

Zhan's self-perception as connected to all other beings can be characterized as an extrovertive mode of mystical experience. Yet, Zhan's intellectual/spiritual search was directed not only outward, into the world of nature, but also inward. It was this second more calm, reflective, and intellectual mode of searching for one's genuine selfhood that, according to Zhan, had to be reached though silence. Intriguingly, this mode was also articulated by Zhan in terms of a "reversed" search. Yet, this time the attention should have been redirected not from the painted image to one's selfhood, but even further—from observing a person's physical face into the depth of one's own being:

> O, Shengzhai! You see my face, but cannot see your own face; I cannot see my face, yet [I] can see your face. How is it that when one observes another, [one's vision] is clear; when one observes oneself, [one's vision] is blurry. Shengzhai, Shengzhai! Why not to forget each other within that [realm which is] outside of one's bodily form and, turning one's sight inward, to observe the beauty of our original face?[22] Could [we try] facing each other [grasp in profound] silence that which cannot be expressed in words [in order to] meditate one another through spirit? (Zhan 1555, *juan* 22, 27)

The text of this laudatory script differs in tone from the examples discussed earlier. Instead of a somewhat ecstatic expression of feelings experienced when observing the sun, it presents the reader with an intellectual reflection on the nature of selfhood. The text does not refer to Zhan's painted image. Instead, it concentrates on the way people perceive themselves and others. Noting that one cannot see one's own face yet seems to see clearly the face of the other, Zhan pointed out that the image of one's face perceived by an observer is only a superficial capturing of one's external features. This is evident because Zhan proposed his friend and painter, Zhang Shengzhai 張省齋, to forget what he observes and together with the object of his observation (it is with Zhan himself) turn they eyes inward, observing themselves in a reversed manner.

The introvertive mode of turning one's sight inward and grasping the goodness of one's original face in profound silence was almost immediately redirected again, reaching outward. Zhan claimed that observing oneself in a reversed manner would allow one to appreciate the beauty of the genuine self of another person and even to communicate with that person without words, through spirit.[23]

Silent Realization: Understanding Principle, Reestablishing Dao

While Zhan's search for the genuine self was accompanied by mystical silence, the most significant feature of Zhan's mysticism was yet another notion—that of silent realization (*moshi* 默識). Unlike silent appreciation of one's own self or silent communication in spirit, silent realization was directed not to discovering one's genuine selfhood, but rather to understanding and grasping "Heavenly principle" (*tianli* 天理).

Discovering one's genuine self through the mystical experience of unity was only a first step in the process of the appreciation of the existential principle that underlies the phenomenological reality. For Zhan Ruoshui, this principle was to be searched for by means of reading and contemplating the Confucian scriptures. Yet, in order to be able to understand the Confucian message, students had first to come to grips with their genuine selfhood and then turn to reading and contemplating the authenticity of Confucian truths. Silent realization was supposed to occur not outside of Confucian intellectual engagements, but rather within the realm of Confucian learning:

> In learning one should seek reaching things by oneself (*zide* 自得) and this is all. If one reaches it by oneself, then "[all processes taking place under Heaven] will come to the same (successful) issue, though by different paths; there is one result, though there might be a hundred anxious schemes."[24] If so, then the sayings of righteous persons of the past will be [the part] of my own learning and thinking. It does not have to be uniform, does not have to be different, it all comes to the same "one." What is this "one?" It is principle. What should we trust/believe in? Trust/believe the principle and this is all! But the taste/understanding of it comes from silent realization; it is not something that tongue and brush can exhaust. When one still did not meet [this understanding], one just needs to trust himself and to nourish himself, seeking in this way to reach things by oneself, for the sake of reestablishing this [Confucian] Dao of ours.[25]

This passage clarifies that unlike the authors of the *Daodejing* and the *Zhuangzi*, Zhan did not seek to attain private freedom from restrains of society by means of promoting mystical unity with all things within the universe. Rather, his goal was clearly public and distinctively Confucian: to reestablish the Confucian Dao.[26]

MYSTICAL VISIONS OF ŚAṄKARA AND ZHAN RUOSHUI: COMPARATIVE OUTLOOK

The discussion above reveals the existence of interesting parallels between Hindu and Confucian mysticisms, represented by the scholarship of Śaṅkara and Zhan Ruoshui. Both Śaṅkara and Zhan Ruoshui claimed that realization occurs in silence and does not depend on the intellectual effort. Yet, both considered the intellectual preparation as necessary for attaining *jñāna* and *moshi*. Both scholars made a connection between attainment of silent realization and a transformed self-perception; both used the analogy of reflection (in a mirror or by a painted image) to distinguish between one's real/genuine self, revealed through silent realization, and one's illusory or not genuine self.[27] Both Śaṅkara and Zhan Ruoshui suggested that in order to understand one's real/genuine selfhood, there is a need to turn one's sight inward. Yet, both also claimed that the realization of one's real/genuine selfhood leads to the expansion of the realm perceived as one's self and results in unity with all other beings.

The differences between the worldviews of these two scholars are also apparent. Even though Śaṅkara's and Zhan Ruoshui's mystical visions contain introvertive and extrovertive modes of experiences, the introvertive mode is central for Śaṅkara's mystical method, while Zhan Ruoshui's experiences are primarily of the extrovertive type. Śaṅkara addressed one's intellectual/spiritual search in a somewhat cool and detached manner, while Zhan Ruoshui's records are characterized by a greater emotionality and warmth.[28]

More importantly, the goals of mystical realization in Advaita Vedānta and Confucianism were different. In Advaita Vedānta, the goal of attaining *jñāna* was the discovery of one's real self and a realization of a complete unity between Ātman and Brahman. Such unity was a unity through identity, which implied the disappearance of the subject-object distinction. Mystical silence was a direct result of this unity: it originated in the absence of the distinction between the perceiver and the perceived.

In Confucianism, as represented by Zhan Ruoshui, understanding the nature of one's genuine self, although important, did not constitute the goal of silent realization. The goal of *moshi* was in understanding the Heavenly principle and in grasping the Dao. The unity promoted by Zhan Ruoshui was not the unity through identity with the Dao or other beings. Rather, it was seen as a communion based on the fact that all beings share the same essential nature (*xing* 性). Zhan's "I" was centered and personal, yet essentially connected to the world around him through *xing*.

This approach differed from the model of unity promoted by Daoist thinkers, because it did not imply the dissolution of one's private self within the world of nature.[29] It also differed significantly from the model of unity promoted by Śaṅkara, because unlike Ātman and Brahman, Zhan's genuine "I" or "self" was not the Dao. In Confucian settings, one could internalize Dao and come to resemble Heaven and Earth, yet one could not *become* Dao or Heaven. A certain duality between the perceiver (even the one who fully realized his genuine selfhood) and that which had to be realized (Dao or principle) was always preserved. Silence accompanied Confucian realization because the experience itself could not be intellectualized and put into words. Yet, it did not imply the disappearance of the subject-object distinction.

The character of intellectual/spiritual transformation in two traditions was also different. Unlike Hindu *jñāna,* which implied moving from the darkness of illusion (*māyā*) to the light of realizing the reality of one's own self,[30] Confucian silent realization did not presuppose such a movement. The concept of illusion was absent from the Confucian worldview. The world of nature and human society were considered as objective, existing independently from one's subjective perceptions. To grasp the objective principle of this objective world was the sole purpose of Confucian *moshi*.

POST SCRIPTUM: "*TAT TVAM ASI* IN CONTEXT" AND UNITY IN *XING*

As it has been shown, despite the existence of similarities in the philosophical argumentation employed by Śaṅkara and Zhan Ruoshui, the models of mystical unity in Advaita Vedānta and Confucianism differed in their nature. The Advaitic unity implied the full identification of Ātman and Brahman, which allowed Śaṅkara to claim that Śvetaketu was, in fact, Brahman. In the Confucian model, the connection between one's self and other beings was not perceived as unity through identity, but rather as a communion through the common essential nature—*xing*.

While these differences hold true within the framework of Śaṅkara's and Zhan Ruoshui's scholarship, one further similarity between the two traditions may be somewhat concealed by Śaṅkara's interpretation of the Upaniṣads. Like many other commentators after him, Śaṅkara interpreted *tad* in the phrase *tat tvam asi* (that thou art) philosophically as *sat*, referring to Being (Brahman) and the "finest essence," without being bothered by the fact that *tad* (that) and *tvam* (thou) disagreed syntactically.[31] Yet, as insightfully noted by Brereton (1986, 98), in the context of the original statement in the Chāndogya Upaniṣad *tad* is neuter, whereas *tvam*, as well as *aṇiman-* (finest essence), are not. Brereton suggests that this disagreement implies a deeper significance. He claims that *tad* does not refer to the "finest essence" or Brahman, but rather to an existential condition of being "pervaded by the finest essence" (Brereton 1986, 109). He therefore translates the passage containing the phrase *tat tvam asi* as follows: "That which is this finest essence, that the whole world has as its self. That is the truth. That is the self. In that way are you, Śvetaketu" (Brereton 1986, 109).

This suggests that the teaching of Uddālaka consisted not in claiming that Śvetaketu was the "very fineness which ensouls all this world," but rather that he, like all other beings in the world, was in a condition of living and being nurtured by the same existential essence. For Śvetaketu, as well as for others, this essence was the self, "for everything exists by reference to it" (Brereton 1986, 109).

While it is beyond my expertise to discern whether or not such an interpretation may challenge the traditional perception of selfhood or of mystical unity in Advaita Vedānta, it seems that the claims of unity through appreciation of the common existential essence make it reasonable to see it as comparable, at least to a certain degree, to the Confucian model of unity through communion in *xing*.

Like Zhan Ruoshui, who encouraged his students to observe the mountains "with/through one's self," perceiving the growth of grass and trees as a growth of their own essential nature, Uddālaka encouraged his son to understand that he, Śvetaketu, like the banyan tree, exists because he contains within himself that "finest essence."

NOTES

1. This article was written during my stay as a Hans Jensen-Minerva fellowship holder at the International Consortium for Research in the Humanities "Fate, Freedom and Prognostication: Strategies of Coping with the Future in East Asia and Europe," University of Erlangen-Nuremberg, Germany. I would like to express my gratitude to the Minerva Foundation and to the International Research Consortium in Erlangen for their support. I also would like to thank Dr. Sven Sellmer for generously answering my questions on Hindu philosophy. As well, my thanks are extended to Professors Ping-yi Chu, Ping-tzu Chu, Marc Kalinowski, Joachim Gentz, and Fabrizio Pregadio for their help to resolve some of my questions regarding Chinese sources.

2. Generally, scholarly research on Chinese mysticism deals mainly with the early Daoist tradition. See Yearley 1983; Kohn 1991, 1992; Roth 1995; 2003. For criticism of an undifferentiated application of the term "mysticism" to Daoism, see Reiter 1996. For studies addressing in addition to Daoist thought some aspects of Confucian mysticism, see Ching 1983; Wu 1995; Trauzettel 1998. For studies dealing explicitly with the Confucian philosophical mysticism, see Chen 1991, 390–415; 2008, 145–186. For a book-length study that explicates the importance of the mystical perception of reality in Chinese settings, connecting it to the issue of political power, see Ching 1997.

3. For more on the meanings of Dao in Daoism and Confucianism, see Cheng 2003.

4. Ineffability and noetic quality were defined by James (1936) as two essential and sufficient characteristics of the mystical experience. James's classification is still accepted by the majority of scholars in the field, see Dupré 2005.

5. For the discussion on the meaning of this phrase, see Gupta and Wilcox 1984; Myers 1993; Lipner 2000.

6. With reference to Śaṅkara's commentary to Bṛhadāraṇyaka Upaniṣad 2.3.6, see Alston 1990, 376.

7. Roth (1995) applies Stace's theory to the interpretation of the mystical experience in the *Zhuangzi*.

8. *Lunyu* 7.2; *Xicizhuan* 1.12. In the context of *Xicizhuan*, the emphasis was not on realizing, but rather on "completing in silence" (*mo er cheng zhi* 默而成之). See also Li 2004.

9. Zhan Ruoshui (Zhan Ganquan 湛甘泉) had a successful official career and significant scholarly influence. He founded at least thirty-seven Academies. Ac-

cording to Deng (2004, 161), the number of Academies could be as much as fifty and comparable only with the number of Academies founded by Zhu Xi 朱熹 (1130–1200). For more on Zhan Ruoshui's life and thought, see Fang 1976; Ching 1976; Wood 2003; Chin 2003; Chung 2001. For the discussion of the "realm of the ineffable" (*wuyan de jingjie* 無言的境界) in Zhan Ruoshui's thought, see Qiao 1993, 202–219.

10. During his lifetime, Zhan made three trips to Mt. Heng in 1544, 1553, and 1556. Fang 1976, 39.

11. Chen Xianzhang, *Baisha Quanji* 白沙全集, *juan* 3 (available online at the Hanquan Database of Ancient Texts (Palace Museum, Taipei, Taiwan): 210.69.170.100/s25/ (last retrieved: July 2012).

12. Zhan Ruoshui, "You Nanyue ji" 遊南嶽記. I use the version of this text as appears in Zhan's "Yueyou jixinglu" 嶽遊紀行錄. See Zhan 1555, *juan* 33, 15. My references to page numbers in this source are according to the electronic edition.

13. Shao Yong, *Guanwu neipian* 觀物內篇, chap. 12. "Observing things with/through things" was explained by Shao as "not observing things with/through one's self" (*bu yiwo guanwu* 不以我觀物). See Shao 2010, 49. See also Wyatt 2003a, 2003b.

14. For the concepts of "I" and "self" in pre-modern China, see Bauer 1990, 31–36, 60–72; Trauzettel 1990. For the discussion about the idea of "expanded self" in Chinese philosophy, see Bloom 1985.

15. I translate and interpret the version of the text as it appears in *juan* 33 of Zhan 1555. The version of the text as appears in *juan* 4 of the same collection has the character *zhi* 知 (to know) instead of *shi* 失 (to lose). The character *zhi* 知 does not suit the inner logic of the text; most likely it is a misprint.

16. These scripts are found in *juan* 22 of Zhan 1555. See also the discussion of some of these scripts in connection to Zhan Ruoshui's perception of selfhood in Bauer 1990, 421–427.

17. In this passage, Zhan signified one's true selfhood using the term *zhenwo* 貞我, possibly in order to distinguish it from the Daoist and Buddhist concepts of *zhenwo* 真我 (one's real or true self). *Zhen* 貞 has connotations of purity, stability, sincerety, and uprightness. I translate it as "one's genuine self."

18. Reference to *Liezi*, chapter 8.

19. Reference to *Houhan shu* 後漢書, "Li Gu zhuan" 李固傳 [The Biography of Li Gu].

20. For an alternative translation, see Bauer 1990, 424.

21. For a discussion of the mirror symbol in Chinese mysticisms, assessed from a comparative perspective, see Ching 1983.

22. I translate here the Chinese term *fanguan* 反觀 as "to observe, turning one's sight inward." The term *fanguan* was also employed by Shao Yong. For Shao, *fanguan* and "observing things with/through things" were identical in meaning. In my understanding, the difference between Shao's and Zhan's approaches was connected mainly to their interpretation of one's "self" or "I" (*wo*). While Shao used *wo* in a "negative" sense, meaning mainly one's "selfish self," Zhan's *wo* also implied a positive meaning of one's genuine self. For a summary of the scholarly views on *fanguan* and for the discussion of its meaning in Shao Yong's thought,

see Katz 2009, 204–210, 272–284. Bauer (1990, 423) translates *fanguan* in this passage as "uns gegenseitig betrachten" (to observe/contemplate each other).

23. For another passage, emphasizing the importance of silence in facilitating communication in spirit, see "You Nanyue ji" as appears in *Yueyou jixinglu* (Zhan 1555, *juan* 33, 23).

24. Reference to *Xicizhuan* 2.5. James Legge's translation.

25. "Da Zheng jinshi qifan" 答鄭進士啟範, in Zhan 1540, *juan* 8, 25. On the concept of *zide*, see de Bary 1991, 43–69.

26. The importance of silent realization for reestablishing of the Confucian Dao was most poignantly discussed by Zhan in an essay entitled "Records on the Hall of Silent Realization," written at the age of ninety-four. Zhan claimed that silent realization constitutes the essence of the sagely teaching and a basis for Confucian transmission of Dao. See "Moshi tang ji" 默识堂记, in Zhan 1681, *juan* 18, 233–234.

27. While both scholars distinguished between real/genuine and unreal/not genuine selves, their understanding of what the unreal or not genuine meant was different. For Śaṅkara, one's unreal self was illusory: it was a result of a self-perception distorted by the power of *māyā*. For Zhan Ruoshui, one's not genuine self was not illusory and unreal as such. It was not genuine, because it was not yet purified through the process of Confucian self-cultivation.

28. It is interesting to see how Śaṅkara and Zhan Ruoshui discussed one's selfhood using the symbol of the sun. While Śaṅkara compared the real self, reflected in the intellect, to the sun reflected in water (*U.S.*, 14.33), Zhan Ruoshui contemplated his own self as seen in the sun.

29. On the difference between Daoist and Confucian attitudes to one's selfhood, see Trauzettel 1997, 9.

30. For the role of Śaṅkara in developing the concept of *māyā*, see Radhakrishnan 1914.

31. As Brereton (1986, 102) notes, "According to Śaṅkara's comments in the *Brahma-sūtra-bhāṣya*, the pronouns refer to a single reality which is called Being (*sat*)."

BIBLIOGRAPHY

Albert, Karl. 1996. *Einführung in die philosophische Mystik*. Darmstadt: Wissenschaftliche Buchgesellschaft.

Alston, A. J., trans. 1990. *The Thousand Teachings (Upadeśa Sāhasrī) of Śrī Śaṃkarācārya*. London: Shanti Sadan.

Bauer, Wolfgang. 1990. *Das Antlitz Chinas: Die Autobiographische Selbstdarstellung in der chinesischen Literatur von ihren Anfängen bis Heute*. München and Wien: Carl Hanser.

Bloom, Irene. 1985. "On the Matter of the Mind: The Metaphysical Basis of the Expanded Self." In *Individualism and Holism: Studies in Confucian and Taoist Values*, edited by Donald Munro (Ann Arbor: Center for Chinese Studies, University of Michigan), 293–330.

Bock, Rudolf. 2003. *Lao-tzu und Chuang-tzu. Der philosophisch-mystische Taoismus.* Münster: Principal Verlag.
Brereton, Joel P. 1986. "'Tat Tvam Asi' in Context." *Zeitschrift der Deutschen Morgenländischen Gesellschaft* 136: 98–109.
Chen Lai 陳來. 1991. *Youwu zhi jing: Wang Yangming zhexue de jingshen* 有無之境: 王陽明哲學的精神 [Between *being* and *non-being*: The spirit of Wang Yangming's philosophy]. Beijing: Renmin.
——. 2008. *Song-Ming ruxue lun* 宋明儒學論 [On Confucianism of Song and Ming dynasties]. Hong Kong: Joint Publishing.
Chen Xianzhang 陳獻章. *Baisha Quanji* 白沙全集 [Complete Works of Baisha]. Electronic edition. Available at the Hanquan Database of Ancient Texts (Palace Museum, Taipei, Taiwan): 210.69.170.100/s25/ (last retrieved: July 2012).
Cheng, Chung-ying. 2003. "Dao (Tao): The Way." In *Encyclopedia of Chinese Philosophy*, edited by Antonio S. Cua (New York and London: Routledge), 202–206.
Chin, Annping. 2003. "Zhan Ruoshui (Chan Jo-shui)." In *Encyclopedia of Chinese Philosophy*, edited by Antonio S. Cua (New York and London: Routledge), 851–854.
Ching, Julia. 1976. "A Contribution on Chan's Thought." In *Dictionary of Ming Biography*, edited by L. Carrington Goodrich and Chaoying Fang (New York and London: Columbia University Press), vol. 1, 41–42.
——. 1983. "The Mirror Symbol Revisited: Confucian and Taoist Mysticism." In *Mysticism and Religious Traditions*, edited by Steven T. Katz (Oxford: Oxford University Press), 226–246.
——. 1997. *Mysticism and Kingship in China: The Heart of Chinese Wisdom.* Cambridge and New York: Cambridge University Press.
Chung Tsai-Chun 鍾彩鈞. 2001. "Zhan Ganquan zhexue sixiang yanjiu" 湛甘泉哲學思想研究 [Investigation of the philosophical thought of Zhan Ganquan]. *Zhongguo wenzhe yanjiu jikan* 中國文哲研究集刊 [Bulletin of the Institute of Chinese Literature and Philosophy] no. 19: 345–405.
De Bary, Wm. Theodore. 1991. *Learning for One's Self: Essays on the Individual in Neo-Confucian Thought.* New York: Columbia University Press.
Deng Hongbo 鄧洪波. 2004. *Zhongguo shuyuan shi* 中國書院史 [History of Chinese Academies]. Shanghai: Dongfang chuban zhongxin.
Deutsch, Eliot and Rohit Dalvi, eds. 2004. *The Essential Vedānta: A New Source Book of Advaita Vedānta.* Bloomington: World Wisdom.
Dupré, Louis. 2005. "Mysticism [First Edition]." In *Encyclopedia of Religion*, edited by Lindsay Jones (Detroit: Macmillan Reference USA), vol. 9, 6341–6355.
Fang, Chaoying. 1976. "Chan Jo-shui." In *Dictionary of Ming Biography*, edited by L. Carrington Goodrich and Chaoying Fang (New York and London: Columbia University Press), vol. 1, 36–41.
Gupta, Bina and William C. Wilcox. 1984. "'Tat tvam asi:' An Important Identity Statement or a Mere Tautology." *Philosophy East and West* 34.1: 85–94.
James, William. 1936. *The Varieties of Religious Experience: A Study in Human Nature.* New York: The Modern Library.
Katz, Sophia. 2009. "The Poetry of Unrestrained Sageliness: Shao Yong and a Tradition of Ruist Philosophical Mysticism." PhD diss., The Hebrew University of Jerusalem.

Kohn, Livia. 1991. *Taoist Mystical Philosophy: the Scripture of Western Ascension*. Albany: State University of New York Press.

———. 1992. *Early Chinese Mysticism: Philosophy and Soteriology in the Taoist Tradition*. Princeton: Princeton University Press.

Li Xin-ping 黎馨平. 2004. "Shilun *Zhouyi* yu *Lunyu* zhongde yumo guan" 試論《周易》與《論語》中的語、默觀 [On the voicing out and silence in the *Zhouyi* and the *Analects of Confucius*]. *Zhouyi yanjiu* 周易研究 [Zhouyi studies], no. 2004/2: 38–41.

Lipner, Julius J. 2000. "The Self of Being and the Being of Self: Saṅkara on 'That You Are' (Tat Tvam Asi)." In *New Perspectives on Advaita Vedānta: Essays in Commemoration of Professor Richard De Smet, SJ*, edited by B. J. Malkovsky (Leiden: Brill), 51–69.

Mahārṣi, Ramaṅa. 2006. *Talks with Sri Ramana Maharshi*. Tiruvannamalai: Sri Ramanasramam.

Myers, Michael W. 1993. "Tat tvam asi as Advaitic Metaphor." *Philosophy East and West* 43.2: 229–242.

Qiao Qingju 喬清舉. 1993. *Zhan Ruoshui zhexue sixiang yanjiu* 湛若水哲學思想研究 [Investigation of the philosophical thought of Zhan Ruoshui]. Taipei: Wenjin.

Radhakrishnan, Sarvepalli. 1914. "The Vedanta Philosophy and the Doctrine of Maya." *International Journal of Ethics* 24.4: 431–451.

Reiter, Florian C. 1996. "Aspekte der 'Mystik' in China." *Zeitschrift für Religionswissenschaft* 4: 19–34.

Roth, Harold. 1995. "Some Issues in the Study of Chinese Mysticism: A Review Essay." *China Review International* 2.1: 154–173.

———. 2003. "Bimodal Mystical Experience in the 'Qiwulun 齊物論' Chapter of the *Zhuangzi* 莊子." In *Hiding the World in the World: Uneven Discourses on the* Zhuangzi, edited by Scott Cook (Albany: State University of New York Press), 15–32.

Shao Yong 邵雍. 2010. *Shao Yong ji* 邵雍集 [Collected works of Shao Yong]. Beijing: Zhonghua.

Stace, Walter. 1960. *Mysticism and Philosophy*. Philadelphia and New York: Lippincott.

Trauzettel, Rolf. 1990. "Denken die Chinesen anders? Komparatistische Thesen zur chinesischen Philosophiegeschichte." *Saeculum* 41.2: 79–99.

———. 1997. "Mystik im chinesischen philosophischen Denken." *Minima sinica* no. 2: 1–16.

———. 1998. "Abendländische und chinesische Mystik: Komparatistische und kontrastive Thesen." In *Komparative Philosophie. Begegnungen zwischen östlichen und westlichen Denkwegen*, edited by Rolf Elberfeld (München: Fink), vol. 4, 255–270.

Venkatesananda, (Swami). 1993. *Vasiṣtha's Yoga*. Albany: State University of New York.

Wood, Alan T. 2003. "Zhan Ruoshui 湛若水." In *RoutledgeCurzon Encyclopedia of Confucianism*, edited by Xinzhong Yao (London and New York: RoutledgeCurzon), vol. 2, 795–796.

Wu, Kuang-ming. 1995. "Chinese Mysticism." In *Mysticism and the Mystical Experience*, edited by Donald H. Bishop (Selinsgrove: Susquehanna Univ. Press), 230–259.

Wyatt, Don J. 2003a. "Guan wu 觀物 (Observation of Things)." In *RoutledgeCurzon Encyclopedia of Confucianism*, edited by Xinzhong Yao (London and New York: RoutledgeCurzon), vol. 1, 233–234.

——. 2003b. "Shao Yong 邵雍: 1011–1077." In *RoutledgeCurzon Encyclopedia of Confucianism*, edited by Xinzhong Yao (London and New York: RoutledgeCurzon), vol. 2, 539–541.

Yearley, Lee. 1983. "The Perfected Person in the Radical Chuang-tzu." In *Experimental Essays on Chuang-tzu*, edited by Victor H. Mair (Hawaii: University of Hawaii Press), 125–139.

Yegnasubramanian, S. 2004. "Dakṣiṇāmūrti Stotram of Adi Śaṅkara" (Part 1. Introduction and *dhyAnaslokas*), *Eternal Truth: Journal of Sringeri Vidya Bharati Foundation* (USA) 6.3–4: 29–33. Accessible online at: www.svbf.org/journal/vol6no3-4/10_dakshina.pdf (last retrieved: July 2012).

Zhan Roushui 湛若水. 1540. *Quanweng daquan* 泉翁大全 [Great compendium of Mr. (Gan)quan], *juan* 8 (1540 edition, preserved in National Central Library, Taipei, Taiwan). Available via Scripta Sinica database in an electronic edition, prepared by Prof. Chung Tsai-Chun of the Institute of Chinese Literature and Philosophy, Academia Sinica.

——. 1555. *Ganquan xiansheng xubian daquan* 甘泉先生續編大全 [Sequel to the great compendium of Mr. Ganquan], *juan* 22 and 33 (1555 edition, preserved in the National Central Library, Taipei, Taiwan). Available via Scripta Sinica database in an electronic edition, prepared by Prof. Chung Tsai-Chun of the Institute of Chinese Literature and Philosophy, Academia Sinica.

——. 1681. *Zhan Ganquan xiansheng wenji* 湛甘泉先生文集 [Collected literary writings of Mr. Zhan Ganquan], *juan* 18 (1681 edition). Available through the database of Berlin State Library, Berlin, Germany.

4

Impermanence and Immortality

The Concept of pañca-skandha *in Buddhism and in Twofold Mystery Daoism*

Friederike Assandri

BUDDHISM AND DAOISM IN EARLY MEDIEVAL CHINA

Ever since its teachings reached China in the first centuries CE, Indian Buddhism entered into fruitful interaction with Chinese thinking and religion; an interaction that shaped the development of Buddhism in China as well as that of Daoism.

Daoism, with its roots going back to teachings of the *Daodejing* attributed to Laozi, developed from various traditions that referred to Dao as origin and rule of all that is. Its first known social organization was created in Sichuan by the followers of the Way of the Heavenly Masters after a revelation of Taishang Laojun, the deified Laozi, to their leader in 142 CE. This movement spread from Sichuan to northern China, and as of the fourth century CE also to the south. In southern China existed older local traditions, going back presumably to the Masters of Esoterica (*fangshi* 方士) of the Han dynasty, who claimed the origin of their teachings in Dao. One of their major concerns was longevity and immortality. In the fourth and fifth centuries these different Daoist traditions and Buddhism saw intense interaction, leading among others to the appearance of the important Daoist scriptural corpora of the *Shangqing* and *Lingbao*. Competition with Buddhism spurred a trend toward integration, which eventually changed Daoism from different competing traditions into an institutionalized religion, vying with Buddhism and Confucianism to become the "first teaching" of the state. When in 589 the Sui dynasty reunited the Chinese empire and set up their capital in Chang'an,

Buddhists and Daoists were both established as major players in the capital. In this environment, Twofold Mystery teaching flourished—a Daoist teaching best known for its use of *tetra lemma* logic, which Mādhyamika Buddhism had brought to China, which also co-opted many other Buddhist concepts. Yet, it retained distinct Daoist characteristics, in particular in its soteriology. Where Buddhism considered all life as suffering and aimed at transcending the world to achieve liberation from the cycle of birth and death in complete cessation (*nirvāṇa*), Daoism saw death as the main problem to be overcome and aimed at eternal life.

Twofold Mystery thinkers expressed their ideas in commentaries to philosophical texts like the *Daodejing* as well as in sacred scriptures like the *Benji jing* (Scripture of Original Beginning). They were initiated into the lore of sacred Daoist scriptures, including the *Shangqing* and *Lingbao* scriptures, the techniques of alchemy, visualization and meditation practices, dietetics and exercises that would lead to long life, and also the traditions of philosophical inquiry into Dao. They strove actively to integrate all these different strands into a coherent worldview. Twofold Mystery teaching was a product of the intellectual and cultural exchange of two originally fundamentally different systems of thought, Indian Buddhism and Chinese Daoism.

Co-option of concepts and terminology might suggest cases of influence or plagiarizing;[1] yet, a close look at some instances of co-option of terms and concepts, other than creating labels of plagiarism, on the contrary can serve to underline fundamental differences. One such instance is the concept of the five aggregates (*pañca-skandha, wuyin* 五陰, *wuju* 五聚 or *wuyun* 五蘊), which come temporarily together and thereby create the illusion of a "self." As a core concept of Buddhism, it was introduced in China with the earliest translations of Buddhist texts,[2] it figured prominently in the very popular *Heart sūtra*, and was discussed also in the seventh century.[3]

We find the concept in an influential Daoist scripture of the seventh century, the *Benji jing*. This raises an obvious question: Why would Daoists, whose overriding concern was overcoming death and reaching immortality, incorporate a theory which proves the "non-existence of self?"

A look at the function of the concept in the soteriological frameworks of Buddhism and Daoism underscores one of their major differences in philosophical outlook and soteriology: the realization of impermanence vs. the quest for immortality.

THE FIVE AGGREGATES IN BUDDHISM

In his very first sermon, the *Setting in Motion of the Wheel of the Law*, explaining the first of the Noble Truths, the Buddha says:

> This O monks is the noble truth of suffering: birth is suffering, old-age is suffering, disease is suffering, death is suffering, union with what one dislikes is suffering, separation from what one likes is suffering, not obtaining one's wish is suffering—*in brief the five kinds of objects of attachments* (upādānaskandha) *are suffering.*[4]

The "five kinds of objects of attachments," or, as they are more commonly called, "five aggregates," are at the core of the Buddhist teaching, closely related to the interpretation of being or existence as suffering (*duḥkha*), impermanent (*anitya*), and not-self (*anātman*).[5]

Focused on an analysis of the condition of man and the reasons for his suffering, this Buddhist theory postulated that the self does not have a real substance, but is only an aggregate of five components, namely form (*rūpa, se* 色), sensory reception (*vedanā, shou* 受), perception (*saṃjñā, xiang* 想), mental processing (*saṃskāra, xing* 行), and consciousness (*vijñāna, shi* 識), which are kept together by desire and ignorance of their true empty nature.

Form (*rūpa, se* 色) refers to the organs of the senses, and also to the external "things" or fields, with which the organs establish contact. Reception (*vedanā, shou* 受) arises when the six internal organs (eye, ear, nose, tongue, body, mind) get into contact with external objects, (sight, sound, smell, taste, touch, mental object). The first five organs have separate objects (the eye turns to things that can be seen, the ear to things that can be heard, etc.), the mind instead aims at all six objects together. This contact results in a sensory reception, which can be good, bad, or neutral. Perception (*saṃjñā, xiang* 想) then occurs when the mind, considered as the sixth sense, connects the sensation derived from the sensory reception with a conscious discernment of an external object. Mental Processing (*saṃskāra, xing* 行) then 'brings together' the perception with conscious will, and this finally results in consciousness (*vijñāna, shi* 識), also of the self. Thus the illusion of self is constructed in momentary processes of the "coming together" of these five aggregates.

> When she was questioned about the nature of a being (*sattva*), the nun Vajirā replied: "What do you mean by saying 'being'? Your doctrine is false. This is merely an accumulation of changing formations (*saṃskāra*): there is no being here. Just as wherever parts of the chariot[[6]] get together, the word 'chariot' is used, so equally, wherever there are the five aggregates, there is being; such is common opinion. Everything that is born is just suffering; suffering is what remains and what disappears, nothing else arises but suffering, no other thing than suffering ceases to be."[7]

What keeps the illusion together is desire and ignorance of its true condition. Ignorance of this true nature or self, namely that it is nothing but a temporary aggregate of five components, makes people give in to desire instead of eliminating it, thus continuing their suffering in Saṃsāra. If instead desire is removed and the insubstantiality of self is realized, the five components have nothing that holds them together. The illusion of self disappears and salvation is obtained.

> Thus I have heard. Once the Buddha stayed in the Jetavana-anāthapiṇḍada-ārāma of Śrāvastī. At the time, the World-honored One told the monks: [Physical] form (*se* 色) is not 'self.' [. . .] Reception, perception, mental processing and consciousness (*shou* 受, *xiang* 想, *xing* 行, *shi* 識) are also exactly like this. Monks! What does this mean? Is form permanent or impermanent? The monks answered the Buddha: "It is impermanent, World-honored One!" "Monks! If something is impermanent, is it suffering?" The monks answered the Buddha: "It is suffering, World-honored One!" "If something is impermanent, suffering, it is transient, O learned disciples, can you consider this as there being a self, a distinct self, that is there, or not?" The monks answered the Buddha: "No, World-honored One!" "Reception, perception, mental processing and consciousness are also exactly like this. [. . .] O learned disciples, you have to meditate on these five aggregates as they truly are not self, and why they are not self. Having thus scrutinized, then there will be nothing in all the worlds to cling to. Because there is no clinging, there will be no attachment. Because there is no attachment, one can realize Nirvāṇa."[8]

Scrutiny of the five aggregates in meditation in order to realize they are not-self, impermanent, and suffering, leads to insight into the insubstantiality of the self. This will eliminate the desire or clinging, which holds the aggregates together creating an illusory "self," and bring about release from suffering, liberation from the cycle of life and death, and complete cessation in Nirvāṇa.

THE CONCEPT OF FIVE AGGREGATES IN THE DAOIST *BENJI JING*

Given the general propensity of Daoist teachings to affirm that individual immortality is attainable, this concept that proves the impermanence and insubstantiality of the self seems to run contrary to Daoist teachings. Yet, we find it in some early Tang Daoist texts,[9] most importantly in the *Benji jing*:

> Born from the true father and mother,[10] one proceeds aimlessly to increase and grow and physical form enters the womb as embryo.
>
> From the worldly parents one is born and raised, this completes all organs. Therefore, it is called aggregate of form (*seju* 色聚).
>
> Once the six organs are completed, they come in contact with the six dusts [i.e., external objects] and bring forth six kinds of consciousness; this is called the aggregate of consciousness (*shiju* 識聚).

Since one in vain chooses external objects and discriminates unreal appearances, like: this is male, this is female, mountains and forests, etc. all these are born from the deliberations of the mind, this is why they are called the aggregate of deliberation (*xiangju* 想聚).

Pouring out from the aggregate of deliberation, in vain the differentiation between hating and loving are generated, contesting good and bad, beautiful and ugly are accepted in the mind, this is why it is called the aggregate of the mind (*xinju* 心聚).

Since the generating minds are already manifest, then there arises with regard to what is perceived greed and desire or hate and rejection, ignorance and stupidity and all the evil and vices create counterproductive actions that influence the future lives (karma), bad and fortunate retribution go back and forth without end, this is why it is called the aggregate of deeds (*xingju* 行聚). Aggregate means that small things aggregate together and become solid, [thus] *they create a cover that obscures the beings and lets them live in darkness*.[11] [Meng Anpai quotes this in *Daojiao yishu* and adds "This is the meaning of the five aggregates."[12]]

The sequence of the aggregates listed does not follow the common Buddhist version, which lists consciousness last; yet there are Buddhist precedents for this: Jingying Huiyuan 淨影慧遠 (523–592) in his *Dacheng yizhang* pointed out that the common sequence of the *skandha* is based on an ordering scheme that runs from coarse to subtle, but that the Chengshi 成實[13] teachings offer a different scheme based on chronology:

In the teachings of the Chengshi the arising of the *skandha*s has its chronological order and is not contemporaneous. How is its order? First it explains the aggregate of form (*se* 色), next consciousness (*shi* 識), then deliberation (*xiang* 想), then reception (*shou* 受) and lastly bringing together (*xing* 行). Why is this so? The arising of the mind consciousness must necessarily rely on the six faculties. Among them, five consciousnesses rely on five faculties of form. The will/mind consciousness is of one kind, it relies on the faculty of thought. If we speak from the viewpoint of plurality, consciousness is brought forth relying on form. Therefore consciousness is explained second. What originates from the consciousness is distinguishing and apprehending perceptive forms. Therefore next deliberation is explained. From the apprehending perceptive form arises the feeling of agreeable, disagreeable, or neither disagreeable nor agreeable. Therefore next the reception is explained. From the *dharma*s one receives arise desire and dislike and so on. Therefore next he explains mental processing (*saṃskāra*).[14]

The sequence of the *Benji jing* seems to follow this scheme; the interpretation corresponds essentially with this version, however, there is a significant terminological change: the *Benji jing* replaces the term *shou* (reception), with the term *xin* (heart/mind). Nevertheless, the explanation referring to the arising of like and dislike is consistent with the Buddhist explanation.

In the Daoist vision of the physical and psychological human being, the *xin* (mind/heart) was the physical seat of both, feelings and thinking, and therefore the "place," from where discernment, like and dislike arose.[15]

This passage of the *Benji jing* suggests that Daoists co-opted the five aggregate theory in their teachings, possibly following a version of the Chengshi teachings, which emphasized a chronological order of the activity of the *skandhas*. Why?

THE FIVE AGGREGATES' ROLE IN A DAOIST VISION OF SALVATION IN TWOFOLD MYSTERY TEACHING: COSMOGONY AND SALVATION

To analyze the function of the use of the five aggregates in this Daoist context, we need to look at the conceptual frame of Twofold Mystery soteriology. In the Daoist frame of mind, death was the major problem humans had to face; religious transformation of the Daoist, from alchemists to proponents of "mystic" teachings like Twofold Mystery, ideally should overcome this problem, prolonging life and reaching immortality. The way to this goal was theoretically clear—reiterated from the ancient *Daodejing* to meditative and alchemical practices—the adept had to reach Dao. Yet, the ancient teachings were often vague on the details of this way, and it was here that there was space for the adoption of new tenets and concepts, also from Buddhism.

In accordance with the teachings of the *Daodejing*, Twofold Mystery thinkers considered Dao as the origin, creative force, and ontological substance of all being. Epistemologically, the fact that Dao embraces all being entailed the logical conclusion that Dao must be "non-being" or "nothing," because anything that "is" would necessarily exclude its opposite.[16] Yet, Daoists in medieval China never understood this non-being of Dao as a negation of being; for them it was origin and substance of being. Twofold Mystery thinker's soteriological proposition followed logically from the concept that Dao is the origin of all being: If the process of cosmogony is the linear fashion in which being emerges from Dao, retracing this process backward step by step would necessarily lead back to Dao.

Cheng Xuanying, in the first chapter of his *Daodejing* commentary, says:

> *What we call the limitless great Dao is the true nature of all beings*. What is the great Dao? It is the guideline of empty nonbeing, it is the *origin of creation and change*, . . . it is the root of the light of the spirit, and the source of natural becoming. . . . Before the primordial *qi* and the great emptiness, in absolute stillness, what could have been there? The subtlest essence (*jing* 精) arose, and the True One (*zhenyi* 真一) emerged. The True One moved the spirit

> (*shen* 神) and the primordial *qi* transformed itself. The primordial *qi*, that is the being in the center of nonbeing, [and at the same time] it is the nonbeing in the center of being. . . . Original nonbeing is spirit. At the height of *emptiness* the *spirit* is born. Original nonbeing is *qi*. The *spirit* moves and the *qi* transforms. *Qi* is *originally without qualities*. It coagulates, and [that's how] *form* emerges. *Form* is originally without *feelings*. It moves and is utilized and [that's how] *it looses its inner nature*. Form becomes complete and the inner nature moves *[this is what] drives one ever farther away from the Dao. This is why one is given over to life and death, and moves away from yin and yang; and [no-one] can stop [this process] by himself. It is not so, that the Dao is [first] there, [when man is born], and then forgotten [when he begins to decay].*[17]

The process of transition from nonbeing to being, which initiates cosmogony, at the same time inevitably and almost mechanically pushes human beings away from Dao, from the eternal source of all being. It is thus exactly the process of the generation of being, which is the cause for human mortality.

However, this process does not cause a complete rupture of human beings and Dao, Dao is also ontological substance of all that is, and therefore it is "true inner nature." Working in the frame of the traditional Chinese assumption of a correspondence of microcosm and macrocosm, Twofold Mystery thinkers emphasized that the Dao of the macrocosm exists equally within the microcosm of the human being, where it is called Dao-nature (*daoxing* 道性).[18] Dao-nature, like Dao in the macrocosm, is "out of itself so" (*ziran* 自然),[19] ineffable non-being that is source and ontological substance of all being. It is the "true inner nature" of beings. The *Benji jing* dedicates the fourth chapter to this important concept, and it is here that we find the concept of *pañca-skandha*.

The fact that Dao is also ontological substance or "true inner nature" of human beings is a prerequisite of the soteriological proposition:

> Dao-nature is true reality. . . . [Therefore,] it is called non-action (*wuwei* 無為). It is naturally of itself so; it cannot be caused to be so. It cannot but be so, therefore, it is called "of itself so." Realizing this true nature, everybody says, this is realizing the Dao. Understanding this in the mind, realizing and seeing it, this is completing the highest great Dao. All beings should be able to attain this enlightenment but since they are on the contrary *covered and clouded by tribulations*, they cannot manifest understanding. [Yet,] since the principle [that is the Dao-nature] exists [in them], they must be able to attain it. The Principle has no fixed form; this is why one calls it "nature." [20]

It is Dao-nature, the immanent presence of Dao in all beings, which ensures the possibility of return to Dao. However, Dao-nature is not manifest in beings because they are "covered" and clouded by tribulations. "Tribulations" refers to the movements and vexations of the mind, arising from the very movement that initiates when the mind or feelings begin to exert influence on form, and, as Cheng says, "push one ever farther away from Dao." This is why Cheng's soteriological proposition names "forgetting the feelings" as a crucial moment of the return to Dao:

> This is why the Dao can bring forth being from nonbeing. How should it not be [also] capable of making being the same as nonbeing! Once being is the same as nonbeing, then *being will not end*. Therefore, *what brings forth the ego is the Dao, what brings about the end of the ego, are the feelings*. If only one can forget the *feelings*, then one completes one's inner nature. Is *the inner nature complete*, then the [outer] form becomes complete. Is the *form* complete, then the *qi* will be complete. Is the *qi* complete, then the spirit is complete. Is the *spirit* complete, then the *Dao* is complete. . . .[21]

In Cheng Xuanying's interpretation, the feelings—situated together with cognition in the faculty *xin* (mind/heart)—initiate the "movement" that leads to the loss of the "inner true nature," namely "Dao." This is the ultimate cause of human mortality, of the perishing of the "form." Since return to Dao proceeds in a linear fashion step by step retracing the process of becoming, the "forgetting of the feelings" implies stopping the movement that feeling—and cognition, as both are seated in the *xin*—have initiated. If this can be achieved, then form, which is the physical form of the body, can be perfected and then the more subtle components of life, *qi* and spirit, will be in perfect shape and Dao, the "true nature," origin of being and consequently the eternal source of life can be reached. Therefore in the cosmogonic sequence, Cheng Xuanying says "Form is originally without feelings. It moves and is utilized and [that's how] *it looses its inner nature*." In the soteriological proposition, he writes: "If only one can forget the *feelings*, then one *completes one's inner nature*. Is the *inner nature* complete, then the form becomes complete."

In this vision of the relation of cosmogony and soteriology, where the process of cosmogony is what causes man's distancing from Dao and therefore has to be reversed, the moment when feelings and mind initiate the movement that pushes man away from Dao is crucial. And it was exactly this moment, which the *pañca-skandha* theory analyzed in detail step by step, providing thus a chronologically reversible sequence in much more detail then the traditional Chinese conceptions, which only suggested a rather general "making still" (like dead ashes etc.) of the mind and the feelings.

CONCLUSION

The concept of the interaction of the *pañca-skandha* was one of the core concepts of the earliest teachings of the Buddha. It explained the non-existence of self; the realization of which was a major step for the Buddhist toward salvation, understood as complete cessation in Nirvāṇa.

The same concept was employed in Daoist texts of the early seventh century. Yet far from proving the non-existence of self, in the Daoist context the concept turned into the detailed explanation for how conscious thinking and feelings initiate movement. This explanation was needed—and had been missing in the traditional Daoist lore—because this moment had to be retraced in the reverse order in order to reach unity with Dao and immortality.

NOTES

1. All of this has been leveled especially against Daoism since the early medieval times by Buddhists, and also by twentieth century scholars.

2. For example, T 32 *Foshuo sidi jing* and T 105 *Wuyin biyu jing*, both translated by An Shigao, second century CE.

3. In 647 Xuanzang translated the *Dacheng wuyun lun* T 1612; his disciple Huiyin 會隱 presented it in a court debate against Daoists in 658 (see *Ji gujin Fo Dao lunheng*, T 2104, 4.387c).

4. Lamotte 1988, 28–29, citing *Saṃyutta* I, p. 135. Compare *Foshuo sidi jing*, T 32, 814c10–14.

5. The connection between these concepts is reiterated over and over in the agamas. the third part of the *Saṃyutta Nikāya* (ch. 22–34) is dedicated to this concept. Compare *Za ahan jing*, T 99, 1, 4c–2, 8a.

6. Compare the famous simile of the chariot in the beginning of the *Milindapañha* in Nyanaponika 1998, 50–52.

7. Lamotte 1988, 28–29, citing *Saṃyutta* I, p. 135.

8. *Za ahan jing*, translated by Gunabhadra (394–468), T 99, 2, 7b22–c10.

9. *Tai-shang lingbao zhihui guansheng jing*, DZ 350, 1; *Daomen jingfa xiangcheng cixu*, DZ 1128, 1.7, 3.7; *Taishang lingbao yuanyang miaojing*, DZ 334, 10.6; *Taishang dongxuan lingbao shangpin jiejing*, DZ 454, 7.

10. This refers to Dao, or more concretely to "original *qi*" (*yuanqi*). Compare Steavu-Balint 2010, 210, citing from *Sanhuang sanyi jing* in *Dongshen badi miaojing jing*, DZ 640: "Father and mother are originally joined; in this state they are known as Primal Pneuma (*yuanqi* 元炁), but by responding to transformations, they embody their distinct forms and are called 'father' and 'mother.'"

11. *Benji jing*, 4, P 2806, lines 193–203; Wan 1998, 424.

12. *Daojiao yishu*, DZ 1129, 4: 1ab.

13. The Satyasiddhi school. Its main exposition, the *Chengshi lun* (T 1646), was translated by Kumārajīva.

14. *Dacheng yizhang* T 1851: 623b27–c05.

15. Professor Charles Willemen, in a personal e-mail communication Nov. 11th 2011 confirms that there is no Buddhist precedence for the use of *xin* instead of *shou* in the Abhidharma sequence of the five aggregates.

16. Wang Bi in the third century expressed this epistemological consideration systematically. Cf. Wagner 2003, 57–60.

17. *Daode jing kaiti xujue yishu* of Cheng Xuanying, in Yan 1983, 295–297.

18. Sharf (2002, 68) and Kamata (1966, 61–154) have rightly argued that the concept of Dao-nature owes much to the concept of Buddha-nature. However, it is also possible to read this concept in the light of the traditional Chinese conception of correspondence between macrocosm and microcosm, which permeates much of Daoist thinking.

19. This attribute is associated with Dao in the *Daode jing* (ch. 25).

20. *Benji jing*, ch. 4, P 2806; Wan 1998, 423.

21. *Daode jing kaiti xujue yishu* of Cheng Xuanying, ch. 1, 297.

BIBLIOGRAPHY

Benji jing 本際經 (*Scripture on Original Time*): Wan 1998.

Boisvert, Mathieu. 1995. *The Five Aggregates. Understanding Theravada Psychology and Soteriology*. Waterloo: Wilfried Laurier University Press.

Chengshi lun 成實論 (*Satyasiddhi-śāstra*) T 1646.

Dacheng wuyun lun 大乘五蘊論 (*Mahāyāna Treatise on the Five Skandhas*) T 1612.

Dacheng yizhang 大乘義章 (*Chapters on the Doctrines of Mahāyāna*) by Huiyuan 慧遠 T 1851.

Daode jing kaiti xujue yishu 道德經開題序決義疏 (*Commentary, preface and expose on the Daode jing*) by Cheng Xuanying 成玄英: Yan 1983, 295–297.

Daojiao yishu 道教義樞 (*Pivotal Meaning of the Daoist Doctrine*) by Meng Anpai 孟安排 DZ 1129.

Daomen jingfa xiangcheng cixu 道門經法相承次序 (*Order of Succession of the Daoist Scriptural Legacy*) DZ 1128.

Dongshen badi miaojing jing 洞神八帝妙精經 (*Scripture of the Wondrous Essence of the Eight Emperors of the Dongshen Canon*) DZ 640.

DZ: *Zhengtong Daozang* 正統道藏. Shanghai: Shanghai shangwu yinshuguan, 1923–1926. (Reprint 1962. Taibei: Yiwen yinshuguan.) The numbers follow the work numbers in Shipper Verellen. 2004. *The Taoist Canon. A Historical Companion to the Daozang*. Chicago & London: University of Chicago Press.

Foshuo sidi jing 佛說四諦經 (*Sūtra on the Four Noble Truths*) T 32.

Ji gujin Fo Dao lunheng 集古今佛道論衡 (*Critical Evaluations of Buddhism and Daoism of Past and Present*) by Daoxuan 道宣 T 2104.

Kamata Shigeo 鎌田茂雄. 1966. "Dōsei shisō no keisei katei" 道性思想の形成過程. *Tōyō bunko kenkyūjo kiyō* 東洋文庫研究所記要 4: 61–154.

Lamotte, Etienne. 1988. *History of Indian Buddhism from the Origins to the Śaka Era*. Louvain: Institute Orientaliste, Peters Press.

Nyanaponika, ed. 1998. *Milindapañha. Ein historisches Gipfeltreffen im religiösen Weltgespräch*, translated by Nyanatiloka. Bern, München, Wien: Otto Wilhelm Barth Verlag.

Saṃyutta Nikāya Part 3: *Khandha-vagga*, edited by M. Leon Feer. London: Henry Frowde for the Pali Text Society, 1890.

Sharf, Robert. 2002. *Coming to Terms with Chinese Buddhism, A Reading of the Treasure Store Treatise*. Honolulu: University of Hawaii Press.

Steavu-Balint, Dominic. 2010. "The Three Sovereigns Tradition: Talismans, Elixirs, and Meditation in Early Medieval China." PhD diss., Stanford University, accessed May 10, 2012 , purl.stanford.edu/sz439qw2285.

T: *Taishō Shinshū Daizōkyō* 大正新修大藏經. 100 vol. Tokyo: Taishō issai-kyō kankō kai, 1929–1934.

Taishang dongxuan lingbao shangpin jiejing 太上洞玄靈寶上品戒經 (*Lingbao Scripture on the Supreme Rules*) DZ 454.

Taishang lingbao yuanyang miaojing 太上靈寶元陽妙經 (*Marvelous Scripture of Primordial Yang of Highest Numinous Treasure*) DZ 334.

Taishang lingbao zhihui guanshen jing 太上靈寶智慧觀身經 (*Lingbao Scripture on Wisdom and the Contemplation of the Body*) DZ 350.

Wagner, Rudolf G. 2003. *Language, Ontology, and Political Philosophy in China*. Albany: SUNY.

Wan Yi 萬毅. 1998. "Dunhuang daojiao wenxian Benji jing lu wen ji jieshuo" 敦煌道教文獻《本際經》錄文及解說. In *Daojia wenhua yanjiu* 13, edited by Chen Guying (Beijing: Sanlian), 367–484.

Wuyin piyu jing 五陰譬喻經 (*Sūtra on the Metaphor of the Five Aggregates*) T 105.

Yan Lingfeng 嚴靈峰. 1983. *Jingzi congshu* 經子叢書, vol 6. Taibei: Xuesheng shuju.

Za ahan jing 雜阿含經 (*Saṃyuttanikāya, Connected Discourses*) T 99.

II

ETHICS

5

Li and *Dharma*

Gandhi, Confucius, and Virtue Aesthetics

Nicholas F. Gier

By the term *dharma* . . . I understand nothing short of moral virtue.

—Bimal Krishna Matilal (Matilal 2002, 50)

Elegant is the *junzi* 君子; he is as if cut, as if filed; as if chiseled, as if polished; how freshly bright; how refined. . . .

—*The Book of Odes* (#55)

Neither Gandhi nor Confucius were interested in metaphysics, so the most fruitful approach for our comparative study will be to focus on their ethics. I will propose that Hindu *dharma* and Confucian *li* are closer in meaning than most scholars have believed, and this convergence allows for a constructive comparative analysis. While the concept of *li* than leads easily to the virtues, scholars have rarely viewed *dharma* in these terms. *Dharma* has generally been understood as strict duty, a set of obligations by which all good Hindus, Jains, and Buddhists must live.

If *dharma* is duty, then Hindu ethics should conform to something like Kantianism, but B. K. Matilal maintains that is not really the meaning of *dharma.* Matilal quotes Robert Lingat favorably when he maintains that *dharma* is never "imposed" but simply "proposed"; and he paraphrases Louis Dumont idea that *dharma* "reigns from above without actually governing the world" (Matilal 2002, 42). Both of these descriptions are intriguing but vague, but when Matilal states that *dharma* is "open ended," a rule- or duty-based ethics appears unlikely and the stage is set for a *dharma* virtue ethics.

DHARMA AS VIRTUE

In most instances caste duties are actually explained as virtues, as in this list for *brahmins* in the *Parāśara Smṛti*: "Assiduous work, the bridling of the passions, compassion, liberality, truthfulness, . . . discipline, generosity, righteousness, . . . [and] wisdom. . . ." (Arokiasamy 1986, 25). This virtue ethics is further explained by the development of character traits (*lakṣaṇa*) by which a person's virtues are revealed. In the *Vanaparva* of the *Mahābhārata* King Nahuṣa asks Yudhiṣṭhira what *dharma* is, and he defines it as the virtues of truthfulness, generosity, forgiveness, goodness, kindness, self-control, and compassion (Matilal 2002, 54). Going completely against caste determinism, Yudhiṣṭhira contends that a *śūdra* having these qualities would actually be a *brahmin*, and if a *brahmin* lacks them he would be a *śūdra*. Gandhi and others who proposed to reform the caste system have always had good evidence for their cause.

Rather than being abstract and deontological, *dharma* is, as Häcker (1965, 99) proposes, "radically empirical" and it can be conceived only through experience. Even though social customs stand third behind *śruti* and *smṛti* on many Hindu textual lists, it could be argued that they are actually the true source of *dharma*. For example, this passage from the *Mahābhārata* gives priority to customs: "*Dharma* has its origin in good practices and the *Vedas* are established on *dharma*" (*Vana Parva* 27.107; Kuppuswamy 1977, 17). Furthermore, Āpastamba's *Dharmasūtra* begins: "And we shall explain the accepted customary laws, the authority for which rests on the acceptance by those who know the law and on the Vedas"; and "he should model his conduct after that which is unanimously approved in all regions by Āryas [two upper castes] who have been properly trained" (*The Dharmasūtras* 1.1.1; Olivelle 1999, 7). Häcker (1965, 99) contends that "this is the most concrete and most precise definition of the Hindu concept of *dharma* that I know." In *The Laws of Manu* (12.110–111) Matilal discerns the same "rational-democratic" principle in the provision that a jury of ten men would convene and resolve disputes about the law (Matilal 2002, 78).

Some passages of *The Laws of Manu* define *dharma* as custom not duty. The righteous king "should ordain (as law) whatever may be the usual custom of good, religious twice-born men, if it does not conflict with (the customs of) countries, families, and castes" (*The Laws of Manu* 8.46; Doniger and Smith 1999, 156). The king was to honor local custom even though it might contravene *smṛti*. This analysis supports the theory that laws are indeed abstracted from customs and the practice of the virtues, and only if this axiological priority was honored could a healthy flexibility and tolerance of different customs and virtues flourish. Stanley Tambiah has discovered this type of moral polity in ancient Sri Lanka: "The polities modeled on mandala-type patterning had central royal domains surrounded by satellite principalities and provinces replicating the center on a smaller scale and at the margins had even more autonomous tributary principalities" (Tambiah 1992, 175). Tambiah calls this type of government "pulsating galactic polities," and he believes that this form of political organization is better at integrating minorities, respecting their customs, and generating tolerance.

This idea of autonomous principalities is very much like Gandhi's village republics, but he seems to have a far less hierarchical view: "There will be ever-widening, never-ascending circles. . . . an oceanic circle whose centre will be the individuals. . . . [and] the outermost circumference will not wield power to crush the inner circle" (Gandhi 1961, 73). In other pronouncements, however, Gandhi envisions that these circles will ascend to a "world federation of free nations," which would provide for "the prevention of aggression and exploitation by one nation over another, the protection of national minorities, the advancement of all backward areas and peoples, and the pooling of the world's resources for the common good of all" (Gandhi 1959, vol. 86, 190).[1] This sharing of resources indicates much stronger economic cooperation than the United Nations, and is more in line with contemporary World Federalists.

DHARMA, LI, AND *ETHOS*

A reference to Aristotle is useful at this point in the analysis. We can propose an equivalence among *dharma,* Confucian *li,* and Greek *ethos* as social customs, and with the aid of practical reason (*phronēsis*), this *ethos* becomes particularized as unique character traits (*ēthos*) and the moral virtues. *Dharma* is like *li* in two other respects: it started as religious rite ("rituals, study of scripture, and austerities"), and grew to pertain to every aspect of daily life. Frank Edgerton defines *dharma* as "propriety, socially approved conduct, in relation to one's fellow man or to other living beings" (Edgerton 1965, 30).

I believe that the best translation of *li* is "propriety," and Ames and Rosemont draw a good point from the Latin *proprius,* "making one's own as in property" (Ames and Rosemont 1998, 51–52).[2] This makes *li,* as Ames and Rosemont contends, "profoundly different from law or rule [because it] is this process of making the tradition one's own" (Ames and Rosemont 1998, 51). This means that *li* can be personalized and stylized, and this parallels the Indian tradition where one is expected to match one's own nature (*svabhāva*) with one's own *dharma* (*svadharma*). As Austin Creel phrases it:

> One's *dharma* is the total situation in which he finds himself; it is the law of his own being, the proper function of nature or constitution. . . . It is his

> appropriate function; it is the manifestation in social existence of his actual capacities. *Dharma* in this sense is deemed not an external code but the inner law of a being. (Creel 1977, 4–5)

This inner law, however, is not something akin to Kant's rational autonomy, which as J. N. Mohanty observes, is far too abstract and impersonal compared to "the innate characteristics of the individual,"(Mohanty 2007, 53) which is designated in Sanskrit as *svabhāva*.

Aristotle's practical reason is the ability to perceive "finely and truly" any situation, whereas Buddhists would call it the virtue of mindfulness and Confucius holds that it is the "appropriate conduct" (*yi* 義) that allows us to put *li* into practice (*Analects* 15.18). Without *yi* Confucian morality would be a mere moralism based on strict conformity to social norms (*li*). Therefore, for a contemporary virtue ethics one could formalize the Confucian position as *ren* + *yi* + *li* = *ren**. *Ren* 人 means the physical person, who, in the process of personally adapting (*yi*) social customs (*li*), becomes a virtuous person *ren** 仁, a homophone of *ren* with the number 2 added to the character *ren*. The literal meaning is therefore "two peopleness" and the ethical meanings are human excellence and benevolence. The social-relational nature of the Asian self stands in instructive contrast to those Euro-American ethical systems built on strict personal autonomy.

Just as every Chinese makes a personal appropriation of *li* by means of *yi*, so may every Indian do the same with *dharma*. Matilal states that the *dharma* "cannot be known as universally fixed," and that "our practical wisdom has a sort of malleability" so that it can adjust to changing situations and circumstances (Matilal 2002, 33). Therefore, *dharma* can indeed be a general guide for action, but it must always be contextualized and individualized. Such a proposal has obviously gone beyond the confines of traditional Hinduism, even the revised caste system envisioned by Gandhi, where a son, although free from discrimination, would stay within the vocation of his father. Gandhi's challenge to his *satyagrahis*, however, appears to inspire the freedom of the Hindu ascetic, whose *dharma*, according to Purushottama Billimoria, "is the correlate of his own innate constitution of which he is master," and "what he should do and not do . . . is left entirely to his own determination" (Billimoria 2007, 39). This is certainly the most radical way of developing one's *svadharma* according to one's *svabhāva*.

THE DANCING *RU* 儒: AN AESTHETICS OF VIRTUE

Most Euro-American philosophy has unfortunately severed the time-honored connections between truth, goodness, and beauty. A Chinese poet of the *Book of Odes* conceives of moral development as similar to the manufacture of a precious stone. At birth we are like uncut gems, and we have an obligation to carve and polish our potential in the most beautiful ways possible. The *ren** person is a work of fine art, something wholly unique and distinctive. Whereas the craft potter takes thousands of mugs from the same mold, the ceramic sculptor makes one singular work.

The Confucians were both dancers and expert musicians, and it is the performing arts that are the best model for a contemporary aesthetics of virtue. Confucian sages were moral virtuosos who used their *yi* to create their own unique style of appropriating the social patterns of their community (*li*). This achievement is both moral and aesthetic because it results in the embodiment of the good (*li*) and the personal creation of an elegant, harmonious, and balanced self. Confucius claimed to have the ability to read the character of composers by listening to their music. It is also said that in his later years Confucius put the *Book of Odes* to music in the proper way, presumably based on a correlation between notes and virtues (*Analects* 9.15).

For Confucius the beauty of the sage kings lies in their virtue; the beauty of any neighborhood is due to the goodness of its residents; a person without *ren** could not possibly appreciate music; and a society without *li* and music would not be just; indeed, *li* cannot be perfected without music. Gandhi once said that he could not "conceive of an evolution of India's religious life without her music" (Gandhi 1969, 266). He would also have celebrated the fact that the *Analects* 11.1 reports that the fusion of *li* and music first came with the commoners and then was adopted by the nobility. One is reminded of the fact that many of the most memorable melodies in European music came from folk (in many instances Gypsy) music.

Although he was not at all as active in the arts as Confucius, Gandhi is committed to the same ancient unity of truth, goodness, and beauty. More so than Confucius, Gandhi is committed to prioritizing truth: "Truth is the first thing to be sought for, and Beauty and Goodness will then be added unto you" (Gandhi 1927, vol. 12, 386). Gandhi's focus was also more on the inner beauty of the pure heart rather than natural or artistic beauty. "Purity of life is the highest and truest art. . . . The art of producing good music from a cultivated voice can be achieved by many, but the art of producing that music from the harmony of a pure life is achieved very rarely" (Gandhi 1933–1956, vol. 6, 10). Confucius would certainly have agreed with this statement. Gandhi rejected the concept of art for art's sake and its amoral aestheticism and there is no question that Confucius would have concurred that art must be an ally of the good life or it loses its value. While in England Gandhi experienced the controversy surrounding Oscar Wilde, and he joined Wilde's critics with the charge that he was guilty of "beautifying immorality" (Gandhi 1927, vol. 6, 377).

Confucians believed that heaven's highest virtue is *cheng* 誠 (sincerity, being true), with beauty and goodness following close behind. The sage and saint are sincere in the same way that heaven is: they are both constant and predictable; they are both true to themselves and true to the present age. Gandhi may have subordinated beauty to both truth and goodness so as to forestall any philosophy of life that would place the acquisition of artworks before the basic needs of the people. Gandhi believed that for the masses to appreciate beauty it must come through truth. "Show them Truth first and they will see beauty afterwards. Whatever can be useful to those starving millions is beautiful to my mind. Let us give today the vital things of life and the graces and ornaments of life will follow" (Gandhi 1927, vol. 6, 386).

In this passage Gandhi's passion for justice appears to have led him to reduce beauty to utility. He may, however, have a more sophisticated aesthetics in mind, one in which form follows function, one that is manifested in the exquisitely beautiful and simple Shaker furniture. (The Shakers were charismatic and celibate Christians who originated in England but had their greatest following in the United States.) Gandhi relates asceticism to aesthetics in the following way: "Asceticism is the highest art. For what is art but beauty in simplicity and what is asceticism if not the loftiest manifestation of simply beauty in daily life, shorn of artificialities and make-believe? That is why I always say that the true ascetic, not only practices art but lives it" (Gandhi 1969, 69).

Gandhi once asked a disciple if a "woman with fair features was necessarily beautiful?" The initial affirmative answer was quickly withdrawn when Gandhi followed with "even if she may be of an ugly character?" (Gandhi 1927, vol. 6, 377) For Gandhi beauty is always "an index of the soul within." He also observed that although they say that Socrates was not a handsome man, "to my mind he was beautiful because all his life was striving after Truth . . ." (Gandhi 1927, vol. 6, 377). M. Kirti Singh has remarked that Gandhi was perhaps as ugly as Socrates, "yet there was a rare spiritual beauty that shone in his face" (Singh 1994, 136). This is a moral beauty that comes from the courage of being true to one's self and being true to others. Gandhi's virtue aesthetics is best summed up in this passage: "Life must immensely excel all the parts put together. To me the greatest artist is surely he who lives the finest life" (Singh 1994, 135).

Gandhi's favorite Hindu scripture was the *Bhagavadgītā*, but the god Kṛṣṇa offers the greatest challenge to those who would claim him as a moral exemplar. One is reminded of when Karna's chariot became stuck in the mud, and Kṛṣṇa urged Arjuna to violate the rule of engagement and kill his enemy's general. Nonetheless, Matilal declares that this "dark Lord" is a "paradigmatic person . . . in the moral field," who "becomes a perspectivist and understands the contingency of the human situation" (Matilal 2002, 34), both necessary elements of virtue ethics. He also describes him, as opposed to the rigid Rāma or Yudhiṣṭhira, as an "imaginative poet" in the moral realm: "He is the poet who accepts the constraints of meters, verses, and metaphors. But he is also the strong poet who has absolute control over them. . . . He governs from above but does not dictate." This guarantees that Kṛṣṇa's "flexibility never means the 'anything goes' kind of morality" (Matilal 2002, 34). While it is highly doubtful that Kṛṣṇa was the model for Gandhi's "experiments in truth" (modern science was the most likely source), Matilal's description of the great Lord's contextual ethics provides instructive similarities and strengthens the case for virtue ethics.

I propose that the fine arts give us a very rich analogue for the development and performance of the virtues. Most significantly, this analogy allows us to confirm both normativity and creative individuality at the same time. Even within the most duty bound roles one can easily conceive of a unique "making one's own" of the Latin root of "propriety." There are a number of good examples in which we can speak of *yi* as personal appropriation without allowing a single variation in *li*. For example, even though judges interpret the same set of laws, their judicial decisions will have a very distinct personal style and character. Similarly, even though violin virtuosos are reading the same musical score, each of them will give the piece a unique interpretation. We should assume that the dances the Confucians performed had a set choreography, but we could easily imagine each having particular styles as varied as all classical ballerinas do. Even the younger brother who defers to his elder brother will have his own style of performing this duty, his own *dharma* (*svadharma*).

Moral aesthetes may be tempted to judge those who are not well formed in body or in action as morally unfit and not suitable for human interaction. For example, the beggars on the streets of large Indian cities are not a pretty sight, and an aesthetics of virtue might lead one to be less compassionate toward them. Both Confucius and Gandhi remind us, however, that moral beauty is primarily an inner quality. The external beauty of some aesthetes may blind us to the fact that they may be too glib and too self-conscious about the gems they have created. Natural moral beauty is never showy and ostentatious; if it is, it is false and only a semblance of virtue. In answer to the conundrum of the evil artist, Gandhi's answer is as good as that of any professional philosopher I know: "That only means that Truth and Untruth often coexist: good and evil are often found together. In an artist [sometimes] the right perception of things and the wrong coexist" (Gandhi 1927, vol. 6, 377).

YI, PRACTICAL REASON, AND EXPERIMENTS IN TRUTH

It is the virtues and practical reason that allows us to navigate the river of law with its constant flow and identity but also its shifting banks and channels. Not only does practical reason guide us in choosing a mean relative to us, it also allows us to suspend the law when it is in danger of becoming "an ass" à la Dickens. Matilal observes that *dharma* "gets fulfilled in novel and mysterious ways" (Matilal 2002, 42), so it may be expressed even in the violation of law or duty. Confucius never insisted on a strict interpretation of *li*: for example, he was willing to embrace a man without relatives and to include him in a universal human family (*Analects* 12.5). Strict conformity to *li* can sometimes make a person an irresponsible fool, as one of Mencius's examples demonstrates. *Li* forbids any man from touching a woman not directly related to him; but Mencius stipulates that, if your sister-in-law is drowning, then by all means you should extend your hand to save her. This is precisely how Aristotle's relative mean operates (right time, right place, right manner, etc.) and also how the Confucian concept of *yi* should work as a personal appropriation of the norms of *li*.

Tu Weiming is very helpful in demonstrating that *yi*, like *phronēsis*, allows us to apply the universal to the particular:

> Explicitly defined as fitness and appropriateness, *yi* mediates between the universal principle of humanity and the particular situations in which the principle is concretely manifested. . . . *Yi* is the human path (*renlu* 人路) through which one's inner morality becomes properly realized in society. This involves a practical judgment based upon the holistic evaluation of objective conditions. (Tu 1989, 52)

"Right" rather than the traditional "righteousness" is a much better translation of *yi*, as long as we realize that this would always mean what is right for us or right for our conditions.

Commentators as well as his own disciples bemoan the fact that the Master never defined *ren** very well. The answer to this puzzle is that Confucius was simply being honest about how context-dependent the virtues actually are. Therefore, what was *ren** for one person may not be *ren** for another. Ames and Rosemont explain it well: "Confucius based his specific response on the question on the specific perspective—lived, learned, experienced—from which he thought the disciple asked it" (Ames and Rosemont 1998, 5). For one disciple Zilu, Confucius advised him to wait before he acted on what he had learned, whereas for Ranyou he urged him to act. When asked the reason for the contrary advice, Confucius said: "Ranyou is diffident, and so I urged him on. But Zilu has the energy of two, and so I sought to rein him in" (*Analects* 11.22). What we see here is Confucius's own experimental method (recall that *dharma* is "radically empirical") by which his disciples could test their actions according to their temperaments and circumstances.

The comparison to Gandhi's "experiments in truth" is eminently instructive. Gandhi's ethics of nonviolence (*ahiṃsā*) cannot possibly be rule based; rather, it must be based on the development of virtues that are formed within the vocations and the various situations in which we find ourselves. Human life is a continuous "experiment in truth" in which we all act out of distinctively personal behavorial styles that do not lend themselves to the mechanical application of moral rules.

Some of Gandhi's exceptions to *ahiṃsā* would appear extreme and unacceptable even to contemporary proponents of euthanasia. Gandhi proposed that a dying man must euthanize his handicapped child if he thought that no one would care for her. If his own son were suffering from rabies and there was no cure, then he should be euthanized (Gandhi 1927, vol. 8, 395). In both cases it is more important to relieve pain and preserve personal dignity than to follow lock-step the rule of nonviolence. This means that in many cases passive *ahiṃsā* is actually *hiṃsā*. If a man who runs amuck and threatens to kill others, Gandhi insists that he must be killed; furthermore, the killer should "be regarded a benevolent man" (Gandhi 1927, vol. 8, 385). Gandhi once told a Jain friend that *ahiṃsā* was not absolute and that one should always be "capable of sacrificing nonviolence for the sake of truth" (Gandhi 1933–56, vol. 4, 49). If people cannot be true to themselves without defending themselves and others, then violence may be necessary.

CONCLUSIONS

As I close this chapter I would like to propose that the best option in this time of great moral crisis is a return to the virtue ethics of the ancients. Moral rules are too abstract and too rigid, and it is difficult to apply them to complex situations and decisions. Gandhi would support a multiculturalism that calls for equal respect for and within all of Tambiah's "pulsating galactic polities." This pluralistic, multicultural vision would honor all the various cultural ensembles of virtues. The tension between the virtues of pride and humility or different ideas of modesty stand as instructive examples of how Asian and European cultures differ. Even though I believe that virtues have axiological priority, moral rules, abstracted as they are from the virtues, still have normative force. This means that international pressure can be brought to bear on people who do not honor human rights and whose practices offend basic human sensibilities.

As opposed to a rule based ethics, where the most that we can know is that we always fall short of the norm, virtue ethics is truly a voyage of personal discovery. Ancient virtue ethics always aim at a personal mean that is a creative choice for each individual. Virtue ethics is emulative—using the sage or savior as a model for virtue—whereas rule ethics involves conformity and obedience. The emulative approach engages the imagination and encourages personal styles and thoroughly grounds individual moral action and responsibility. Such an ethics naturally lends itself to Matilal's moral poets and an aesthetics of virtue: the crafting of a good and beautiful self, a unique gem among other gems.[3]

NOTES

1. This comes from a statement of the Congress Party on August 8, 1942, which Gandhi reaffirms by quoting it in an article in the *Bombay Chronicle* (April 18, 1945).
2. Unless otherwise noted all references to *The Analects* come from this translation.
3. Parts of this chapter have been adapted from Gier 2004.

BIBLIOGRAPHY

Ames, Roger T. and Henry Rosemont, trans. 1998. *The Analects of Confucius: A Philosophical Translation*. New York: Ballantine Books.

Arokiasamy, Soosai. 1986. *Dharma, Hindu and Christian according to Roberto de Nobili*. Rome: Editrice Pontificia Universita Gregoriana.

Billimoria, Purushottama. 2007. "Introduction to Part A: Early Indian Ethics—Vedas to the Gītā; *Dharma*, Rites to Right." In *Indian Ethics: Classical Traditions and Contemporary Challenges*, edited by P. Billimoria, J. Prabhu, and R. M. Sharma (Surrey, UK: Ashgate, 2007), vol. 1.

Creel, Austin B. 1977. *Dharma in Hindu Ethics*. Columbia, MO: South Asia Books.

Doniger, Wendy and Brian K. Smith, trans. 1999. *The Laws of Manu*, New Delhi: Penguin Books, 1999.

Edgerton, Frank. 1965. *The Beginnings of Indian Philosophy*. Cambridge, MA: Harvard University Press.

Gandhi, Madan. 1969. *A Gandhian Aesthetics*. Chandigarh: Vikas Bharati.

Gandhi, M. K. 1927. *Young India*. 11 volumes. New York: Viking Press.

———. 1933–1956. *Harijan*. M. H. Desai, ed. 25 volumes. New York: Garland Publishing Co.

———. 1959. *The Collected Works of Mahatma Gandhi*. 100 volumes. New Delhi: Government of India Publications.

———. 1961. *Democracy: Real and Deceptive*. Ahmedabad: Navajivan.

Gier, Nicholas F. 2004. *The Virtue of Non-Violence: from Gautama to Gandhi*. Albany, NY: State University of New York Press.

Häcker, P. 1965. "Dharma im Hinduismus." *Zeitschrift für Missionwissenschaft und Relgionswissenschaft* 49.

Kuppuswamy, Bangalore. 1977. *Dharma and Society*. Columbia, MO: South Asia Books.

Matilal, B. K. 2002. *The Collected Essays of Bimal Krishna Matilal: Ethics and Epics*, edited by Jonardon Ganeri. New Delhi: Oxford University Press.

Mohanty, J. N. 2007. "*Dharma*, Imperatives, and Tradition: Toward an Indian Theory of Moral Action." In *Indian Ethics: Classical Traditions and Contemporary Challenges*, edited by P. Billimoria, J. Prabhu, and R. M. Sharma (Surrey, UK: Ashgate).

Olivelle, Patrick, trans. 1999. *The Dharmasūtras: The Law Codes of Āpastamba, Gautama, Baudhāyana, and Vasiāṭha*. New York: Oxford University Press.

Singh, M. Kirti. 1994. *Philosophical Import of Gandhism*. New Delhi: South Asian Publishers.

Tambiah, Stanley J. 1992. *Buddhism Betrayed: Religion, Politics, and Violence in Sri Lanka*. Chicago: University of Chicago Press.

Tu, Weiming. 1989. *Centrality and Commonality*. Albany, NY: State University of New York Press, 1989.

6

Ethics and Metaphysics in the *Bhagavadgītā* and Classical Chinese Thought

Ithamar Theodor

While getting acquainted with Chinese thought, I found a striking similarity between the Indian and Chinese traditions, and have subsequently decided to explore this further.[1] As such, this chapter aspires to bring together Indian and Chinese Ethics and Metaphysics, and highlight their similarities. In my work on the *Bhagavadgītā* (Theodor 2010), I have tied together ethics and metaphysics based upon the *Guṇa Doctrine*; in this chapter I aspire to take this a step further and highlight its Chinese counterpart.

THE *BHAGAVADGĪTĀ'S GUṆA DOCTRINE* AND ITS CHINESE COUNTERPART

The theory underlying the Yoga and Sāṅkhya schools considers nature to consist of three qualities or strands, called *guṇa*s; the three qualities are named *sattva* representing goodness and transparency, *rajas* representing passion and desire, and *tamas* representing ignorance, indolence, and darkness. The three *guṇa*s comprise human nature, and they bind the soul to mind and matter, or to the subtle and gross bodies. As opposed to the soul which remains steady and unchanging, the *guṇa*s constantly interact among themselves, and unite in various combinations; as such, sometimes goodness prevails, sometimes passion, and sometimes darkness. The three *guṇa*s not only interact with each other rather they balance each other and a variety of combinations are created. In general, the *rajas guṇa* tends to be over active while the *tamas guṇa* tends to be the opposite, that is, over passive; the *sattva guṇa* paves a path which may be considered a kind of a "middle way," and as such it acts as a balancing force. This balanced position does not merely offer an average or a sum total of the other two forces, rather it opens the gate, so to speak, to spirituality and enlightenment.

As the *guṇa*s are so dominant and govern every aspect of life, this world is sometimes called "the world of the *guṇa*s." As the three *guṇa*s comprise human nature, they are reflected through each and every thought, word, or deed. As such, the way one thinks, speaks, and acts reflects upon the combination of the conditioning *guṇa*s. This concept offers a unique division of human and even non-human existence which groups together various aspects of life, such as various psychological components, activity and adherence to duty, social grouping, eating habits, and cosmological divisions. The *guṇa* of goodness is characterized by knowledge and happiness, and adherence to duty for the sake of duty; it represents the intellectual social group or the brahmins and, cosmologically, leads to the higher planets. The *guṇa* of passion is characterized by desire and attachment, and with adherence to duty for the sake of its fruits or for some ulterior gain. When mixed with a larger amount of goodness it represents the ruling class, and when mixed with a somewhat lesser amount of goodness, it represents the mercantile and farming class; cosmologically it leads to the middle planets. The *guṇa* of ignorance is characterized by darkness, indolence, and madness and it involves the negligence of duty; it is more dominant among the productive social class and cosmologically it leads to the lower planets.

There has been a tendency in western scholarship of the *guṇa*s, to dichotomize them into "good" and "bad." In other words, sometimes there is a reading of the *sattva guṇa* as being good in ethical, ontological, and epistemological terms, whereas the *rajas guṇa* and the *tamas guṇa* are described as diametrically opposed or being similarly bad. There is no doubt a hierarchy underlying the *Guṇa Doctrine* and assuming that *rajas* is higher than *tamas*, and that *sattva* is higher than both. However, sometimes this hierarchical structure was perhaps over dichotomized, so to speak, under the influence of Neo Hindu trends, expressing some apologetic tendencies toward Western ethical notions. It is to be noted that beside the hierarchical aspects of the *Guṇa Doctrine*, it has a balanced aspect as well. Accordingly, the *guṇa*s constantly interact among themselves and their interaction creates a kind of a natural balance underlying the whole of existence. Perhaps the present attempt to bring the *Bhagavadgītā (Bg)* into dialogue with classical Chinese philosophy will help to emphasize these balanced aspects of the *Guṇa Doctrine.*

In looking for the Chinese counterpart, it seems that the terms *yin* 陰 and *yang* 陽 are close in many ways to the *guṇa*s, in that they are explanatory categories characterizing the relationships and interactions among immediate concrete and particular phenomena and things of the world. *Yin* and *yang* describe the relationships that are constitutive of unique particulars, and provide a vocabulary for capturing various subtleties. The complementary nature of the opposition captured in this pairing expresses the mutuality, interdependence, diversity, and creative efficacy of the dynamic relationships that are deemed immanent in and valorize the world. The full range of difference in the world is deemed explicable through this pairing (Peerenboom and Ames 1995, 985–986). *Yin* and *yang* are terms used to express a contrastive relationship that obtains between two or more things; *yin* is the shady side of a hill, and *yang* is the sunny side. *Yin* is represented by darkness, cold, contraction, passivity, and fading, whereas *yang* is represented by light, heat, expansion, activity, and growth (Ron 2006, 37). Among the *guṇa*s, it seems that the two *guṇa*s of *rajas* and *tamas*, roughly translated as passion and ignorance, best correspond to the terms *yin* and *yang*, in that *rajas* tends to be active and restless, whereas *tamas* tends to be dark and obscure:

> When *rajas* is dominant, greed, vigorous activity, venture, restlessness, and yearning are born. O descendant of Kuru, when *tamas* is dominant, obscurity, inertia, insanity, and confusion are born. (Theodor 2010, 112)

The *yin-yang* vocabulary describes how things hang together in their dynamic and always changing relationships. Importantly, these relationships that define things are intrinsic and constitutive (Ames 2003, 846). Given that *yin-yang* must always refer to a particular time and place, such correlations are always unstable. In fact, the Book of Changes appeals to *yin-yang* as a way of articulating the process of ceaseless change, succession and alteration within which the human experience is played out (Ames 2003, 846). The *Bg* offers a similar idea according to which there is a constant tension between the three *guṇa*s; as such, at different times different *guṇa*s prevail:

> *Sattva* prevails when it overcomes *rajas* and *tamas;* similarly *rajas* prevails by overcoming *sattva* and *tamas*, and *tamas*—by overcoming *sattva* and *rajas.* (*Bg* 14.12–13, Theodor 2010, 112)

The *yin-yang* vocabulary seems to be universal and timeless; the *Bg* carries another similar idea according to which the transformations of the *guṇa*s are beginningless:

> Know material nature and the conscious entity to be both without beginning; know too that the transformations as well as the *guṇa*s originate from material nature. (*Bg* 14.10, Theodor 2010, 107)

Also, the *guṇa*s themselves are universal and all encompassing:

> There is no being neither on earth, nor among the gods in heaven, free from these three *guṇa*s born of material nature (*Bg* 18. 40, Theodor 2010, 136).

Apparently, a process of ceaseless changes between the *guṇa*s takes place, which is rather similar to the way the *yin* and *yang* constantly correlate. Accordingly, nature is characterized by unlimited combinations of the *guṇa*s, or alternatively of *yin-yang*, and these determine, categorize, and constitute the natural world and human psychology.

SPIRITUAL HUMANISM: *GUṆA* AND CONFUCIAN ETHICS

The *Guṇa Doctrine* has notable ethical characteristics, as it aspires to elevate or sublimate one's deeds and character, and bring them to the level of *sattva* or goodness. The *Guṇa Doctrine*'s ethics follow a simple principle, according to which every action could possibly be performed in three states or modes: in goodness or *sattva*, in passion or *rajas*, and in ignorance or *tamas*. Out of these three states the first mode is recommended, the second state is worse, and the third state is the worst. The *Bg* offers a variety of examples and one such textual example will be presented, looking into the subtleties of charity:

> Charity is held to be of the nature of goodness when the gift is bestowed upon one who has not performed a prior service, with a sense of duty and conviction that it ought to be given, and when offered at the proper place, at the proper time and to a worthy person. But when charity is given in expectation of some gain, with its fruits in mind or offered grudgingly, that gift is considered to be of the nature of passion. That charity given at the wrong time and place, to an unworthy person, without paying respect and with contempt is said to be of the nature of darkness. (*Bg* 17.20–22, Theodor 2010, 127)

We may not offer a commentary on this, as it seems that the principle is self evident; however, suffice it to say that this principle of sublimating one's activities through adherence to the *sattva guṇa* or mode of goodness, is the central principle underlying the doctrine of action for which the *Bg* is famous, and that this indeed offers a sense of humanistic spirituality, that is, a notion of spirituality attained through a pure performance of one's humanistic action.

Confucianism too furthers a notion of immanent spirituality which is similarly deeply related to ethics. Confucianism no doubt offers a profound sense of religiosity and spirituality which may be considered in the realm of "religious or spiritual humanism." As such, Confucianism identifies the moral or virtuous with the religious or transcendental. The Confucian discussion of human nature and the state of the heart and mind are concerned with life fulfilled in this world, as opposed to life in the other world. Similarly, it is concerned with the process of self-transformation or self-transcendence through moral cultivation and social engagement, as opposed to the possibility of salvation from this world. This is somewhat similar to the ethical aspects of the *Guṇa Doctrine* which are concerned mainly with refining human life in this world through a constant endeavor for self cultivation. In a sense, the question "how to become good" in the Confucian tradition becomes as resourceful and profound as the question "how to be saved" in many other religious traditions. In this sense, the search for the morally perfect is also the search for a "transcendental breakthrough," breaking through one's moral limitations as an ordinary human being (Yao 2000, 157). As spirituality and ethics are bound together in the Confucian worldview, there is no call for an escape from the world, nor a seeking of an extraordinary lifestyle of asceticism. This too is somewhat similar to the ethical aspects of the *Guṇa Doctrine* which considers the "gate to spirituality" to be found in a balanced moral and social behavior, as opposed to extreme asceticism. This humanistic ethical view of reality is indeed related to a wider, cosmic vision. As such, in the perspective of the possibility of being transformed and cultivated in everyday life, Confucianism establishes its optimism and confidence in human destiny on a solid ground, and by bringing individuals' growth in line with cosmic evolution, Confucians locate their concept of immortality (*buxiu* 不朽) (Yao 2000, 158).

At the heart of the classical Confucian worldview was a profound commitment to humanness and civility, and pursuing them was considered actually pursuing a spiritual path (Tucker 2003, 9). Confucians identify "immortality" with sagehood or moral superiority; in the Confucian view, the world is not dichotomously divided between good and evil, heaven and hell, but between the civilized and the barbarian, the learned and the ignorant, the cultivated and the uncultivated. Life as a whole is a process of development from the latter to the former, the goal of which is to become a sage or a person of virtue (Yao 2000, 158–159). As such, they advocated cultivating oneself to embody the attributes just described. Confucius used *ren* 仁 often translated as "humaneness" or "benevolence," to refer to the ethical ideal encompassing all these desirable attributes (Shun 1997, 140). Humaneness is considered to be "a person-making process"; a dynamic force for creating and renovating one's self and others. The Confucian discourse on humaneness is related to the human potential and the constant attempt to realize it; moreover, humaneness is considered the essential qualification of a person of virtue or the *junzi* 君子. *Junzi* has been translated as "a person of virtue," "a superior man," "a princely man," "an ideal man," or "a gentleman." Confucius expanded the term to signify the totality of superior human qualities and the embodiment of humaneness. For him, a man cannot be a *junzi* if he doesn't manifest humaneness; "a *junzi* who parts company with humaneness does not fulfill that name. Never for a moment does a *junzi* quit humaneness" (Yao 2000, 214).

The *Bg* offers a similar view, and describes the "person of virtue" through a variety of examples. Here is an example of this principle, illustrated through three kinds of agents; the first agent described is influenced by the *guṇa* of goodness is parallel to the *junzi,* whereas the second and the third agents described are parallel to the vulgar person:

> An agent is said to be of the nature of goodness when he is free from attachment and self-absorption, determined, courageous and enthusiastic, and unchanged in success or failure. An agent is considered to be of passionate nature when he is passionate, covets the fruits of his actions, greedy, harmful, impure, and absorbed in joy and sorrow. He who is undisciplined, vulgar, stubborn, crooked, vile, indolent, dejected, and procrastinating, such an agent is said to be of the nature of darkness (*Bg* 18.16–28, Theodor 2010, 134).

This is, in many ways, a major confluence between Confucian thought and the *Bg*, or from a wider point of view, between Chinese and Indian thought. Apparently both traditions highlight the position of the "person of virtue" at the heart of their ethical systems. A deeper look reveals that being a "person of virtue" is not a static position rather it is deeply related to the spiritual state, represented by the *Sattva Guṇa* and the Dao respectively.

DAO: THE WAY OF THE SUPERIOR PERSON

The Way (*Dao* 道) is fundamental to the Confucian view of the world, concerning the question of the ultimate meaning of human existence. Confucian masters focus on how to apply the principle governing Heaven and Earth to human life and society and on how to find the Way to maintain or restore the harmony of the world. In this process, the original meaning of Dao as a road or a path is enriched to mean the universal Way applicable and existent in every corner of the universe. The universal Way is understood to originate from Heaven and Earth and therefore be the source of the meaning and value of human life (Yao 2000, 139–140). Understood as such, the Way is the foundation of a harmonious universe, a peaceful society, and a good life, and without it the transformation of the universe would break down, human society would fall into chaos, and the state would weaken and collapse (Yao 2000, 140).

Translated into the realm of human action, the term *wu-wei* 無為 signifies a natural mode of action which is action in harmony with the Dao or the Way (Littlejohn 2011, 65). The Way is not distinct from human beings and cannot be separated from human life, since it exists in daily life, in ordinary behavior, and in mundane matters (Yao 2000, 140). This is of course very much similar to the state of *sattva guṇa* or goodness, which balances the two other lower *guṇa*s, which offers an ethical or humanistic path leading to immanent spirituality, and which, on a cosmological level, offers a state of prosperity, harmony, and peace. The external manifestation of Dao is humaneness, which is considered to be "a person-making process," a necessary quality of human beings and a dynamic force for creating and renovating one's self and others.

The Confucian discourse on humaneness is always related to what humans can become and humaneness is considered the essential qualification of a person of virtue, *junzi*. As mentioned, the *junzi* is a qualitative term denoting someone who has an ongoing commitment to personal growth as it is cultivated and expressed through leadership in his community. *Junzi* refers literally to the son of a ruler, that is, to a prince; a royal heir undergoing practical and moral training leading to the assumption of kingship. This is transferred, within the context of the idealized Confucian vision, to every person who by his ongoing moral and personal character is rendered fit, hypothetically at least, to participate in the great enterprise of ordering the world. The term captures in one expression the two semantics values: nobility of birth and nobility of spirit (Plaks 2003, 109). The *junzi* is not characterized in terms of specific skills or expertise, but by recourse to the quality of his interactions with others. Confucius repeatedly draws a contrast between the socially expansive and inclusive *junzi*, and the disintegrative and retarding characteristics of what he terms "the small person" (*xiaoren* 小人). This "small person" is motivated by selfishness and thus detracts from the effective coordination of the community (Hall 1997, 219–220).

At a lower level, a *junzi* is someone free from violence, whose bearing is completely sincere and whose speech lacks vulgarity. The Way (*Dao*) is the only thing that a *junzi* seeks, even if his doing so brings him into poverty. The contrast between a *junzi* and a *xiaoren* (a small man) is the contrast between a person of virtue and a mean or vulgar person. This contrast is manifest in all areas of life. In terms of a psychological character, the former is broad-minded while the latter is partisan. In terms of behavior, the former always aims at what is righteous while the latter understands only what is profitable. Internally, the former is calm and at ease while the latter is full of distress and ill at ease. In personal relations, the former only makes demands upon himself, while the latter makes demands upon others. On the surface, the qualities of a *junzi* are common and secular. However, together the integrated qualities constitute an ideal personality that Confucius strived hard to achieve.

DHARMA AS AN ETHICAL AND METAPHYSICAL FRAMEWORK

Similar to Confucianism which considers ethics to merge with metaphysics and cosmology, Indian thought, too, makes these connections. As such, its fundamental term for ethics ties together individual ethics, social and political ethics, spirituality, as well as cosmology. The term *dharma* is central to Indian thought, and may be translated as religion, duty, morality, justice, law, and order. *Dharma* retains much of this total sense of the cosmic status quo and the specific acts of all manner of beings which enforce it. *Dharma* is not only external to the human being, rather it is perceived as comprising the essence or nature of everything. As such, it aspires to place everything—not only the human being but the whole of phenomena, in its proper place. *Dharma,* in Hinduism and of course in the *Bg,* is the cosmically or "religiously" determined activity of all existing beings to maintain the normal order in the world, and can therefore be rendered "norm." However, *dharma* should not be thought of as something static, but as a balance which is constantly being struck. It retains the connotation of powerful activity operating in the universe, and even constituting this universe, representing its essence or idealized form. These activities called *dharma* are imposed as a kind of natural law on all existent beings in the universe; as such, the human being's initiating of such activity is not a moral act contingent on his disposition, but an innate characteristic, that which makes a being what it is, assigning the part it is to play in the universal concert. It is the *dharma* of the sun to shine, of the pole to be fixed, of the rivers to flow, of the cow to yield milk, of the brahmin to officiate and teach, of the *kṣatriya* to rule, of the *vaiśya* to farm (Van Buitenen 1957, 36).

Dharma aspires to establish human society on a solid moral foundation and, as such, it defines the human being through two parameters which are the personal and professional statuses. The personal status is defined through one's relation to family life, and it is comprised of a division of human life into four stages. As such, one spends his childhood and youth as a celibate student, a *brahmacārī,* practicing austerity and discipline while living devoid of possessions under the direction of the *guru.* Later he enters the stage of married life called *gṛhastha,* and fulfils the four aims of life.[2] Once his children have grown up, he gradually returns to the more renounced mode of life practiced during youth through the *vānaprastha* stage, and at last one becomes a *sannyāsī*, and renounces the world altogether, to meet death in a detached and enlightened state of mind.

The second parameter defining the human being is the professional one; *dharma* defines four groups which cover the entire range of proper occupations. The first group is that of the Brahmins; this is the intellectual class, comprised of teachers, priests, philosophers, and intellectuals characterized by qualities such as self-restraint, austerity, purity, honesty, and wisdom. The second group is that of the *kṣatriya*s; this is the ruling class comprised of kings, nobles, generals, and administrators characterized by heroism, determination, expertise, fighting spirit, generosity, and leadership. The third group is that of the *vaiśya*s or the agriculture and mercantile class; they support society through establishing a firm economic foundation based upon agriculture and trade. The fourth group, the *śūdra*s, comprise the working and serving class, which includes artisans and craftsmen. The system itself is considered to be of a divine origin, and moreover, is not artificially enforced upon human society, rather springs from natural categories and human nature. As such, the Supreme states in the *Bg* that "the four social classes were created by me according to the divisions of the *guṇa*s and modes of work" (*Bg* 4.13, Theodor 2010, 50).

The relations between *dharma* and the *guṇa*s have two aspects; the external and the internal. The external aspect defines one's *dharmic* duty, roughly speaking, by determining the type of one's body and mind. In other words, brahmins are influenced mainly by *sattva, kṣatriya*s by a mixture of *sattva* and *rajas, vaiśya*s by a somewhat lower mixture including a larger amount of *tamas,* and *śūdra*s, having the largest amount of *tamas* constituting their nature. The internal aspect is more subtle, and refers to the attitude by which one follows his *dharmic* duty; this perhaps is the deeper determining factor of one's ethical and spiritual position. Accordingly, one can perform his *dharmic* duty in three different states of mind; in *sattva,* in *rajas* and in *tamas*. This principle is rather subtle and as such, the *Bg* provides numerous examples meant to illustrate it. Here is an example concerning the practice of austerity:

> This threefold austerity is said to be of the nature of goodness when performed with deep faith by persons disciplined through *yoga*, expecting no fruit in return. Austerity is said to be of the nature of passion when hypocritically performed for the sake of winning reverence, honor and distinction; it is ephemeral and unstable. Austerity is said to be of the nature of darkness when performed out of obscure notions and self-torture, or with the aim of harming others. (*Bg* 17.17–19, Theodor 2010, 127)

Apparently there are different types of austerities determined by one's nature which is defined by one's constituent of the *guṇa*s. Once one's type of austerity is determined, there could be three basic mental dispositions as to how the particular type of austerity is to be practiced. When it is practiced in discipline and faith, it is in goodness. When practiced for the sake of profit and honor, it is in passion, and when practiced out of self torture or for the sake of harming others, it is in ignorance.

CONFUCIAN METAPHYSICS AND *DHARMA*; BOTH CONNECTING HEAVEN AND EARTH

According to the Confucian Understanding, the world is sustained by or structured around three foundations, which are also termed the three powers of the universe: *tian* 天 (heaven), *di* 地 (earth), and *ren* 人 (humans). These three powers work together in an organic cosmos so the "Heaven, Earth and Humans are the origin of all things." Heaven generates them, Earth nourishes them, and humans perfect them (Yao 2000, 139). Important as Heaven is for Confucianism, there seldom seems to be a consensus concerning what Heaven is. The character for Heaven (*tian*) is traditionally defined as the "Supreme Ultimate" (Yao 2000, 142). Among many of its meanings, three are most frequently referred to in a Confucian context. In its metaphysical and physical connotation, Heaven, often in conjunction with, and/or in opposition to, the Earth, refers to the universe, the cosmos, the material world, or simply, nature. Applied in the spiritual realm, it signifies an anthropomorphic Lord or a Supreme Being who presides in Heaven, and rules over or governs directly the spiritual and material worlds. In moral context, it is understood to be the source of ethical principles and the supreme sanction of human behavior. Most importantly, the Confucian Heaven functions as the Ultimate Reality, to which human beings are answerable with respect to fulfilling their destiny. This also defines citizenship in political terms, as the Confucian notion of citizenship is defined through submission to the mandate of Heaven. The Way of Heaven predetermines the Way of Humans and underlies the Way of Harmony. The diverse spiritual, ethical, and natural meanings of Heaven establish the Way of Heaven as the foundation of Confucian views of the world, the universe and human society (Yao 2000, 142). The conception of Heaven as the Supreme Being is closely related to the understanding of Heaven as a set of moral principles. These two aspects are the two closely related sides of Confucian doctrine: Heaven is supreme because it is the embodiment and source of moral virtues, and Heaven can generate and bring out illustrious virtues (in humans) because it is the ultimate principle of transcendence. The close relationship between its moral and its transcendental implications distinguishes Heaven as the Confucian Ultimate from the God of theistic traditions. The Way of Heaven lies primarily in the moral path which people lead in their life.

The Confucian discussion of Heaven lays down a solid foundation for its metaphysical view of the world, its understanding of Earth links the present to the past, and its approach to humankind seeks the full realization of human potentiality. The three dimensions of the universe share the same nature, and their relationships are characterized by harmony rather than opposition or confrontation. This is somewhat similar to the concept of *dharma* inherent in which are universal aspirations, or the idea of uniting the natural world and human society all under one harmonious framework, encompassing nature, society, and the individual's duty under the principle of *sattva guṇa*. Similar to the Confucian idea that the cosmic order is generated by Heaven, the *Bg* holds a similar view according to which *dharma* has its source in the Supreme. Accordingly it is the Supreme who descends to earth to establish *dharma*.

> Indeed whenever a decline in *dharma* occurs, and a surge of *adharma*—then I myself appear. To rescue of the good and the pious, to destroy evil doers, and to re-establish *dharma*, I myself descend age after age. (*Bg* 4.7–8, Theodor 2010, 49)

In other words, *dharma* has its source in the Supreme, and similar to the Chinese concept, it descends to earth, and shapes human society as well as human duties according to the *guṇa*s. Then it is left for humans to perfect *dharma* through self cultivation, that is, the constant attempt to become established in *sattva guṇa* by following one's duty in a *sattvic* way.

Heaven is believed to have constructed human life and endowed humans with their nature. As the creator of humans, Heaven is believed to regulate the Way of Humans and commands humans to practice humaneness and righteousness, to be ashamed of what is shameful, and not to be concerned, like the birds and beasts, solely with existence and profit (Yao 2000, 145). As the Supreme Being with the power to sanction moral behavior, Heaven naturally becomes the centre of gravity in Confucian theories and practices with regard to religion, politics, ethics, history, literature, and the way of life, and as such could also be considered to be a "moral absolute." Confucians are determined to fulfill their mission in the world for they believe that those who are obedient to Heaven are preserved, while those who are against Heaven are annihilated. This idea, too, is similar to the idea of *dharma* which protects the good and the pious and annihilates the evil doers. At any rate and returning to Chinese thought, Confucians devote their life to learning, education, and the transmission of ancient culture because of their belief in the Mandate of Heaven which can be known through learning, divination, and observation (Yao 2000, 147).

THE ATTITUDE OF FOLLOWING ONE'S DUTY AS DETERMINING ONE'S MORAL POSITION

Heaven endows humans with the Mandate, by which the world can be ruled justly. Some of them, and specifically the mythical sages and the superior persons, seem to embody within themselves the holistic power of heaven (Schwartz 2003, 59). Just rule can be exercised only if the people are satisfied in a moral way. Heaven's generating power is understood as "conferring" on the people their (moral) nature, so that they can follow and develop the Way from their own nature in a variety of ways. This idea is also fundamental to the *Bg's* moral doctrine, according to which one's moral duty of *Dharma* springs from one's own nature. As Heaven embodied in human nature is identified with the Way, cultivation of the Way becomes the source of Confucian doctrine and instruction. It is believed that instruction and education of this kind will lead to goodness, truth, and perfection in general, and to personal integrity and sincerity, family loyalty and responsibility, communal reciprocity and sound commonsense in particular (Yao 2000, 147–148). It may be observed that besides Heaven's ethical aspects it has a natural aspect too and this is closely related to the conception of *qi* 氣, the vital material force (Yao 2000, 151). As mentioned, this is similar to *dharma*'s natural aspects, too, according to which *dharma* manifests in the taste of water or the light of the sun.

The Confucians believed that the way to bring about order is to restore and maintain certain traditional values and norms, which serve as the basis for an orderly society in ancient times. These include various attributes within the family and state, such as affection for and being filial toward parents, a reverential attitude toward elders, loyalty to superiors, and kindness as well as a caring attitude toward those below oneself. They also include rules of behavior governing the interaction between people in recurring social contexts, such as the way to conduct sacrifices, marriage ceremonies and funerals, the way for hosts and guests to interact, as well as various obligations one has toward another person in virtue of the different positions the two occupy within the family or state. The term *li* 禮, which often refers to such rules, is often translated as "rites" because it originally referred to the rites of sacrifice, and even when used more broadly to refer to various rules of conduct, it still emphasizes the ceremonial (Shun 1997, 139–140). Similar to *li*, *dharma* also serves as a framework encompassing a large body of social rules of conduct, preserving and transmitting human culture. *Dharma* had its source in the ancient Vedic term *ṛta* which carries a similar notion of a sacrificial word order. This term connects the Vedic sacrificial world with the human codes of conduct, and creates an ethos according to which adherence to human duty is a type of a sacrifice, and should be conducted in similar ways, such as acting without regard to the fruits.

The Confucians did not adopt the traditional values and norms uncritically. They emphasized the importance of having the proper attitude in following the rules of *li*, an attitude akin to the reverential attitude involved in sacrifices. One should pay serious attention to those with whom one interacts, be cautious about one's demeanor and appearance, and yield to others in matters that bring good or honor. The traditional rules of *li* may be suspended in states of emergency or adapted to cope with changing circumstances. Underlying the advocacy of traditional values and norms is a sense of what is proper, or *yi* 義, which provides a basis for assessing and adapting such values and norms (Yao 2000, 140). In practicing *dharma* one faces a similar nuance, in which one is faced by a particular circumstance out of which a particular duty or required mode of behavior emanates. Then, his actual attitude or mode of behavior in that circumstance determines his state of *sattva* or alternatively his lack of it (Theodor 2010, 127). There are many subtleties here, but it could be stated that the general tension is between acting out of duty, as opposed to the lower mode of acting for the sake of profit. An example of this principle may be found in the *Bg*'s articulation of action:

> It is said that an action is of the nature of goodness when performed according to the injunctions of *dharma*, without attachment, devoid of attraction or repulsion, by one who desires not its fruits. But action performed to satisfy one's own desires, accomplished by great effort or accompanied by an exaggerated ego notion, is said to be of the nature of passion. An action performed without considering future consequences, loss or injury to others, disregarding one's ability to accomplish it, and undertaken out of delusion, is said to be of the nature of darkness. (*Bg* 18.23–25, Theodor 2010, 134)

Apparently the main dichotomy here is between two modes of action; in the first mode, action is performed out of a sense of duty, and in a state of equal-mindness or indifference to the result being pleasant or unpleasant. In the second mode, action is performed with some end or profit in mind, and as such cannot be indifferent to the results or the fruits. This is similar to the relation between the ethical ideal and ordinary self interest in Chinese thought; on the one hand, Confucians acknowledged a potential conflict between ethical pursuits and ordinary self interest, and advocated subordinating the latter to the former. One should not be tempted by wealth and honor, or swayed by poverty and obscurity, to deviate from ethical pursuits. Instead, one should willingly accept the adverse circumstances of life, including even death, should these be unavoidable consequences of proper conduct. On the other hand, especially in the political context, they believed that self cultivation will also bring about certain ordinary objects of pursuit; for example, one who has cultivated one's ability and character will likely be appreciated and employed by others and as a result attain ranks in government (Shun 1997, 141).

In summary, it seems that the *Bhagavadgītā* offers a universal worldview springing from the *guṇa*s. This worldview intertwines both ethics and metaphysics, as on the one hand, it explains how society is constructed, and then on the other hand, it sets an ethical ideal to follow, aspiring to raise the human being to the platform of *sattva*, and hence to spiritual humanism. It seems that with some variations, Classical Chinese thought holds a view which indeed is strikingly similar.

NOTES

1. I would like to thank my colleague Gad Isay for helping me grasp some of the subtleties of Confucian thought.
2. Following *dharma* and contributing to the maintenance of the social order, accumulating wealth, satisfying desires, and eventually turning one's attention toward liberation from birth and death.

BIBLIOGRAPHY

Ames, R. T. 2003. "Yin and Yang," in Cua, A. (ed.), *Encyclopedia of Chinese Philosophy* (London and New York: Routledge), 846–847.

Hall, D. L. 1997. "The Way and the Truth," in Deutsch, E. and Bontekoe (eds.), *A Companion to World Philosophies* (Malden and Oxford: Blackwell Publishers), 214–224.

Lau, D. C., trans. 1979. *Confucius: The Analects.* Hong Kong: The Chinese University of Hong Kong Press. 1992 reprint.

Littlejohn, R. L. 2011. *Confucianism: An Introduction.* London and New York: I. B. Tauris.

Peerenboom, R. P. and Ames, R. T. 1995. "*Yin Yang*," in Audi, R. (ed.), *The Cambridge Dictionary of Philosophy*, 2nd Ed (Cambridge: Cambridge University Press, 2001 reprint), 985–986.

Plaks, A, trans. 2003. *Ta Hsueh and Chung Yung*. London: Penguin Books.

Ron, G. 2006. *Health: The Chinese Way* (in Hebrew). Hod Hasharon: Astrolog Publishing.

Schwartz, B. I. 2003. "The Ethical and the Meta-Ethical in Chinese High Culture and Thought," in Tu, W. and Tucker, M. E. (eds.), *Confucian Spirituality* (New York: The Crossroad Publishing Company), vol. 1. 56–61.

Shun, K. L. 1997. "Ideas of the Good in Chinese Philosophy," in Deutsch, E. and Bontekoe (eds.), *A Companion to World Philosophies* (Malden and Oxford: Blackwell Publishers), 139–147.

Theodor, I. 2010. *Exploring the Bhagavadgītā: Philosophy, Structure and Meaning*. Surry: Ashgate.

Tucker, M. E. 2003. "Introduction," in Tu, W. and Tucker, M.E. (eds.), *Confucian Spirituality* (New York: The Crossroad Publishing Company), vol. 1, 1–35.

Van Buitenen, J. A. B. 1957. "Dharma and Moksha." *Philosophy East and West* 7.1–2: 33–40.

Yao, X. 2000. *An Introduction to Confucianism*. Cambridge: Cambridge University Press.

7

Communal Moral Personhood and Moral Responsibility in the *Analects* and the *Bhagavadgītā*

Alexus McLeod

Moral responsibility is often seen as inextricably linked to moral agency, such that only an entity with the ability to produce some action can be held morally responsible for that action. There has been much debate in the contemporary literature on moral responsibility concerning the question of *collective* action and responsibility—that is, the possibility that responsibility for action could belong to a community rather than an individual.[1] In much of this literature, the assumption is made that in order to bear moral responsibility, an entity must have moral agency. That is, an entity must be the kind of thing capable of reflection, willing, choice, and intentional action based on this choice.[2]

In this chapter I discuss two ethical systems that do not accept this claim, and which, I argue, offer plausible positions on which moral agency and moral responsibility come apart. Both systems, I argue, have a conception of what I call *moral personhood,* distinct from moral agency, which allow for entities to bear moral responsibility without agency. In particular, a view of moral personhood involving a communalistic conception of moral personhood, collectively instantiated and directly connected to moral responsibility, can be found both in the early Chinese text *Lunyu* (more commonly known in the west as the *Analects*) and in the classical Indian text *Bhagavadgītā* (hereafter *Gītā*).[3] Both texts offer conceptions of moral personhood that take integration into community (in different ways, which I will discuss below) as the central determinant of moral personhood, and reject the requirement of agency for moral responsibility.[4] The focus on moral personhood, rather than moral agency, that we see in the *Analects* and the *Gītā* points to the centrality of communal contextualization, role, and harmony in moral action and responsibility, alternatively to the Kantian ethical tradition that locates moral action and responsibility in autonomy and rationality.[5] In both the *Analects* and the *Gītā,* the moral person is a communally contexualized entity, where the moral value of acts, attitudes, and dispositions are determined by the characteristic types of acts, attitudes, and dispositions of the relevant community. Below, I briefly outline the positions of the *Analects* and the *Gītā,* and show how such positions offer clear alternatives to the account of agency and moral responsibility in the Kantian ethical tradition.

WHAT IS MORAL PERSONHOOD?

Before looking to the texts in question, it is helpful to give some brief explanation of this concept of moral personhood contained in both texts.[6] Moral personhood is connected with the concept of the person as moral entity,[7] with the identity of the individual as moral being independently from consideration of action and causal role in action. Moral personhood primarily makes the entity the recipient of *moral responsibility.* One is responsible for certain actions insofar as one is the person connected with such action. However, one does not have to have *produced* the relevant action, in terms of agency. The moral person is one who can undergo and aims to undergo self-cultivation to construct itself into an ideal moral entity, with certain ideal moral qualities. The scope of moral personhood is variable—a person might be an individual human being, or an entire community.

My reason for considering moral personhood here rather than agency is that the concept of agency is so soiled with the notions of choice, will, autonomy, and rationality (and even more broadly construed "internal states") as central that it creates a bias from the beginning against views of moral responsibility and the individual that assume a different account of what makes us morally responsible or gives us moral qualities. So while *agency* focuses one's properties insofar as they concern production of action, moral personhood deals with moral *identity* independently of action and how this identity bears on both agency/responsibility. To hold that a thing can have moral value or even moral responsibility independently of the capacity to act severs the connection between moral responsibility and agency, and (in the case of the *Analects* at least) ties it to moral personhood. Thus, moral personhood is a more basic concept than agency.

Although their accounts differ (as we will see below), in both the *Analects* and the *Gītā,* moral personhood is fixed by *communal,* non-individual features of an individual, rather than the autonomous features of the individual stressed in Kantian ethics. For Kant, and much of western ethics thereafter, moral responsibility is attained insofar as one's acts are produced by features of the agent severed from or not determined by characteristics of their communities. Insofar as one's action is determined, it is not autonomous and thus outside of the realm of the moral. For the *Analects* and *Gītā,* however, moral responsibility attains insofar as one attains moral personhood, which is a matter of integrating into and acting from a *communal* basis, such that the moral person is *less* autonomous than the ideal Kantian agent. Individual moral agency as basis for moral responsibility is rejected in both the *Analects* and the *Gītā.*

MORAL PERSONHOOD IN THE *ANALECTS*

In the case of the *Analects,* the concept of moral personhood is linked to the developed social individual integrated (in the right way) into a larger communal entity, and whose moral responsibility, action, and identity are linked to the community with which they are integrated. We will see that this is slightly different from the conception of moral personhood in the *Gītā,* although it shares common features. A person, on the Confucian view, gains features of individual character as derivative from *communal* dispositions, where the individual's features can be thought of as manifesting wider group regularities. The person, in this sense, for the Confucian, is not an *autonomous individual,* but rather a representative of a communal entity. The *character* of the person, according to the Confucian view, is derivative of the character of the community, such that communal dispositions or patterns of action are in part due to the contribution of the individual to the shared collective actions and abilities that underlie this disposition.[8]

The five passages discussed below from the *Analects* help give us a sense of this conception of moral personhood. We learn how personhood is understood through consideration of the application of moral properties, and in the *Analects* moral properties are primarily *communal* rather than individual. In the case of one of the most important (perhaps *the* most important) moral properties in the *Analects,* that of *ren* 仁 (humanity),[9] the *Analects* takes it as primarily a communal moral concept that belongs to individuals only in a derivative sense. The view of moral personhood in the *Analects* is that *all* moral properties of individuals are like this. Not only is moral agency dependent on being a member of a community, but the features of one's character and dispositions are based on wider features of the community of which one is part.

In *Analects* 4.1, we see a statement of the necessity of being in a *ren* (humane) community for the attribution of the property:

> The master said, "Living in the midst of *ren* is beautiful. If one does not reside in *ren*, how can one therein obtain knowledge?"[10]

The community having a certain property (in this case, *ren*) is necessary in order for the individual to have access to another property (here, *knowledge*). Although by itself this passage does not show that one gains the property of knowledge through being a member of a community and that *ren* attaches to the community primarily (because it could simply be that one has to be around a community full of *ren* individuals as it is conducive to individual virtue), read in conjunction with the passages below it becomes more plausible that 4.1 refers to a communal requirement for possession of moral properties. 4.25 reads:

> The master said, "moral excellence (*de* 德) is not alone, it of necessity (*bi* 必) has neighbors."

Having neighbors is seen as a necessary condition of moral excellence, similar to the way that being in a *ren* community is described as a condition for gaining knowledge in 4.1. Note here that the statement of 4.25 is given necessity by the term *bi* ("necessarily"). It is not simply helpful or generally efficacious to have neighbors, but in every case, necessarily, moral excellence does not come about without neighbors. Other passages show that being a member of a community is responsible for more than just attainment of virtue, but *all* features of our character. 4.7, for example, reads:

> The master said, "the mistakes of people (*ren* 人) are in each case (*ge* 各) attributable (*yu* 於) to their group (*dang* 黨). Observe their mistakes, and you will know whether humanity (*ren* 仁) obtains."

Here, we see a stronger connection made between personhood and community. Not only is *virtue* linked to the community one belongs to, but *vice* is also so linked. More than this, we see in 4.7 that membership in community is a necessary condition of having *negative* moral properties. It is "in each case" (*ge*), according to this passage that moral mistakes are attributable to one's community. This makes community membership a necessary feature for the attribution of vice, in addition to virtue. It is by observing one's mistakes, which are attributable to their group, that one can discover whether *ren* obtains. If both positive and negative moral properties are attributable to one's community, then *all* moral properties are attributable to one's community. And this is independent of whether the individual has control over the actions or attitudes in question, and thus independent of agency.

Membership in community is a necessary feature for personhood, but there are also levels of moral quality of persons. Not all persons are ideal persons, and Confucius speaks about the sage and the *junzi* 君子 in different ways than he speaks about the *xiaoren* 小人 (petty person). While communal membership is a threshold condition for personhood, one's moral value *as* person depends on one's degree of commitment to the community, the commitment to and skill with which one performs one's communal role(s), and the virtues cultivated within the social context. 6.30 explains how a person achieves positive moral properties such as *ren*:

> As for the *ren* person, desiring to establish himself he establishes others, desiring to achieve he helps others achieve. To be able to make oneself close (*jin* 近) to others and to identify with them can be called in the area of *ren*.

That is, it is through increased commitment to and identification with others that one gains positive moral qualities. The way to achieve *ren* is to increase one's commitment to mutual support, and to gain sympathetic understanding through the strengthening of one's identification of others, some minimal degree of which is necessary for personhood. Finally, 12.1 explains the moral development of the person, again pointing us to greater integration into a community:

> Yan Yuan asked about *ren*. The master said, "Turn away from yourself (*ji* 己) and return to ritual (*fu li* 復禮)—this is *ren*. If for only one day one could turn away from oneself and return to ritual, the entire world would return (*gui* 歸) to *ren*. Becoming *ren* is caused by oneself—how can it be caused by others?"

Being a member of a community is a necessary condition for personhood, but the way to *ideal* personhood is to perfect that membership, which is a matter of lessening one's concern with individual desires and projects and integrating more deeply into communal projects and concerns, via ritual. This is "turning away from the self and returning to ritual," and represents a continual process of developing the person. Personhood and moral development are ultimately linked to communal membership, activity, and concern. At the threshold, one cannot possess moral properties or even have a defined human identity without community and some level of basic communal commitment.

MORAL PERSONHOOD IN THE *GĪTĀ*

In the *Gītā*, the concept of moral personhood is less clearly shaped by patterns of communal action. Instead, we see a concept of communal moral personhood in use through the notion of the identity of the person on the basis of *dharma*, or "sacred duty." We can see through an examination of the concept of *dharma* and its role in personhood that the *Gītā* does have a communal and role based conception of personhood similar to what we find in the *Analects*, although the exact relationship required between the individual and the larger community from which the individual gains moral features is quite different in the *Gītā*, as I explain below.

Chapters 2, 3, and 18 most clearly develop the idea of *dharma* as connected to identity and moral personhood, supplemented by positions and arguments elsewhere in the *Gītā*. One of Kṛṣṇa's first arguments to Arjuna, after explaining the impossibility of his killing that which is truly important in those he must fight (that is, the *ātman*, which is imperishable), is that failing to fight will be to neglect Arjuna's duty as a *kṣatriya*, and that there are a number of negative consequences of this (*Gītā* 2.31–36).

It ought to strike us as interesting that this consideration is placed where it is. Although one may suggest that the consideration of *dharma* is given as a conventional argument before the more central philosophical content of the *Gītā* is explained in later chapters, I think we have reason to think something deeper than that is going on here. Of course, performance of Arjuna's *dharma* to fight in the necessary battle is the major aim of Kṛṣṇa's instruction in the *Gītā* as a whole, but the reasons given in the chapter 2 can be instructive about a major feature of *dharma*—that is, its role in person-making.

Dharma performed in a certain way involves a disposition that is fixed and constituted by certain communal patterns of action, rather than individual choice, will, or rationality. What one does when they adhere to *dharma* is to act in ritually specified ways *for* ritually specified reasons. It is also the case that the aim of *dharma* and thus the aim of the person is in some sense the ordering of the community. This approaches the idea of communal commitment, membership, and role as necessary for personhood as discussed in consideration of the *Analects* above. *Dharma* aims at ordering the community and expanding or perpetuating the community, and one is a person insofar as they are engaged in this communally aimed project.

Kṛṣṇa explains throughout the *Gītā* that liberation is made possible through *sacrifice* (*yajña*), that is, through action performed without attachment to the fruits, or results, of action,[11] but rather done as devotion, which leads to knowledge and the realization of the ultimate identity of one's self (*ātman*) and the universal self or spirit (*Brahman*), as discussed in the *Upaniṣads*. Why, however, isn't liberation possible by just performing *any* action without attachment to the fruits? Kṛṣṇa explains in chapter 3 that performing one's *dharma* helps to keep the world in order. There is something special about *dharma* that requires it for liberation, rather than any action done as devotion. Presumably Arjuna cannot gain liberation through deserting from battle and wandering off into the woods but without attachment to the fruits of this action—it is not possible for Arjuna to be a *yogī* (one who is well disciplined via sacrifice) and neglect his *dharma*. We must consider why this is, as well as a controversy surrounding this issue that comes up in later *Gītā* commentaries. In 3.8, Kṛṣṇa says:

> You should perform the actions that you are obliged to perform, because action is better than inaction. Without action, you would not be able to maintain your body's health. It would surely fail.[12]

Krishna then moves on to explain the social basis of *dharma* linked to the notion of the well-being or health of a whole (social) organism.

> Long ago Prajāpati, the Lord of Creation, brought forth all creatures along with sacrifice, and he said, "by means of sacrifice you will grow and multiply. Let sacrifice be your wish-fulfilling cow! Make the gods flourish by means of it, and let the gods make you flourish as well! Make yourselves flourish for each other's sake. You will reach the highest good . . ." (*Gītā* 3.10–11).

Sacrifice, in the performance of one's duty without attachment to the fruits of action, is a social glue, and draws the individual away from more selfish concerns toward a concern for the community in general. Through sacrifice in terms of moving away from selfish attachment, one aids the community, "by this growing and multiplying" (*anena prasaviṣyadhvam*). It is the *dharma* and one's performance of such that allows for the functioning of the community, and is basic thus for personhood, but the *thriving* of the community requires something beyond mere performance of *dharma*. We see here that sacrifice also plays a role, just as commitment to ritual for the Confucians plays the role of reducing selfish motivations that might undermine communal wellbeing.

Kṛṣṇa makes the point that failure to act would cause the structure to collapse. If he himself did not act, he says, the entire world would collapse. The preservation of the world and all within it is dependent on Kṛṣṇa's own *proper* action. He attributes this in part to his causal influence over others.

> If I myself did not engage in action relentlessly at every moment, Arjuna, all mankind would follow in my path. All these worlds would collapse if I myself did not perform my work . . . (*Gītā*, 3.23–24).

Likewise, the preservation of the society is dependent on everyone performing his or her duties. In addition to the direct results of one's own duties being performed (*kṣatriyas* must engage in battle in order for states to be protected, for example), there are also secondary results, in that one who adheres to *dharma* influences others around them to also so act. This is very similar to the Confucian notion of *de* 德 (virtue), the moral potency gained through commitment to ritual, which has a power over others. As in the Confucian case, mere performance of duty alone does not generate this influence, but performance of duty *with the right motivation* generates it. In this way, we can think of the generation of something like "virtue" as a part of the picture in both the *Analects* and *Gītā* of how the initially socially construed person becomes idealized. One is a *person* insofar as one has and adheres to (in some sense) a *dharma*, and the generation of virtue is a matter of coming to have the right motivations and mental states concerning one's performance of duty.

A consideration of the *guṇa*s, or natural qualities, can be helpful here. All people have characters in accord with one of the three *guṇa*s—and all three *guṇa*s are consistent with the performance of *dharma*. It is not only the *sattvic* person who performs his or her duties, rather it is this person who performs his or her duties for the right reasons, acting in sacrifice, and on the path to liberation. The other kinds of person, the *rajasic* and *tamasic*, perform *dharma*, but for different reasons. The person who adheres to his or her duty because of the honor it will bring, for example, is the *rajasic* person, while the one who adheres to duty because of the physical pleasure attached or for some other lowly reason is the *tamasic* person. The petty and corrupted person still performs *dharma*—insofar as they are a person and moral agent, they play a role in the preservation and growth of community, but they are to a greater or lesser extent deficient in their understanding and motivation.

Matthew MacKenzie (2001) notes what he calls the "decentralizing" aspect of agency in the *Gītā*, contrasting this with the Kantian view that locates agency in autonomy and rationality. I agree with this contrast, and my position is that insofar as the *Analects* and the *Gītā* both present pictures of the ideal person as *less* rather than more autonomous in that they are integrated more deeply into the community, the key difference here concerns the conception of personhood underlying these ethical theories. Autonomy is neither an ideal nor even a baseline for personhood in the thought of the *Analects* and *Gītā*. Indeed, a person who succeeds at becoming fully autonomous (like the hermits in *Analects* 18) on these views surrenders their personhood, losing something essential to being human. Part of what is contained in our very nature (*xing* 性 for Confucians, *prakṛti* in the *Gītā*) is our *sociality*, and we are determined by this sociality. As humans we can never completely escape from it (just as Kant claims it is in human nature to be rational), and to neglect or reject it is to become more like a non-human animal than a human.

Ramesh Patel notes this aspect of the concept of *dharma* in the wider Indian tradition. "Hinduism," he says, "defines humans as animals with the sense of [*dharma*] and regards a human without this sense as a mere brute. It is striking that the intelligence or the ability to think is not considered essential in defining a human here; the prime emphasis is laid rather on the ability to relate with other humans in a naturally fulfilling way" (Patel 1991, 78–79).

Moral personhood is at issue in the discussion of action in chapter 18. The moral person, as the source of both agency and moral value and responsibility, is broader than the individual human being. As I will argue below, when we focus on moral personhood rather than agency, we see that free will and autonomy are not necessary for moral responsibility.

MacKenzie notes a possible problem with the picture of moral responsibility in the *Gītā*, which brings out this important feature of my approach. In Rāmānuja's commentary on the *Gītā*, he addresses a possible objection connected to 18:15, which takes the "five causes" to be the source of an individual's action. If this is the case, it seems to deny free will and the autonomy that is its basis. Rāmānuja responds to this objection, attempting to salvage free will and soften the force of the non-agent causes of action (*adhiṣṭhānam, kartā, kāraṇam, prāṇas, paramātmā*), by claiming that these factors do not *determine* but only *inform*. He says:

> The Supreme Lord impels the *jīva*s [individual selves] according to their nature and tendencies from previous activities and does not interfere in the free will or invalidate the injunctions or ordinances of the Vedic scriptures in any way.[13]

As MacKenzie points out, this response is insufficient, as *Gītā* 18.61 seems to explicitly assert that the divine causal factor is determinative, not merely guiding. It reads:

> The Lord is present in all beings, Arjuna, he dwells in the territory of the heart. With his magical power, his *māyā*, he makes all things revolve like the paddles of a watermill.[14]

While MacKenzie takes the proper response to this difficulty to concede that since free will is undermined, the liberated person, who is discussed in Book 18, "is *not* a moral agent and is *not* morally responsible in the normal way" (MacKenzie 2001, 145), I think more can be said. Given what I have argued above about the communal based conception of personhood in the *Gītā*, we can see the liberated person as an idealized person in a similar sense to that of the *Analects*. The individual as agent becomes less active and the other causal factors play a greater role in the liberated person, but this does not undermine either the moral personhood or the moral responsibility of the individual. The non-agent factors, including the tendencies of the nature of an individual fixed by the *paramātmā* (Supreme Lord), can determine action, while responsibility is retained. Indeed, we might see the *Gītā*'s insistence on the determination of human behavior by the machinations of the divine to be a statement of the kind of social and material determinism the Confucians also took notice of. The fact that I tend to read books about philosophy and history in my free time rather than watch movies surely has something to do with facts about my psychological makeup, which can be explained by biological and environmental facts that I had no control over whatsoever. If we want to make sense of morality in a deterministic world, we can hardly do better than the compatibilist position outlined in the *Gītā*.

In addition, the person determined by the divine impulse, as in part *constituted by* this divine impulse, has a moral status connected to it. This is what the liberated person realizes—that what "I" am is in actuality a construct far beyond the local features of this mind and body, but involving a much broader source of identity that includes the entirety of the divine, and thus other individuals as well. As we saw in the case of the *Analects*, facts about my moral identity have much more to do with aspects of my life that are outside my individual control and related to role, responsibility, and community.

Autonomy, as the *Analects* and the *Gītā* both so masterfully point out, need not play any role in the generation of *my* action. I can stray from what is required of me due to having a bad family or upbringing,[15] being a part of an unvirtuous community, or simply by being in the wrong place at the wrong time. This does not, however, mean that I take on no moral responsibility for doing acts caused by the confluence of these things. To claim that it does begs the question, as it simply *assumes* that a Kantian view of agency, in which autonomy is required for moral responsibility, must be correct.

Indeed, the proponent of the communal/role based view of personhood will have a ready and naturalistically respectable argument at hand to employ against the Kantian position. Insofar as we accept scientific determinism as an explanation of action in the physical world, and our bodies, as physical objects, exist within this order, how could we as (at least partially) constituted by the physical truly be autonomous from other persons, events, and things in the way Kant suggests the moral agent must be? It will not help by positing a transcendent soul connected with and guiding the body, because how can we explain how this thing interacts with a category of thing in a world otherwise completely physically determined? And even if one does not want to push this kind of radical determinism, it does at least seem inconsistent with basic scientific facts about human behavior to hold that we can ever be as truly independent of causative environmental features as the Kantian position holds that moral agents are. The fact is that human psychology and behavior is highly dependent on environmental features, including relationships, situations, and roles.[16] And this is a fact much more consistent with the views of moral personhood and responsibility found in the *Analects* and the *Gītā* than it is with the Kantian position that continues to guide much contemporary western thought about moral responsibility and action.

NOTES

1. Including the work of Margaret Gilbert on "plural subjects," Michael Bratman on collective action and intention, Larry May, Peter Copp, Peter French, Raimo Tuomela, and others.

2. In particular, the notion that something like *intention* is necessary to explain moral responsibility, a dominant view among philosophers working in this area today, with some exceptions, such as Marion Smiley, whose position is closer to my own (and that contained in the two texts I cover in this chapter).

3. We do not have precise dates for the construction of either text, and it is quite possible that both texts were results of the accretion of material over many years from different sources. Although issues of dating are controversial in the case of both texts, it is generally thought that the construction of the *Analects* took place somewhere between 500 and 100 BCE, and that the construction of the *Gītā* took place somewhere between 400 BCE and 200 CE. The late boundary is based on the seeming familiarity of the *Gītā* with Buddhism, Jainism, Sāṅkhya, and Yoga. See Deutsch and Dalvi 2004, 60.

4. These are not the only two texts or traditions offering such positions, but I confine myself to these two in this chapter because of their surprising similarities as well as due to the fact that these similarities are not often noticed, as little comparative work has been done between Chinese and Indian philosophical texts.

5. This is given in Kant's formulations of the categorical imperative in his *Groundwork of the Metaphysics of Morals*.

6. Although there is no single term in either texts that corresponds to "moral personhood," there is a clear sense in which such a *concept* is developed in both texts. Van Norden (2007) offers a convincing argument against what he calls the "lexical fallacy" (that if a text does not have a term translatable as the term for some concept, it does not discuss that concept).

7. This conception is related to Locke's (1979, II.27: 26) "forensic" notion of personhood that links personhood to the attribution of responsibility for action.

8. I offer a more detailed account of this view and argument for its plausibility as an interpretation of the *Analects* on personhood in McLeod (2012).

9. A distinct concept from the similarly pronounced *ren* 人 ("human," "person").

10. All translations from the Chinese are my own.

11. Although *yajña* originally refers to ritual sacrifices in a more conventional sense, Krishna uses the term in a primarily ethical sense. This is similar to the Confucian ethical transformation of ceremonial terms such as *li* 禮 (ritual).

12. *Gītā* 3.8. This and the following translations from the *Bhagavad Gītā* are from Thompson (2008).

13. Rāmānuja's Commentary on *Gītā* 18.15, see Adidevananda 2001.

14. *Gītā* 18.61. Part of the problem that arises for Rāmānuja's account is that if we take 18:61 seriously, it is hard to see how the appeal to actions in previous lives helps—presumably the Lord also controlled and determined action in these lives as well. The determinism will go as far back as one's moral action in general, and at no point do we see an autonomous free will.

15. As Aristotle insists throughout the *Nicomachean Ethics*.

16. This is continually driven home by situationist psychological experiments like Milgram's "Obedience to Authority" experiments, Zimbardo's Stanford Prison Study, and others. Doris (1998; 2005), arguing against the conception of character traits often endorsed by virtue ethicists in philosophy, draws on these studies, as does Harman (1999). There has been an enormous amount of philosophical discussion of situationism and its implications for virtue ethics in recent years.

BIBLIOGRAPHY

Adidevananda, trans. 2001. *Śrī Rāmānuja-Gītā-Bhāṣya*. Madras: Sri Ramakrishna Math.

Cheng Shude程樹德. 2008. *Lunyu jishi* 論語集釋. 2nd ed. Beijing: Zhonghua shuju.

Deutsch, Eliot and Rohit Dalvi, eds. 2004. *The Essential Vedānta: A New Sourcebook of Advaita Vedānta*. Bloomington: World Wisdom.

Doris, John. 1998. "Persons, Situations, and Virtue Ethics." *Nous* 32 (4): 504–530.

———. 2005. *Lack of Character: Personality and Moral Behavior*. Cambridge and New York: Cambridge University Press.

Harman, Gilbert. 1999. "Moral Philosophy Meets Social Psychology: Virtue Ethics and the Fundamental Attribution Error." *Proceedings of the Aristotelian Society* 99: 315–331.

Locke, John. 1979. *An Essay Concerning Human Understanding*, edited by Peter Nidditch. Oxford and New York: Oxford University Press.

MacKenzie, Matthew. 2001. "The Five Factors of Action and the Decentering of Agency in the *Bhagavad Gītā*." *Asian Philosophy* 11.3: 141–150.

McLeod, Alexus. 2012. "*Ren* as a Communal Property in the *Analects*." *Philosophy East and West* 62.4: 505–528.

Patel, Ramesh. 1991. *Philosophy of the Gītā*. New York: Peter Lang Publishing.

Thompson, George, trans. 2008. *The Bhagavad Gītā: A New Translation*. New York: North Point Press.

Van Norden, Bryan. 2007. *Virtue Ethics and Consequentialism in Early Chinese Philosophy*. Cambridge and New York: Cambridge University Press.

8

Ethics of Compassion

Buddhist Karuṇā *and Confucian* Ren

Tim Connolly

Compassion for the suffering of others, according to John Hick, is the common core of the great ethico-religious traditions. In Buddhism, especially the Mahāyāna branch, compassion (*karuṇā*) is arguably the most significant virtue. The Buddha taught "out of compassion for beings," and as the Mahāyāna philosopher Śāntideva writes, "It is through Great Compassion (*mahākaruṇā*), O Lord, that all the Buddha-qualities are encompassed for *bodhisattvas*" (Quoted in Keown 1992, 189). Confucianism for its part also may be described as an ethic of compassion. The main virtue in the *Analects* is *ren* 仁—translated as "humaneness" or "benevolence"—and Confucius says that to be *ren* means to "care for others" (*Analects* 12.22). His disciple Mencius further claims that "humans all have the feeling of compassion (*ce yin zhi xin* 惻隱之心)," and that "the feeling of compassion is *ren*" (*Mencius* 6A7).

Yet the virtue of compassion may differ from one tradition to another in terms of its range and intensity, motivation, and relation to other central teachings. Whereas Buddhist *karuṇā* is linked to insights about the nature of personal identity and aimed at all sentient beings, Confucian *ren* is rooted in particular human relationships, with the feelings of love and goodwill that we innately experience for those closest to us, especially our parents, as its basis. This has led to some consternation on the part of scholars looking at both traditions. Charles Goodman argues that the emphasis on familial relationships "would be out of place in any interpretation of Buddhist ethics" (Goodman 2009, 71). Damien Keown similarly contends that Buddhism's lack of consideration for family and society makes it the "mirror image" of Confucianism (Keown 1996, 345n14). Despite the common emphasis on the virtue in both traditions, then, we are compelled to ask whether the Buddha and Confucius would be able to comprehend, much less endorse, each other's teachings about compassion.

In this essay, I examine *karuṇā* and *ren* by placing them alongside one another. Let me first say something about the range of this comparison. While Buddhism eventually entered China and directly encountered Daoist and Confucian philosophies, I find it more instructive to compare Buddhist and Confucian ideas about compassion as they developed independently of one another. Hence I primarily explore the nature of compassion in the classical Confucianism of Confucius and Mencius and in Buddhism as it developed in India—though as anyone who has studied the arrival of Buddhism in China knows, there is much more to the story than this. I begin by discussing the meaning of compassion in each tradition, and then turn to issues regarding its basis and scope.

COMPASSION AS SUFFERING-WITH

Aristotle defines compassion (*eleos*, "pity") as a feeling of pain at an evil that has befallen someone else (*Rhetoric* 1385b13–14). This definition is reflected in the derivation of the English word "compassion," from Latin *cum* and *patior*, together meaning "to suffer with." Both Confucian and Buddhist thinkers share this basic conception of compassion. In the Theravāda text the *Visuddhimagga*, *karuṇā* is identified with "not being able to bear (seeing) others suffer." In like fashion, Mencius's discussion of compassion is prefaced with the statement that "All men have hearts which cannot bear to see the suffering of others." In contrast to Aristotle, however, both Confucian and Buddhist traditions make compassion into a central virtue, and in some cases even claim it as the basis of political life.

In one of the many passages in the *Analects* that discuss *ren*, Confucius defines the concept by means of the so called "negative Golden Rule": "Do not impose upon others what you yourself do not desire" (*Analects* 12.2). This aspect of *ren* he names *shu* 恕, or "sympathetic understanding." When one of his students asks him if there is "one word that can serve as a guide for one's entire life," Confucius responds that this word is *shu*, and again gives his formulation of the negative Golden Rule (*Analects* 15.24). A text from a later commentary illustrates how reflecting on one's own negative desires provides a basis for understanding the positive desires of others:

> The fact that you yourself hate hunger and cold allows you to understand that everyone in the world desires food and clothing. The fact that you yourself hate labor and exertion allows you to understand that everyone else in

> the world desires rest and ease. The fact that you yourself hate poverty and deprivation allows you to understand that everyone in the world desires prosperity and sufficiency (Singerland 2003, 183).

Several passages in the *Analects* depict Confucius's personal concern for the suffering of other people. In one passage he tells his students his three main aspirations, the first of which is "to bring comfort to the aged" (*Analects* 5.26). Another describes his reaction when the nearby stables (possibly his own) burn down: "When the Master returned from court, he asked, 'Was anyone hurt?' He did not ask about the horses" (*Analects* 10.17). This story indicates that Confucius lived his life in such a way that the suffering of others mattered far more to him than valuable possessions.

Confucius's disciple Mencius provides a foundation for Confucian sympathy for others' suffering by locating it among our basic human dispositions. This is famously illustrated in his story of the child and the well:

> The reason why I say that all humans have hearts that are not unfeeling toward others (*bu ren ren zhi xin* 不忍人之心) is this. Suppose someone suddenly saw a child about to fall into a well: anyone in such a situation would have a feeling of alarm and compassion (*chu ti ce yin zhi xin* 怵惕惻隱之心)—not because one sought to get in good with the child's parents, not because one wanted fame among their neighbors and friends, and not because one would dislike the sound of the child's cries. From this we can see that if one is without the feeling of compassion, one is not human. (*Mencius* 2A6)

The term *ren* 忍 in the passage is ambiguous—meaning either "cruel" or "unfeeling" on the one hand, or "to bear" or "endure" on the other—and thus the key phrase for understanding Mencian compassion can be rendered as either "not being cruel [or unfeeling] to others" or "not enduring [the sufferings of] others."[1] In the same passage, Mencius endorses a method of government based on this feeling, one in which the ruler himself is incapable of enduring the sufferings of others (*bu ren ren zhi zheng* 不忍人之政). Compassion is thus not just a personal ethic for the Confucian but also a principle for ordering society in general.

Compassion plays a significant role in the Buddha's life and teachings as well. In the Buddha's own description of himself, the term occupies a central position: "Rightly speaking, were it to be said of anyone: 'A being not subject to delusion has appeared in the world for the welfare and happiness of many, out of compassion for the world, for the good, welfare, and happiness of gods and humans,' it is of me indeed that rightly speaking this should be said" (Ñāṇamoli and Bodhi 1995, 104). Significantly, the Buddha often characterizes the teaching of his doctrines as motivated by compassion. In one discourse, he recounts a period of inaction in which he did not teach, believing that his views might be too subtle and counterintuitive for others to understand. But then the deity Brahmā Sahampati appears before him and beseeches him, and the Buddha goes forth to teach, "out of compassion for beings" (Ñāṇamoli and Bodhi 1995, 261).[2]

In the Theravāda branch of Buddhism, compassion is the second of the four "divine abidings" (*brahma-vihāra*). These are four states of mind considered godlike because they are the most worthy attitudes to have toward other beings, the sorts of mindsets that the Brahma deities have (Buddhaghosa 1999, 313). Chapter IX of Buddhaghosa's *Visuddhimagga* defines the four as follows: loving-kindness (*mettā*) is concerned with wishing well for others, compassion (*karuṇā*) with "not being able to bear (seeing) others suffer" and "quiver[ing] at the pain of others," sympathetic joy (*muditā*) with rejoicing in others doing well, and equanimity (*upekkhā*) with recognizing the equality of all beings (Buddhaghosa 1999, 310–311). While all four states have to do with regard for others, *karuṇā* is defined in a way that is nearly identical to the Mencian *bu ren ren zhi xin*, and Buddhaghosa (1999, 310) similarly opposes it to the vice of cruelty.

Further, in explaining *karuṇā*, the *Visuddhimagga* gives a thought-experiment that can be placed alongside Mencius's story of the child at the well:

> [F]irst of all, on seeing a wretched man, unlucky, unfortunate, in every way a fit object for compassion, unsightly, reduced to utter misery, with hands and feet cut off, sitting in the shelter for the helpless with a pot placed before him, with a mass of maggots oozing from his arms and legs, and moaning, compassion should be felt for him in this way: "This being has indeed been reduced to misery; if only he could be freed from this suffering!" (Buddhaghosa 1999, 308–309)

Both examples imagine the plight of a helpless other as means of making us reflect on the nature of compassion. As Buddhaghosa (1999, 310–311) says later in the text, "[Compassion's] proximate cause is to see helplessness in those overwhelmed by suffering." Nonetheless, each author has a different aim: whereas Mencius wants to show how feelings of compassion naturally arise in certain situations, Buddhaghosa's illustration serves to introduce us to a meditative technique for developing compassion. According to the Buddhist author, one is supposed to begin with exercising a compassionate outlook toward the miserable person, and then proceed through a series of additional exercises until one learns to "pervade all beings" with compassion. This includes even the happy person, since he is subject to the same cycle of suffering.

Martha Nussbaum (1996, 28) has argued recently that compassion is not an emotion but rather a "certain sort of reasoning." A significant disagreement between early Confucian and Buddhist views of compassion, brought to light by the passages from Mencius and Buddhaghosa, would be on this point. *Ren* is based on our pre-reflective natural tendencies. As Mencius says, "That which people are capable of without learning is their genuine capability. That which they know without pondering is their genuine knowledge" (*liang zhi* 良知; Mencius 7A15). Buddhism, on the other hand, conceives of suffering-with-others within the broader context expressed in the First Noble Truth: that sentient beings are caught up in a cycle of suffering. As one Mahāyāna text puts it, ". . . [A] wise man sees deeply that sentient beings are sinking in the ocean of suffering, the immense ocean of repeated birth and death. He invokes compassion because he wishes to rescue them."[3] According to this conception, suffering is caused by illusions about the nature of reality, and the Buddha's teachings help to ease people's suffering by telling them the truth. As such *karuṇā* is closely connected with a kind of wisdom or insight (*prajñā*). This wisdom, in contrast to Mencius's "genuine knowledge," must be both learned and pondered.

COMPASSION, SELF, AND OTHERS

The foremost illusion about the nature of reality, according to Buddhist philosophers, is the illusion of self. This brings us to the next aspect of our comparison: the radically divergent views about personal identity which underlie Confucian and Buddhist attitudes toward other people's suffering. In early Confucianism, the individual person is viewed in the context of specific relationships. Ethical practice takes place within a broader conception of "human roles" (*ren lun* 人倫): the proper interactions between father and children, ruler and minister, husband and wife, elder and younger siblings, and friends (*Mencius* 3A4). *Ren* is developed especially through the practice of filial piety (*xiao* 孝), the proper behavior and attitude towards one's parents and elders.[4] For the Buddha, who left his family in order to seek Enlightement, compassion depends on not making distinctions among beings. The *Sūtra of the Upāsaka Precepts* distinguishes between compassion before and after one has realized this fundamental truth of the no-self (*anattā*): ". . . [B]efore attaining bodhi, [sentient beings in] one's observations have boundaries [so one's compassion is called compassion]. After attaining bodhi, sentient beings in one's observations are boundless, so one's compassion is called great compassion."[5] Since *ren* is based precisely on distinctions between beings, would it therefore constitute a lower level of compassion for the Buddha?[6]

The Chinese character for *ren* is made up of two components: the radical meaning "person" (*ren* 人) and the number two (*er* 二). This suggests a central meaning of human relatedness, which several translators have attempted to capture by rendering it as "humanity" or "humaneness." In the *Analects*, Confucius says that "Virtue (*de* 德) is never solitary; it always has neighbors" (*Analects* 4.25). In a later chapter, he responds to a sage who has removed himself from human society, and recommends that Confucius do likewise, with the following retort: "A person cannot flock together with the birds and the beasts. If I do not associate with the followers of men, then with whom would I associate?" (*Analects* 18.6)

Other passages emphasize that a person develops *ren* only by maintaining the right sort of relationships with others. Of particular importance is one's conduct toward one's parents. As one important passage states, "The gentleman applies himself to the roots. 'Once the roots are established, the Way will grow.' Might we not say that filial piety and respect for elders constitute the root of Goodness" (*Analects* 1.2). In pre-Confucian China, filial piety was worshiped, and Confucius makes the requirements for practicing it even more stringent.[7] Without a familial context in which to practice it, a person's *ren* is rootless.

Similarly, for Mencius, the feeling of compassion (*ce yin zhi xin* 惻隱之心) refers not only to concern for the suffering of others in general, but also to familial affection (Kim 2010, 419–421). Affectionate feeling for one's parents begins early, and eventually can be developed into full-fledged virtue: "Among babes there are none that do not know how to love their parents. . . . Treating one's parents as parents is *ren*" (*Mencius* 7A15). Infants do not have to reason their way into loving their parents, just as the person seeing the infant on the edge of the well does not have to think about the situation in order for feelings of alarm and compassion to arise. Further, for the early Confucians, understanding and developing this aspect of ourselves connects us with a deeper moral order in the universe. As Mencius declares, "To fully understand one's heart (*xin* 心) is to understand one's nature (*xing* 性, literally "inborn heart"). To understand one's nature is to understand Heaven (*tian* 天). To preserve one's heart and nourish one's nature is the way to serve Heaven" (*Mencius* 7A1).

The doctrinal counterpart to the relational self in Buddhist metaphysics is expressed in the principle of "dependent origination" or "conditioned arising": the belief that nothing exists in its own right, but rather all things exist as a series of mutually interdependent processes. This applies to the "self" as well: it is made up of the so-called "five aggregates (*skandha*)"—material form, sensation, perception, volition, and consciousness—and at bottom these amount to processes rather than substances. Śāntideva (1995, 8.101–103) provides an argument connecting the doctrine of no-self with compassionate behavior:

> The continuum of consciousness, like a queue, and the combination of constituents, like an army, are not real. The person who experiences suffering does not exist. To whom will that suffering belong?
> Without exception, no sufferings belong to anyone. They must be warded off simply because they are suffering. Why is any limitation put on this?

This argument appears to begin from the premise that suffering is bad in itself (and hence should be "warded off"). Now most of us believe that the suffering which we ourselves experience is worse than the suffering experienced by others, for the simple reason that we seem to feel this suffering *more*. Yet if one denies this common belief that there are distinct individuals experiencing suffering, and is still committed to the premise that suffering is bad and worth eliminating, then it does not matter with whose suffering one begins. Nor will one engage in the sort of self-serving behavior that ordinarily stands in the way of the compassionate outlook. As Goodman (2009, 50) writes, "An experiential realization of the truth of no self can eliminate our belief in the significance of the distinction between self and other, and thereby eradicate our selfishness; in the process, this realization will also remove our attachment to false views that interfere with compassion. . . . Seeing beyond the illusion of self allows our natural compassion to shine forth."

In doing away with the boundary between self and others, however, the no-self doctrine also eliminates distinctions that the early Confucians would see as necessary to the development of compassion, such as those between son and father, younger brother and elder brother, and members of one's immediate family and strangers. In practice, the Buddha saw family life as an obstacle to that of the enlightened person, and taught that his students should leave their homes first if they wanted to embark on the path of the compassionate life:

> On hearing the Dhamma [a householder or householder's son] acquires faith in the Tathāgata. Possessing that faith, he considers thus: "Household life is crowded and dusty; life gone forth is wide open. It is not easy, while living in a home, to lead the holy life utterly perfect and pure as a polished shell. Suppose I shave off my hair and beard, put on the yellow robe, and go forth from the home life into homelessness." On a later occasion, abandoning a small or large fortune, abandoning a small or a large circle of relatives, he shaves off his hair and beard, puts on a yellow robe, and goes forth from the home life into homelessness (Ñāṇamoli and Bodhi 1995, 448).

Confucius and Mencius, for their part, would find it difficult to endorse this method of developing compassion. As Mencius puts it, "There have never been those who are *ren* who abandoned their parents" (*Mencius* 1A1).

THE SCOPE OF COMPASSION

This brings us to the question of scope: who deserves our compassion? Do we owe it to some (such as our close relatives or friends) more than others? In keeping with the Buddha's just-mentioned instructions, the Mahāyāna *Inquiry of Ugra* warns against special regard for one's son: "If for his sake I bring forth excessive affection toward that son of mine while not doing the same toward other beings I will be deviating from the training prescribed by the Buddha" (Quoted by Goodman 2009, 74–75). Additionally, Asaṅga and other Mahāyāna writers emphasize that the bodhisattva possesses greater concern for those who are violent and immoral than for those who are peaceful, since the former are suffering more (Asaṅga 1986, 69). Early Confucianism, on the other hand, has ample room for familial obligations, and Confucius and Mencius reject treating strangers or enemies with any special regard.[8]

Buddhists and Confucians further disagree on whether the scope of compassion extends to non-human animals. As mentioned above, the Buddha taught "out of compassion for beings." According to Buddhist teachings about the cycle of rebirth (*saṃsāra*), although the human level of existence is elevated due to the human's capacity for Enlightenment, humans form a continuum with non-human animals, with humans having experienced past births as animals, and animals as humans. The first of the Five Precepts thus forbids killing any sentient being.[9] The Buddha relates this prohibition to compassion: "[A]bandoning the killing of living beings, he abstains from killing living beings; with rod and weapon laid aside, gently and kindly, he abides compassionate to all living beings" (Ñāṇamoli and Bodhi 1995, 448–449).[10]

The early Confucian tradition takes a hierarchical view of the beings toward whom one should practice *ren*. As Mencius sums up the Confucian doctrine of "graded" or "partial" love, "Gentlemen, in relation to animals, are sparing (*ai* 愛) of them but are not benevolent (*ren* 仁) toward them. In relation to the people, they are benevolent toward them but do not treat them as kin (*qin* 親). They treat their kin as kin, and then are benevolent toward the people. They are benevolent toward the people, and then are sparing of animals" (*Mencius* 7A45). We may see further the contrast between Confucian partial love and Buddhist regard for all sentient beings when we consider Mencius's criticism of the teachings of Mozi, who advocated impartial treatment of all human beings. Mozi argued, for instance, that sons who are truly filial would best serve their parents by going out and taking care of other people, since then others will respond in like fashion. But as Mencius counters, impartial compassion means "not to have a father. To not have a father . . . is to be an animal" (*Mencius* 3B9). If Mencius thinks Mohist impartiality toward human beings is so far off, he would be even more skeptical of the Buddhist kind of impartiality.

Interestingly, nonetheless, the neo-Confucian philosopher Wang Yangming shows how Mencius's thought-experiment regarding the child and the well can be made into an argument for adopting a compassionate attitude toward other sentient beings, and even toward inanimate objects:

> It may be objected that the child belongs to the same species. Again, when [the man who observes the child about to fall into the well] observes the pitiful cries and frightened appearance of birds and animals about to be slaughtered, he cannot help feeling an "inability to bear" their suffering. This shows that his humanity forms one body with birds and animals. It may be objected that birds and animals are sentient beings as he is. But when he sees plants broken and destroyed, he cannot help a feeling of pity. This shows that his humanity forms one body with plants. It may be said that plants are living things as he is. Yet even when he sees tiles and stones shattered and crushed, he cannot help a feeling of regret (Chan 1963, 659–660).

This line of thought is not without basis in early Confucian texts. One passage in the *Analects* portrays Confucius's care in avoiding the undue infliction of pain on the birds and fish when he is hunting (*Analects* 7.27, on one interpretation). Further, the *Mencius* tells the story of a king who is unable to bear the suffering of an ox that is about to be slaughtered, and argues that the king should extend this attitude toward his subjects (*Mencius* 1A7). As Rodney Taylor (2006, 297) argues, "The *junzi* 君子 [Confucian gentleman] cannot bear to see the suffering of others; moreover, the scope of their moral perception encompasses not only fellow humans but also the lives of other sentient creatures." While the sufferings of one's parents and elders have priority, Confucian compassion can be extended to all beings capable of suffering.

CONCLUSION

Would the Buddha and Confucius endorse each other's views regarding compassion? Owen Flanagan (2007, 32) suggests that compassion has the same overall purpose in both traditions, and the difference lies mainly in how it is developed: "[I]n Confucianism *ren* . . . is rooted in the family and designed to spread outward. In Buddhism *karuṇā* and *mettā* . . . start as universal values but focus on those close-to-us for familiar practical reasons. The goal, a good loving world, is perhaps the shared end." Yet as we have seen, there are significant philosophical barriers to reconciling the two views of compassion. The first and foremost of these on the Confucian side is the emphasis on particular human relationships. Mencius criticizes thinkers far less radical than the Buddha when he thinks they are undercutting basic familial bonds. If familial bonds are a necessary component of *ren*, and the Buddha abandoned his family and taught others to do likewise in order to pursue Enlightenment, then the Buddha cannot be counted as *ren*. On the Buddhist side, the notion of a higher-order compassion which rises above the illusion of selfhood seems to consign early Confucian *ren* to a lower level—unenlightened compassion rather than "great compassion." These differences are not merely a matter of how the practice of compassion is developed, but rather of deeply engrained views regarding the nature of reality and our place within it.

In spite of these differences, philosophers in both the Confucian and Buddhist traditions recognize that human beings have the capacity to be deeply moved by the suffering of others, and attempt to give this capacity and its development a central place in our ethical life. Both Mencius and Buddhaghosa, as we saw, ask us to imagine a person who is completely helpless in the face of suffering. They contend that the feeling we have in such a case is a worthy one, and challenge us to reflect on how we might cultivate it further. At the head of either tradition, Confucius and Buddha serve as the unparalleled exemplars of the compassionate life. Although the disagreements between their views run deep, taken together they offer us a rich array of resources for the advancement of compassion-centered ethics.

NOTES

1. See Kim (2010, 412–413) for discussion of the two renderings.
2. See Keown (1992, 73–76) for discussion of the Buddha's motivation as sympathy and compassion for all beings; refer to Harvey (2001, 267) for background on the Brahmā Sahampati.
3. *Sūtra of the Upāsaka Precepts*, Ch. III. Mahāyāna philosophers in turn emphasize the *bodhisattva* ideal of helping all beings achieve freedom from this cycle. Śāntideva captures this in his maxim that, "One should do nothing other than what is either directly or indirectly of benefit to living beings . . ." (Śāntideva 1995, 5.101). Asaṅga's "Chapter on Ethics" in turn teaches the "eleven modes" by which a bodhisattva works to bring about the welfare of sentient beings. The first of these is ministering to those who are suffering: nursing the sick, aiding the blind and deaf and amputee, and helping to eradicate any suffering that arises from sensory desire (Asaṅga 1986, 54).
4. For further discussion, see Connolly 2012.
5. *Sūtra of the Upāsaka Precepts*, Ch. III.
6. Goodman (2009, 6) divides the development of *karuṇā* into distinct stages. At the first and lowest stage, compassion is an emotional reaction to the suffering of others that has not yet realized that there is no "self" or "others." At the

second level, one realizes that the distinctions between individuals are illusory, and thereby acts to eliminate the suffering of all. These two levels correspond to the pre-bodhi and post-bodhi stages in the passage just quoted. However, there is also a third and final level, at which one realizes the emptiness of all things—that nothing exists, or alternatively, that nothing has any intrinsic character (Goodman 2009, 124–125). On this understanding, Confucian compassion would be two steps removed from the fully enlightened kind.

7. See especially *Analects* 2.7, where he criticizes the filiality of his contemporaries. For discussion of this point, see Knapp 1995, 206.

8. For instance, when asked whether someone should requite injury with kindness, Confucius responds, "With what, then, would one requite kindness?" (*Analects* 14.34) Mencius for his part contends that if you hear an altercation outside your window it is acceptable to bar your door (rather than going outside to help), if the altercation involves someone who is not your family member (*Mencius* 4B29).

9. Though Buddhist attitudes toward vegetarianism and animal sacrifice are rather complicated; see Harvey (2000, 156 ff.) for discussion.

10. I owe the reference to Harvey 2000, 69.

BIBLIOGRAPHY

Analects of Confucius = Slingerland 2003.

Asaṅga. 1986. *Asaṅga's Chapter on Ethics with the Commentary of Tsong-Kha-Pa: The Basic Path to Awakening; The Complete Bodhisattva*, trans. by Mark Tatz. Lewiston, NY: The Edwin Mellen Press.

Buddhaghosa, Bhadantācariya. 1999. *The Path of Purification (Visuddhimagga)*, trans. by Bikkhu Ñāṇamoli. Seattle, WA: BPS Pariyatti Editions.

Chan, Wing-tsit. 1963. *A Source Book in Chinese Philosophy*. Princeton, NJ: Princeton University Press.

Connolly, Tim. 2012. "Friendship and Filial Piety: Relational Ethics in Aristotle and Early Confucianism." *Journal of Chinese Philosophy* 39: 71–88.

Flanagan, Owen. 2007. *The Really Hard Problem: Meaning in a Material World*. Cambridge, MA: MIT Press.

Goodman, Charles. 2009. *Consequences of Compassion: An Interpretation and Defense of Buddhist Ethics*. Oxford and New York: Oxford University Press.

Harvey, Peter, ed. 2001. *Buddhism*. London and New York: Continuum.

———. 2000. *An Introduction to Buddhist Ethics*. Cambridge and New York: Cambridge University Press.

Keown, Damien. 1992. *The Nature of Buddhist Ethics*. New York: St. Martin's Press.

———. 1996. "Karma, Character, and Consequentialism." *Journal of Religious Ethics* 24: 329–350.

Kim, Myeong-seok. 2010. "What *Ceyin zhi xin* (Compassion/ Familial Affection) Really Is." *Dao: A Journal of Comparative Philosophy* 9: 407–425.

Knapp, Keith. 1995. "The *Ru* Interpretation of *Xiao*." *Early China* 20: 195–222.

Mencius of Mencius = Van Norden, Bryan W. 2008. *Mengzi, with Selections from the Traditional Commentaries*. Indianapolis, IN: Hackett Publishing Company.

Ñāṇamoli, Bhikkhu and Bikkhu Bodhi, trans. 1995. *The Middle Length Discourses of the Buddha: A New Translation of the Majjhima Nikāya*. Boston, MA: Wisdom Publications.

Nussbaum, Martha. 1996. "Compassion: The Basic Social Emotion." *Social Philosophy and Policy* 13: 27–58.

Śāntideva. 1995. *The Bodhicaryāvatāra*, trans. by Kate Crosby and Andrew Skilton. Oxford and New York: Oxford University Press.

Slingerland, Edward. 2003. *Confucius: Analects, with Selections from the Traditional Commentaries*. Indianapolis, IN: Hackett Publishing Company.

Sūtra of the Upāsaka Precepts. Available online at www.sutrasmantras.info/sutra33a.html (accessed 12/15/2011).

Taylor, Rodney. 2006. "Of Animals and Humans: The Confucian Perspective." In Paul Waldau and Kimberley Patton eds., *A Communion of Subjects: Animals in Religion, Science, and Ethics* (New York: Columbia University Press), 293–307.

9

Why "Besire" Is Not Bizarre

Moral Knowledge in Confucianism and Hinduism

Yong Huang

In this chapter, I shall challenge Gilbert Ryle's famous distinction between knowledge-that and knowledge-how, particularly when these two types of knowledge are seen as exhaustive of all knowledge. I shall first start with a discussion of Confucian conception of moral knowledge as something other, or more, than both knowledge-that and knowledge-how. In neo-Confucianism, such moral knowledge is not knowledge about morality but is itself moral, which is in contrast to what they call knowledge of seeing and hearing. While one who possesses the former is inclined to act accordingly, one who possesses the latter is not. So what is unique about moral knowledge is that it includes its possessor's disposition or inclination to act accordingly, which is not included in either knowledge-that or knowledge-how in Ryle's distinction. However, this Confucian conception of moral knowledge as including disposition and inclination to act is not acceptable to contemporary Humeans, for whom disposition or inclination belongs to what they regard as desire, which is not part of any knowledge or belief but works together with belief to cause a person to act. In their view, a mental state that includes both belief and desire, the mental state of besire, is bizarre in light of Anscombe's view about the opposite directions of fit between belief and the world on the one hand and between desire and the world on the other. Then, I shall argue in what sense this single mental state of besire is not bizarre. Finally, I shall try to show that this Confucian conception of moral knowledge is similar to the spiritual or liberative knowledge, which includes moral knowledge, in the Vedānta tradition of Hinduism: they are both knowledge that not merely informs but also transforms their possessors; they both include belief and desire, which constitute a single mental state of besire; and they both can only be acquired through a person's inner experience and not merely by reading books or listening to lectures. I shall conclude the essay with a brief summary.

CONFUCIAN MORAL KNOWLEDGE: OTHER (OR MORE) THAN KNOWING-THAT AND KNOWING-HOW

Gilbert Ryle has made the famous distinction between knowledge-that and knowledge-how. Knowledge-that is the knowledge that something is the case, and knowledge-how is the knowledge about how to do something. There are similarities between these two types of knowledge, as we can learn, find out, or forget both types of knowledge. However, Ryle emphasizes their differences: "we never speak of a person believing or opining how, and though it is proper to ask for the grounds or reason for someone's acceptance of a proposition, this question cannot be asked of someone's skill at cards or prudence in investments" (Ryle 1968, 28). We can say that knowledge-that is propositional knowledge, while knowledge-how is practical knowledge.

With this distinction in mind, in his book, *Eastern Philosophy*, Ram Prasad Chakravarthi claims that knowledge in Confucianism is primarily a knowledge-how in contrast to knowledge-that, since "Confucianism concentrates on the cultivation of a life of ritual precision, proper engagement with society, and the search for an ordered state" (Chakravarthi 2005, 200); and such a conception of practical knowledge has its triumph in Neo-Confucianism, which is a practical learning with two dimensions: the inner dimension concerning self-cultivation and one's conduct toward others, and the outer dimension concerning the social-political ordering of the country (Chakravarthi 2005, 210). It has to be said that Chakravarthi, while not an expert in Confucian philosophy, is not alone in this respect. Many well-known scholars of Confucianism hold a similar view (see, for example, Raphals 1992, 9; Wong 1989; Kupperman 2005).

Given the fact that Confucians are primarily concerned with moral knowledge, and they have undoubtedly put great emphasis on moral self-cultivation, it is clear that knowledge in Confucianism is not merely propositional and theoretical knowledge-that. Indeed, if knowledge-that and knowledge-how have exhausted all possible types of knowledge, I would certainly also agree that moral knowledge in Confucianism is knowledge-how rather than knowledge-that. However, what I would like to challenge in this essay is precisely the assumption that these two types of knowledge have exhausted all types of knowledge, and consequently I would also like to challenge the characterization of Confucian moral knowledge as knowledge-how. In contrast, I would like to claim that it is other (or more) than knowledge-that and knowledge-how. To do this, I shall take a close look at knowledge in Confucianism, particularly neo-Confucianism, where Chakravarthi claims that there is a triumph of knowing-how, and I will use Wang Yangming 王陽明, one of the two greatest neo-Confucians (with Zhu Xi 朱熹 being the other), as an example.

In Wang Yangming, this moral knowledge, according to Mencius, is called *liangzhi* 良知, literally "good knowledge" or, simply, "moral knowledge." However, it is not the knowledge about the "good" or "moral"; rather it is the knowledge itself that is good or moral. This is made most clear when he compares *liang* 良 (goodness) of knowledge with *shan* 善 (goodness) of human nature: "because no human's nature is not good (*shan*), so no one's knowledge is not good (*liang*)" (Wang 1996, 65). In Wang's view, just as Mencius claims, such knowledge, as a distinguishing mark of being human, is what one is born with without the need to learn. Yet, except in rare cases (of sages), it is often clouded by one's selfish desire. So moral cultivation for Wang is "*zhi liangzhi* 致良知": to recover the good knowledge by getting rid of these selfish desires.[1] To understand the unique feature of Wang's *liangzhi*, it is important to relate it to the well-known neo-Confucian distinction between knowledge of/as virtue (*dexing zhi zhi* 德性之知) and knowledge from seeing and hearing (*wenjian zhi zhi* 聞見之知), first made by Zhang Zai 張載 but more fully developed by Cheng Yi 程頤. According to Cheng Yi, "knowledge from seeing and hearing is not knowledge of/as virtue. It results from the contact between one thing and another thing and therefore is not internal. The knowledge of those erudite and skillful persons belongs to this. Knowledge of/as virtue does not rely upon hearing and seeing" (Cheng and Cheng 1989, 317).

Clearly, here knowledge from hearing and seeing is roughly equivalent to Ryle's knowledge-that, but is knowledge of/as virtue equivalent to Ryle's knowledge-how? Against the popular interpretation, my answer to this question is negative. In terms of the origin, knowledge from seeing and hearing is external knowledge: either directly by our sense perception of the external things or indirectly through listening to others and reading books; in contrast, knowledge of/as virtue is internal knowledge, as it can only come from one's inner experience.[2] Thus, Cheng Yi claims that "learning, generally speaking, cannot be obtained by knowledge from hearing. One can obtain it only by its being apprehended in one's own heart/mind (*mo shi xin tong* 默識心通). If a learner wants to learn something, the learner has to be sincere in seeking the illumination from the principle (*li* 理). The best way to get it is the sudden enlightenment" (Cheng and Cheng 1989, 178). Because it is internal, it is not something that can be communicated by language (Cheng and Cheng, 1253) or that can be taught by a teacher or learned by reading classics. Rather it has to be acquired through one's own inner experience. It is in this sense that Cheng Yi emphasizes the importance of "getting it by oneself" (*zide* 自得): "in learning, what is most important is to get it by oneself. As one does not get it from outside, it is called getting it by oneself" (Cheng and Cheng 1989, 316).

What is unique about knowledge of/as virtue, in contrast to knowledge from hearing and seeing, is that it inclines its possessor to act accordingly: "When knowledge is profound, action will be thorough. No one ever knows without being able to act. If one knows without being able to act, the knowledge is superficial. Because they know the danger, people do not eat poisonous herbs when hungry, and do not tread on water and fire. People do evil things simply because they lack knowledge" (Cheng and Cheng 1989, 164). Here, Cheng claims that, on the one hand, people cannot do moral things or do immoral things only because they lack knowledge of/as virtue, and, on the other hand, people who have knowledge of/as virtue will necessary act morally and refrain from acting immorally.

It is precisely this aspect of moral knowledge that Wang Yangming wants to emphasize with his idea of *liangzhi*: "there has never been one who knows and yet does not act. To know and yet not to act is without knowledge" (Wang 1996, 5). Such knowledge that inclines one to act Wang calls *liangzhi* or, more precisely, the *liangzhi* that has not been clouded by selfish desires. This is in contrast to the type of knowledge that does not incline one to act. Thus he states, "one knows what is good and yet does not act according to this good knowledge (*liangzhi*), or one knows what is not good and yet does not refrain from doing it according to this good knowledge, only because one's good knowledge is clouded, and one does not make an effort to recover this knowledge" (Wang 1996, 124). This is an important aspect of Wang's well-known idea of unity of knowledge and action: genuine knowledge necessarily inclines a person to act.[3]

To illustrate this type of knowledge that inclines one to act accordingly, Wang uses the famous analogy from the Great Learning, one of the Confucian classics:

> The Great Learning shows us what are genuine knowledge and genuine action. It asks us "to love the good as we love the beautiful color and to hate the evil as we hate the bad odor." Here seeing the beautiful color belongs to knowledge, while loving it belongs to action. However, at the very moment one sees the beautiful color one has already loved it; it is not the case that

> one decides to love it only after seeing it. Similarly, smelling the bad odor belongs to knowledge, while hating it belongs to action. However, at the very moment one smells the bad odor, one has already hated it; it is not the case that one decides to hate it only after smelling it. (Wang 1996, 5–6)

Here Wang emphasizes that our knowledge of a flower as beautiful is necessarily accompanied with our natural inclination to love it; and our knowledge of an odor as smelly is necessarily accompanied by our natural tendency to it. In his view, our moral knowledge, *liangzhi*, is similar: our genuine knowledge of something as good must be accompanied by our natural tendency to it, and our genuine knowledge of something as bad must be accompanied by our natural dislike for it. It is in this sense that he claims that "one becomes a sage if he or she loves the good as he or she loves beautiful flower and hates the evil as he or she hates the bad odor" (Wang 1996, 102).

It is noteworthy that, in such a situation, as one acts according to one's natural tendency, whether when doing moral things or not doing immoral things, one does not fight against one's natural inclinations contrary to what one does or does not do and therefore can take delight in being moral. For this reason, Wang also emphasizes the importance of joy in moral action. He wrote a short essay, entitled, "The Greatest Joy Comes from Doing Moral Things," in which he states:

> a superior person takes delight in getting the Way, while an inferior person takes delight in satisfying his or her desires. However, in inferior persons' satisfying their desires, I also notice their suffering. . . . Concerned [about how to cover up their immoral deeds] and worried [about being found out] throughout their life . . . where do they really find joy? Superior persons do moral things, and therefore, looking up, they don't feel guilty; looking down, they don't feel ashamed; during the day, no persons criticize them, and in the night, no ghosts are blaming them. . . . What other joy can match it! (Wang 1996, 1012)

There are at least two things noteworthy about Wang's use of the analogy of beautiful color and smelly odor to explain our attitude toward moral good and evil. First, since seeing the beautiful color and loving it (or smelling the bad odor and hating it) are not two separate mental states, knowing what is good and desiring to do the good (or knowing what is evil and hating it) are not two separate mental states either. In other words, *liangzhi*, good knowledge, will naturally incline a person to act accordingly. This is the point we have been emphasizing all along. Second, when there is a beautiful color, one naturally loves it; and when there is a bad odor, one naturally hates it. Here no imperative is needed, categorical or hypothetical, autonomous or heteronomous. We will feel pain, indeed, if we are ordered to love the bad odor and hate the beautiful color. Similarly, with *liangzhi* being not clouded by selfish desire or recovered from such selfish desires, when we do good things and avoid doing evil things, we also feel natural and pleasant, without any feeling of hesitance or need for imperative; we would feel pain, indeed, if we are asked to do evil things and not to do good things.

With such an understanding of moral knowledge in Confucianism in mind, let us revisit Ryle's distinction between knowing-that and knowing-how. Suppose that we know that we ought to love our parents. As knowing-that in Ryle's distinction, such a propositional knowledge is entirely compatible with our not actually loving parents. This is what Neo-Confucians call knowledge from seeing and hearing. Now also suppose that we know how to love our parents (for example, by keeping them warm in the winter and cool in the summer). As knowing-how in Ryle's distinction, it is also perfectly compatible with our not actually loving our parents. In other words, neither knowing-that nor knowing-how, as Ryle defines them, inclines us to act according to our knowledge. Even if we know that we ought to love our parents (having knowledge-that) and know how to love our parents (having knowledge-how), we may still fail to love our parents.

This is quite understandable. We all know that, for example, riding bicycles is more environmentally friendly, and it is more important for us to take care of our environment than to save some time by driving cars; and we also know how to ride bicycles; still we may decide to drive cars instead of riding bicycles. However, as we have seen, moral knowledge in Confucianism, knowledge of/as virtue or *liangzhi,* is precisely the knowledge that inclines us to act according to such knowledge. If our knowledge that we ought to love our parents is the knowledge of/as virtue, and not knowledge from seeing and hearing, then we will not only naturally learn how to love our parents (i.e., seek knowledge-how), if we don't know how to love them yet, but will take delight in loving them and feel pain for our failure to do so. It is in this sense that I claim that moral knowledge in Confucianism cannot be simply characterized as either knowing-how or knowing-that: it includes both but has something additional; it is more than knowing-that and knowing-how. What is this additional thing? As we have seen, it is the inclination or disposition that a person with moral knowledge has to act according to such knowledge.

It is important to point out, however, that this inclination or disposition is different from the disposition that Ryle attributes to knowing-how. For example, he also says that competences and skills of a person with knowledge-how are "second natures or acquired dispositions" (Ryle 1968, 42), not only in the sense that "when they [people with knowledge-how] perform these operations [make and appreciate jokes, talk grammatically, play chess, fish, argue], they *tend to* perform them well, that is, correctly or efficiently or successfully" (Ryle 1968, 28; emphasis added), but also in the sense that "if he makes a mistake, he is *inclined not* to repeat it, and if he finds a new trick effective, he is *inclined* to continue to use it and to improve on it" (Ryle 1968, 42; emphasis added). The difference between the disposition in Wang Yangming's *liangzhi* in particular and Confucian moral knowledge in general on the one hand and the disposition in Ryle's knowledge-how on the other is that a person with knowledge-how tends, is inclined or disposed, to do things well when they do them, while a person with *liangzhi* not only tends, is inclined or disposed, to do moral things well when they do them but also tends, is inclined or disposed, to do moral things. In other words, while both a person with Ryle's knowledge-how and a person with Confucian moral knowledge tend to do things well when they do them, the former does not necessarily have the disposition to do things he or she can do well, while the latter is disposed to do them.

CONFUCIAN MORAL KNOWLEDGE: BESIRE BUT NOT BIZARRE

From the Humean point of view, a still dominant view in contemporary philosophy of action, philosophy of mind, and moral psychology, Confucians are perhaps both confused and confusing in their claim that knowledge of/as virtue or *liangzhi* is other or more than knowing-how and knowing-that. What they consider as "more" or "other" than knowing-how and knowing-that, as we have just seen, is the inclination or motivation to do things one's moral knowledge tells one it is right to do. However motivation is not knowledge and does not belong to knowledge, whether it is knowledge-that or knowledge-how, but something other than knowledge: desire. According to Humeans, in order for an action to take place, both belief and desires are needed: belief tells one what to do, and desire motivates the person to do it. Without desire, one's belief will not incline him or her to act; without belief, one's desire will not tell him or her what action to take and how to take the action.

Although there are some contemporary philosophers of action who are not Humeans and even are claimed (either by themselves or by others) to be anti-Humeans, most of them still agree that belief and desire are separate mental states. They are anti-Humeans only in the sense that they try to provide different explanations of action than the Humean one. On the one hand, we have those anti-Humeans who, as cognitivists or rationalists, claim that knowledge alone can motivate a person to act and there is no need for desire in this explanation. For example, Thomas

Scanlon argues that "a rational person who judges there to be compelling reason to do A normally forms the intention to do A, and this judgment is sufficient explanation of that intention and of the agent's acting on it (since this action is part of what such an intention involves). There is no need to invoke an additional form of motivation" (Scanlon 1998, 33–34).[4] On the other hand, we have those anti-Humeans who, as noncognitivists or emotivists, claim that all that is involved in our action is desire or emotion. For example, A. J. Ayer argues that if "moral judgment" is indeed a judgment (belief), it cannot be about morality and therefore cannot result in action (in other words, belief has nothing to do with action); if it is indeed about morality, then it cannot be a judgment. Moral statements are really not statements but "are simply expressions of emotion which can be neither true nor false" (Ayer 1946, 103); moreover, Ayer adds, "it is worth mentioning that ethical terms do not serve only to express feeling. They are calculated also to arouse feeling, and so to stimulate action" (Ayer 1946, 108).

It is true that there are also a small number of anti-Humeans who claim that one's action can be explained neither by belief alone (as claimed by cognitivist anti-Humeans) nor by desire alone (as claimed by emotivist anti-Humeans) but by both belief and desire, not as two separate mental states (as claimed by Humeans) but as one single mental state, a state which includes both belief and desire. J. E. J. Altham even coined the word "besire" to designate such a mental state (see Altham 1987). For example, John McDowell claims that action is not explained by a reason and an independent desire; rather it is explained by a single mental state that is both appetitive (desire) and cognitive (belief). He developed this view most clearly in his argument with Bernard Williams on whether reason for action is internal or external. As a Humean, Williams is an internalist, claiming that any reason or belief one has for action must be related to what exists in one's "subjective motivational set," which includes desires and other motivating elements, before it can cause an action (see Williams 1981). Williams here is primarily arguing against such externalist of moral reasons as Thomas Scanlon, who claims that moral reasons are self-sufficient and can cause a person to act without any additional mental state of desires. McDowell tries to steer a way between these two positions. He agrees with Williams that both belief and desires are needed to cause a person to act. However, he disagrees with Williams's view that belief and desire are two separate mental states. Instead they are produced simultaneously as one single mental state. Thus he claims that,

> if we think of ethical upbringing in a roughly Aristotelian way, as a process of habituation into suitable modes of behavior, inextricably bound up with the inculcation of suitably related modes of thought, there is no mystery

> about how the process can be the acquisition, simultaneously, of a way of seeing things and of a collection of motivational directions or practical concerns, focused and activated in particular cases by exercises of the way of seeing things. (McDowell 1998, 101; see also Platts 1979, McNaughton 1988, chapter 7, and Dancy 1993, 20)

However, such a conception of the single mental state, besire, that includes both belief and action has been seriously challenged and regarded as something bizarre by Humeans. The problem for them is that belief and desire are two very different mental states. Belief tells us what to do, and desire motivates us to do it. Belief represents the world, and so it is either true or false depending upon how well it represents the world; if it does not fit the world, it (belief) has to be changed to fit the world. In contrast, desire does not represent the world, and so, whether it is satisfied or not, it is neither true nor false; when it does not fit the world and is not satisfied, it (the desire) does not have to be changed. In contrast, we often want to change the world to fit our desires. Thus G. E. M. Anscombe uses the direction of fit to explain the difference between belief and desire. There is a need for fit both between the world and belief and between the world and desire. However, the directions of fit in these two cases are different. The fit between the external world and belief is obtained by changing the belief to fit the world: the direction here is from the mind to the world; in contrast, the fit between the world and desire is obtained by changing the world to fit the desire: the direction of fit here is from the world to the mind (Anscome 1957, Section 2).

Now, these Humeans ask: if there is such a single mental state that includes both belief and desire, the mental state of besire, then what is the direction of fit between this mental state and the world? As a belief, we need to change the mental state to make the belief fit the world; however, as a desire, we have to change the world to fit the mental state. Yet, since besire is one single mental state that includes both belief and desire, we will be at a loss about what to do to obtain the fit between this mental state and the world, as there are two opposite directions of fit at work here at the same time: to change the mental state to fit the world or to change the world to fit the mental state? (see discussion in McNaughton 1988, 109). It is in this sense that some Humeans claim that besire is a self-contradictory concept (Smith 1994, 118) and is something simply bizarre (see discussion in Little 1997, 66).

Although neo-Confucians in general and Wang Yangming in particular, in their discussion of moral knowledge, didn't employ the vocabulary, particularly belief, desire, and besire, in the contemporary debate between Humeans and anti-Humeans, their conception of moral knowledge, knowledge of/as virtue or *liangzhi*, is clearly neither merely belief nor purely desire but is a single mental state that includes both belief and desire; it is besire. However, is it indeed bizarre? Neo-Confucians of course think not. Their response can take at least two steps.

The first step is simply to show that, whether bizarre or not, the mental state of besire as a matter of fact does exist. In this respect, I think Wang Yangming has already made a convincing case in his use of the analogy between *liangzhi* and seeing/loving the beautiful color (or smelling/hating the bad odor) in the Great Learning. Our recognition of a color as beautiful and our loving it are one single mental state: it is neither that we first believe it is beautiful and then a desire arises to love it, nor that we first have a desire to love it and then we believe it is beautiful; we cannot love it if we don't at the same time believe it is beautiful, and we cannot believe it is beautiful if we don't at the same time love it. In the neo-Confucian view, genuine moral knowledge, *liangzhi* or *dexing zhi zhi*, is a similar single mental state of belief and desire, the state of besire. We will not believe that, for example, we ought to love our parents if we don't have the desire to love them at the same time; and we will not desire to love our parents if we don't believe that we ought to love our parents. It is neither that we first believe that we ought to love our parents and then a desire arises to love them, nor that we first desire to love our parents and then we believe that we ought to love our parents. It is at one and the same time, the time when our *liangzhi* is recovered, that we believe that we should love our parents and we desire to love our parents. Take away the belief, no desire is left, and take away the desire, no belief is left. So belief and desire are one and the same single mental state: besire.

Regarding this first step, we need to keep two things in mind. On the one hand, to say that moral knowledge is one single mental state that includes both belief and desire, neo-Confucians do not have to claim that this is the only mental state, thus denying the existence of the mental state of belief alone or the mental state of desire alone. As a matter of fact, the knowledge of hearing and seeing they talk about is a mental state of belief not accompanied by a desire to act according to this belief; and what they regard as the action in the dark is caused by the mental state of desire not accompanied by a corresponding belief. What they would argue is only that, in addition to belief and desire, besire is an equally legitimate although more desirable mental state. On the other hand, to say that moral knowledge is a single mental state of besire is not to say that moral knowledge is the only candidate for such a mental state. Clearly, one's knowledge that a flower is beautiful and one's desire to love it, just as one's knowledge that an odor is bad and one's desire to hate it, also constitutes a single mental state of besire. More interestingly, it is possible that there is a mental state extremely opposite to moral knowledge, call it "immoral" knowledge, which may also be a single mental state of besire. As we can see, moral knowledge is closely related to a virtuous person, as a virtuous person is one who possesses moral knowledge, the knowledge that inclines him or her to act accordingly. A virtuous person differs from the person who performs what Kant regards as the most typical moral actions: a person who does a morally good thing not because the person has the desire to do it but simply because the moral law commands him or her to do it. It is in this sense that such a person, as Kant acknowledges, is often not a happy person. In contrast, a virtuous person does the virtuous things, willingly, joyfully, and therefore with a great ease. Now the opposite of such a virtuous person is neither a person who does moral things in a Kantian sense nor a person who simply does immoral things but a person who does immoral things willingly, joyfully, and with a great ease. For example, a person who believes that women are inferior to men has a natural desire to discriminate against women, where his belief and desire may also constitute a single mental state of besire. The person will then engage in activities discriminating against women spontaneously, joyfully, and with a great ease.

The second step that neo-Confucians can take in responding to the criticism of besire as bizarre is to show that besire is indeed not bizarre, to show, in other words, that there are no two opposite or contradictory directions of fit between besire and the world. To do so, there is a need to distinguish between two different types of belief, one factual and one normative. Suppose I believe that the sun turns around the earth but actually the sun does not turn around the earth, then it is true that my belief has to be changed to fit the world. However, if I believe that people ought to love their parents, then even if there is no single person in the world who loves his or her parents, my belief that people ought to love their parents does not necessarily turn out to be false. In other words, it does not mean that I have to change my belief into one that people ought to not love their parents. In contrast, I ought to do what I can to make people love their parents, as long as it is within their power to love their parents, so that the world can be changed to fit my belief. The distinction between our factual beliefs and normative beliefs is actually made by Kant, who distinguishes between reality in theoretical reason and reality in practical reason. In the former, the reality of something is the cause of our knowledge of it and our knowledge has to fit the reality; in the latter, however, the reality of something is inseparable from our belief in it and our willingness and ability to act accordingly. To discern the reality in the latter sense, according to Kant, is "only to discern the possibility or impossibility of willing the action by which a certain object would be made Real, provided we had the ability to bring it about" (Kant 1956, 59).[5]

About this second step, we also need to keep something in mind. In the passage quoted above, Kant has a proviso: "provided we had the ability to bring it about." This proviso is necessary. When we say that we ought to change the world to fit our normative belief, in contrast to changing our descriptive belief to fit the world, we are not saying that we can hold whatever normative belief, however absurd it is, and demand the world to fit it. For example, we cannot hold a normative belief that human beings ought to be immortal and then try to change the world so that it can fit our belief. The reason is that it is impossible for humans to be immortal, or it is not within our ability to change the world so that it can fit our beliefs. This is really what the slogan "ought implies can" means: what we think people ought to do must be something that they can do (although it is not necessarily what people actually do, as people may not do what they can do), so that when people do not do what we believe that they ought to do, we can blame them in order to make them do it (i.e. change the world to fit our belief). For example, according to Owen Flanagan's principle of minimal psychological realism, we need to "make sure when constructing a moral theory or projecting a moral ideal, that the character, decision processing, and behaviour prescribed are possible, or are perceived to be possible for creatures like us" (Flanagan 1991, 34). This, however, is not unique to moral beliefs, which require that the world be changed to fit them; desires are the same. When we say that we change the world to fit our desires, it also means that our desires must be realistic. If we desire that we will never die, then perhaps we can never change the world in such a way that it will fit our desire.

When Humeans claim that besire is bizarre because there are conflicting directions of fit between besire and the world, they apparently only have the factual belief in mind. The direction of fit between factual belief and the world and that between desire and the world are indeed opposite, and so it would indeed be bizarre if they exist in one single mental state. However, the direction of fit between moral belief and the world and the direction of fit between moral desire and the world can be perfectly consistent. When no one in the world loves his or her parents, my desire that people love their parents of course requires that the world be changed to fit my desire so that people can start to love their parents; similarly when no one in the world loves his or her parents, my belief that people ought to love their parents does not automatically become false; rather the lack of the fit between my belief and the world in this particular case shows that the world is not what it ought to be and so has to be changed to fit my belief. Here, the world has to fit both our desire and our belief: the directions of fit in these two cases are thus consistent, as both are from the world to the mind.

MORAL KNOWLEDGE IN HINDUISM

It is my hunch that something similar to Confucian moral knowledge, which as a besire is more than knowing-that and knowing-how, is also present in Hinduism. As my knowledge of Hinduism is very limited, my discussion in this section must be parenthetical and so cannot go much beyond this hunch.

The ultimate goal of Hinduism is *mokṣa*, the final release from the cycle of life and death and the eventual identification between self and Brahman. Particularly relevant to the topic of this essay is the way emphasized by the Vedānta school, the way of cognition or knowledge. For example, Śaṅkara claims that release is the result of knowledge, for "release is not something which is to be brought about, but something whose nature is permanently established, and is reached through knowledge" (Śaṅkara 1989, III.iv.51), "immortality can be viewed as the result of the knowledge of the self" (Śaṅkara 1989, I.iv.22), perfect knowledge "is the door to perfect beatitude" (Śaṅkara 1989: I.iv.22), and "the cognition of the unity of Brahman is the instrument of final release" (Śaṅkara 1989, II.i.14). Here the knowledge in question is the knowledge that "thou art that!" or "that art thou!" (Śaṅkara 1989, I.iv.22), that is, I am Brahman, and my self is identical to Brahman.

While knowledge in Vedānta is primarily spiritual knowledge, whose goal is the final release, at least two things are certain in relation to morality: (1) it also includes moral knowledge, and (2) whether as spiritual knowledge or moral knowledge, it is not merely a propositional knowing-that or technological knowing-how. About (1), since the knowledge to be sought is that my self, just like the self of anyone else, is identical to Brahman, there is no difference between my self and the self of anyone else. Thus any immoral actions on my part betray my lack of the knowledge necessary for the final release, since all immoral actions are predicated on the assumption that there is a separation between my self and those of others. For this reason, S. Radhakrishnan rejects the contrast between the spiritual person in the Hindu tradition and a virtuous person in the Greek tradition. According to this contrast, while a virtuous person in the Greek tradition is one whose possession of knowledge makes him or her to do virtuous things, a spiritual person in the Hindu tradition is the one whose possession of knowledge makes it pointless for the person to do any virtuous things, since one does the virtuous things in this world of Maya, which his or her spiritual knowledge tells him or her is unreal. In contrast, S. Radhakrishnan claims that people with spiritual knowledge are those "who have risen above their selfish egos," for whom "morality becomes the very condition of their being, and law I fulfilled in love. There is no possibility of evil-doing in them" (Radhakrishnan 1962, 228).

About (2), S. Radhakrishnan states,

> this knowledge is not merely intellectual any more than ignorance is error. Ignorance . . . and selfish desire . . . are two phases of one phenomenon. . . . Only when a man rises to dispassion and acts without selfish attachment is he really free. The ego is the knot of our continued state of ignorance, and so long as we live in the ego we do not share in the delight of universal spirit. In order to know the truth we must cease to identify ourselves with the separate ego shut up in the walls of body, life, and mind. . . . Again, the delivery from the illusion is not achieved by means of abstract knowledge. (Radhakrishnan 1959, 95)

With this R. P. Chakravarthi agrees. For him, while such knowledge is essentially knowledge that *ātman* is Brahman, it is not simply a philological and philosophical grasp of the meanings of "*ātman*," "is," and "Brahman." In contrast,

> the intimacy with a piece of knowledge must carry with it qualities that transform its relationship with that knowledge. These qualities must inform not only a certain attitude towards that knowledge, but also more generally the dispositions, priorities, values and concerns of the subject of knowledge. The surrounding life-work of that subject makes the significance of knowledge—in terms of the effect it has on the subject—radically transformative, in a way that 'mere' knowledge of philosophical content does not. (Chakravarthi 2007, 103)

This view of Radhakrishnan and Chakravarthi is well grounded in the Upaniṣads as well as in Śaṅkara's writings. For example, the Upaniṣads distinguish two types of knowledge: "the lower of the two consists of the Ṛgveda, the Yajurveda, the Sāmaveda, the Atharvaveda, phonetics . . . whereas the higher is that by which one grasps the imperishable" (*Muṇḍaka Upaniṣad* 1.1.4–5). In other words, the knowledge in question, knowledge of Brahman, is not something you can acquire by studying the Vedas, as it is not a bookish knowledge.[6] The difference between lower knowledge and higher knowledge is whether it can transform the person who possesses the knowledge. For example, we learn from the Upaniṣads that "the seers, sated with knowledge, when they have attained him, become free from passion and tranquil, and their selves are made perfect" (*Muṇḍaka Upaniṣad* 3.2.5).[7] The transformative power of knowledge is clearly affirmed here as in Confucianism. Śaṅkara makes a much more Confucian-sounding statement: "the man who has once comprehended Brahman to be the Self, does not belong to this transmigratory world as he did before. He, on the other hand, who still belongs to this transmigratory world as he did before, has not comprehended Brahman to be the Self" (Śaṅkara 1989, I.i.4).[8] It is Confucian-sounding as it reminds us of what

Wang Yangming says: a person who truly knows does not do evil things, and a person who does evils things does not really know. In other words, just as for Wang Yangming whether a person really has moral knowledge or not is not measured by the person's ability to recite or even explain the knowledge but by the person's actual inclination to act morally, so for Śaṅkara whether a person truly knows Brahman or not is not measured by the person's analytical understanding of "thou art that" but by the person's actual detachment from this world. Clearly, such knowledge is not disinterested knowledge, whether it is knowing-that or knowing-how, but is an existentially transformative knowledge, knowledge that transforms its possessor.

What kind of transformation does the person who knows that his self is Brahman undergo? According to the Upaniṣads, such a person will exhibit a number of remarkable features, which include (1) having no bewilderment or sorrow: "When in the self of a discerning man, his very self has become all beings, what bewilderment, what sorrow can there be, regarding that self of him who has become all beings?" (*Īśā Upaniṣad* 7); (2) having no desires: "it is when they come to know this self that Brahmins give up the desire for sons, the desire for wealth, and the desire for worlds" (*Bṛhadāraṇyaka Upaniṣad* 3.5); (3) having no fears: "One who knows that bliss of Brahman, he is never afraid" (*Taittirīya Upaniṣad* 2.4); (4) freedom from evil: "A man who knows this, therefore, becomes calm, composed, cool, patient, and collected. He sees the self (*ātman*) in just himself (*ātman*) and all things as the self. Evil does not pass across him and he passes across all evil. He is not burnt by evil; he burns up all evil. He becomes a Brahmin—free from evil, free from stain, free from doubt" (*Bṛhadāraṇyaka Upaniṣad* 4.4.22);[9] and thus (5) being purified: "the ascetics who have firmly determined their goal through a full knowledge of the Vedānta, have their being purified by the discipline of renunciation" (*Muṇḍaka Upaniṣad* 3.2.6)

If we regard such a transformation, as well as the behavior of the person who undergoes such a transformation, all caused by the relevant knowledge, as action or at least, as Radhakrishnan calls it, inner action (Radhakrishnan 1959, 107), then the following claim made by Kumārila, meant to be a criticism of the Vedānta school's emphasis on knowledge, is off the point: "right cognition does not enter into opposition with the potential for action. Though it is accepted that lack of right cognition brings about [wrong] actions, as it does attachment and the like (i.e., obstructions to a proper life), they are not removed by [right] cognition" (cited in Chakravarthi 2007, 105). Apparently, in this criticism, the type of knowledge that Kumārila has in mind, whether it is moral knowledge or spiritual knowledge, is the sort of knowledge that neo-Confucians would call knowledge of hearing and seeing, not the type of knowledge that Vedānta emphasizes, which neo-Confucians would call knowledge of/as virtue, one unique feature of which is to incline the knower to act accordingly. Clearly, a person who acquires the knowledge that "I am Brahman" in the Vedāntic sense will not do anything that is selfish. As we have seen above, for Śaṅkara, a person who knows is no longer attached to the world, and a person who is attached to this world does not know. With such a clear statement, how can Kumārila say that right knowledge cannot remove actions inconsistent with such knowledge? In Vedanta, not only wrong belief will lead to wrong actions and true belief will lead to right actions, which Kumārila acknowledges, but true belief can also remove the wrong actions, and wrong beliefs will block right actions.

So knowledge as a means to *mokṣa* in Hinduism, just like moral knowledge in Confucianism, is something more than knowing-that and knowing-how, as neither knowing-that nor knowing-how can cause existential transformation of the knower. Then can we also regard knowledge in the Vedānta school of Hinduism as a mental state of besire, a state that includes both belief and desire? In appearance, we cannot, as one of the remarkable features of a person who possesses such knowledge, as we have seen above, is being desireless. However, we need to note that in both Upaniṣads and Śaṅkara, there is a distinction between two kinds of desires. The desires that a person who acquires knowledge as the means to the final release no longer has are all worldly desires, the desires for sons, for the wealth, and for the world. However, there is a different desire such a person must have: "As a man embraced by a woman he loves is oblivious to everything within or without, so this person embraced by the self (*ātman*) consisting of knowledge is oblivious to everything within or without. Clearly this is the aspect of his where all desires are fulfilled, where the self is the only desire, and which is free from desires and far from sorrows" (*Bṛhadāraṇyaka Upaniṣad* 4.3.21). In other words, just as a lover who has no other desires except the desire to love his or her lover, a person who knows Brahman has no other desires except the desire for being Brahman. As Sarasvati Chennakesavan points out, "to attain salvation, man must first desire it. The ancient seers attained *mokṣa* because they desired it with a burning intensity" (Chennakesavan 1976, 203).

This distinction between the worldly desires to be extinguished and the spiritual desire necessary for salvation is made clear by Śaṅkara, when he talks about the antecedent conditions for the inquiry into Brahman, which include "the discrimination of what is eternal and what is non-eternal, the renunciation of all desire to enjoy the fruit (of one's actions) both here and hereafter, the acquirement of tranquility, self-restraint, and the other means, and the desire of final release" (Śaṅkara 1989, I.i.1).[10] Here, it is striking that two of the four conditions mentioned are precisely to renounce the worldly desire and to acquire the desire for final release respectively. Moreover, in Śaṅkara's view, these two conditions are closely connected: we need to acquire the desire of knowing Brahman because it destroys our worldly desires: Knowledge "springs up only in so far as learning destroys the obstacles in the way of knowledge" (Śaṅkara 1989, III.iv.27). So without the desire for knowing Brahman, the worldly desires cannot be destroyed; and one who wants to keep the worldly desires is unlikely to have the desire for salvation. It is in this sense that we can legitimately claim that knowledge as the means of the final release in Hinduism, just like moral knowledge in Confucianism, is not only something more than knowing-how and knowing-that but that the reason it is more than these two types of knowledge is precisely that it is the single mental state of besire, a mental state that includes both belief and desire.

Now, because knowledge in Vedānta is a besire, the way to obtain it, just as the way to obtain moral knowledge in Confucianism, is not merely a business of intellectual exercise. For example, Śaṅkara claims that "in matters to be known from scripture mere reasoning is not to be relied on" (Śaṅkara 1989, II.i.11). What we need instead is a kind of deep meditation. Thus Śaṅkara tells us: "From the devout meditation on this Brahman there results as its fruit, final release" (Śaṅkara 1989, I.i.4). This is also confirmed by the following passage in the Upaniṣads: "not by sight, nor by speech, nor by any other sense, nor by austerities or rites is he grasped. Rather the partless one is seen by a man, as he meditates, when his being has become pure, through the lucidity of knowledge" (*Muṇḍaka Upaniṣad* 3.1.8). Such a way of knowing is similar to the inner experience in Confucianism. Thus we are told that "He who, his spirit purified by contemplation / Plunges into the *ātman*—what measureless blessedness he feels! / That for the expression of which words are of no avail / Must be experienced within in the inmost heart" (*Maitrī Upaniṣad* 6.34; cited in Deussen 1966, 352). Since this is an inner experience, knowledge cannot be imposed from the outside but must be gained by oneself. Thus, responding to the question of what is the meaning of those Vedic passages which speak of the highest Brahman as something to be seen, to be heard, and so on, Śaṅkara replies that they aim

> not at enjoining the knowledge of truth, but merely at directing our attention to it. . . . Even when a person is face to face with some object of knowledge, knowledge may either arise or not; all that another person wishing to inform him about the object can do is to point it out to him. . . . True knowledge . . . can neither be brought about by hundreds of injunctions nor be checked by hundreds of prohibitions. (Śaṅkara 1989, III.ii.21).[11]

This is essentially the same idea of self-getting (*zide*) in Confucianism.

CONCLUSION

In this essay, I have argued that Confucian moral knowledge and Hindu spiritual knowledge, which includes moral knowledge, cannot be regarded as either knowledge-that or knowledge-how. It is true that they contain both knowledge-that and knowledge-how, as a person who possesses Confucian moral knowledge and Hindu spiritual knowledge not only knows what to do but also knows how to do it. However, they also contain something that is not contained in either knowledge-that or knowledge how, for a person possessing both knowledge-that and knowledge-how certainly knows what to do and how to do it but is not necessarily inclined to do it. A person with Confucian moral knowledge and Hindu spiritual knowledge, however, has the inclination to act accordingly. So not only does such knowledge contain, to use the vocabulary of contemporary philosophy of action, both belief and desire, but belief and desire are not two separate mental states: they form a single mental state of besire. Such a mental state of besire is not bizarre as claimed by contemporary Humeans, as the direction of fit between this mental state of besire, both as belief and as desire, and the world is from the world to the mind: when there is conflict between the world and mind, we demand that the world be changed to fit the mind.[12]

NOTES

1. I here understand "*zhi liangzhi*" as to get rid of selfish desires to recover *liangzhi*, which differs from a common understanding. For example, according to Mou Zongshan 牟宗三, "*zhi*" means to extend or expand, equivalent to Mencius's "expansion" (*tui* 推) of the four beginnings (see Mou 2001, 161). I think such an understanding ignores an important difference between Mencius and Wang Yangming. For Mencius, since we are only born with the four beginnings, we need to expand them. For Wang, however, we are already born with the full *liangzhi*. The trouble is that it is clouded by selfish desires, and so moral cultivation aims to remove such selfish desires to restore, and not expand, the *liangzhi*. In this respect, I think Julia Ching is right to point out that Wang's *liangzhi* can neither be increased nor decreased (see Ching 1976, 73). Another common interpretation is that *zhi liangzhi* is to apply *liangzhi* in action. However, as Chen Lai 陳來 has pointed out, for Wang, *liangzhi* is a type of knowledge that has already included action (see Chen 1991, 111–112). In my view, *liangzhi* continues to exist even when it is clouded by selfish desires. However, because it is clouded by selfish desires, it cannot function normally and thus cannot incline a person to act accordingly. Thus there is a need for *zhi liangzhi*, that is, to recover *liangzhi* by getting rid of the selfish desires, so that it can incline a person to act accordingly.

2. While knowledge of/as virtue may be acquired independently of any knowledge of seeing and hearing, neo-Confucians also acknowledge that knowledge of seeing and hearing, that is, intellectual knowledge, may be transformed into knowledge of/as virtue, if it is not merely understood by mind but also experienced by heart. For a more detailed discussion about the relationship between these two types of knowledge, see Huang 2008.

3. Sometimes Wang claims that knowledge itself is action, that is, a mental action. In this case, this mental action itself, just like bodily action, calls for an explanation in terms of belief and desire or simply besire, as we shall argue in the next section.

4. To show that desire is not necessary or sufficient for action, Scanlon also mentions situations where we do things we do not have desire to do or we do not do what we have desire to do (Scanlon 1998, 39).

5. This Kantian distinction is stated in a more easily understandable way by John Rawls, also a Kantian: "practical reason is concerned with the production of objects according to a conception of these objects . . . while theoretical reason is concerned with the knowledge of given objects" (Rawls 1993, 93).

6. It is in this sense that Radhakrishnan claims that "the attitude of the Upaniṣads is not favorable to the sacredness of the Vedas," as "it is recognized that the Vedic knowledge is much inferior to the true divine insight, and will not liberate us" (Radhakrishnan 1962, 149). Of course, this does not mean that knowledge of the Vedas has nothing to do with knowledge of the Self or Brahman (see Forsthoefel 2002, 58–62). What it means is that the study of the Vedas merely as texts, not combined with one's inner experience of what is said in these texts, will not result in the transformative knowledge of the self. This is quite consistent with the neo-Confucian view of the role the Confucian classics play in one's self-cultivation.

7. All references to the Upaniṣads are from Olivelle 1996.

8. Skoog also claims that such knowledge can "bring about a whole new way of being, a total psychological transformation in which one's sense of personal identity and one's perception of the world undergo a dramatic and radical alternation" (Skoog 1986, 30).

9. Śaṅkara also points out that complete comprehension of Brahman, as the highest end, "destroys the root of all evil such as ignorance" (Śaṅkara 1989, I.i.1).

10. In another place, Śaṅkara states that one's knowledge that "I am Brahman" leaves "nothing to be desired because the state of consciousness . . . has for its object the unity of the universal Self. . . . [T]here is nothing else which could be desired in addition to the absolute unity of Brahman" (Śaṅkara 1989, II.i.14).

11. In this connection, Kim Skoog points out that this spiritual knowledge, which he calls liberative knowledge, does not operate "on the cognitive level of human awareness. Simply to tell someone of their ignorance or to attempt to realize one's own ignorance (on a cognitive level) does not immediately bring about the removal of this 'ignorance.' It is only upon reflection and direct experiencing of truth that one gains liberation—a process that is non-cognitive in nature" (Skoog 1986, 27).

12. This essay originates from an invitation from Professor Jiang Tao to present a paper at the Chinese and Indian Religious Traditions unit of American

Academy of Religion at its annual meeting in 2010. While I was doing my sabbatical at Chinese University of Hong Kong in the Spring of 2011, Professor Yao Zhihua read and commented on an earlier version of this paper, from which I benefited greatly. I also presented part of this paper at Soochow University of Taipei and Tunghai University of Taizhong as well as American Philosophical Association Annual Meetings in Washington, D.C. I benefited from questions raised by audiences in these locations. Thanks also go to Eric Hutton, who read and commented on an earlier version of this chapter, which made me rethink a number of issues. I posted some ideas of this chapter at the blog "Way, Weft, and Way" and benefited greatly from comments posted there. Finally, I would like to thank the two editors of this volume, not only for their extraordinary effort to bring this significant volume into completion, but also for their valuable comments on the penultimate version of this chapter.

BIBLIOGRAPHY

Altham, J. E. J. 1987. "The Legacy of Emotivism." In *Fact, Science, and Morality: Essays on A. J. Ayer's* Language, Truth, and Logic, edited by Graham Macdonald and Crispin Wright. Oxford: Blackwell.

Anscombe, G. E. M. 1957. *Intention*. Oxford: Blackwell.

Ayer, A. J. 1946. *Language, Truth, and Logic*. New York: Dover Publications.

Chakravarthi, Ram Prasad. 2005. *Eastern Philosophy*. London: Weidenfeld and Nicolson.

———. 2007. *Indian Philosophy and the Consequences of Knowledge*. Hampshire, England: Ashgate.

Chen, Lai 陳來. 1991. *The Realm of Being and Nonbeing: The Essence of Wang Yangming's Philosophy* 有無之境: 王陽明哲學的精神. Beijing 北京: Renmin Chubanshe 人民出版社。.

Cheng, Hao, and Cheng Yi. 1989. *Collections of the Two Chengs* 二程集. Beijing: Shangwu Yingshuguan.

Chennakesavan, Sarasvati. 1976. *Concepts of Indian Philosophy*. Columbia, MO: South Asia Books.

Ching, Julia. 1976. "A Contribution on Chan's Thought." In *Dictionary of Ming Biography*, edited by L. Carrington Goodrich and Chaoying Fang (New York and London: Columbia University Press), vol. 1, 41–42.

Dancy, Jonathan. 1993. *Moral Reasons*. Oxford: Blackwell.

Deussen, Paul. 1966. *The Philosophy of the Upanishads*. New York: Dover Publications.

Flanagan, Owen. 1991. *Varieties of Moral Personality: Ethics and Psychological Realism*. Cambridge, MA: Harvard University Press.

Forsthoefel, Thomas A. 2002. *Knowing beyond Knowledge: Epistemologies of Religious Experience in Classical and Modern Advaita*. Burlington, VT: Ashgate.

Huang, Yong. 2008. "How Is Weakness of the Will Not Possible? Cheng Yi's Neo-Confucian Conception of Moral Knowledge." In *Educations and Their Purposes:*

A Conversation among Cultures, edited by Roger T. Ames and Peter D. Hershock. Honolulu: University of Hawaii Press.

Little, Margaret Olivia. 1997. "Virtue as Knowledge: Objections from the Philosophy of Mind." *Noûs* 31: 59–79.

Kant, Immanuel. 1956. *Critique of Practical Reason*. New York: Macmillan Publishing Company.

Kupperman, Joel L. 2005. "Morality, Ethics, and Wisdom." In *A Handbook of Wisdom: Psychological Perspective*, edited by Robert J. Sternberg and Jennifer Jordon. Cambridge: Cambridge University Press.

McDowell, John. 1998. *Mind, Value, and Reality*. Cambridge, MA: Harvard University Press.

McNaughton, David. 1988. *Moral Vision: An Introduction to Ethics*. Oxford and New York: Blackwell.

Mou, Songsan 牟宗三. 2001. *From Lu Xiangshan to Liu Jishan* 從陸象山到劉蕺山. Shanghai 上海: Shanghai Guji Chubanshe 上海古籍出版社。.

Olivelle, Patrick, trans. 1996. *Upaniṣads: A New Translation*. Oxford and New York: Oxford University Press.

Platts, Mark de Bretton. 1979. *Ways of Meaning: An Introduction to a Philosophy of Language*. London, and Boston: Routledge and Kegan Paul.

Radhakrishnan, S. 1959. *Eastern Religions and Western Thought*. New York: Oxford University Press.

———. 1962. *Indian Philosophy*. Vol. 1. New York: Macmillan.

Raphals, Lisa. 1992. *Knowing Words: Wisdom and Cunning in the Classical Traditions of China and Greece*. Ithaca, New York: Cornel University Press.

Rawls, John. 1993. *Political Liberalism*. New York: Columbia University Press.

Ryle, Gilbert. 1968. *The Concept of Mind*. New York: Barnes and Noble.

Śaṅkara. 1989. "The Vedānta Sūtras with the Commentary by Śaṅkarācārya." In *A Sourcebook in Indian Philosophy*, edited by Sarvepalli Radharkrishnan and Charles A. Moore. Princeton: Princeton University Press.

Skoog, Kim. 1986. *The Epistemological Status of Liberative Knowledge (with Special Reference to Advaita Vedanta)*. PhD Dissertation, University of Hawaii at Manoa.

Smith, Michael. 1994. *The Moral Problem*. Oxford and Cambridge, MA: Blackwell.

Wang, Yangming. 1996. *Complete Works of Wang Yangming* 王陽明全集. Beijing: Hongqi Chubanshe.

Williams, Bernard. 1981. "Internal and External Reasons." In his *Moral Luck: Philosophical Papers, 1973–1980*. Cambridge: Cambridge University Press.

Wong, David. 1989. "Universalism versus Love with Distinctions: An Ancient Debate Revived." *Journal of Chinese Philosophy* 18: 241–272.

III

BODY, HEALTH, AND SPIRITUALITY

10

Yoga and Daoyin

History, Worldview, and Techniques

Livia Kohn

Yoga, the eight-limb system associated with Patañjali's *Yogasūtras*, and Daoyin, the Daoist practice of guiding (*dao* 導) the *qi* and stretching (*yin* 引) the body, at first glance have a lot in common. They both focus on the body as the main vehicle of attainment; they both see health and spiritual transformation as one continuum leading to perfection or self-realization; and they both work intensely and consciously with the breath. In both Yoga and Daoyin, moreover—unlike in Taiji quan and the majority of Qigong forms—physical stretches and movements are executed in all the different positions of the body, while standing, moving, sitting, and lying down. Postures are often sequenced into integrated flows and named either descriptively or after various animals.

In both systems, too, practitioners follow certain basic ethical rules and guidelines for daily living, geared to create an environment best suited to personal transformation. They learn the exact way to execute postures and movements, they gain awareness and control of their respiration, and they work to adjust the breath in accordance with the body postures. Adepts moreover use the strengthening of the muscles, loosening of the joints, and awareness of internal energies to enter into states of absorption and deeper meditation, relating actively to spiritual powers and seeking higher levels of self-realization.

Does that mean, then, that Yoga and Daoyin represent essentially the same system, just expressed in Indian and Chinese forms? Do they pursue the same goal, use the same methods, and reach similar stages, just formulated in different languages and terminologies? Is there, maybe, even a historical overlap, a mutual influence between the two systems that might explain their closeness? Or are the similarities coincidental—predicated upon the fact that all bodies move and stretch and breathe and that certain exercises are essentially good for us—and mask a deeper layer of complex and sophisticated differences in worldview, history, social role, and practice?

To answer these questions, I will look at the philosophical foundations of both practices, at historical origins and sociological settings, at their developments over time, and at the way they relate healing to spiritual realizations. I conclude with a look at their concrete practices and a general evaluation of their similarities and differences.

PHILOSOPHICAL FOUNDATIONS

The body in Yoga forms an integral part of a body-mind continuum that cannot be separated and is seen as one. This continuum is one aspect of the material world ground, known as *prakṛti*. *Prakṛti* is real and eternal, dynamic and creative, inert and primordial (Eliade 1969, 31). It is the underlying substance of all that exists, the "noumenal matrix of creation," "the realm of the multitudinous phenomena of contingent existence" (Feuerstein 1980, 29). It lies deep underneath the surface of natural everyday reality, representing its ultimate ground and creative potential, yet it is also the concrete, material world as it exists with all its different forms, modes, and transformations. *Prakṛti* at the root of all being is not accessible by ordinary sensory means but can be reached through yogic introspection after long periods of training and meditative immersion.

So far, *prakṛti* sounds amazingly like Dao. Literally "the way," the term indicates how things develop naturally, nature moves along in its regular patterns, and living beings continuously grow and decline. Dao is the one power underlying all. The fundamental ground of being, it makes things what they are and causes the world to develop. Mysterious and ineffable, it cannot be known but only intuited in tranquil introspection. As the *Daodejing* says:

> Look at it and do not see it: we call it invisible.
> Listen to it and do not hear it: we call it inaudible.
> Touch it and do not feel it: we call it subtle. . . .
> Infinite and boundless, it cannot be named; . . .
> Vague and obscure,
> Meet it, yet you cannot see its head,
> Follow it, yet you cannot see its back. (ch. 14)

Beyond this, like *prakṛti,* Dao also manifests actively in the material, natural world and is clearly visible in rhythmic changes and patterned processes. On this, the phenomenal level, it is predictable in its developments and can be characterized as the give and take of various pairs of complementary opposites, as the natural ebb and flow of things as they rise and fall, come and go, grow and decline, emerge and die (Kohn 2005, 10). Like practitioners of Yoga, Daoists and Daoyin practitioners locate the human body-mind in the underlying cosmic continuum, as it is both the root of creation and manifest in the phenomenal world. Practitioners of either system strive to increase awareness of the fundamental structure and organization of reality, deepening their understanding of the fluid nature of the phenomenal world and encouraging the development of intuitive faculties that allow a greater appreciation of the underlying ground.

There is, therefore, a basic commonality in the elementary worldview underlying Yoga and Daoyin. However, there are also major differences. Unlike in Daoism, the Yogic ground of *prakṛti* is equipped with particular characteristics, qualities, or aspects known as *guṇa*s, which are the ultimate building blocks of all material and mental phenomena. These are *sattva,* intelligence or luminosity that can reveal the ultimate but may also lead to attachment to knowledge and happiness; *rajas,* motor energy, passion, and activity which bind people to wealth and pleasures; and *tamas,* static inertia or ignorance that creates sloth, laziness, and delusion (Eliade 1969, 31; Feuerstein 1980, 33; Worthington 1982, 51).

These three condition psychological and physical life, and each manifest in five further aspects of reality. That is to say, *sattva,* the intelligent quality of *prakṛti,* appears in the five senses of perception, that is, hearing, seeing, touching, smelling, and tasting. The motor energy or *rajas* of the primordial ground is activated in the five organs of action, that is, hands, feet, speech, excretion, and reproduction. And the inert quality of *tamas* appears in the five *tanmātra*s or birth states of the five elements—ether, gas, light, liquids, and solids—which join together to create the material world (Mishra 1987, xxv; Feuerstein 1980, 30).

In Daoism, on the contrary, Dao manifests in the two complementary forces yin and yang 陰陽 which originally described geographical features and were first used to indicate the shady and sunny sides of a hill. From there they acquired a series of associations: dark and bright, heavy and light, weak and strong, below and above, earth and heaven, minister and ruler, female and male, and so on. In concrete application, moreover, they came to indicate different kinds of action:

Table 10.1.

yang	active	birth	impulse	move	change	expand
yin	structuring	completion	response	rest	nurture	contract

In addition, the ongoing flux and interchange of yin and yang was understood to occur in a series of five phases, which were symbolized by five materials or concrete entities:

Table 10.2.

minor yang	major yang	yin-yang	minor yin	major yin
wood	fire	Earth	metal	water

These five energetic phases and their material symbols were then associated with a variety of entities in the concrete world, creating a complex system of correspondences. They were linked with colors, directions, seasons, musical tones, and with various functions in the human body, such as energy-storing (yin) organs, digestive (yang) organs, senses, emotions, and flavors. The basic chart at the root of Chinese and Daoist cosmology is as follows:

Table 10.3. A talisman used in Highest Clarity practice. Source: Zhenzhai lingtu.

yin/yang	*phase*	*direct.*	*color*	*season*	*organ1*	*organ2*	*emotion*	*sense*
lesser yang	wood	east	green	spring	liver	gall	anger	eyes
greater yang	fire	south	red	summer	heart	sm. int.[1]	exc. joy[2]	tongue
yin-yang	earth	center	yellow	spleen	stomach	worry	lips	
lesser yin	metal	west	white	fall	lungs	lg. int.[3]	sadness	nose
greater yin	water	north	black	winter	kidneys	bladder	fear	ears

Notes:
1. Small intestine.
2. Excessive joy.
3. Large intestine.

Daoyin practice, as much as other forms of Daoist body cultivation, accordingly aims to create perfect harmony among these various forces and patterns, which guarantees health and long life. Going beyond this harmony, adepts also hope to enter a deeper awareness of and oneness with the Dao at the center of creation, finding perfection through resting in and flowing along with the root of all being.

Yogic practice, in a quite different mode, does not work toward harmony with the *guṇa*s and their various aspects, but sees them as obstacles that have to be overcome in order to reach the highest goal. The highest goal, moreover, is not the attainment of *prakṛti* in its aspect as the creative root of the world, but to go beyond *prakṛti* altogether to a level that is unique to the Indian system and has no matching counterpart in China. This level is described variously as *puruṣa*, *ātman*, *Brahman*, and *īśvara*.

Puruṣa is best known from *Ṛgveda* hymns as the cosmic giant whose body is dismembered to create the world, a story that appears in Chinese folklore as the myth of Pangu 盤古 but which has little impact on Daoist practice (see Lincoln 1975; Mair 2004, 91).[1] *Puruṣa* is the original man, the cosmic creator, the cause of all material being and existence of the universe, the source of the source, the power behind even the underlying ground (Feuerstein 1980, 16). A representation of the sheer awareness that transcends even pure consciousness, *puruṣa* is the authentic, ultimate being of humanity, the far-off and detached seer of all ongoing psychic and physical processes, the perfect knowledge of all, the ultimate mirror of reality that is utterly apart, completely other, unmoving, unthinking, unfeeling, and unintending (Feuerstein 1980, 19–20).

In this latter sense, the notion of *puruṣa* in the *Ṛgveda* is very similar to the concept of *ātman* in the *Upaniṣads;*[2] their key concept of *ātman*, which is used interchangeably with *puruṣa* in yogic texts, indicates the soul or true self, a transcendent autonomous principle that is unique, universal, fundamentally real, solidly substantial, and eternally free. Originally referring to the extended self, that is, the social and individual personality, *ātman* first included the physical body as much as social status, family, and self-image. In the *Upaniṣads*, however, it came to be seen on a more sophisticated meditative level as the core of the individual's inner being, the divine moment within. Ultimately indestructible, *ātman* exists from the beginning of time and to the end of all eons. However often reincarnated and immersed in *prakṛti*, it remains forever free from evil, grief, hunger, thirst, old age, and death.

Ātman is so far beyond the senses and the intellect that it cannot be described, but one can pursue a state of consciousness that allows a glimpse. The *Māṇḍūkya Upaniṣad* distinguishes four kinds of consciousness—waking, dreaming, deep sleep, and meditative trance—noting that only the latter is a state that is awake yet completely free from bodily concerns (Worthington 1982, 25). Like the wind, the clouds, lightning, and thunder, this state is present but does not rely on a tangible body that is subject to the limitations of the *guṇa*s. Only in meditative trance can one experience the deepest inner nucleus of one's being, the ultimate true self or *ātman*. Deeply serene, one can allow the true self to shine forth in bright radiance (see Cope 2000). As the *Bṛhadāraṇyaka Upaniṣad* says:

> The true nature of the ultimate self is to be free from fear, free from desire and evil. As lovers in deep embrace forget everything, and only feel peace all around, so man where he embraces his true self feels peace all around. In that state there is neither father nor mother, there are no gods, no worlds, no good, and no evil. He neither sees, hears, tastes, smells, knows, nor touches. Yet he can see, for sight and he are one; he can hear, for sound and he are one. . . . (Worthington 1982, 16)

Ātman, moreover, is to be realized as ultimately one with *Brahman*, the universal cosmic energy that is at the root beyond creation, is completely separate and different from all that exists materially, and is perceptible with the senses. *Brahman* is described as being in the world like salt is in water or like clay is in statues (Worthington 1982, 18), but in its original form it is utterly beyond description. It is

> not coarse, not fine, not short, not long, not glowing like fire, not adhesive like water, not bright, not dark, not airy, not spacious, not sticky, not tangible. It cannot be seen, nor heard, not smelled nor tasted. It is without voice and wind, without energy and breath, without measure, without number, without inside, without outside. (Worthington 1982, 25)

Brahman is the cosmic counterpart, the larger version of *ātman*, and a key doctrine of the ancient Indian thought that both are originally one. The goal of Yoga, then, as much as of other Indian ascetic practices and philosophies, is to fully realize that one's innermost, original, and perfect self is the same as the innermost, original, and perfect power of the universe. This is classically expressed in the phrase "Tat tvam asi!" (Thou art that!).

The practice of Yoga accordingly is to move through different layers of the apparent self as created by and perceptible through *prakṛti* to come to the ultimate true self which is *puruṣa*, the original man, *ātman*, the innermost soul, and *Brahman*, the underlying power of the universe. The key layers of the apparent self are the five so-called sheaths (*kośa*). They are: the physical body that is nourished by food; the etheric body that exists through vital energy or *prāṇa*; the astral body made up from thoughts and intentions; the causal body consisting of pure intellect and knowledge; and the ultimate bliss body, true self, or *ātman* (Cope 2000, 68; Mishra 1987, 49; Worthington 1982, 23).

Yogic practice aims to reach oneness with *Brahman*, to return to the purity of the original soul, and to recover the true self. Firm, fixed, permanent, and eternal, this true self is thus the person's ultimate identity. Originally one with the deepest transcendent ground of all, human beings have forgotten this identity through their karmic involvement with the world and the sensory experience of *prakṛti*. Through Yoga they can recover the innate stability, wholeness, and permanence of the cosmos within and return to the essential substance of their being.

To do so, in additional to regular practice, they also have to have strong devotion to *īśvara*, the lord, a personalized form of *Brahman* who can extend grace and support to the practitioner. Omnipresent and omnitemporal, he remains pure, distant, and incomprehensible, yet in the yogic system "the grace of the deity is a necessary precondition for the recompense of ascetic exertion" (Feuerstein 1980, 4). *Īśvara* is innate cosmic enlightenment, coessential with the innermost self, the personified power that creates, upholds, and withdraws. Yoga is, therefore, essentially theistic (Eliade 1969, 16). Grace and devotion are key factors for success, and *īśvara-praṇidhāna*, "refuge in the lord," is one of the five *niyamas*, the mental attitudes to be cultivated as the very foundation of the practice, which also include purity, contentment, austerity, and self-study.

With this strong otherworldly and theistic orientation, Yoga in its philosophical foundations is clearly different from the underlying vision of Daoyin. The Daoist universe is complex in its own way, similarly presupposes several layers of existence, and acknowledges the pervasive presence of an underlying ground; but it does not propose the substantial, eternal presence of something totally other. Daoist practice, as a result, remains within the realm of energetic refinement and transformation. Practitioners transmutate into pure spirit, a subtle form of energy that flows at high velocity and allows easy transformations, celestial consciousness, and supernatural powers, but that is not utterly different from the world or a permanent, firm, unchanging entity of a transcendent nature.

The emphasis on the stability and permanence of the true self and the ultimate state in Yoga thus stands in radical contrast to the refinement into subtler and faster energetic flows in Daoyin. This difference, moreover, is also expressed in the execution of postures—a strong focus on stability and holding in Yoga as opposed to a sense of flow and easy movement in Daoyin—and in the role of the mind, which is the key subject of transformation in Yoga and an adjunct to transformation in Daoyin. Beyond that, the difference also manifests in the historical and social development of the two traditions.

HISTORY AND SOCIETY

The historical origins of the two systems could not be more different. Yoga comes from the ancient Indian hermit tradition which "rejected the world as it is and devalued life as ephemeral, anguished, and ultimately illusory" (Eliade 1969, 18). Daoyin, on the other hand, arose as part of Han-dynasty medicine which encouraged people to relish the world in all its aspects, to find greater health, and to enjoy their physical and social pleasures. Both traditions have, in the course of their history, moved into the other realm—Yoga becoming a vehicle for health and Daoyin being integrated into the quest for immortality—but their origins and social bases remain far apart.

The earliest document on Yoga is the *Yogasūtras* of Patañjali, who may or may not be identical with a well-known Sanskrit grammarian who lived around 300 BCE. The date of both author and text is unclear, and some scholars have placed them as late as the third century CE, but all agree that the text is later than the *Upaniṣads* and early Buddhism and probably came after the *Bhagavadgītā* (Worthington 1982, 55). The text divides into four main sections on Yogic Ecstasy, Discipline, Miraculous Powers, and Isolation (Eliade 1969, 12), and consists of 196 *sūtras* or short half-sentences that are more mnemonic aids than clarifying explanations (Taimni 1975, viii). It is largely philosophical in nature and inherits key doctrines from the *Vedas* and *Upaniṣads*.

For example, an important *sūtra* that is often cited among yogis today appears right in the beginning: "Yoga is the cessation of the modifications of the mind" or the "abolition of all states of consciousness" (I.2). I. K. Taimni writes a four-page explanation on this short phrase, dwelling on every word and reaching the conclusion that its intended meaning refers to the overcoming, through yogic practice, of the various states and delusions of the mind that are conditioned by the *guṇa*s and thus opening the way to the appreciation and realization of *ātman* (1975, 6–10). Mircea Eliade sees the phrase as describing the gradual overcoming and elimination of all errors, delusions, and dreams, then of all normal psychological experiences, and finally even of all parapsychological powers to the point of complete cessation (1969, 51). Confirming this, the text moves on to explain the various trance states in the depth of meditative absorption and the need to overcome the *guṇa*s and identify fully with *puruṣa*. As this example shows, the text is brief in phrasing and often obscure. Thus Georg Feuerstein says: "Their extreme brevity and conciseness renders the *sūtra*s almost unintelligible to the uninitiated" while at the same time guaranteeing "the great degree of flexibility witnessed in the diverse traditions" of Yoga (1979, 21).

In contrast to this rather obscure and philosophical writing, the earliest works on Daoyin are immensely practical in nature and can be precisely dated. Found among manuscripts unearthed from southern China, they include the silk manuscript *Daoyin tu* 導引圖 (Exercise Chart) and the bamboo tablets of the *Yinshu* 引書 (Stretch Book).

The *Daoyin tu* was found at Mawangdui, in the tomb of the Marchioness of Dai, the wife of a local lord who died in 168 BCE. The text consists of forty-four color illustrations of human figures performing therapeutic exercises that are explained in brief captions (see Fig. 10.1). The figures are of different sex and age, variously clothed or bare-chested, and shown in different postures (mostly standing) from a variety of angles. In many cases, they have one arm reaching up while the other stretches down, one arm moving forward while the other extends back, possibly indicating rhythmical movement.

There is some variety among them. Two figures are in a forward bend, one with head lowered, the other with head raised. Another is bending slightly forward with a rounded back and hands hanging down toward

Figure 10.1. The Mawangdui "Exercise Chart." Source: Daoyin tu.

the knees. Yet another has one arm on the ground and the other extended upward in a windmill-like pose (Harper 1998, 132). The captions are often illegible, but among them are the well-known "bear amble" and "bird stretch," showing a figure walking in a stately fashion with arms swinging and one bending forward with hands on the floor and head raised, respectively.

The lack of written explanations is somewhat alleviated by the *Yinshu*, which consists entirely of text. It was found in a manuscript at Zhangjiashan 張家山, also in Hunan, in a tomb that was closed in 186 BCE. The text divides into three parts: a general introduction on seasonal health regimens; a series of about a hundred exercises, divided into three sections; and a conclusion on the etiology of disease and ways of prevention (see Fig. 10.2).

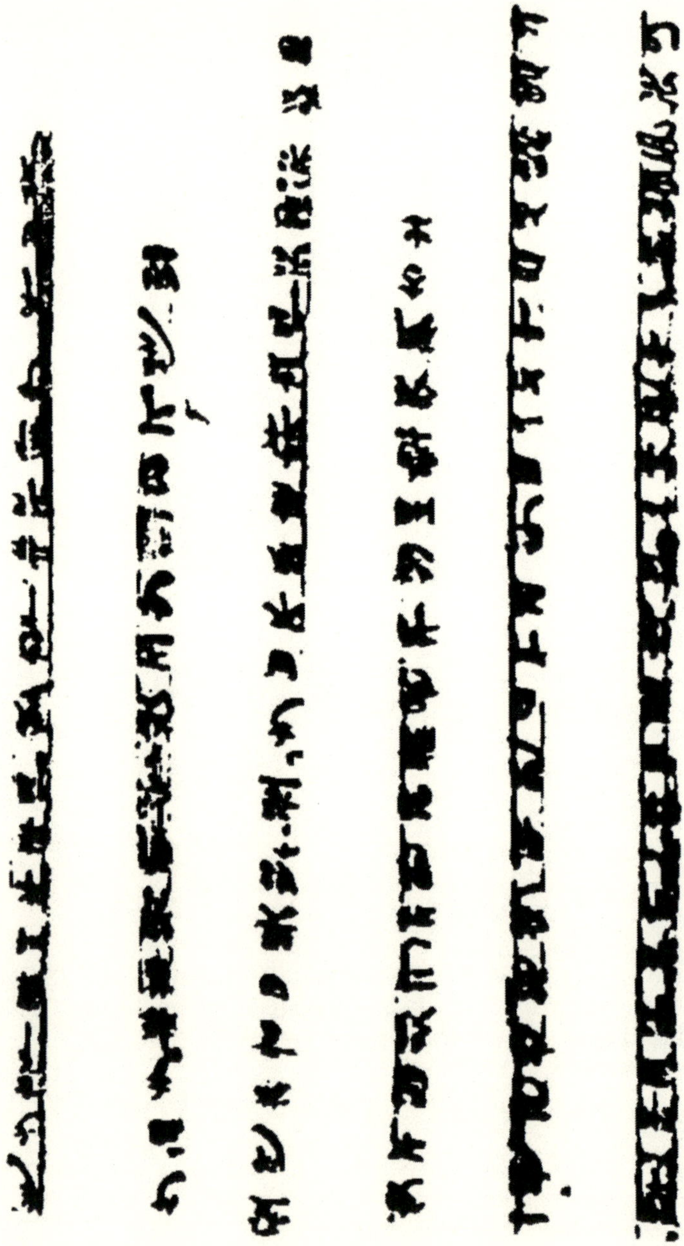

Figure 10.2. The bamboo slips of the "Stretch Book." Source: Yinshu.

The first part on seasonal health regimens discusses hygiene, diet, sleep, and movement as well as adequate times for sexual intercourse. It is ascribed to Pengzu 彭祖, a famous immortal of antiquity, said to have lived over 800 years. It says, for instance:

> Spring days. After rising in the morning, pass water, wash and rinse, clean and click the teeth. Loosen the hair, stroll to the lower end of the hall to meet the purest of dew and receive the essence of Heaven, and drink one cup of water. These are the means to increase accord. Enter the chamber [for sex] between evening until greater midnight [1 a.m.]. More would harm the *qi*. (Engelhardt 2001, 215; Harper 1998, 110–11)

This places the practice firmly in the home of a wealthy aristocrat with leisure to pursue long life and well-being and the inclination to perform proper hygiene and develop bodily awareness. It also assumes that the practitioner lives in society and has a wife or concubine for bedroom activities. The scene could not be further removed from the kind of hermit setting that lies at the foundation of Yoga.

Following a general outline of daily routines, the middle part of the *Yinshu* provides concrete practice instructions, describing and naming specific moves. For example:

> "Bend and Gaze" is: interlace the fingers at the back and bend forward, then turn the head to look at your heels (#12).
>
> "Dragon Flourish" is: step one leg forward with bent knee while stretching the other leg back, then interlace the fingers, place them on the knee, and look up (#19).
>
> "Pointing Backward" is: interlace the fingers, raise them overhead and bend back as far as possible (#29).[3]

Following forty exercises of this type, the text focuses on the medical use of the practices. It often repeats instructions outlined earlier and in some cases prescribes a combination of them. For example, a variation of lunges such as "Dragon Flourish" is the following, which can be described as a walking lunge:

> To relieve tense muscles: Stand with legs hip-width apart and hold both thighs. Then bend the left leg while stretching the right thigh back, reaching the knee to the floor. Once done, [change legs and] bend the right leg while stretching the left leg back and reaching that knee to the floor. Repeat three times (#46).

Another variant of the lunges is recommended to relieve *qi*-disruptions in the muscles and intestines. Lunging with the left foot forward and the right leg back, one goes into a twist by bending the right arm at the elbow and looking back over the left shoulder. After three repetitions on both sides, one is to maintain the lunge position while raising one arm at a time and then both arms up as far as one can (each three times), bending the back and opening the torso (#68). The idea seems to be that by stretching arms and legs one can open blockages in the extremities while the twisting of the abdominal area aids the intestines.

Exercises like these in the medical section of the text also include breathing techniques, notably exhalations with *chui, xu,* and *hu* (three forms of the six breaths) to strengthen the body and to harmonize *qi*-flow, as well as exercises in other than standing positions, such as seated, kneeling, or lying down. For example, to alleviate lower back pain, one should lie on one's back and rock the painful area back and forth 300 times—if possible with knees bent into the chest. After this, one should lift the legs up straight to ninety degrees, point the toes, and—with hands holding on to the mat—vigorously lift and lower the buttocks three times (#55).

An example of a kneeling practice is the following:

> To relieve thigh pain. Kneel upright, stretch the left leg forward while rotating the right shoulder down to bring them together with some vigor. Then stretch the right leg forward while rotating the left shoulder down to bring them together. Repeat ten times. (#50)

Following this detailed outline of concrete exercises, the *Yinshu* concludes its third part with a list of twenty-four brief mnemonic statements. After this, it places the practice into a larger social and cultural context. It notes that the most important factors in causing diseases are climatic excesses:

> People get sick because of heat, dampness, wind, cold, rain, or dew as well as because of [a dysfunction] in opening and closing the pores, a disharmony in eating and drinking, and the inability to adapt their rising and resting to the changes in cold and heat. (Engelhardt 2001, 216)

This harks back to the seasonal regimen in the beginning of the text, restating the importance of climatic and temporal awareness in the way one treats the body. The proper way of treating the body, however, as the text points out next, is accessible mainly to "noble people" of the upper classes, who fall ill because of uncontrolled emotions such as anger and joy (which overload yin and yang *qi*). "Base people," whose conditions tend to be caused by excessive labor, hunger, and thirst, on the contrary, have no opportunity to learn the necessary breathing exercises and therefore contract numerous diseases and die early.

This, as much as the fact that the manuscripts were found in tombs of local rulers, makes it clear that Daoyin practice in Han China was very much the domain of the aristocracy and upper classes and aimed predominantly at alleviating diseases and physical discomforts, providing greater enjoyment of daily luxuries and faster recovery after raucous parties (Engelhardt 2000, 88; 2001, 217; also Harper 1998, 381). Also, the very existence of the texts with their detailed instructions shows that the practices were public knowledge and accessible to anyone with enough interest and financial means to obtain them.

Historical records show that medical and philosophical materials were often collected by aristocrats. Some searched out already written works and had them transcribed; others invited knowledgeable people to their estate and had them dictate their philosophical sayings and medical recipes to an experienced scribe. While knowledge was transmitted orally in a three-year apprenticeship from father to son in professional medical families or from master to disciple among itinerant practitioners and within philosophical schools, the dominant tendency was to offer this knowledge to society at large, and there was little concern for the establishment of close-knit hierarchies or esoteric lineages (Harper 1998, 61).

The situation in Indian Yoga is much different. As the *Yogasūtras* reflect, the masters' knowledge, however practical, was closely guarded and formulated in obscure philosophical phrases. Disciples had to commit fully to their teacher, and together with faith in the grace of *īśvara* had to have total trust in and obedience to the guru who, as representative of the ultimate, possessed powers far beyond ordinary knowledge (see Arya 1981; Hewitt 1977). Also, since the goal of Yoga was the attainment of complete cessation of mentation and the realization of the transcendent true self, it could not be undertaken within society—let alone be used for the enhancement of ordinary pleasures. The only way to freedom and beatitude in Yoga, as Mircea Eliade points out, was to withdraw from the world, detach from wealth and ambition, and live in radical self-isolation (1969, 21).

Socially, therefore, Yoga took place in a completely different context than Daoyin. Yogic practitioners were not aristocrats trying to stay healthy and have more fun, but radical ascetics who denied themselves even the most basic human comforts. The ascetic hermit (*sādhu*) would give up all products of culture and live in the wilderness, not even "stepping on ploughed land," the symbol of human domination over nature (Olivelle 1990, 133). He—very few if any female ascetics are mentioned from the early stages (Ghurye 1964, 40)—would eat only uncultivated foods, such as fruits, berries, roots, and herbs; wear bark, leaves, and animal skins; leave his hair unkempt and his nails growing; and imitate animals in his behavior—notably deer, cows, pigeons, fish, snakes, and dogs. Returning to a state of primal origin, before the plow and social hierarchies, he would find paradise for himself in utter independence from society (Olivelle 1990, 134–35). Thus he could attain the freedom of mind and body necessary for ultimate release.

Typically such ascetics undertook a variety of practices, which are still familiar among the yogis of today.

> There are those who squatted on their heels, others who lay on beds of thorns, ashes or grass, others who rested on a pestle. . . . One was avowedly following the vow of exposing himself to the elements, especially to the sun and the rain. Another with the help of a long staff was carrying out the austerity of standing on one leg. (Ghurye 1964, 39–40)

This contrasts vividly with the description of the ideals of Daoyin from a fourth-century text, which through its very warning of the enticements of sensuality and beauty shows just how much its practitioners were exposed to them. It says,

> The method of nourishing longevity consists mainly in not doing harm to oneself. Keep warm in winter and cool in summer, and never lose your harmony with the four seasons—that is how you can align yourself with the body. Do not allow sensuous beauty, provocative postures, easy leisure, and enticing entertainments to incite yearnings and desires—that is how you come to pervade the spirit. (Stein 1999, 169)

Rather than subject themselves to extremes, practitioners of Daoyin matched the changes of nature, creating harmony in the body and in society instead of leaving the family and restructuring the body to the point of complete cessation. The physical and breathing exercises of the two systems, however apparently similar, in their original setting thus served completely different purposes, were executed in completely different social milieus, and found expression in completely different kinds of documents.

HEALING AND TRANSCENDENCE

As history moved along, this original contrast between the two traditions began to dissolve to a certain degree. Daoyin became part of the Daoist enterprise of the attainment of immortality and Yoga, as we know all too well from its popularity today, turned into a major method for health and well-being. How and when did this change occur?

In the case of Daoyin, it had to do with the arising of various organized Daoist groups that adopted some self-cultivation methods practiced by Chinese hermits (see Kohn 2001). Most prominent among them was the school of Highest Clarity (Shangqing 上清), which arose in the 360s, when two brothers of the aristocratic Xu family hired the medium Yang Xi 楊 羲 (330–386) to establish contact with Xu Mi's 許謐 wife who had died in 362 to find out about her fate in the otherworld. She appeared to tell them about her status and explained the overall organization of the heavens. She also introduced the medium to various other spirit figures who revealed methods of personal transformation, meditations, visualizations, and alchemical concoctions; gave thorough instructions on how to transmit the texts and their methods; and provided prophecies about the golden age to come (see Strickmann 1981).

The Xu brothers wrote down everything Yang Xi transmitted, however disparate it may have seemed, and created a basic collection of sacred texts. They shared their new revelations with their immediate neighbors and relatives, thus establishing the first generation of Highest Clarity followers (Robinet 1984, 1:108). They developed a spiritual practice that also included a daily routine of stretches, breathing, and self-massages in combination with the use of talismans and incantations—all to purify their bodies and to enhance their vigor for the great endeavor of becoming immortal.

How Daoyin functioned in the daily practice of these would-be immortals is described in the *Baoshen jing* 寶神經 (Scripture on Treasuring the Spirit, DZ 1319; trans. Kohn 2012, 52–73. See Robinet 1984, 2:359–62). The text says:

> When you get up in the morning, always calm your breath and sit up straight, then interlace the fingers and massage the nape of your neck. Next, lift the face and look up, press the hands against the neck while moving the head back. Do this three or four times, then stop.[4]
>
> This causes essence to be in harmony and the blood to flow well. It prevents wind or wayward *qi* from entering the body. Over a long time it will keep you free from disease and death.
>
> Next, bend and stretch; extend the hands to the four extremes [up, down, right, left]; bend backward and stretch out the sides; and shake out the hundred joints. Do each of these three times. (6a)

These and similar morning practices were further accompanied by incantations that implored the deities and perfected to support the practitioner and enhanced their visions of divine ascension. An example is:

> My spirit and material souls receiving purity,
> My five spirits [of the inner organs] are restful and at peace.
> I return in a flying carriage to visit [the heaven of] Jade Clarity,
> Ascend to Great Nonbeing and journey with the sun.
> Becoming a perfected, I merge in mystery with emperors and lords. (2b)

Figure 10.3. A talisman used in Highest Clarity practice. Source: Zhenzhai lingtu.

The practice also involved the use of talismans, written in red ink on yellow paper in imitation of the sacred writings of the otherworld. Adepts used them either by placing them on themselves or by burning them and drinking the ashes (*Baoshen jing* 16b) (see Fig. 10.3).

The morning practices of Daoyin in Highest Clarity served several goals: dispersal of obstructive and demonic forces, self-purification in the face of the divine, clarity of vision and keenness of hearing to open otherworldly perception, extension of life expectancy to have more practice time, and preparation for ascension through visualizations of gods and heavens (see Robinet 1993).

Variations of the practice include:

- bends and stretches known from the medical manuscripts as well as deep breathing to release stale *qi* and absorb new energy;
- self-massages of the face, eyes, and ears;
- saliva swallowings to harmonize *qi* in the body and calm the viscera;
- visualizations of the inner organs with the body gods.

In this religious Daoist context, therefore, the practice of Daoyin was transformed into an aspect of spiritual purification, including but not limited to the maintenance of health and extension of life. Although the setting was still aristocratic and mundane, it has come much closer to Yoga, leading to extensive explorations of the unseen world and deep absorptive trance states.[5]

Yoga, on the other hand, moved in the opposite direction, leading to a greater emphasis on health benefits and a wider spread among people within society. Two movements in particular took the tradition into a more secular environment and transformed it into a popular form of self-therapy. The first is known as Laya Yoga. It arose toward the end of the first millennium CE as part of the tantric adoption of Yoga and focused on utilizing the energy that arises in the body after prolonged meditation.

This energy, called *kuṇḍalinī*, was thought to lie dormant at the base of the spine. If awakened properly, it would begin to move from here, rising up along the spine through three major *nāḍis* or energy channels. Along the way it would open the seven *cakras* or energy centers until it reached the top of the head where it would unify with cosmic consciousness and exit the body (see Tab. 10.4). By activating *kuṇḍalinī*, the belief was, people could bring their energetic system into balance and reach greater health, endurance, and well-being (Worthington 1982, 100–102).

The seven *cakras*, moreover, were associated with various colors, geometric forms or *yantras*, deities, and personality types. They are:[6]

Table 10.4.

Name	*Location*	*Color*	*Yantra*	*Personality*	*Deity*
Root	perineum	red	square	survival	Brahmā
Sacral	abdomen	orange	semi-circle	creativity	Viṣṇu
Central	solar plexus	yellow	triangle	ego/confidence	Rūdra
Heart	chest/thyroid	pink	star	love/compassion	Īśa
Throat	throat/pineal	blue	triangle	logic/thought	Śiva
Brow	third eye	violet	circle	intuition	
Crown	top of head	gold	triangle	spirituality	

Activating the *cakras* through a mixture of physical practices, breathing exercises, and meditations, practitioners hoped to find perfect balance in their energetic system to create health, vigor, and long life. As history moved on, however, the practice was once more reintegrated with the higher spiritual goals of Patañjali's *Yogasūtras* and practitioners came to aspire to advanced stages of evolution, reaching out to complete transcendence and the true self. Even the awakening of the *kuṇḍalinī* eventually came to be described as a mystical, supernatural experience. As the modern mystic Krishna Gopi records:

> I experienced a rocking sensation and then felt myself slipping out of my body, entirely enveloped in a halo of light. I felt the point of consciousness that was myself growing wider, surrounded by waves of light. I was not all consciousness, without any outline, without any idea of a corporeal appendage, without any feeling or sensation coming from the senses, immersed in a sea of light. (1985, 143)

Therefore, while Laya Yoga may have begun as a secularized form of energy transformation, it eventually recovered the spiritual aspects of classical Yoga and became an important part of the tantric tradition (see Feuerstein 1998a).

This is not quite the case in the other therapy form of Yoga, known as Haṭha Yoga and named after a combination of *ha*, the sun, and *ṭha*, the moon, meant to indicate the joining and harmonizing of the two basic forms of energy in the body (Yasudian and Haich 1965, 20).

Haṭha Yoga goes back to a group known as Nāth yogis who flourished in northern India from the tenth century onward. Founded by Gorakṣanāth, this group placed great emphasis on physical fitness, developed various forms of martial arts, and engaged in psychic experiments. Rather than remain aloof from society, they made attempts at reform, treating women and outcasts as equals and trying to unite Hindus and Buddhists. Their efforts were not greatly appreciated by the ruling classes, and they were soon relegated to a lower caste. Still, the legendary Gurkha fighters are said to be their heirs, and their transformation of Yoga into an art of practical living has had a profound impact on the tradition (Worthington 1982, 129).

The main document of the Nāth yogis is the *Haṭhayoga-pradīpikā* (Light on Hatha Yoga), which was compiled in the fifteenth century on the basis of the notes and instructions of earlier masters by Svātmārāma Swāmī, also known as Divātmā Rām. Arranged in five sections on Initial Practices, Stepping up Energy, Overcoming Limitations, Manifesting Self, and Corrective Treatments, it is written like the *Yogasūtras* in a series of short instructions that need further personal instruction (Worthington 1982, 129).

Unlike the *Yogasūtras* and more like the early Daoyin manuscripts, however, the *Haṭhayoga-pradīpikā* is eminently practical and quite concrete. It warns against excesses that will hinder the practice, including overeating, exertion, useless talk, extreme abstinence, public company, and unsteadiness of mind. Instead it encourages persistence, knowledge, courage, and determination (Worthington 1982, 130). It follows the eight limbs of the *Yogasūtras* but places a stronger emphasis on moral discipline and the physical practices than on deep absorptions and meditative trances. It supports the five *yamas* or restraints—against killing, stealing, lying, sexual misconduct, and attachments—and the five *niyamas* or proper mental attitudes: purity, contentment, austerity, self-study, and refuge in the lord (Iyengar 1976, 31–40). Continuing along the eight limbs, the text then provides detailed instructions on the performance of fifteen key postures or *āsanas* and moves on to a discussion of breath control or *prāṇayāma* (Eliade 1969, 65).

Haṭha Yoga has become dominant in the practice of Yoga today and for many people means the creation of perfect health, defined as the state of natural equilibrium of all energies and the free flow of *prāṇa*, the inner life force that smoothes out irregularities and preserves health, the power of gravity, attraction, repulsion, electricity, and radioactivity (Yasudian and Haich 1965, 30, 53).

Prāṇa is more concrete and more tangible than *kuṇḍalinī*; present in everyone and everything, it does not need to be awakened. Very much like *qi*, it is omnipresent, flows through energy channels in the body, and is activated through conscious breathing and controlled physical movements. People tend to neglect and waste their *prāṇa*, straining it through exhausting labor, excessive sexuality, and draining mental work. Daoists would agree with this. Haṭha Yoga, like Daoyin, accordingly teaches to use and store vital energy to the maximum, thereby enhancing health and extending long life (Yasudian and Haich 1965, 36, 31).

The proper use of *prāṇa* ultimately leads to the complete control over the body and mind, the ability to counteract various outside influences through internal energy work and to overcome and eventually eliminate all sorts of harmful emotions, such as rage, fear, grief, sorrow, fright, jealousy, despondency, and pessimism (Yasudian and Haich 1965, 37). While this may again sound very much like the program of Daoyin or even Qigong, the ultimate goal of Haṭha Yoga is formulated once more in the classical vision as the ultimate transformation of consciousness. As B. K. S. Iyengar notes:

> Yoga is the method by which the restless mind is calmed and the energy directed into constructive channels. . . . The mind, when controlled, provides a reservoir of peace and generates abundant energy for human uplift. . . .

> [Eventually] the seer, the sight, and the seen have no separate existence from each other. It is like a great musician becoming one with his instrument and the music that comes from it. Then the yogi stands in his own nature and realizes his true self, the part of the Supreme Soul within himself. (1976, 20, 22)

DIVERGENT TECHNIQUES

Taking all this information together, we can now begin to answer the questions posed in the beginning. Are Yoga and Daoyin essentially the same but formulated differently? Or are they two separate traditions that have very little in common? It should be clear by now that in their original social setting, cosmological speculation, and textual formulation they are very different indeed, although they share some basic notions about the nature of existence and propose similar physical practices. In the course of history, on the other hand, they have come a bit closer to each other, Daoyin being used in a more spiritual context and Yoga transforming into popular therapy. This shift has also led to a certain change in key concepts, Laya and Haṭha Yoga emphasizing notions of internal vital energy that are very much like *qi*, and Highest Clarity and later Daoists engaging in deep trance states with the hope to reach otherworldly dimensions.

To conclude this discussion, I would now like to take a closer look at the actual practices and their commonalities and differences. First, quite obviously, both Yoga and Daoyin support a moderate and simple lifestyle, a nutritious and natural diet, freedom from strong emotions, and clarity in daily living. They have a basic moral code, formulated as the *yamas* and *niyamas* in Yoga and apparent in Daoism in various sets of precepts for lay followers, priests, and monastics (see Kohn 2004).

Both also prescribe a fairly straightforward exercise regimen that, combined with deep, abdominal and chest-expanding breathing, can be executed in all different positions of the body. Exercises include bends and stretches, most commonly forward bends, backbends, lunges, and twists, as well as some weight-bearing practices, such as pull-ups and push-ups. Many of these basic exercises are part and parcel of any workout routine and will be familiar to athletes and gym-users everywhere. They have been proven effective for health over many centuries and in all different cultures, just as a moderate life style and good moral foundation have been helpful all along.

So far, both systems do not contradict each other, nor are they different from other health enhancing methods, whether they emphasize the physical or the spiritual. Their effectiveness is not questioned, nor is their general applicability. Beyond this, however, things become more complicated. Both Yoga and Daoyin have more complex postures and sequences that are not at all alike in name or execution.[7]

Daoyin variously makes use of ropes and swings, which are not found in Yoga. Yoga, on the other hand, places a great emphasis on inversions and balancing poses which are strikingly absent in Daoyin. Also, with the exception of the meditation known as "Standing Like a Pine Tree," Daoyin tends to encourage movement, while Yoga demands holding—sometimes for periods of ten, twenty, or thirty minutes. This, of course, goes back to the ultimate goal in Yoga of reaching a level of complete inner stability that allows the awareness of the eternal true self, contrasted with the aim of Daoists to become one with the flow and to find perfect harmony by moving along with the patterns of Dao.

A similar set of differences also applies to the breathing practices associated with the two systems, *qifa* 氣法 in Daoyin and *prāṇayāma* in Yoga. Both encourage holding of the breath—called *biqi* 閉氣 in Daoyin and *kumbhaka* in Yoga—for the opening of energy channels. Both use a method of directed breathing to alleviate discomforts and distress, and both guide energy up the spinal column. Yet, in general Daoyin works with the systematic circulation of *qi* throughout the body, while Yoga focuses on the concentrated use of breath in the nostril, sinus, and throat areas.

For example, one form of Daoyin breathing is called "swallowing qi" (*yanqi* 咽氣). According to the *Huanzhen xiansheng fu neiqi juefa* 幻真先生服內氣訣法 (Master Huanzhen's Essential Method of Absorbing Internal *Qi*, DZ 828),[8] this involves lying flat on one's back with the head slightly raised and the hands curled into fists. In this position, adepts inhale through the nose, allow the breath to reach the mouth, mix it with saliva by moving the tongue and cheeks, and swallow it down, guiding the *qi* mentally to reach the stomach and spread from there into the various inner organs. To help the movement, practitioners massage the passageway of the breath by rubbing the chest and belly (2b–3b).

In an extension, they also "guide the *qi*" (*xingqi* 行氣) by first taking the swallowed saliva-breath mixture into the lower elixir field, then entering it into two small caverns at the back and imagining it moving up the body in two strands to enter the Niwan Center or upper elixir field in the head. From here they allow it to stream into all parts of the body, "through hair, face, head, neck, and shoulders into the hands and fingers; from the chest and the middle elixir field at the heart into the five inner organs and down along the legs to thighs, knees, calves, heels, and soles" (3b–4a). As they do so, all congestions of blood and blockages of *qi* are successfully dissolved, paving the way for the refinement of *qi* into subtler energetic forces.

A yet different variant is called "surrendering to qi" (*weiqi* 委氣), which is described as flowing mentally along with the qi in the body wherever it may go in a state of deep absorption, "where there is no spirit, no conscious awareness; deep and serene, the mind is one with the Great Void" (5b–6a). This in turn causes the body to become independent of nostril breathing as the *qi* will begin to flow through the pores of the skin. In an extension of this heightened power of *qi*, adepts can then spread it to other people in a form of laying-on of hands to create healing and greater harmony with the Dao.

In contrast to these breathing practices, Yoga followers use the breath to heighten awareness, to calm the mind, and to cleanse the air passages (see Loehr and Migdow 1986). To give a few examples, there is a popular form known as *ujjayi* breathing, often called the "ocean-sounding breath." It involves the tightening of the muscles at the back of the throat, allowing the air to flow slowly and making a soft, rasping noise, said to stimulate the endocrine and thyroid glands and increase mental alertness (Yasudian and Haich 1965, 120). A breath that calms the mind and balances energy channels is *nāḍi-śodhana*. Also called "alternate nostril breathing," it is done by alternately closing off one nostril with the fingers or thumb of the right hand. Encouraging long, calm inhalations and complete, deep exhalations, this is very soothing and aids the integration of the two brain hemispheres.

Another classic yogic breath is *bhastrikā*, which means "bellows." In this exercise, the breath is pushed in and out quickly and powerfully ten times, after which it is held in for five to ten seconds. It is said to help with colds, destroy phlegm, relieve inflammation of the nose and throat, and over longer periods may cure asthma (Yasudian and Haich 1965, 122). The "skull-polishing" breath, finally, is called *kapālabhātī*. It cleanses and tones up the nasal passages, expels bacteria, and increases concentration. For this, practitioners breathe in deeply and then expel the breath in short bursts from the lungs through the nose while vigorously contracting the abdominal muscles and pushing the diaphragm upward. They continue for thirty to fifty repetitions, then exhale completely, hold the breath out while "securing the locks" by tightening the muscles in pelvis, belly, and throat, then inhale and hold the breath in (Yasudian and Haich 1965, 120–21).

This brief overview of the best known breathing practices in the two systems shows just how significantly different they are in both form and purpose. Daoists mix the breath with saliva and guide it internally to effect opening of *qi*-channels while Yogis work with strong, deep inhalations and exhalations to cleanse specific physical channels.

The difference is further enhanced by the vast variety in cleansing procedures in the two traditions. Daoists practice daily hygiene by washing the face, rinsing the mouth, and cleaning the teeth. They also expel stale *qi* upon waking in the morning. To do so, they close the eyes and curl their hands into fists. Lying down flat, they bend the arms and set the fists on the chest, while placing the feet on the mat to raise the knees. From here, they lift the back and buttocks, hold the breath in, and pound on the abdomen to make the stale *qi* in the belly flow back out through the mouth (*Huanzhen juefa* 1ab).

Yogis likewise wash and rinse and clean their teeth, but in addition they also gargle, rub the base of the tongue and cleanse it with butter, and clean the hole in the skull by massaging the third-eye area. They clean the interior of the chest by inserting a plantain stalk through the mouth into the esophagus and the nasal passages, hoping thereby to remove phlegm, mucus, and bile. They may also swallow a fine cloth about three inches wide, allowing it to reach the stomach, then pull it out again, or they might guide a thread through the nostrils into the mouth to open the sinuses. For intestinal sweepings, they push water in and out of the rectum or insert a stalk of turmeric into the colon (Wood 1971, 126–28). All these are methods quite unique to the Indian tradition that have no documented counterpart in China.

CONCLUSION

Given the enormous differences in historical origins, fundamental worldview, and applied techniques, it is safe to conclude that Yoga and Daoyin are indeed two radically different systems of body cultivation. This is despite the fact that there are certain basic similarities in body postures and energy circulation (Mair 2004, 88; 1990, 140–48); that there was rich cultural contact between Persia, India, and China already in the first millennium BCE; that evidence shows the use of various technical Sanskrit terms in Chinese (Mair 2004, 92); and that Buddhist masters undoubtedly brought physical and breathing practices to China in addition to scriptures and meditations in the first few centuries CE (see Despeux 1989; Eliade 1958).

In spite of all this, examining the deeper levels of the two systems, it becomes clear that Yoga and Daoyin are completely at odds in the way they deal with the body:

- They see the body differently: Yogis strive to control and overcome its characteristics, while Daoyin followers hope to align with it and perfect its functioning.
- They use the body differently: Yogis change its natural patterns and ultimately aim to keep it quiet and stable for the unfolding of mental purity and a vision of the true self, while Daoyin practitioners enhance its natural functioning with the expectation of refining its energetic structure to greater levels of subtlety and thus reaching the perfection of the Dao.

- They heal the body differently: Yogis accept health as a byproduct and necessary condition for more advanced stages and—with the exception of Haṭha practitioners—tend to scorn the pursuit of mere bodily well-being and successful functioning in society, while Daoyin masters—again with some exceptions in later Daoist circles—emphasize health, long life, and the experience of mundane pleasures and see them as a key motivation of the practice, more spiritual states being possible but not essential.

Both systems, when followed at a basic level, can help people find wellness in their bodies, peace in their minds, and balance in their lives. They both fulfill an important role in modern technological and hyperactive societies. However, when it comes to higher spiritual goals, their visions, organizational settings, and practices are vastly divergent.

NOTES

1. The *Ṛgveda* is the oldest and most important of the four Vedas, which go back to about 3000–2000 BCE, and served as the key sacrificial hymnbooks of Indo-Aryan culture, a parallel culture to the ancient Indus Valley civilization. Without spelling out philosophical doctrines, the texts imply notions of self-effacement and purity. See Kinsley 1989; Feuerstein 1998a.

2. A collection of over a hundred philosophical writings based on the hermit tradition that dates from around 600 BCE and are considered among the most sacred scriptures of Hinduism (see Kinsley 1989).

3. These translations are based on the original text. It is published with modern characters and some punctuation in Wenwu 1990; Ikai 2004.

4. The same exercise is still part of the Daoyin repertoire today. It appears under the name "Immortal Imitating Tall Pine Standing Firmly in the Wind" in Ni Hua-ching's regimen (1989, 60). Here the posture proposed is to sit cross-legged.

5. This more spiritual form of Daoyin practice has persisted in the Daoist tradition, leading to the integration of gymnastic exercises into later forms of Daoist meditation and immortality practice, including the complex system of inner alchemy—the creation of an elixir and immortal embryo within the body—which still is the dominant form of Daoist spiritual practice today (see Berk 1986; Despeux 1988). On the other hand, it has also recovered its medical origins in the practice of Qigong, which since the 1950s has adopted Daoist techniques into a health regimen for the masses and spread successfully not only throughout China but also in East Asia and the West (see Kohn forthcoming).

6. See Wood 1971, 153–55; Worthington 1982, 104–06; Yasudian and Haich 1965, 93–95.

7. One exception is figure 44 on the *Daoyin tu*, shown with legs in lunge position and arms extended and named "Warrior Pointing," which is strikingly similar to the Yoga pose known as "Warrior II."

8. The text has a preface dated to the mid-Tang period. It also appears in the *Chifeng sui* 赤鳳髓 (Marrow of the Red Phoenix) of the late Ming. It is translated by Despeux 1988, 65–81 and summarized in Kohn, forthcoming.

BIBLIOGRAPHY

Arya, Usharbudh. 1981. *Mantra and Meditation*. Honesdale, PA: Himalayan Institute.

Berk, William R. 1986. *Chinese Healing Arts: Internal Kung-Fu*. Burbank, Calif.: Unique Publications.

Cope, Stephen. 2000. *Yoga and the Quest for True Self*. New York: Bantam.

Despeux, Catherine. 1988. *La moélle du phénix rouge: Santé et longue vie dans la Chine du seiziéme siècle*. Paris: Editions Trédaniel.

———. 1989. "Gymnastics: The Ancient Tradition." In *Taoist Meditation and Longevity Techniques*, edited by Livia Kohn, 223–61. Ann Arbor: University of Michigan, Center for Chinese Studies Publications.

Eliade, Mircea. 1958. *Yoga: Immortality and Freedom*. New York: Pantheon Books.

———.1969. *Patanjali and Yoga*. New York: Funk & Wagnalls.

Engelhardt, Ute. 2000. "Longevity Techniques and Chinese Medicine." In *Daoism Handbook*, edited by Livia Kohn (Leiden: E. Brill), 74–108.

———. 2001. "*Daoyin tu* und *Yinshu*: Neue Erkenntnisse über die Übungen zur Lebenspflege in der frühen Han-Zeit." *Monumenta Serica* 49: 213–26.

Feuerstein, Georg. 1979. *The Yoga-Sūtra of Patañjali*. New Delhi: Arnold Heinemann.

———. 1980. *The Philosophy of Classical Yoga*. New York: St. Martin's Press.

———. 1998a. *Tantra: The Path of Ecstasy*. Boston: Shambhala.

———. 1998b. *The Yoga Tradition: Its History, Literature, Philosophy and Practice*. Prescott, AZ: Hohm Press.

Ghurye, G. S. 1964. *Indian Sadhus*. Bombay: Popular Prakashan.

Gopi, Krishna. 1985. *Kundalini: The Evolutionary Energy in Man*. Boston: Shambhala.

Harper, Donald. 1998. *Early Chinese Medical Manuscripts: The Mawangdui Medical Manuscripts*. London: Wellcome Asian Medical Monographs.

Hewitt, James. 1977. *The Complete Yoga Book*. New York: Schocken Books.

Ikai Yoshio 豬飼祥夫. 2004. "Kōryō Chōkasan kanken Insho yakuchūkō" 江陵張家山漢簡引書釋註. Draft paper. Used by permission of the author.

Iyengar, B. K. S. 1976. *Light on Yoga*. New York: Schocken Books.

Kinsley, David R. 1989. *Hinduism: A Cultural Perspective*. Englewood Cliffs, NJ: Prentice Hall.

Kohn, Livia. 2001. *Daoism and Chinese Culture*. Cambridge: Three Pines Press.

———. 2004. *Cosmos and Community: The Ethical Dimension of Daoism*. Cambridge, Mass.: Three Pines Press.

———. 2005. *Health and Long Life: The Chinese Way*. In cooperation with Stephen Jackowicz. Cambridge, Mass.: Three Pines Press.

———. 2008. *Chinese Healing Exercises*. Magdalena, NM: Three Pines Press.

——. 2012. *A Source Book in Chinese Longevity*. St. Petersburg, FL: Three Pines Press.
Lincoln, Bruce. 1975. "The Indo-European Myth of Creation." *History of Religions* 15: 121–45.
Loehr, James E., and Jeffrey A. Migdow. 1986. *Breathe In, Breathe Out: Inhale Energy and Exhale Stress by Guiding and Controlling Your Breathing*. Alexandria, VA: Time Life Books.
Mair, Victor. 1990. *Tao Te Ching: The Classic Book of Integrity and the Way*. New York: Bantam.
——. 2004. "The Beginnings of Sino-Indian Cultural Contact." *Journal of Asian History* 38.2: 81–96.
Mishra, Rammurti S. 1987. *Fundamentals of Yoga: A Handbook of Theory, Practice, and Application*. New York: Harmony Books.
Ni, Hua-ching. 1989. *Attune Your Body with Dao-In: Taoist Exercises for a Long and Happy Life*. Malibu, Calif.: Shrine of the Eternal Breath of Tao.
Olivelle, Patrick J. 1990. "Village vs. Wilderness: Ascetic Ideals and the Hindu World." In *Monastic Life in the Christian and Hindu Traditions,* edited by Austin B. Creel and Vasudha Narayanan, 125–60. Lewiston, NY: Edwin Mellen Press.
Robinet, Isabelle. 1984. *La révélation du Shangqing dans l'histoire du taoïsme*. 2 vols. Paris: Publications de l'Ecole Française d'Extrême-Orient.
——. 1993. *Taoist Meditation*. Translated by Norman Girardot and Julian Pas. Albany: State University of New York Press.
Stein, Stephan. 1999. *Zwischen Heil und Heilung: Zur frühen Tradition des Yangsheng in China*. Uelzen: Medizinisch-Literarische Verlagsgesellschaft.
Strickmann, Michel. 1981. *Le taoïsme du Mao chan; chronique d'une révélation*. Paris: Collège du France, Institut des Hautes Etudes Chinoises.
Taimni, I. K. 1975. *The Science of Yoga*. Wheaton, Ill.: Theosophical Publishing House.
Wenwu 文物. 1990. "Zhangjiashan Hanjian Yinshu shiwen" 張家山漢簡引書釋文. *Wenwu* 文物 1990/10: 82–86.
Wood, Ernest. 1971. *Yoga*. Harmondsworth: Penguin.
Worthington, Vivian. 1982. *A History of Yoga*. Boston: Routlege & Kegan Paul.
Yasudian, Selvarajan, and Elizabeth Haich. 1965. *Yoga and Health*. New York: Harper and Row.

11

The Emergence of Classical Medicine in Ancient China and India

Wei Zhang

The term "classical medicine" is used here to designate the two emergent medical systems in the ancient civilizations of China and India roughly between the last few centuries BCE and the early centuries CE. The new medical systems in both traditions distinctively departed from the previous "religious medicine" endorsed by religious beliefs and sanctified by ritual practices. In the Indian subcontinent the understanding of the somatic body, and health and illness, had gone through a paradigm shift from that of "a magico-religious to empirico-rational" as some modern scholars observed (Zysk 1991, 26). The emergence of the new medical system largely owed to the rise of the heterodox and wandering ascetic (*śramaṇa*) movement, as well as to the rise of Buddhism (Zysk 1991, 21–27). In China, the proto-scientific systemization of medical knowledge and the expansion of the medical canon were accompanied by the rise of the individual schools of thinkers, who debated about natural philosophy and cosmological order, and explored the inner ecology of the body during the latter part of the Warring States (403–221 BCE) and early period of Han dynasty (206–220 BCE).

There are further "parallel" moves that seemed to have characterized the emergence of classical Chinese and Indian medicine. First, the understanding and handling of the human body—in both healthy and diseased state, became an independent field of inquiry and practice. Second, the early medical practitioners or shaman-healers or priests were gradually replaced by a new group of so-called "medical specialists," who possessed not only the healing skills, but theories of medicine that were ranked as "equal" to the other branches of learning. In China, those medical specialists were known as "scholars of medicine," and their counterparts in India were called *vaidya* or "men of knowledge." Third, in both China and India, the emergence of classical medicine was marked by compilation of the two respective bodies of medical literature, distinct from the respective corpus of religious and ritual and deviational texts; later on, both of them acquired canonical status in the respective medical traditions.

Here, I shall only provide a brief survey on the contents and styles of those two canonical medical literatures. The present editions of these two medical canons are respectively known as the *Yellow Emperor's Inner Classic* or *Inner Classic* (*Neijing*) in China, and the Caraka's *Compendium* (*Caraka-saṃhitā*) in India. The early layers of the texts in the *Inner Classic* were perhaps being compiled in the second or the first century in China. The earliest composition of the *Compendium* was said to take place in about the third or second century BCE, though, it did not begin to circulate until the Gupta dynasty (320–480 CE), according to Dominik Wujastyk (2003, 4), a contemporary translator of the Āyurveda texts. Both canons were composed in conversational styles. And the conversations primarily took place between the royal patron and the chief physician in ancient China, or the ancient sages and their disciples in ancient India. The *Inner Classic* was attributed to the Yellow Emperor, the legendary sage-king of the first Chinese dynasty of the Xia, who was also invoked to "author" a number of other classical texts. In India, the discussion of medicine was largely casted in the teaching and dialogue of the sage Ātreya to his disciple Agniveśa. There was no mentioning of the name of Caraka in the *Compendium*, however. The name Caraka was only mentioned in later Chinese Buddhist historiography, as the royal physician and one of the three close friends to the famous Yuezhi King of the Kushan Empire, Devaputra Kaniṣka (Wujastyk 2003, 3–4).

The contents of the two medical canons clearly reflected the expansion of medical knowledge and therapeutic techniques. A comparative assessment of the organization and contents of the *Inner Classic* and *Compendium* reveal some interesting differences as well as similarities in terms of the scope and theoretical commitment of those two medical systems. The *Compendium* contains one hundred and twenty segments which are classified into eight sections. The first section is called the "rules" (*sūtra*) that encompasses various topics on the qualities of food substances, dietary regiments, etiology, and therapies or treatment options. It also outlines the scope of medicine and responsibilities of physicians. The second section describes in details the symptomatic expressions of eight major diseases. The third section offers the discussion of general pathology, as well as nutritional information on various qualities of the food substances. Section four discusses in modern medical terminology, the subjects of "anatomy," "embryology," and "heredity." Section five discusses the diagnostic principles and guidelines for deriving the prognosis of certain diseases. From sections six through eight, there are collections of general and specific therapeutic formulas. Medical reasoning or medical "epistemology" is included mainly in sections one and four.

In the modern edition, the *Inner Classic* contains two "books" entitled as the "Basic Questions," and "The Spirit Pivot." Each book in turn consists of eighty one "chapters." The second book is primarily concerned with the theories and application of the needling therapies and pulse diagnosis, but not to the exclusion of the discussion of medical theories. For the medical humanists, the first book, "the Basic Questions," provides the most interesting information on medical worldviews, cosmology, climatology, local ecology, and typology—all of which are regarded as the integral processes of the physiological function and pathological alternation of the human somatic body. In the following, I shall discuss the Chinese and Indian medical conceptions of the human body, the understanding of the states of health and illness, as well as the "disease causations" or medical epistemology, based on the information provided by the *Inner Classic* and the *Compendium*.

MEDICINE AS A CULTURAL CRITIQUE OR PARADOX OF PROGRESS

First, I would like to expound on a critical thesis that seemed to have informed both of the medical system's self-perception of their respective conditions of emergence. I suggest that both Chinese and Indian traditions seemed to adopt a critical attitude in their respective self-understanding of the nature of the emergent medicine. For both, the new medical systems, departing from the previous religious and healing traditions, naturally require a self-justification of their emergence and purposes, hence a different medical philosophy and ethics. Apparently, the social and cultural conditions in ancient China and India were quite different from one another at the time; yet the perception of the new medicine as a testimony to the "fall" of humanity, that is, the deterioration of the social morality and existential conditions seemed to be a "shared" vision in both traditions. Already, in the earlier Vedic India, the healing of the physical ailments and the handling of the physical body in general had presented a tension with the fundamental religious convictions about ritual purity and pollution. One of the main social factors attributing the rise of Indian classical medicine were the emerging community of unorthodox wandering aesthetics, as well as the establishment of Buddhist monastic community, as I mentioned earlier. It is only in the latter contexts that the direct contact with the "polluted" body and its various diseased states became possible. The tension between the practice of medicine and that of religion clearly persisted in the classical periods as well, so much so that it compelled the later Āyurvedic physicians to continue to defend the goals of medicine in secular terms. That is, medicine served only those who wished to retain health, but not those who aspired to achieve virtue (*dharma*). The term *Āyurveda,* literarily means the "science of long life," concerned with prolonging the natural life span and bringing it to the "ripe of the age." Defining medicine exclusively as a secular discipline dedicated to sustaining health and achieving long life, physicians were able to perform very different roles than their predecessors such as ritual specialists and shaman healers. Although, the term *Veda* was retained in medical discourses and some still traced the root of classical medicine to a specific *Veda,* i.e. *Atharva Veda,* for the most part, as some contemporary scholars argued, the classical *Āyurveda* did not build upon the foundations of the Vedic religions. One telling example was that there was no mentioning of the doctrine of three humors in Vedic literature, which, in fact, was the centerpieces of the *Āyurveda* (Wujastyk 2003, xxix).

However, we find in *Compendium* that the attitude toward medicine was not unproblematic; the general perception of the emergence of the new knowledge of the therapeutics reflects a different type of ambivalence. The new medicine was not an anti-thesis to religion or religious practices as such, but rather a "negative" testimony to the "fall" of humanity; the declining of physical strength or weakened constitutions of the body, which was perceived as a correlate with the corruption of personal and social morality as well as the natural environment. The texts in the *Compendium* described that human beings had suffered a fall from the "Golden Age" and descend into the next "Silver Age." There was no *need* for medicine in the Golden Age. The physical constitutions and bodies of the inhabitants were "solid as the condensed essence of mountains," and their looks were "radiant" and minds "exalted." The good health of people correlated with the good moral virtues. People of the Golden Ages were kind, generous, and free from anger, greed, depression, delusion, and so on. The good health and virtues were also blessed by the favorable geo-climatic environment. At that time, the earth and other elements were at their best, and the growth yielded were the most ripening with "unimaginable savor" (Wujastyk 2003, 43). The Silver Age anticipated the rise of medicine and "justified" the need for it. The social customs and personal morals had deteriorated, that is, the "greed led to perfidy, from perfidy came lying . . . lust, anger, hatred, cruelty . . ." and so on. The corruption of personal and social morality led to the declining of the public health. There also disappeared the "goodness in the earth" and qualities of its yields. The weakening of the physical constitutions and the afflictions of the population further worsened by the environmental and ecological deteriorations, subjected the inhabitants of the Silver Age to the "besiegement of fire and wind" and the attack of diseases such as "fever and so forth" (Wujastyk 2003, 44). All of which called for more aggressive measures that the new medicine seemed to be able to offer.

A very similar perception of the degraded world order and human conditions that called for the new medical interventions was presented by the Chinese medical authors. The new medicine—the invasive needling and "poisonous" drug therapies, were "undesirable" but "necessary" response to the deteriorating social customs; excessive drinking, overeating, physical exertions, sexual indulgence, and most importantly the negligence of the natural laws. That is, according to testimony of the medical writers, the physical alignments of the body were no longer treatable by the earlier "soup" therapies administered by the ancient sage-healers. Thus, the expansion of the medical canon, the new therapeutic techniques, and herbal remedies, were not mere accomplishments of human civilization, or an indicator of social "progresses." In the first treaties on the "Natural Truth in Ancient Times," the Yellow Emperor observed that the physical conditions of the people at the time were "decrepit and failing" at the age of fifty (Veith 2002, 97), and the average life span of the population was greatly reduced. The situations contrasted sharply to that of the ancients of the high and middle antiquities. According to the Emperor, the ancient worthies either overcame physical mortality or lived up to one hundred years of age. For instance, the "true men" in the high antiquity, were indeed "immortals"—having understood the natural laws and working order of *yin* and *yang*, they lived as long as the heaven and earth. The descending from the high to middle antiquity, continuing on to the time of the "sages" and "men of virtues," seemed to be on a downward spiral, from a medical point of view. The Yellow Emperor observed that the "sapients" in the middle antiquity still had the options of departing from the world and retiring from "mundane affairs" (Veith 2002, 101), hence lived up to an unlimited age. Yet the "sages" and the "virtuous men" who preferred to be involved with the human affairs and society, only lived up to one hundred years of age. Worse still, men of the present age had neither the options of withdrawing from the worldly affairs and its vanity, nor knowledge of the natural laws, both of which were essential for the preservation of the spirit and body, eventually had their physical constitution weakened and the natural life span shortened.

In sum, there was a self-critical evaluation of the emergence of medicine in both ancient China and India. The new medicine was not wholeheartedly celebrated as a "progress" of the human civilization in either tradition. Rather, it was presented as a cultural critique of the social and environmental deteriorations, personal moral laxity, and the public health crisis.

THE BODY IN CLASSICAL CHINESE AND INDIAN MEDICINE

However, the new medical systems in both China and India did offer much more information on the human somatic body. It was with the rise of classical medicine that the human body was first *systematically* organized in terms of its somatic constituents and ontogenetic processes. Both systems demonstrated familiarity with vital organs, musculoskeletal structures, tissues and bodily fluids, as well as the complex pathways of circulations. The medical organizations of the somatic constituents in both traditions overlapped in some aspects with that of modern anatomy and physiology. However, classic Chinese and Indian medicine placed more emphasis on mapping the complex network of physiological system energetic of the living body, rather than the structural properties and locations of the organs in the postmortem biopsy.

There are some noticeable differences in those two systems regarding the basic understanding and presentation of the body. First, in the *Āyurveda*, the investigation of the body included both the prenatal (hereditary and embryology), as well as the postnatal, to the extent of mental phenomena and what was called "consciousness." In the *Inner Classic*, there was no discussion of the prenatal life. The postnatal life was conceptually divided in a number of seven-year (for female) or eight-year (male) cycles, with the corresponding stages of physiological changes. Second, in terms of organization, the somatic constituents were structured in terms of three distinct but interactive "humors" or *doṣas (tridoṣa-vidyā)*, which were known as *vāta*, *pitta*, and *kapha* in the system of Indian medicine. The humors were not specific organs or anything substantial in nature. According to some modern Āyurvedic practitioners, there was no "direct perception of these *doṣa*s," since those humors "do not exist on the physical planes." However, their presence and influence can be ascertained or inferred through the qualities and modalities of the energetic interaction of three semi-fluids: "bile, phlegm and other bodily secretions" (Svoboda and Lade 2000, 50). The healthy human body is said to have an *appropriate* mixture and *right* amount of total *doṣa*s that sustain the physical "vitality, adaptability and immunity" (Svoboda and Lade 2000, 50). An unhealthy person is then said to "under-produce" or "over-produce" a certain *doṣa*, thus an impropriate mixture of the three *doṣa*s. The three *doṣa*s are also employed as three "categories" or conceptual "models" for correlating various organs, tissues, senses organs, orifices, and specific somatic regions and so on. For instance, *vāta* correlates with the nervous system and the vital organs of heart and lungs, as well as the secondary organs such as bladder and large intestine, and lastly, skins tissues and the bones, and pelvis and ears. *Pitta*, also correlates with the neurological system; but different vital organs, the liver and spleen, as well as endocrine glands and blood; secondarily, gallbladders, small intestines, and skin and eyes. *Kapha,* correlates the vital organs of kidneys and the vital regions of head, neck, and chest; secondarily, the stomach, joints, lymph nodes, and body fat. External to the body, the three *doṣa*s correlate and represent specific qualities and flavors (of food or drug substances) that directly interact with the bodily *doṣa*s through ingestion and subsequent metabolic processes. For instance, *vāta* correlates such qualities as dry, cold, light, clear, and rough; *pitta,* the qualities of fluid, hot, and slightly oily, and *kapha,* the qualities of cold, soft, smooth, and oily. Theoretically, each set of qualities (along with their corresponding flavors) represented by a specific *doṣa,* has the impact on the network energetic of the corresponding somatic system that was also correlated and represented by the same *doṣa.* For instance, a food or medical substance with bitter flavor and one or combined qualities of the dry, cold, light, clear, and rough, could directly affect the dynamic functions of the energetic network of the vital or nervous system, the heart and lungs, as well as the secondary organs of the bladder and large intestine—all of which were correlated and represented by *vāta.* Quantitatively, the over-consuming or under-consuming of a particular set of qualities of food or medicine (in addition to other factors) would potentially contribute to a certain physical alignment. Clearly, the organization of the human body defies the modern anatomical and physiological systematic reductions. More importantly, the body in the Āyurvedic medicine was typically presented as interactive energetic systems within the somatic body. Further, the body is in open communication with the external influences, that is, the food, medicine, and perhaps poisonous substances, ingested or consumed, for instance. The environmental factors, as well as the mental images grasped by the sense organs were also said to have also an impact on the network functions of the three respective *doṣa*s. In the absence of a "substance anatomy," the ancient Indian medical thinkers outlined a network of energetic impact between the three systems of somatic constituents, and their interactions with the specific configurations of the qualities and motions, which either reinforce or undermine the performances of those three *doṣa*s.

Similar to the Āyurvedic authors, the medical writers of the *Inner Classic* also imagined the body as a dynamic and energizing network of system interactions. But more specifically, the body was thought to have "inhabited" a specific biological sphere under a specific configuration of geo-climatic influence, hence, an "embodiment" of the local ecology or a microcosm of the macrocosmic and planetary forces. There were various "triune" models such as the "three burners" (of the upper, middle, and lower), and "three treasures" (of the spirit, essence, and vitality) were used, in addition to the famous "dual" model of *yin* and *yang,* for correlation of various somatic constituents or energetic systems of the body. But the more complex and latest models were known as the "five phase-energetic," a modern appropriation of the classic Chinese term of "five phases" or *wuyun* 五運. The five phase-energetic models represent both macrocosmic and microcosmic energetic configurations. Within the somatic body, the five phases of bio-energetics, named as liver, heart, spleen, lungs, and kidneys, respectively, were not merely directly perceivable postmortem anatomical entities. Rather they were perceived as the five vitally different but interrelated physiological processes, involving the proper functions of certain vital viscera and their complementary and secondary organs, the corresponding tissue, bones, blood, and other bodily fluids (even certain psychic-emotion states), and finally, their five respective transportation routes known as the meridians that the hepatic, cardiovascular, and other somatic system energetic circulate. For instance, the liver phase-energetic network includes primarily the function of the hepatic obit and its complementary organ of the gall bladder; secondarily, that of the tendons and ligaments, the sensory organs of eyes, the emotional state of anger, and the hepatic meridian pathways. In the absence of the speculation of prenatal life and embryology such as that in the Indian medical system, the Chinese medical thinkers focused their investigation on the postnatal life only. The beginning of the somatic body or life was imagined as a kind of emergence of various "onto-genic" processes, evolved and developed from the direct interactions with the information and feedback of various geo-climatic impacts, the seasonal energetic influences, and the growing cycles and their nutritional and pharmacological qualities of their respective yields.

In sum, both Chinese and Indian medical theorists and practitioners held an evolutionary and developmental view of the makeup of the somatic body. The somatic constituents are not understood as substantial entities in mutually isolating anatomical locations, but the integral processes of the somatic network of bio-energetics. The somatic energetics is not a closed system but living organisms that constantly receives feedback from the external ecological and biological environments. Neither the three *doṣa*s nor the five phases of bio-energetics should be regarded as mere *substantial* anatomic entities either, but "names" designating the three or five bio-energetic systems that make up a living body.

VIEWS OF HEALTH AND ILLNESS

The notion of health is not treated as a *formal* concept in either Chinese or Indian classical medicine. Instead, the state of the health is considered in both systems as a state of "dynamic equilibrium," fluctuating with both internal and external biological and ecological environments. In the *Compendium*, Caraka qualifies health of the body as a state of "concordance." The state of concordance contrasts to the unhealthy state of the body which is characterized as "discordance" (Basham 1976, 22). Here, the term concordance does not stand for a "hemostasis," but a state of dynamic balancing among the three humors within the somatic body as well as that of the outside of the body. For the Chinese medical thinkers, the notion of health was also referred to as a state of dynamic balance or balancing (*ping* 平). In the *Inner Classic*, the healthy person was called "man of balance" (*pingren* 平人). As in Indian medicine, the somatic balance or the state of health in Chinese medicine was also treated as a functional capacity of self-sustaining and self-adjusting, in relation to the changing energetic both within and without the body. Theoretically, for both medical systems, since the external geo-climatic influences and biological environment are in constant flux or in a constant state of transformation, the body is thus required to realign itself constantly in relation to or against the changing external influences, to strike a "new" balance or concordance.

For both Chinese and Indian medical theorists, the influx of informational exchange between the somatic body and the larger ecological and biological environments can temporarily offset the healthy state or the immunity of the body, leading to the (re)occurrence of the physical alignments. For instance, in the Āyurvedic system, the consumption of the improper amount or quantity or quality of food substance at an improper time framework, or the indigestion of the food substance and mental images, could offset the balance of the three *doṣa*s. In particular, it would either dry out or damp the "digestive fire" of the body, hence, further hinder the metabolic process. According to the classical Chinese "medical cosmology," outlined in the *Inner Classic*, a specific "unseasonal" influence, in both temporal and quantitative terms, could undermine or overwhelm the specific physiological balance or immunity. For instance, a delayed spring may yield an insufficient amount of sunlight and below normal temperature, which would in turn compromise the defense system of the hepatic system, contributing to the (re)occurrence of various liver diseases. Therefore, from both Chinese and Indian medical views, the state of health and illness are not polar opposites, but mutually yielding processes of transformation within the same continuum of the somatic exchange with its external environment.

DISEASE CAUSATION AND RELIGIOUS WORLDVIEWS

Prior to the arrival of the Āyurveda and classical Chinese medicine, physical ailments and suffering were believed to be "caused" by supernatural forces. In the Vedic period, the diseased state of the body was considered a matter of "divine intervention," that is, the visitation of punishing gods such as the god Varuṇa, who inflicted pain on those who disobeyed his command (Basham 1976, 18–19). Demons were also seen as the cause of diseases in the later collection of Vedic hymns of the *Atharva Veda*. In the first Chinese historical dynasty of the Shang, the "curse of the ancestors" was identified as the primary cause for a wide range of symptoms from the "toothache" to the "stomach pain" and so on. Later on the certainty of knowing of the specific ancestral spirits directly responsible for the afflictions, hence the ways of addressing them, was replaced by the uncertainty of not knowing who or what caused the illness and suffering. The notion "evil spirit" as an unspecified yet pervasive presence was imagined as a universal pathogenic influence causing the sickness. The coping mechanisms included exorcism, ceremonial and ritual purging and purification, and so on. The shift in disease causality and the changing modalities of coping with physical alignments reflected the social, demographic, and conceptual changes prior to the arrival of classical Chinese medicine (Unschuld 2010, 17–37).

With the arrival of the new medicine, a "materialistic" view of the causes of the diseases in both Indian and Chinese systems began to emerge. For Caraka, what "causes" diseases could be that which is either "internal" or "external" to the body. The disharmony between the three bodily humors was considered an internal cause, for instance. The external causes include the injuries by dangerous creatures and poisonous substances or wounds inflicted by instruments and weapons (Wujastyk 2003, 31). The Chinese medical thinkers identified six "pathogens"—the six patterns of abnormal or unseasonal weather behaviors that could assault the various somatic defense systems.

However, I want to point out that in both Chinese and Indian medical systems, the *underlining* cause for physical alignments was *ontological* rather than *epistemological*. Since the states of health and illness are mutually yielding processes of transformation of the same continuum of the somatic body, the unhealthy state or illness cannot be "caused" by anything external to the somatic continuum. The discordance or unbalance of the body is the temporary or permanent failing of the body's organic responses to the external influence of the climatic and environmental and dietary regiments. In the *Compendium*, Caraka identifies the "self" as the cause of physical decay and affliction. In his word, "man afflicts himself" (Caraka 4.5, in Basham 1976, 22). In the language of modern practitioners, a *doṣa* thus means a "defect" (Basham 1976, 22). Similarly, the Chinese medical writers perceived the corporeal body as that which was *predisposed* to physical afflictions. The ontological imperfection of the somatic body was recognized from the onset of the medical discussion in the *Inner Classic*. As long as there is a change, the body is subjected to the unbalanced influences. The Yellow Emperor stated that it was only the "true men" who were not susceptible to any influences of irregularity and changes, thus not immune to diseases and aging.

We may have a better understanding of the inherent imperfection of the *doṣa*s, or predisposed (or genetic) susceptibility to diseases in both Indian and Chinese medicine, if we trace their perceptions to the respective religious/philosophical traditions. According to the thinkers of the school of Sāṅkhya, the physical body, consisting of the three *doṣa*s, was the metamorphoses of the grosser forms of a more "primordial" being, *puruṣa*, hence flawed or "imperfect." In the Sāṅkhya cosmogony, all of the physical and material bodies evolved from the ultimate body of *puruṣa*, known as the ultimate reality. However, there are degraded stages of separation. First, from this absolute and indivisible singularity of *puruṣa* comes what is known as *prakṛti*, or relative reality; it is through the latter, that the absolute reality is actively perceived and universal awareness known as *mahat* arises. This infinite cosmic awareness then gives rise to the limited self-awareness that is called ego (*ahaṃkāra*). It is from the plane of the ego that the three *doṣas* and sense organs evolve and are perceived as individualized bundles of egos, endowed with three functional attributes: equilibrium, activity, and inertia. The Chinese Daoists presented a very similar version of the world-becoming that was also characterized by a degraded process from the singularity to duality and to plurality. The well-known verses in *Daodejing* read, "from the Dao 道 (the ultimate), comes the one" (the singularity or totality of the cosmic energetic *qi* 氣); "from the one, comes the two" (splitting of the heaven and earth or yang *qi* and yin *qi*). And "from the two, comes the three" (the triad of the heaven, earth, and man), and finally, the "three gives birth to the myriad things." There is an implicit paradox which underlies this Daoist cosmogony. That is, the separation from the ultimate source of Dao gives "birth" to the man and things, enabling the world to come into existence; however, the separation from the Dao, step by step, also brings about disorder and diseases. The true men that both Daoist masters and medical writers spoke of were the ones who had either succeeded in "reversing" the process of world-becoming from the plural forms of life back to the singularity of the Dao, or had never departed from the ultimate source. They were the men of Dao or the "embodiment" of Dao. From a medical point of view, the true men are far superior to the later sages and men of virtues, for the latter lost their naturally endowed life span, which was originally infinitely long; as long as the life of the heaven and earth. The descending from the true men to the sage and virtuous men, typified by the delimiting of the natural life span as well the deterioration of the human condition in general, thus anticipated the arrival of the "physical" medicine. The parallel religious world views in the school of Sāṅkhya and Daoism that anticipated the medial world views of both Indian and Chinese medicine are indeed remarkable.

In conclusion, this chapter discusses the emergence of the classical Chinese and Indian medical systems in terms of their respective historical and cultural contexts. The medical conceptions of the human body, the notions of health and illness, and medical reasoning and disease causation are the chosen topics of the discussion. I suggest that a comparative examination of these aspects of the two great ancient medical systems enables a new conceptual framework to emerge for an integrated inquiry of the scope, objective, theoretical interest, and ethical commitment of these two great medical systems. It may also improve the public understanding of the diversity and distinctiveness of classical Chinese and Indian medicine that are often obscured by lumping them together under an overarching category of "alternative and complementary medicine."

BIBLIOGRAPHY

Basham, A. L. 1976. "The Practice of Medicine in Ancient and Medieval India." In *Asian Medical Systems: A Comparative Study*, edited by Charlie Leslie. Berkeley: University of California Press.

Larson, Gerald James. 1998. *Classical Sāṅkhya: An Interpretation of its History and Meaning*. New Delhi: Motilal Banarsidass Publishers.

Porkert, Manfred. 1974. *A Theoretical Foundation of Chinese Medicine*. Cambridge, MA: The MIT Press.

Svoboda, Robert and Arnie Lade. 2000. *Chinese Medicine and Ayurveda*. Delhi: Motilal Banarsidass Publishers.

Unschuld, Paul. 2010. *Chinese Medicine in China: A History of Ideas*. Berkley: University of California Press.

Veith, Ilza, trans. 2002. *The Yellow Emperor's Classic of Internal Medicine*. Berkeley: University of California Press.

Wujastyk, Dominik. 2003. *The Roots of Ayurveda*. New York: Penguin Books.

Zysk, G. Kenneth. 1991. *Asceticism and Healing in Ancient India: Medicine in the Buddhist Monastery*. New York and Oxford: Oxford University Press.

12

Health, Illness, and the Body in Buddhist and Daoist Self-Cultivation

Joshua Capitanio

In this chapter, I seek to explore the role that concepts of health and illness played in the religious conceptions of the body held by medieval Chinese Buddhists and Daoists. I will argue that, though Buddhist and Daoist views of the body are often strongly contrasted (in medieval China as well as modern scholarship), both traditions display similarly ambivalent attitudes that carry certain implications for religious practice. My analysis will focus on the writings of the Daoist priest Sima Chengzhen 司馬承貞 (647–735) and the Buddhist monk Tiantai Zhiyi 天台智顗 (538–597), both of whom devoted significant space in their works on self-cultivation to detailed discussions of illness and healing.

In analyzing these authors' writings, I treat the medical concepts presented therein as religious knowledge. States of health and illness, when discussed in the context of religious practice, are religiously *significant*—that is, they signify religious realities. Thus, rather than treat statements about medicine in religious literature simply in terms of their *descriptive* functions, I will instead consider the *prescriptive*, normative role that medical knowledge serves when deployed in religious discourse. From such a standpoint, discourses on sickness and treatment can be seen as religious "technologies of the self," which "permit individuals to effect by their own means, or with the help of others, a certain number of operations on their own bodies and souls, thoughts, conduct, and way of being, so as to transform themselves in order to attain a certain state of happiness, purity, wisdom, perfection, or immortality" (Foucault 1997, 225). Regardless of their status as objective realities, "health" and "illness" are also highly subjective categories that describe human experiences. As the sociologist Bryan Turner has suggested,

> The human body is subject to processes of birth, decay and death which result from its placement in the natural world, but these processes are also 'meaningful' events located in a world of cultural beliefs, symbols and practices. . . . Concepts like "illness" and "sickness" are socio-cultural categories which describe the condition of persons rather than their flesh, bones and nerves. . . . It follows that it is plausible to argue that I have an illness, but also that I "do," or perform my illness. (Turner 2008, 55–56)

Thus, in this chapter, I will explore some of the ways in which Buddhists and Daoists in medieval China utilized religious discourse in understanding the religious implications of their own bodily conditions and in "performing" their states of health and illness.

BUDDHIST AND DAOIST BODIES

One way in which medieval Chinese intellectuals called attention to the differences between Buddhism and indigenous forms of religious thought and practice was to sharply contrast their respective views of the body. While Daoists emphasized the maintenance and cultivation of the body as important ideals in the quest for various forms of transcendence, some Chinese criticized Buddhists for disregarding and even defacing their bodies, and cast Buddhism as a religion of death, the *yin* to Daoism's *yang*. There was, in fact, some truth to such depictions. The most dominant paradigm for understanding the body in much of medieval Chinese Buddhist literature was indeed a negative one; in contrast, Daoists did largely tend to regard the body as perfectible and seek to extend its longevity indefinitely through the practice of various spiritual exercises. However, underlying these general models were alternate and seemingly contradictory attitudes: despite regarding the body as naturally subject to disease and existing in a state of constant degeneration, Buddhists did try to attain perfect health and longevity; despite regarding the body as capable of refinement and perfection, Daoists did still attempt to cultivate attitudes of detachment from the body by emphasizing its impermanence and susceptibility to disease.

Such contradictory representations of the body may seem incompatible as medical models for understanding health and illness; however, as religious models designed to inspire certain moods and motivations in the minds of their adherents, they functioned to support two distinct yet complementary modes of religious practice, which William LaFleur (1998, 38) has described as follows: "Cultures, subcultures, and religious institutions position themselves somewhere on a spectrum between one pole, where the body is considered a given, and its opposite, where somatic plasticity is regarded as not only allowed but even desirable, an index to religious identification and involvement." LaFleur (1998, 38) notes that in the first model ("where the body is considered a given"), which he terms the "acceptance mode," "the transformation is entirely *mental*, because in this way even severe bodily deformity or damage can be changed into something with *meaning*" (LaFleur 1998, 38. Emphasis in original). Alternately, the second mode of transformation or "malleation" attempts to reshape the body in some way, either through internal transformation, external modification, or some combination of both (LaFleur 1998, 38–39). Both of these modes of religious practice were important in medieval Chinese Buddhism and Daoism, and both were based upon and reinforced by certain ways of understanding the body.

ACCEPTANCE AND TRANSFORMATION IN BUDDHIST BODIES

A negative view of the body, in which its impermanence and undesirability are emphasized, is arguably the most dominant paradigm expressed in Buddhist literature. This negative view is based on a fundamental conceptual metaphor—the body as a collection of parts—which itself is derived from Indian medical paradigms (Salguero 2008, 139). Zhiyi begins the discussion of illness contained within his massive treatise on meditative practice, the *Great Calming and Contemplation* (*Mohe zhiguan* 摩訶止觀, T 1911), by describing this normative representation of the body:

> To have a body is illness itself. The four snakes have different temperaments; water and fire oppose each other, [like] the owl and the owlet perching together, or the python and the mouse inhabiting the same hole. This poisoned vessel is a heavy burden, a marsh [containing] the various sufferings. The four neighboring states repeatedly invade and plunder each other. When their strength is equal, there is temporary peace, but when a weakness can be exploited, one will be swallowed up. The vicissitudes of the four gross elements can be understood from these metaphors. (*Mohe zhiguan*, T 1911, 46: 106a19–23)

Such statements are not meant to be merely descriptive; rather, as their inclusion in a manual devoted to explaining the practice of Buddhist meditation suggests, they *prescribe* a certain paradigm for accepting one's bodily condition that the practitioner is expected to internalize, through repeated contemplation, as an integral part of their own spiritual transformation. Many Buddhist texts present the body as an obstacle to realization, the locus of both the physical, sensual pleasures that prevent people from entering the religious lifestyle of renunciation and of the subtle attachments to selfhood that obscure true understanding. Thus, an attitude of aversion toward the body was actively cultivated through meditative practice and monastic discipline.

The value of this mode of bodily acceptance, the contemplation of illness as a fundamental condition of the human body, is repeatedly emphasized in Zhiyi's writings. In fact, in one passage within the *Great Calming and Contemplation*, he suggests that this contemplation can lead one through all of the various levels of Buddhist practice as categorized within Zhiyi's Tiantai system, from the lowest level of the *śrāvaka* all the way up to the state that Zhiyi refers to as the "mode of discernment of the inconceivable realm," which represents the apex of Buddhist practice in the Tiantai classification:

> As for [the mode of discernment of] the inconceivable realm, in a single thought one sees illness and mind to be unreal and non-existent. This is none other than the dharma-realm of the nature of reality. . . . Illness is also like this—inexpressible, beyond characteristics, quiescent, clear and pure. For this reason it is called "inconceivable." When one has understood this absolute reality of illness, how could there be happiness or worry? When one engages in this contemplation, [the illness] will be revealed and will vanish. (*Mohe zhiguan*, T 1911, 46: 110 a24–c27)

In this passage, we see where the "acceptance" model of religious practice ends and the "transformation" model begins. Acceptance and contemplation of one's bodily condition can bring about transcendence; more importantly, transcendence properly pursued brings about transformation—freedom from illness. In fact, for all of Zhiyi's rhetorical emphasis on the importance of accepting one's diseased body, the main message behind his various writings on sickness and healing seems to point to the importance of bodily health and the positive role that correct Buddhist practice can play in maintaining health. As he writes in another meditation manual, the *Explanation of the Progressive Methods of the Pāramitā of Meditation* (*Shi chan boluomi cidi famen* 釋禪波羅蜜次第法門, T 1960):

> If one is adept at applying one's mind in the practice of seated meditation, then the four hundred and four illnesses will diminish of their own accord; however, if there is a deficiency in the application of the mind, then the four hundred and four illnesses will be aroused. Therefore, if the practitioner wishes to cultivate himself for the sake of saving others, he should understand well the origins of illness, and know well the inner mental methods of treating illness that can be applied while seated [in meditation]. If he does not know the method of treating illness, then, when one morning he finds himself sick, not only will this be an obstacle to his cultivation of the Way, it will also threaten his greater fate. (*Shi chan boluomi cidi famen*, T 1916, 46: 505b12–19)

Despite the central role that the negative view of the body plays in many Buddhist teachings, longevity and freedom from disease are ideals that are mentioned frequently in Buddhist scriptures and in Chinese Buddhist discourse. As Zhiyi's statements imply, the body is important as a vehicle for Buddhist practice, and correct practice can extend longevity and prevent or treat the arising of disease.

Ultimately, Zhiyi's analysis of health and sickness is a discussion of Buddhist practice. As in the above quotation, good health is equated with the correct practice of meditation, while poor health is seen as a sign of incorrect practice. Of the six categories of illness that Zhiyi analyzes in his *Great Calming and Contemplation*—caused by imbalances among the four gross elements, immoderation in food and drink, improper seated meditation, ghosts and spirits taking advantage, the deeds of *māra*s, and karmic retribution—all but the first two are to be treated by means of various mainstream Buddhist practices such as contemplation, visualization, repentance, incantation, and devotion. More importantly, the bulk of his chapter on illness in the *Great Calming and Contemplation* deals with various methods of calming and contemplative meditation that are not only described as curative methods but also as being able to eliminate illness completely. Thus, he makes such statements as, "by simply practicing *samādhi* single-mindedly, all the various diseases will be eliminated" (*Mohe zhiguan*, T 1911, 46: 110a14–15), or that "the bodhisattva who is ill should use the contemplation of emptiness to regulate and control his mind; when the mind is regulated and controlled, all real sicknesses will be healed" (*Mohe zhiguan*, T 1911, 46: 110c29–111a1). The concept of illness is used as a basis for advocating the practices of both bodily acceptance and transformation, which are revealed in Zhiyi's writings to be complementary: proper acceptance (i.e., contemplation and analysis) of one's sick body becomes the means through which the body can be transformed and made free from disease.

HEALTH AND SICKNESS IN DAOIST SELF-CULTIVATION

When comparing Buddhist medical views of the body with those found in Daoist texts, there appears to be a sharp contrast between the two. However, I argue that both traditions display a similar sort of ambivalence toward the body, though they differ in their emphases. Whereas in Buddhist representations of the body, its impermanence and susceptibility to illness are emphasized in framing practitioners' basic attitudes, Daoists tend to begin by accentuating the body's perfectibility and numinous character; a negative view of the body is introduced in Daoist texts as the basis for more advanced forms of contemplation. For my analysis of

Daoist self-cultivation practices, I will be looking primarily at two works by Sima Chengzhen, the *Treatise on the Essential Meaning of Ingesting Pneumas* (*Fuqi jingyi lun* 服氣精義論, DZ 830)[1] and the *Treatise on Sitting and Forgetting* (*Zuowang lun* 坐忘論, DZ 1036).[2] The first text is primarily concerned with techniques of bodily cultivation—specifically, the ingestion of pneumas (*qi* 氣)—and presents a generally positive view of the body; the second text is concerned with delineating a path for the attainment of transcendence through an ultimate realization of the Dao, in which a certain type of negative attitude toward the body is advocated.

In the introduction to Sima's *Treatise on the Essential Meaning of Ingesting Pneumas*, he discusses the importance of pneuma in Daoist self-cultivation. Following traditional Chinese cosmological and medical theory, he presents the body as composed of the same pneumatic substance as heaven and earth; thus, he argues, the preservation, augmentation, and refinement of bodily pneuma is the most effective means for cultivating transcendence:

> As for the methods of ascending to transcendence, there are many paths that can be studied; however, the essential meanings of all these converge on a single principle. Ingesting the liquid of "flying elixirs," one ascends and soars through the efficacy of the drug; performing purificatory fasts and practicing visualization, winged transformation is achieved as a result. However, medicinal compounds require a great deal of effort and are difficult to pursue; achieving results through practice and study takes many years, during which one can easily go astray. If one seeks that which, when acted upon, brings swift results, and when concentrated upon, is capable of bringing about achievement, harmonizing with the Dao in its empty nothingness, uniting one's Virtue with the divine numen, there is nothing more wondrous than pneuma! . . . Thus, knowing how to inhale and guide the morning mist, to swallow and gargle with wind and frost, to nourish the sources of essence within the five viscera, and to lead their protective [influences] throughout the hundred joints, one will be able to bring peace to the body by dispelling disease, and also to extend harmony and enjoy longevity. (*Fuqi jingyi lun*, DZ 830, 1: 1a–2a)

Here, Sima argues that the cultivation of pneuma is a more effective means of pursuing transcendence than other forms of Daoist practice such as ingesting "flying elixirs"—longevity drugs—or performing fasting rituals and visualization meditations. Moreover, through pneumatic practices one can rid the body of disease. Thus, Sima presents a positive view of the body that informs a transformative mode of religious practice wherein perfect health and transcendence are coterminous goals.

A more detailed discussion of the importance of pneuma in repelling disease is given in a later chapter of this text on "Avoidances and Taboos," in which Sima Chengzhen argues that, as longevity, health, and transcendence can be accomplished through the retention and refinement of these pneumas, one must carefully guard against any outside influence that could cause their depletion:

> With regard to pneuma, the principle is: when taken in, it is difficult to stabilize; when emitted, it is easily exhausted. Being difficult to stabilize, one must preserve it and maintain its integrity; being easily exhausted, one must treasure it and not allow it to leak away. . . . In interacting with others, talking and laughing, one should limit oneself; one's movement and speech should be regulated and measured. Only by esteeming caution in all activities can one avoid loss [of vitality].
>
> With regard to that which constitutes the nature of human beings, their bodies are joined with Heaven and Earth and their pneumas are a mixture of *yin* and *yang*. The flourishing and preservation of their skin, bones, marrow, and viscera, the coming and going of their inhalations and exhalations, and the changes of heat and cold—there are none of these that are not coextensive with the Two Poles [of *yin* and *yang*] and responsive to the Five Phases. Thus, one should know that when Heaven and Earth are in fluctuation, *yin* and *yang* become disordered; when the viscera are not regulated, symptoms of illness appear within their circulatory channels. As for those that strike from the outside, the various illnesses all arise from wind; regarding those that are brought about internally, the various illnesses are all produced from pneuma. Thus, it is said: "When one is tranquil and unmoved, empty and quiescent, perfected pneuma will abide therein; when one's essence and spirit are guarded within, from where could sickness arise?" Trust well these words! (*Xiuzhen jingyi zalun*, DZ 277, 1: 13a–b)

Describing the origins of illness, Sima presents two etiological paradigms here. In the first, disease arises due to the influence of external forces that disrupt the body's natural harmony. In classical Chinese medicine, as described in texts such as the *Inner Canon of the Yellow Thearch* (*Huangdi neijing* 黃帝內經), "wind" (*feng* 風) was regarded as the pathogenic invader *par excellence*:

> For doctors in China, wind represented . . . disease itself, an alien invader. It swept straight *into* the body's interior and harmed by intrusion. Attacking the skin, it might produce chills, headache, a slight fever; as it burrowed deeper, it wrought more intractable, more violent suffering. (Kuriyama 1999, 251)

Winds were believed to literally enter the body through minute openings such as pores and hair follicles. However, their influence could be mitigated by the cultivation of pneuma and the maintenance of a proper lifestyle—"Persons conducting their life 'in clarity and purity' will be unaffected; their 'flesh and skin structures are firmly closed up and resist' the impact of wind" (Unschuld 2003, 186).

For the second paradigm, Sima states that illnesses also arise internally, from imbalanced pneumas. In classical Chinese medical and religious literature, such imbalances are generally described as occurring when an individual becomes mentally or emotionally disturbed—again, most often as a result of external factors. As one Han-dynasty text, the *Huainanzi* 淮南子, states,

> The sage relies on his mind: the multitude relies on their desires. The superior person manifests aligned vital energy [pneuma]; the inferior person manifests aberrant vital energy. That which inwardly goes along with one's nature and outwardly accords with what is right, and which in its movements complies with natural guidelines and is not bound up in external things, this is the aligned vital energy. That which is stimulated by fragrances and tastes, excited by sound and color, evoked by pleasure and anger, and which if you are not careful leads to trouble, this is the aberrant vital energy. Aberrant and aligned vital energy injure one another; desire and nature interfere with one another. Both cannot be established together. When one flourishes, the other falls away. Therefore the sage relinquishes desire and preserves his nature. (Roth 1991, 637)

Thus, though diseases may be produced within the body by aberrant pneuma, such aberration is not a natural condition; rather, it is generally brought about by improper engagement with the external world.

Both etiological models suggest the importance of maintaining a certain type of lifestyle that is conducive to the nourishment and cultivation of pneuma, so as to ward off disease. In Sima's writings, that lifestyle is a religious lifestyle—that is, one in which the individual accords with the Dao—and the goal of freedom from illness thus becomes a religious goal:

> If one can preserve [pneuma] and cause it to reside [within the body], then one's divine numen will become resplendent. If one can restrict one's expenditure [of pneuma], then its potential will be fully realized. Moreover, if I use my mind to direct my pneumas, order my body, and combat my illnesses, how could they not be healed? If one practices the ingestion [of pneumas] and abides in tranquility, then [these pneumas] are easily preserved, and can be used to suppress and treat all of the various illnesses and irritations. (*Xiuzhen jingyi zalun*, DZ 277, 1: 18a–b)

Thus, Sima is here presenting an essentially positive view of the body, albeit one in which the fragility of its natural state of harmony is given particular emphasis in order to underscore the importance of certain modes of behavior as part of a program of religious self-cultivation.

Yet, while the techniques presented in the *Treatise on the Essential Meaning of Ingesting Pneumas* suggest a positive understanding of the body, Sima's *Treatise on Sitting and Forgetting* (*Zuowang lun*, DZ 1036) expresses a more negative view, in which illness is regarded as a fundamental condition of the body:

> If there is suffering or disease, one should first understand through observation that it originates in the fact that one has a personal body. Without a body the vexations would have no place to dwell. As the *Daode jing* states: "If I had no personal body, what vexations would I have?" . . . Thus when one "makes one's body like dried wood and one's mind like dead ashes" all the various diseases will be duly eradicated. (Kohn 1987, 101–102, see also 53–55)

Here, Sima presents a different perspective wherein the body is the locus of disease, based on an interpretation of the thirteenth chapter in the received version of the *Daodejing*. In order to understand the significance of this negative representation of the body, we must place it within the larger soteriological system that Sima advocates. In a text appended to Sima's *Treatise*,[3] a seven-fold process for the refinement of the body is outlined:

1. All conduct and activity in line with the occasion,
   Appearance and complexion in harmony with inner joy.
2. Diseases and nervousness gradually diminish,
   Body and mind become light and clear. . . .
3. Forestalling the tendency of untimely death
   One returns to the prime and recovers life. . . .
4. Extending life to several thousand years:
   Become an immortal. . . .
5. Refining the body to pure breath:
   Become a realized one. . . .
6. Refining the breath to pure spirit:
   Become a spirit man. . . .
7. Refining the spirit to unify with the Dao:
   Be the perfect man! (Kohn 1987, 140–141)

While adepts on the lower stages of self-cultivation are concerned with attaining longevity and refining the physical substance of the body according to transformative models of practice, ultimate transcendence is achieved by unifying the body with the Way and merging into nothingness. In doing so, one is actually casting off the body that is susceptible to illness and gaining eternal life in a body that is constituted entirely of the pure pneumas of the Way. As Sima describes this ideal himself:

> Once the mind is emptied and the spirit like a valley, the Dao alone will come to assemble. Once the Dao has become strong, it imperceptibly works changes in body and spirit. The body pervaded by the Dao and unified with the spirit is what constitutes a spirit man. His spirit and inner nature are empty and fused into one. His bodily structure no longer changes or decays. Once his body is united with the Dao, there is no more life or death. (Kohn 1987, 108)

The key to attaining this state is releasing one's attachment to the body, and that release is attained through the cultivation of an attitude of dissatisfaction. In the *Treatise on Sitting and Forgetting*, Sima describes how to cultivate this attitude by contemplating one's bodily illness:

> Somebody who is horrified by death, for example, should therefore think of his body as the lodge of the spirit. Thus as the body becomes old and sick, as breath and strength decline day by day, it will just be like a house with rotting walls. Once it becomes uninhabitable, it is best to abandon it soon and look for another place to stay. The death of the personal body and the departure of the spirit are a mere change of residence. However, when one hankers after life and loathes death, resisting the natural transformations, one's spirit consciousness will be confused and led into error. (Kohn 1987, 102–103)

With such an attitude, the adept is able to "smash up limbs and body, drive out intellect and perception and experience detachment and oblivion" (Kohn 1987, 107), which creates the conditions through which one is opened up to the pervasive influence of the Way.

We can observe, then, a roughly twofold division of practice and attainment in Sima's presentation of self-cultivation. In the beginning, the adept engages in transformative practices connected with the positive view of the body as perfectible; these can result in the significant extension of one's lifespan. However, at this stage the practitioner must abandon their attachment to the body in order to be capable of refining it into a state of purity by merging with the Dao; it is in the service of this ideal that Sima advocates the "acceptance" model wherein the body is regarded as flawed and undesirable.

CONCLUSION

The above examples from the writings of Zhiyi and Sima Chengzhen are drawn from manuals of meditative practice. In this context, medical ideas are introduced as the basis for contemplative practices designed to induce certain moods and motivations with regard to the body, which carry soteriological significance. In the case of Buddhism, the negative view of the body as susceptible to disease frames the entire Buddhist attitude toward the body, and according to Zhiyi's presentation all levels of Buddhist soteriology can be encapsulated in the reflection on bodily illness. Yet, practitioners are also encouraged to pursue the ideal of bodily transformation and freedom from disease, which is connected with the attainment of higher states of understanding through various religious practices, which also serve as therapeutic techniques. In the case of Daoism, Sima Chengzhen presents a fundamentally positive view of the body in which he advocates certain techniques of bodily transformation based on the refinement of pneuma; these are also therapeutic techniques in that, in the process of approaching transcendence through their practice, they combat and free the practitioner from states of illness. Yet within this model, a negative understanding of the body is also expressed as a foundation for practices of bodily acceptance that are necessary for enabling the practitioner to overcome attachment to their transitory body so that they can merge with the eternal body of the Dao, the final step in the process of attaining transcendence. In both of these paradigms of practice, Buddhist and Daoist, the state of illness is transformed into the *act* of being sick, which is framed as a kind of religious performance, and these attitudes and their related practices serve as technologies of the self by means of which practitioners reshape their perceptions of their own bodies in a manner that is conducive to certain forms of religious behavior.

NOTES

1. In the Zhengtong edition of the Daoist canon, this text has been separated into two separate works, the *Fuqi jingyi lun* and the *Xiuzhen jingyi zalun* 修真精義雜論, DZ 277; see Schipper and Verellen 2004, 368, 373–374.

2. Citations from the *Zhengtong Daozang* 正統道藏 (Beijing: Wenwu chubanshe, 1988) will employ the numbering system used in Schipper and Verellen 2004, abbreviated as DZ.

3. This appendix is a modified version of the *Annotated Scripture of the Cavern-Mystery Canon of the Numinous Treasure on Stabilization and Contemplation* (*Dongxuan lingbao dingguan jing zhu* 洞玄靈寶定觀經注, DZ 400); see Schipper and Verellen 2004, 307.

BIBLIOGRAPHY

Foucault, Michel. 1997. "Technologies of the Self." In *Ethics, Subjectivity, and Truth: The Essential Works of Michel Foucault 1954–1984, Volume One*, edited by Paul Rabinow (New York: The New Press), 223–252.

Kohn, Livia. 1987. *Seven Steps to the Tao: Sima Chengzhen's* Zuowanglun. Nettetal: Steyler Verlag.

Kuriyama Shigehisa. 1999. *The Expressiveness of the Body and the Divergence of Greek and Chinese Medicine.* New York: Zone Books.

LaFleur, William R. 1998. "Body." In *Critical Terms for Religious Studies,* edited by Mark C. Taylor (Chicago: University of Chicago Press), 36–54.

Roth, Harold. 1991. "Psychology and Self-Cultivation in Early Taoistic Thought." *Harvard Journal of Asiatic Studies* 51.2: 599–650.

Salguero, C. Pierce. 2008. "Buddhist Medicine in Medieval China: Disease, Healing, and the Body in Crosscultural Translation (Second to Eighth Centuries CE)."PhD diss., Johns Hopkins University.

Schipper, Kristofer and Franciscus Verellen, eds. 2004. *The Taoist Canon: A Historical Companion to the* Daozang. Chicago: University of Chicago Press.

Turner, Bryan. 2008. *The Body and Society: Explorations in Social Theory, Third Edition.* Los Angeles: SAGE Publications.

Unschuld, Paul. 2003. *Huang Di Nei Jing Su Wen: Nature, Knowledge, Imagery in an Ancient Chinese Medical Text.* Berkeley: University of California Press.

IV

LANGUAGE AND CULTURE

13

Indic Influence on Chinese Language

Guang Xing

The Buddhist impact on Chinese language is enormous. This is mainly due to the translation and introduction of Buddhist scriptures from Sanskrit and other Indic languages. The translation of Buddhist scriptures lasted for more than a thousand years in China as it started in the second century CE and ended by the end of the Song dynasty in the twelfth century. As the Indian ways of thinking are different from the Chinese, so their ways of expression are also different from the Chinese. Therefore, the translators of Buddhist scriptures had to invent and introduce many new words in order to express the highly abstract ideas and concepts in Buddhism apart from finding similar words and concepts in Chinese language. Thus these new words and concepts gradually have been integrated into the Chinese language and some of them even become part of their daily conversation. The translation of Buddhist scriptures in Sanskrit and other Indic languages greatly influenced the semantic and syntax of medieval Chinese as well as enriched the literary genres and rhetoric techniques. The Sanskrit phonetics brought along with Buddhist translation raised the awareness of Chinese people about phonetics in their own language. This triggered an unprecedented interest in linguistic studies, in particular the description and analysis of the phonetic values of Chinese characters. The result is the compilation of numerous rhyme dictionaries which are of great value for the reconstructions of the different stages of the phonetic systems of Middle Chinese.

ENLARGEMENT OF CHINESE LEXICON

According to modern scholar's studies, it is estimated that approximately thirty-five thousand new words entered the Chinese language through the agency of Buddhism (Mair 2004, 154).[1] The distinguished Chinese linguist Wang Li said that the Buddhist terminology contributed to Chinese vocabulary tremendously and some of these terms have already embodied in the blood of Chinese language that people do not even know that they are originally from Buddhist literature (Wang 1990, 678–686). For instance, *shi-jie* 世界 (*loka*) means the world, but ancient Chinese people used *tian-xia* 天下 to mean the world. The Buddhist influence on and contribution to the Chinese lexicon can be summarized, according to Sun Changwu's study, into the following aspects.

The first, many existing Chinese words are used in the Buddhist translation of scriptures, but their connotations are new. Such as the words used to express doctrinal teachings: *kong* 空 (*śūnya*, empty) is used as empty of self nature, but in Chinese it can mean nothing, similar to *wu* 無, which means nothingness; *you* 有 (*asti*, existence) is the opposite of *kong* 空 and it means existence in the Buddhist sense, but in ancient Chinese philosophy it means being. In fact, *you* 有 which means being and *wu* 無 which means non-being are important philosophical terms in ancient Chinese philosophy. *Fa* 法 (*dharma*) is used to denote the Buddhist teaching in general, specific thing in particular, but it can mean regulation, law, et cetera, in Chinese; *xing* 性 (*svabhāva*, nature) is used for the nature of things, but in Chinese it can mean character, gender, sex, et cetera. *Zhiran* 自然 (self-existing) and *wuwei* 無爲 (*asaṃskṛta*, uncompounded) are two words borrowed from Chinese philosophy to express Buddhist meanings as they are similar to Buddhist usage.

The second is the creation of new words by transliteration. There are a large number of such words introduced into the Chinese language with the Buddhist translations. It can be broadly classified into the following two categories and the first and the largest category is proper name such as *fo* 佛 (Buddha, full transliteration is *fotuo* 佛陀), *pusa* 菩薩 (bodhisattva, *putisaduo* 菩提薩埵), *luohan* 羅漢 (*arhat*, *aluohan* 阿羅漢, worthy one), *biqiu* 比丘 (*bhikṣu*, monk), *biqiuni* 比丘尼 (*bhikṣuṇī*, nun), *ta* 塔 (*stūpa*, *tapo* 塔婆).

The second category of transliteration is more complex and Xuanzang gave five reasons for this category (1) for reason of secrecy such as *dhāraṇī*, (2) for reason of numerous meanings such as *boqiefan* 薄伽梵 (*bhagavat*, meaning the *blessed one* or *world-honoured one*), (3) for reason of no such terms in Chinese such as *chan* 禪 (*dhyāna*, *channa* 禪那, meditation), *ye* 業 (*karma*, action), *jie* 劫 (*kalpa*), *niepan* 涅槃 (*nirvāṇa*), *sheli* 舍利 (*śarīra*, relics), *cha-na* 刹那 (*kṣaṇa*, instant), *yanfuti* 閻浮提 (*Jambudvīpa*, the great continent south of Mt. Sumeru) et cetera, (4) for complying with tradition such as *anouduoluo sanmiao sanputi* 阿耨多羅三藐三菩提 (*Anuttarā-samyak-saṃbodhi*, highest supreme enlightenment), *boluomi* 波羅蜜 (*pāramitā*, perfection), and (5) for the rising of goodness such as *bore* 般若 (*prajñā*, wisdom). The largest category is the third, new terms and concepts which are not found in Chinese.

The third is the creation of new words by translating its meaning to express the newly introduced Buddhist concepts. Such words are as *rulai* 如來 (*Tathāgata*, thus come one), *guiyi* 皈依 (*śaraṇa*, to take refuge in), *jingtu* 淨土 (*Sukhāvatī*, Pure Land), *jietuo* 解脫 (*mokṣa*, liberation), *lunhui* 輪回 (*saṃsāra*, round of birth and death), *youqing* 有情 (*sattva*, sentient being), *gongde* 功德 (*puṇya*, merit), *fangbian* 方便 (*upāya*, skilful means), *wuchang* 無常 (*anitya*, impermanence), et cetera.

The best example of this category is the Sanskrit word *tathatā* which means suchness, or the true nature of phenomena. There is no such concept in Chinese philosophy and the translators faced huge troubles in finding a suitable word to express the Indian concept. At first Lokakṣema used *benwu* 本無 to translate it, but it was misleading as *benwu* means that originally there is nothing in Daoist philosophy. It was Kumārajīva who created the new word *zhenru* 真如 to translate this highly philosophical concept.

The fourth is the creation of new words by a combination of transliteration and translation of its meaning or a combination of transliteration of a Sanskrit word and a Chinese word, such as *foqu* 佛曲 (Buddhist song, *fo* 佛 is a transliteration while *qu*曲 is Chinese word), *foxiang* 佛像 (Buddha image) is same; *chanshi* 禪師 (meditation master, *chan* 禪 is a transliteration and *shi* 師 is a Chinese word), *chanfang* 禪房 (meditation hall) is same; *niepanzong* 涅槃宗 (Nirvāṇa School, *niepan* 涅槃 is a transliteration and *zong* 宗 is a Chinese word).

All these words denoting things and concepts are not found in Chinese so the translators had to create new words to express them, but the meanings of some Chinese characters were retained while others were changed completely. However there is a close relationship between the meanings of newly created words and the original meaning of each Chinese character. This means that in the translation of Buddhist scriptures, the original meanings of Chinese characters are borrowed to create new words usually by combination of two or more Chinese characters, but the meanings of the newly created words are completely different from the original meanings of the characters.

The fifth is the new expressions added to the Chinese language through the influence of Buddhism but these are not direct translations from Sanskrit such as *chujia* 出家 (*parivraj*) leaving the family to become a monk; *chushi* 出世, to transcend the world; *tidu* 剃度, ordained by shaving his or her head; *huayuan* 化緣 to beg for food or something else; *kuhai*

苦海, a bitter sea, meaning life is as dangerous as the rough sea; *fang-zhang*方丈, literally means one square *zhang* (= 3.3 meters), but it designates abbot of a monastery.

The sixth is the increase of Buddhist related idioms and phrases. As Buddhism was gradually accepted by Chinese people, Buddhist ideas, thought, and concepts gradually integrated into Chinese language and as a result new idioms and phrases were formulated.

For instance, (1) there are idioms from Buddhist stories such as *tian nü san hua* 天女散花 which means to make a mess of everything, *tian hua luan zhui* 天花亂墜 means to speak things untenable, *shui zhong zhuo yue* 水中捉月 or *shui zhong lao yue* 水中撈月means literally to try to fish the moon out of water, but it obviously means to make futile efforts, et cetera.

(2) There are idioms from Buddhist doctrinal teachings such as *bu er fa men* 不二法門 which means the only way, *yi chen bu ran* 一塵不染 means immaculate, spotless, *si da jie kong* 四大皆空 means literally the four elements of solidity, fluidity, temperature, and mobility are impermanent. This is because according to Buddhist teaching, the human physical body is made of the four great elements, so the human physical body is also empty of self nature and impermanent, just an instrument.

(3) There are idioms from Buddhist similes such as *meng zhong shuo meng* 夢中說夢 which means literally talking about dreams in a dream, actually meaning talking nonsense; *tan hua yi xian* 曇花一現 means to last for a very brief period of time just as the epiphyllum blooming at night, or short lived; *shui yue jing hua* 水月鏡花 means illusions like the moon in the water and flower in a mirror; *xin yuan yi ma* 心猿意馬 originally means that the mind is like a monkey or a horse that is very difficult to bring under control, and is always prone to outside attractions, and now it means that the mind is unsettled and restless.

The seventh is Buddhist proverbs and Buddhist related common sayings. (a) *jiu ren yi ming, sheng zao qi ji fu tu* 救人一命，勝造七級浮屠 means that to save a person is better than building a seven storey stūpa. It means that saving a life is better than other meritorious deeds. (b) *fang xia tu dao, li di cheng fo* 放下屠刀，立地成佛, a butcher becomes a Buddha at once if he gives up his knife. It means that an evil person can become a good person if he realizes his bad deeds. (c) *wu shi bu deng san bao dian* 無事不登三寶殿, one will not come to the shrine room without having to do something. It means that one will not come to you without a purpose. (d) *lin shi bao fo jiao* 臨時抱佛腳, it means that one does a thing without preparation.

INCREASE OF DISYLLABIC AND POLYSYLLABIC WORDS

According to Chinese linguists, there were mostly monosyllabic words and each character is a word to express something in written Chinese in ancient China. But with the translation of Buddhist scriptures there was an increase of many disyllabic and polysyllabic words which played an important role in the development of Chinese language and vocabulary from monosyllabic to polyphony. During the time of the six dynasties from the first century CE to the end of the sixth century CE, a large number of disyllabic and polysyllabic words appeared and were used, and these words were mainly created by Buddhists.

Liang Xiaohong who has made a study of the Buddhist vocabulary says that there was a huge increase of disyllabic words from the Han dynasty to Southern and Northern dynasties and this was mainly brought by Buddhist translations. She gives the following as an example: there are only 2,300 disyllabic words among the 210,000 words of Wang Chong's *Lunheng* written in the Eastern Han dynasty (25–220). But there are 1,541 disyllabic words among 61,000 words of Liu Yiqing's (403–443) *Shisui Xingyu* of the Southern dynasty (Liang Xiaohong 1994, 175). She also gives the following example to show that there are more disyllabic words in Buddhist scriptures than in non-Buddhist texts. One-thousand-five-hundred disyllabic words are found in chapter 3 "Simile and Parable" of Kumārajīva's translation of the *Lotus Sūtra,* which contains 7,750 words. There are 250 more disyllabic words among 1,400 more words of the chapter on "Maitreya's Miracles" of the *Bodhisattva Buddhānusmṛti Samādhi Sūtra* translated by Guṇaśāra in the Southern dynasty. However, there are only 60 more disyllabic words among also 1,400 more words of the chapter on Politics of Liu Yiqing's *Shisui Xingyu.*

Apart from these, Buddhist translators also introduced polysyllabic words such as *pu ti xin* 菩提心 the mind of enlightenment, *gong de shui* 功德水 meritorious water, *zheng si wei* 正思維 right thought, *po luo mi duo* 波羅蜜多 *pāramitā* means perfection, *fei xiang fei fei xiang* 非想非非想 neither thought nor non-thought.

In ancient Chinese language there were few polysyllabic words. So the introduction of polysyllabic words made a huge change in the Chinese language. All this shows that the Buddhist translators created not only a variety of words for the Chinese language but also the ways and methods to create new words by careful synthesis and analysis of the characteristics of Buddhist vocabulary. This makes the Chinese language a powerful tool to express complex abstract ideas and thoughts as well as the finest details of things.

THE INVENTION OF *QIEYUN* AND THE SUMMARY OF THE FOUR TONES

Buddhist scriptures were translated from texts written either in Sanskrit or other Indic languages which are all phonogram languages. However the Chinese is not a phonogram but a logogram language. The phonogram refers to the written symbols which carry the phonetic information, whereas the logograms are those meaning-laden written symbols.

Chinese Buddhist translators learned and some even mastered these phonogram languages in order to help in translation. This in turn promoted the awareness and understanding of phonetic sounds in the Chinese language which is an important step in the development of the Chinese language. The Song scholar Zheng Jiao (1104–1162) said, "The Indians excel in (phonetic) sound so they acquire their knowledge mainly from hearing . . . while the Chinese excel in characters so they acquire their knowledge from seeing (reading)" (Zheng 1987, 352).

Some scholars are of the opinion that the creation of *qieyun* 切韻, a way to get the phonetic sound of a Chinese character, and the formation of the theory of the four tones in Chinese language are closely related to or even directly influenced by Buddhist translation of Sanskrit scripture. Others are of the opinion that Chinese people knew these before the introduction of Buddhism.

Chen Yinque (1890–1969) is the first Chinese scholar who said that the four tones in Chinese language were created after the Buddhist monks' recitation of sūtras (Chen 2001, 367–381). His arguments are as follows:

> (1) The Chinese four tones were created by imitating the three tones of Buddhist recitation of sūtras at the time, which were from the three tones of Vedas in ancient India. (2) The Chinese four tones were created in Yongming's era (489) because King Xiao Ziliang invited many Buddhist monks who were well acquainted with Buddhist recitation to assemble at his home in order to create new Buddhist music (*Nanqi Shu* 1972, vol. 2, 698). (3) There were many Buddhist monks from Central Asia who lived in Jiankang (Today Nanjing) and were learned in Buddhist recitation.

However, other scholars such as Yu Min who wrote papers in 1984 questioned it with a support of Buddhist Vinaya rule that the Buddha prohibited monks from using the heretic (Brahmin) way of reciting the Buddhist sutras (Yu 1999, 43). However, he agreed that Chinese people became aware and understood the four tones in their language because of the Buddhist study of phonetic sound.

Jao Tsung-I wrote a paper in 1987 and he also questions Chen Yinque's ideas, but his questions are mainly concerned with the three tones. Professor Jao argues that (1) there are more than three tones in the Vedas and the ways of the Veda recitation had long been lost before the sixth century CE when the Buddhist monks in China discussed the ways of Buddhist recitation. (2) The four tones existed in Liu Song (420–479). (3) Same as Yu Min, Buddhist Vinaya rule prohibited monks from using heretic ways of recitation. (4) As Buddhists used hybrid Sanskrit and the Brahmin ways of recitation may have been used in the Buddhist recitation of Buddhist hybrid Sanskrit sutras but the link with the Veda recitation is not clear. However, Jao argues that the four tones were created after the fourteen phonetic sounds introduced in the Buddhist *Mahāparinirvāṇa Sūtra* (Jao 1993, 79–92).

Hirata Shoji argues against Yao and Yu Min and says that although Buddhist monks were prohibited from using heretic (Brahmin) way of reciting the Buddhist sutras, this rule was relaxed and Sanskrit, for example, was used by a Buddhist school called Sarvāstivāda later around the first century BCE although during the Buddha's time use was prohibited.

Here let me also add more evidence in support of Hirata's argument concerning the Vinaya rules in Buddhism. The Buddha, just before he passed away, said to Ānanda, his attendant, "When I am gone, let the monks, if they should so wish, abolish the lesser and minor rules."[2] This idea influenced later Buddhists so much that a special Vinaya was established called "Vinaya According to Locality" which means that the lesser and minor rules can be changed according to the location. Yu Min does not know this so his argument is not valid because the rule of not allowing the use of heretic way of chanting was relaxed later and even chanting mantras was also allowed in and after the sixth century when Vajrayāna rose in India.

Aśvaghoṣa (ca. 100 CE), the eminent Indian Buddhist monk scholar, poet and playwright, used both Sanskrit and music to promote Buddhist teachings in the first century (Khoroche 2004, 35). He also popularized the style of Sanskrit poetry known as *kāvya.* This shows that Buddhists already used music or a phonetic sound system to promote the Dharma in the first century CE although there is a rule prohibiting monks to attend musical shows. So Mair and Mei assert that

> Nevertheless, exposure to the Sanskrit language and Indian linguistics for several centuries made the Chinese more aware of the phonological features of their own language. The first fruit was the invention of the *fanqie* method of spelling (namely, taking the initial sound of one character and the final sound of a second character to represent the pronunciation of a third character) (Mair and Mei 1991, 392).

Although the creation or formation of the four tones may not be directly linked to the Veda, Sanskrit influence is quite evident and Sanskrit was introduced in China together with Buddhism. The linguistic study of Sanskrit inspired the Chinese to examine the phonetics in their language. At least, Chinese people became aware of the four tones in their language due to the influence of Sanskrit used in Buddhist scriptures.

Today many Chinese scholars support this idea such as Wang Bangwei who is a specialist in Sanskrit and Buddhist studies at Beijing University. He argues with evidence from historical records that the well known

Chinese literati Xie Lingyun (385–433) was highly involved with the study of the fourteen phonetic symbols in his lifetime (Wang 1998, 631–646).

The *Sui Shu*, the History of Sui dynasty, records this,

> Buddhism reached China since the Latter Han dynasty and there came the foreign letters from Xiyu (western region). It can represent all vocal sounds with fourteen letters. It is concise and compendious and is called the Brahman letters. It differs from our characters which are divided into Eight Styles (of writing) and Six Orders (of formation) (*Sui Shu* 1973, vol. 4, 947).

According to Guanding (561–632), the *Mahāparinirvāṇa Sūtra* translated by Dharmakṣema in the northwestern part of China, was transmitted to the South during the reign of emperor Song Wendi (424–453 in power) who loved the sutra so much that he asked Huiguan, Huiyan, and Xie Lingyun (385–433) to re-edit the scripture (T38: 14). Three of them revised the sutra and divided "the Chapter on Lifespan" into four chapters and "the Chapter on the Nature of Tathāgata" into ten chapters in which there is a chapter on Letters. There are twenty-five chapters in the revised version in contrast to the thirteen chapters in the original translation and it is true when the existing two versions are checked.

According to Fei Zhangfang who was a contemporary of Guangding, the reason for revising the Dharmakṣema's translation is that the original was a literary translation and the language was not polished well for dissemination (T49: 89–90). This means that Huiguan, Huiyan, and Xie Lingyun added the title of the chapter on letters. So Xie Lingyun clearly knew the discussion of letters in the Dharmakṣema's translation of the *Mahāparinirvāṇa Sūtra* in which there is a mention of the fourteen phonetic symbols (T12: 653).

According to Huijiao's (497–554) *Gaoseng Zhuan* (Biography of Eminent Monks),

> Xie Lingyun of Chen County loved Buddhist studies, especially the comprehension of sounds different from ordinary ones. He consulted Huiri (355–439) concerning the letters in sutras and the different sounds with their variations in meaning and he wrote the *Shisi Yinxun Xu* (A Study of the Fourteen Phonetic Symbols). He made it clear by listing Chinese and Sanskrit words so that the written characters have their evidence (T50: 367).

Huijiao's *Gaoseng Zhuan* also informs us that Huiri traveled to many kingdoms up to South India and learned various phonetic symbols, literary genres, and interpretation. It is clear that Xie Lingyun wrote his *Shisi Yinxun Xu* based on the fourteen phonetic symbols in the *Mahāparinirvāṇa Sūtra* after consultation with Huiri. According to Wang Bangwei's study mentioned above, the fourteen phonetic symbols in Xie Lingyun's *Shisi Yinxun Xu* refer to the fourteen vowels of Sanskrit language based on Sarvavarman's *Kātantra*, a Sanskrit grammar book.

As discussed above, it was in such a situation that King Xiao Zilian (460–494) invited many Buddhist monks who were well acquainted with Buddhist recitation to assemble in his home in order to create new Buddhist music (*Nanqi Shu* 1972, vol. 2, 698).

Shen Yue (441–513) and Zhou Yong both were Buddhists who were interested in phonetic symbols. Japanese monk Kūkai (774–835) said in his *Bunkyo Hifuron* (*Wenjing Mifu Lun*), "From the end of [Liu] Song dynasty (420–479) the four tones came into being. Mr Shen wrote an essay to discuss their genealogical table in which he said that it came from Zhou Yong" (Kūkai 1983, 80). According to the *Nanshi*, a historical book, Zhou Yong wrote the *Shisheng Qieyun* (A Study of the Four Tones and Qieyun) (*Nan Shi* 1972, vol. 3, 895).

All these evidences show that Buddhist use of Sanskrit directly influenced the creation of *qieyun*, a way to get the phonetic sound of a word, and the formation of the four tones. It triggered the Chinese interest in linguistic studies. This also indirectly influenced the study and use of rhyme in Chinese poetry.

COMPILATION OF RHYME DICTIONARIES

The Chinese interest in the Sanskrit phonetic symbols gave rise to unprecedented interest in linguistic studies, in particular the description and analysis of the phonetic values of Chinese characters. This resulted in the compilation of numerous rhyme dictionaries. Although these dictionaries were mainly compiled for the purpose of reading and studying Buddhist scriptures, they are also valuable for Chinese linguistic and other historical academic studies.

In fact, there is a tradition of study of the form, the sound, and the meaning of Chinese characters in Chinese history. Chinese Buddhists adopted this tradition and borrowed from non-Buddhist works to compile many rhyme dictionaries. As early as the Northern Qi (550–577), a Buddhist monk named Daohui compiled a book entitled *Yiqiejing Yin* (The Sound of All Scriptures) and later Zhisai compiled *Zhongjing Yin* (The Sound of All Scriptures). But in the Tang dynasty there appeared many important works by eminent Buddhist linguists such as Xuanyin, Huilin, and Fayuan.

Xuanyin was a learned person who was even selected by the emperor as one of the ten leading Buddhist monks who formed the Xuanzang's translation committee. Xuanyin compiled the *Yiqiejing Yinyi* (The Sound and the Meaning of All Scriptures) and explained the difficult Chinese characters in four hundred and fifty six Buddhist texts. According to Daoxuan, Xuanyin was not happy about Daohui's work mentioned above so he compiled his own and quoted from more than a hundred and a dozen Chinese works apart from Buddhist literature (T55: 283). It is a valuable work for modern scholars as his editing and study were of a high quality.

Second, Huilin compiled a work with the same title *Yiqiejing Yinyi* in a hundred fascicles. Huilin was originally from Kashgar and came to China to study under Amoghavajra. So he was learned in Indian phonetics and Confucian texts. Huilin in his work explained the difficult words in one thousand and three hundred Buddhist texts. Just as Xuanyin, Huilin also quoted more than a hundred Chinese works and some of them are lost already. Most of the linguists in Qing dynasty made Huilin's work as their main source book.

Then, in about 1151, during the Song dynasty, Fayuan compiled the well known *Fanyi Mingyi Ji* (A Collection of Chinese Transliteration of [Sanskrit] Names and Terms). It contains 2,040 entries of transliteration of words from Sanskrit with careful explanation of the sources and meaning. The author also quoted more than four hundreds non-Buddhist works.

Another important work entitled the *Fanyu Qianzi Wen* (A thousand Characters of Sanskrit Language) was compiled by Yijing who traveled to India through the South China Sea in the later part of the seventh century. This is a bilingual dictionary. All these Buddhist dictionaries promoted the linguistic study of the Chinese language and introduced new light.

THE USE OF VERNACULAR LANGUAGE

Chinese Buddhists are the first people to use vernacular to translate the Buddhist scriptures in China and this influenced the use of vernacular among the Chinese. Mair (2004, 154) even thinks that later it became the national language of China.

Mair (2001, 30) lists six reasons why Buddhism used vernacular and some of his reasons are quite forceful. I think the main reasons for Buddhism to use vernacular are as follows: The first and the most important reason is the Buddha's language policy. Mair points out that the injunction of the Buddha was to transmit his *dharma* (doctrine) throughout the world in the languages of various regions, rather than in the preclassical language of the Vedas as recorded in the Vinaya (rules of discipline governing the community of monks). Because the Buddha wanted all people, mostly the ordinary, to learn and understand his teaching, Mair calls it the Buddhist egalitarian social values that favor demotic forms of language over elitist, hieratic forms.

It is this sanction of using vernacular language that is reflected in Chinese translation of Buddhist scriptures. According to the preface to the Chinese translation of the *Dharmapāda*, when Vighna came to China in 224 he was invited to translate Buddhist scriptures with his friend Zhu Jiangyan, but the latter had not mastered Chinese yet although he knew

Sanskrit well, so the translation was plain and not elegant. But Vighna said, "The Buddha said, 'Go with the meaning without decoration, take the teaching (Dharma) without ornamentation.' It is good if the translator makes it easy to understand without losing the meaning" (T4: 566). Thus they translated the Buddhist texts in vernacular language. However, this vernacular is, on one hand, coupled with massive borrowing from Indic words and even grammatical usage and syntactic structures and, on the other hand, modified by the Chinese Buddhists who helped in the translations so it became a mixture of vernacular and literary style. Scholars call it Buddhist Hybrid Sinitic or Buddhist Hybrid Chinese.

There are a large number of manuscripts in vernacular language preserved in the Dunhuang cave library which were recovered in the early twentieth century. The entire corpus of vernacular narratives in Dunhuang was referred to as *bianwen* (transformation texts), which includes *jiangjing wen* (sūtra lecture texts, elaborate exegeses of specific scriptures), *yazuo wen* (seat-settling texts, prologues for the sūtra lecture texts), *yinyuan* (circumstances, stories illustrating karmic consequences), and *yuanqi* (causal origins, tales illustrating the effects of karma), et cetera.

The nature of this collection of literatures shows that they were used for public lectures, preachings, tale illustration of Buddhist teachings, and even dramas. As they used vernacular so they were easy to understand and thus it became the best tool for the spread of the Buddhist teaching.

The second major reason for the use of vernacular language is the Chan school's philosophy of not depending upon words and letters, but a special transmission outside the scriptures. Thus the Chan masters transmitted their teaching by word of mouth such as relating enlightening stories called *Gongan*. However, later, the disciples collected the stories and speeches of their masters and compiled them into books called *yulu* (Records of Sayings). As the Chan masters used dialects and even colloquials to instruct their disciples so vernacular language is used in the *Yulun* to record their masters' speeches as they were.

The use of vernacular language in Buddhist literatures was widened in Song dynasty as there are a large number of collections preserved. There are two kinds of such collections: "Denglu" which means the "Record of Lamp" and "Yulu" which means the "Record of Sayings." The representative work of "Record of Lamp" in the Song dynasty is the *Jingde Record of the Transmission of the Lamp* which was composed by Daoyuan during the Jingde era (1004–1007). The representative of the "Record of Sayings" is the *Blue Cliff Record* compiled by Keqing (1069–1135) who wrote short introductions to each story and even added notes and comments to some important stories.

Buddhist use of vernacular language in the "Record of Sayings" also influenced Confucians in the Song dynasty that they also used vernacular with the same literary style as Jiang Fan (1761–1831), a scholar of Qing dynasty, who said, "Chan School had *Yulu* and Song Confucians also had *Yulu*; Chan School used vernacular language (Lit: street language) in their *Yulun* and Song Confucians also used vernacular language in their *Yulu*" (Jiang 1983, 190). Again Qian Daxin (1728–1804) said, "The Buddhist use of *Yulu* started from the Tang dynasty while Confucian use of *Yulun* started from the Song dynasty" (Qian 2000, 488). So we find the Record of Sayings of Song Neo-Confucian Chen Yi 程頤 (1033–1107), Zhang Jiuchen 張九成 (1092–1159), and Zhu Xi 朱熹 (1130–1200). Just as Mair (2004, 156) says, "Thus, with the Buddhist sanctioning of the written vernacular, a sequence of revolutionary developments occurred that radically transformed Chinese literature for all time. Moreover, hand in hand with vernacularization came other Buddhist-inspired developments in Chinese literature."

However, "the mainstream Confucian literati never accepted anything other than Literary Sinitic as a legitimate medium for writing. To them the vernacular was crude and vulgar, beneath the dignity of a gentleman to contemplate," as pointed out by Mair (2004, 156). But ordinary people paid no heed to this opinion and proceeded to use vernacular for dramas, stories, on the foundations laid by the Buddhists of medieval China. Mair (2004, 157) asserts that "it is safe to say that Buddhism legitimized the writing of the vernacular language in China."

In conclusion, the Buddhist impact on Chinese language is enormous from vocabulary to phonetics studies and vernacular. The Sanskrit phonetics triggered the Chinese people's interest in linguistic studies and even compiled rhyme dictionaries. This in turn also influenced Chinese literature.

NOTES

1. This is based on *Bukkyō daijiten* 佛教大辭典 compiled by Mochizuki Shinkō 望月信亨(1869–1948).

2. Dīghanikāya ii, 154. Chinese translations of *Mahāparinirvāṇa Sūtra* of the *Dīrghāgama* (T1, no.1, 26, a28–29), the *Mahīśāsaka-vinaya* (T22, no.1421, 191, b3–4), the *Mahāsaṃghika-vinaya* (T22, no.1425, 492, b5–6), the *Dharmaguptaka-vinaya* (T22, no. 1428, 967, b12–13), and the *Sarvāstivāda-vinaya* (T23, no. 1435, 449, b13–14).

BIBLIOGRAPHY

Chen Yinque 陳寅恪. 2001. "sisheng san wen" 四聲三問. In *Jinmingguan conggao chubian* 金明館叢稿初編 (Beijing: Sanlian shudian), 367–381.

Jao Tsung-I 饒宗頤. 1993. "Yindu boerni xian zhi weituo sansheng lun lue: sisheng wailai shuo pingyi" 印度波儞尼仙之圍陀三聲論略——四聲外來說平議. In *Fanxue ji* 梵學集 (Shanghai: Shanghai guji chubanshe), 79–92.

Jiang Fan 江藩. 1983. *Guochao Hanxue Shicheng Ji* 國朝漢學師承記. Appendix: *Guochao Jingshi Jingyi Mulu* 國朝經師經義目錄 and *Guochao Songxue Yuanyuan Ji* 國朝宋學淵源記. Beijing: Zhonghua Shuju.

Karashima, Seishi. 2006. "Underlying languages of early Chinese translations of Buddhist scriptures." In Christoph Anderl and Halvor Eifring, eds. *Studies in Chinese Language and Culture: Festschrift in Honour of Christoph Harbsmeier on the Occasion of His Sixtieth Birthday*. Oslo: Hermes Academic Publication.

Khoroche, Peter. 2004. "Aśvaghoṣa." In Robert E. Buswell, ed. *Encyclopedia of Buddhism*. Vol. 1. New York: Macmillan Reference USA.

Kūkai, 1983. *Bunkyō Hifuron* 文鏡秘府論. Beijing: Zhongguo Shehui Kexue Chubanshe.

Liang Xiaohong 梁曉虹. 1994. *Fojiao ciyu de gouzao yu hanyu cihui de fazhan* 佛教詞語的構造與漢語詞彙的發展. Beijing: Beijing Yuyan Xueyuan Chubanshe.

Mair, Victor H. 2001. "Language and Script." In *The Columbia history of Chinese literature*, edited by Victor H. Mair (New York: Columbia University Press), 19–57.

———. 2004. "Buddhist Influences on Vernacular Literature in Chinese." *Encyclopedia of Buddhism*, edited by Robert E. Buswell, Jr. (New York: Macmillan Reference USA), vol. 1, 154–157.

Mair, Victor H. and Tsu-Lin Mei. 1991. "The Sanskrit Origins of Recent Style Prosody." *Harvard Journal of Asiatic Studies* 51.2: 375–470.

Nan Shi 南史, vol. 2. Beijing: Zhonghua Shuju, 1975.

Nanqi Shu 南齊書, vol. 2. Beijing: Zhonghua Shuju, 1972.

Qian Daxin 錢大昕. 2000. *Shijiazhai Yangxin Lu* 十駕斋養新錄. Nanjing: Jiangsu Guji Chubanshe.

Sui Shu 隋書, vol. 4. Beijing: Zhonghua Shuju, 1973.

Sun, Changwu. 2006. "The contribution of Buddhism to the development of the Chinese language and linguistics." In Christoph Anderl and Halvor Eifring, eds. *Studies in Chinese Language and Culture: Festschrift in Honour of Christoph Harbsmeier on the Occasion of His Sixtieth Birthday* (Oslo: Hermes Academic Publication), 331–353.

T. *Taishō Shinshū Daizōkyō*, edited by Takakusu Junjiro and Watanabe Kaigyoku. Tokyo: Taishō Issaikyō Kankō kai, 1924–1932.

Vighna, trans. 224. *Dharmapāda*. CBETA.

Wang Bangwei 王邦維. 1998. "Xie Lingyun 'shisi yin xun xu' jikao" 謝靈運〈十四音訓敘〉輯考. In *Beijing daxue bainian guoxue wencui: yuyan wenxian juan* 北京大學百年國學文粹-語言文獻卷 (Beijing: Beijing daxue chubanshe), 631–646.

Wang Li 王力. 1990. *Wangli Wenji: Hanyu Cihui Shi* 王力文集-漢語詞匯史. Jinan: Shandong jiaoyu chubanshe.

Yu Min 俞敏. 1999. "Houhan sanguo fan han duiyin pu" 後漢三國梵漢對音譜. In *Yu Min yuyanxue lunwen ji* 俞敏語言學論文集 (Beijing: Shangwu yinshuguan), 1–62.

Zheng, Jiao 鄭樵. 1987. *Tongzhi Shierlue* 通志二十略. Beijing: Zhonghua Shuju.

14

Magical Alphabet in the Indian and Chinese Minds

From the Garland of Letters to Master Pu'an's Siddham Mantra

Bill M. Mak

The pursuit of a pure and refined language, hence *saṃskṛtam* (*sam* "completely," + √*kṛ* "to do"), by the ancient Indians, was motivated by a practical concern that the Vedas would be efficacious only when properly enunciated. As a result, a highly sophisticated science of phonetics was developed to ensure that the Vedic texts and mantras were correctly pronounced and transmitted.[1] This was the prime motivation for the analysis and arrangement of the Sanskrit syllables, which became in turn the basis for the construction of the written alphabet.[2]

When the Indic languages were first introduced to China through the translation of Buddhist texts starting from the first century CE,[3] the Chinese were fascinated by the Sanskrit language and its alphabet. This fascination continued for centuries in China up to the present day, despite Sanskrit as a language itself was largely forgotten. In this chapter I shall examine the Sanskrit alphabet, how it was conceived by the Indians, and how it underwent a series of transformation in the Chinese minds as it was absorbed into the East Asian culture.[4]

2.0 SANSKRIT *AKṢARA*-S IN INDIA

The Sanskrit syllables, commonly known as *akṣara* (lit. "imperishable"), or *varṇa* (lit. "color"), suggesting likely how they were conceived analytically by the Indian phoneticians, were considered the smallest unit of sound which possesses various phonetic qualities. The study of such basic units of the language, known as *śikṣā* (lit. "training," equivalent roughly to "phonetics" in modern terminology) is considered an important branch of the traditional Vedic lore. Not until the modern time, the highly sophisticated oral tradition of the ancient Indians had made writing an accessory rather than a necessity.[5] The alphabet appeared to have spread in India only after the invention of the Brāhmī script sometime during the first millennium BCE.[6] Unlike in China where writing was much revered, writing was largely utilitarian to the early Indians; later on, exercises of the Sanskrit alphabet were prescribed exclusively to children as part of their elementary education (figure 14.1).

Figure 14.1. Child learning Brāhmī alphabet (Sugh, Haryana, c. second century BCE. Terracotta from Delhi National Museum Collection). Source: Photo by author.

2.1 Phonetic Science of Ancient India

Unlike the Western alphabet which was arranged in no apparent order, the enumeration of Sanskrit syllables or *akṣarasamāmnāya* ("recitation of the alphabet"), known popularly as the *varṇamālā* ("garland of letters"), reflects the phonetic knowledge of the Indians. Phonetic analysis such as the differentiation between vowels and consonants, places of articulation, and features of various sound units were described in early phonetic works such as the *Taittirīya-prātiśākhya*. An example of such analysis is the organization of the twenty-five plosive+nasal consonants known as *pañca-pañca vargāḥ* ("five-by-five square") familiar to the students of Sanskrit:[7]

Table 14.1.

Position of contact (sparśa)	*First: voiceless (aghoṣa), unaspirated*	*Second: voiceless, aspirated*	*Third: voiced (ghoṣavat), unaspirated*	*Fourth: voiced, aspirated (hakāra)*	*Final: voiced, nasal (anunāsika)*
Velar (*hanūmūle*)	ka	kha	ga	gha	ṅa
Palatal *tālau*	ca	cha	ja	jha	ña
Retroflex (*mūrdhani*)	ṭa	ṭha	ḍa	ḍha	ṇa
Dental (*dantamūleṣu*)	ta	tha	da	dha	na
Labial (*oṣṭhābhyāṃ*)	pa	pha	ba	bha	ma

As a pedagogical tool for both phonetics and writing, the alphabet was taught to children through two main methods: 1) enumeration of the alphabet starting from the vowels followed by the consonants as in the *varṇamālā*; 2) various consonant-vowel permutation such as *ka, kā, ki, kī, ku, kū, ke, kai, ko, kau, kaṃ, kaḥ / kha, khā, khi, khī, khu, khū. . . . ptai, pto, ptau, ptaṃ, ptaḥ*. Unfortunately, except for rare fragments such as the "Florence Fragment," (figure 14.2) no "textbook" on Sanskrit or Indic orthography had survived in South Asia, suggesting either that such work was considered too trivial to be canonized, or that it was meant only as writing exercise using sand board rather than the more precious materials such as palm leaves or birch bark.[8] The Chinese, however, took these phonetic/orthographic exercises very seriously, which became an integral part of the traditional Sanskrit studies in East Asia (§3.2).

Figure 14.2. Florence fragment from the collection of Instituto Papirologico "G. Vitelli." Sinhalese script. The fragment contains two main elements copied in repetition: (a) *Varṇamālā* ". . . *(ra)-la-va-śa-ṣa-sa-ha-ḷa (vada) (ki)m[virāma]aḥ k(iṃ) akṣarasoḍasa (v)ada k(iṃ)* . . ." and (b) *Ṣoḍaśākṣarī* ". . . *(kh)ṛ-khṝ-khḷ-khḹ-khe-khai-kho-khau-khām-kaḥ-ga-ghā-ghi-gh(ī)*. . . ." Initial transcription by Jacob Schmidt-Madsen with correction by Rangama Chandawimala. Images courtesy of G. Bastianini. Note the repetition of each line which suggests the text to be some form of writing exercise. It is possibly part of an orthographic textbook which is no longer extant. Although the dating of the Florence fragment is uncertain, Rangama Chandawimala pointed out to me that on orthographical ground the folios are unlikely to be older than the twelfth century. Source: Collection of Instituto Papirologico "G. Vitelli."

2.2 Alphabet as Mnemonics

The alphabet has proved a useful invention and was employed in a number of non-linguistic ways, from practical matters such as inventory[9] and mnemonics, to the esoteric exegesis based on the analyses of words. The Sanskrit alphabet was enumerated notably in a number of early Mahāyāna texts as a kind of "exegetical *dhāraṇī*,"[10] embedded either within the text proper (e.g., *Lalitavistara*) or as an independent chapter known as *Akṣaraparivarta* as in the *Larger Prajñāpāramitā* and the *Avataṃsaka*. In the *Larger Prajñāpāramitā*, we find the description of what is called the "Door of letters" (*akṣaramukham*), a mnemonic device which connects a letter to a certain Buddhist doctrine, for example, "*a*" for "*an-utpanna*" (non-arisen), "*ra*" for "*rajas*" (impurity) and so on:[11]

Moreover, Subhūti, the Great Vehicle of the Bodhisattva, the Mahāsattva, is the "Doors of Dhāraṇī," which is the "Equanimity of the Alphabet," the "Door of Syllables," the "Entrance of Syllables." What are the "Equanimity of the Alphabet," the "Door of Syllables," the "Entrance of Syllables?" The syllable "a" is the door to the insight that all dharma-s are non-arisen from the beginning . . .[12]

punar aparaṃ subhūte bodhisattvasya mahāsattvasya mahāyānaṃ, yad uta dhāraṇīmukhāni, yad utākṣaranayasamatākṣaramukham akṣarapraveśaḥ, katamo 'kṣaranayasamatā akṣaramukham akṣarapraveśaḥ? akāro mukhaḥ sarvadharmāṇām ādyanutpannatvāt . . .[13]

In such a way, the text goes on enumerating forty-two letters, conveniently known as the *Arapacana* alphabet which is most probably of non-Sanskrit origin.[14] Exegetical *dhāraṇī* based on the conventional Sanskrit *varṇamālā* appeared only in later Mahāyāna works such as the *Mahāparinirvāna*, modeled likely upon the *Arapacana*.[15] Textually speaking, however, the two traditions appeared to have developed independently with no apparent crossover. The texts themselves did not provide any discussion on how one related to the other, which as we shall see, causing considerable confusion to the Chinese.

2.3 Alphabet as divinities

Among the Indian, non-Buddhist Sanskrit works such as the Upaniṣad-s and the Purāṇa-s, there appears to be a widespread practice known as *varṇasaṃjñā*, that is, the association of each Sanskrit syllable to a divinity.[16] In the Vaiṣṇava work *Jayākhyasaṃhitā*, we find descriptions of various deities, each linked to a letter:

The letter *ka* is of the highest nature, the lotus and the *Karāla* (referring to Brahma); the letter *kha* is the dwarfish body, the soul of the body and the producer of everything (referring to *garuḍavāhana*, he whose vehicle is the Garuḍa); the letter *ga* is the remover of sickness, the cowherd (*Govinda*) and the carrier of a mace; the letter *gha* should be known as the one with the ray of heat, the one with splendor (*tejasvī*) and possessing heat (hence, the Sun); the letter *ṅa* is the single-tusked (*Gaṇeśa*), the soul of the created and the creator of all beings.

kamalaś ca karālaś ca kakāraḥ prakṛtiḥ parā | | 6.40
khakāraḥ kharvadehaś ca vedātmā viśvabhāvanaḥ
gadadhvaṃsī gakāraś ca govindas sa gadādharaḥ | | 6.41
ghakāraś caiva gharmāṃśus tejasvī dīptimān smṛtaḥ
ṅakāra ekadaṃṣṭraś ca bhūtātmā viśvabhāvakaḥ | | 6.42 [17]

A syllable was conceived as the embodiment of a certain divinity and the *varṇamālā*, or the alphabet as a whole, became thus the totality of the divinity. In their written forms, the Sanskrit letters were turned into objects of worship. Such abstraction and transference of the concept of the divine resulted in the Sanskrit letters becoming one of the favorite themes for the *yantra*-s, a kind of magical diagram which has a long history in India. In the Śaiva tradition, deities consisted of Sanskrit letters are conjured up in various Tantric meditative practices, attesting to some of the highly creative uses of the alphabet in a religious context (figure 14.3).[18] Suchlike religio-philosophical uses of the alphabet were seen also in Esoteric Buddhism, as well as certain strains of early Mahāyāna Buddhism. Although their relations have yet to be clarified, it is beyond doubt that both sprang from the same tradition in ancient India where the alphabet was understood and employed often in a multifaceted and highly nuanced way, that is, both linguistically and non-linguistically.

Figure 14.3. "Synaesthetic icon of the deity Mālinī made up of Gupta characters." Source: Vasudeva 2007: 536.

3.0 SANSKRIT ALPHABET IN CHINA

One of the key features of the Chinese understanding of the Sanskrit alphabet, as in the case of Indian Buddhism in general, is the initial confusion of temporally, geographically, or even ideologically disparate elements and the subsequent need to rationalize and synthesize them into a coherent, inclusive, yet new body of knowledge. Thus the Sanskrit alphabet whose multifarious functions were highly specific yet contextual in India suddenly became one richly nuanced concept as it was as if haphazardly introduced to the Chinese through the translation of the Buddhist texts which lasted through the first millennium.[19] For centuries the Chinese tried to unpack all these meanings associated with the Sanskrit alphabet and in the course of their inquiry, some very surprising ideas about the Sanskrit alphabet and even the Sanskrit language emerged, becoming eventually part of the Chinese's collective conception of the supernatural and the spiritual.

3.1 *Arapacana* and Sanskrit Alphabet in Chinese Mahāyāna Texts

Among the earliest Chinese translations of Buddhist texts containing references to the Indic alphabet are Dharmarakṣa's *Puyao jing* 普曜經 (*Lalitavistara*)[20] and Mokṣala's *Fangguang bore jing* 放光般若經 (*Larger Prajñāpāramitā*),[21] both dated around the third century CE. The alphabet described in these text is of the *Arapacana* type. The earliest exegetical *varṇamālā*, on the other hand, arrived in China somewhat later, and are found in Dharmakṣema's *Daboniepan jing* 大般涅槃經 (*Mahāparinirvāṇa*)[22] and Saṅgabhadra's *Wenshushiliwen jing* 文殊師利問經 (*Mañjuśrīparipṛcchā*),[23] both dated c. fifth century CE. Although the *Arapacana* alphabet is likely of non-Sanskrit origin and at any rate reflects no phonetic knowledge of the Indians like the *varṇamālā* does, its sanskritization, or at least its reinterpretation in a Sanskritic context, must have been quite early as evinced by the Gilgit manuscript of the *Larger Prajñāpāramitā*. At any rate, the *Arapacana* was accepted as an alternate alphabet for the Sanskrit language by the Chinese although its relation with the *varṇamālā* has never been clear to anyone.[24]

The exegetical alphabet, both of the *Arapacana* and the *varṇamālā* variety, in a way brought the concept of the Sanskrit alphabet closer to that of the Chinese characters, namely, that a symbol represents an idea. This in turn allowed the Chinese to formulate their own idea of what the Sanskrit language was, albeit erroneously. From the Chinese point of view, unlike the Chinese characters whose pronunciation was never transparent, the exegetical alphabet represents sounds as well the meanings, which to the early Chinese must have been something of a revelation.[25] In such a way, the phonetic and religio-semantic functions of the exegetical alphabet were comfortably mixed together. While the *varṇamālā* eventually established itself among the learned Chinese Buddhists as the proper Sanskrit alphabet, *Arapacana* continued to inspire generations of Chinese Buddhists, developing into an independent genre of liturgy which is performed even today.[26]

3.2 Studies of Siddham and Magical Sanskrit Alphabet

The proper study of Sanskrit, following the Indian tradition, begins with the study of Sanskrit phonetics through the help of the alphabet and various pedagogical techniques as those we have seen in §2.1. One such pedagogical material which was known to and vigorously studied by the Chinese was the so-called "Siddham Chapters" or *Xitanzhang* 悉曇章 (XTZ), which began to circulate in China as early as the fourth century CE.[27] In describing this text, Yijing 義淨 (635–713 CE) in his *Nanhai jigui neifa zhuan* 南海寄歸內法傳, under the heading of "The Western Methods of Learning" 西方學法, remarked:

> One invented the learner "Chapters of Siddham," called also "Siddhir astu." This is the name of a work of Minor Learning[28] and one merely took [the word meaning] "success and auspiciousness" as title. Basically, there are forty-nine *akṣara*-s and their permutation results in eighteen chapters, with over 10,000 [composite] *akṣara*-s in total, altogether in over 300 verses.[29] In general, one verse is said to contain four *pada*-s and each *pada* eight *akṣara*-s. Furthermore, there are the "large verses" and the "small verses," which are not to be elaborated here. Children of six years learn this [text] in six months and it was said to be taught by Maheśvara (Śiva).[30]

> 創學《悉曇章》，亦云《悉地羅窣堵》。斯乃小學標章之稱，但以成就吉祥為目。本有四十九字，其相乘轉，成一十八章，總有一萬餘字，合三百餘頌。凡言一頌，乃有四句，一句八字，總成三十二言。更有大頌小頌，不可具述。六歲童子學之，六月方了。斯乃相傳是大自在天之所說也。[31]

This textbook of eighteen chapters for the six year olds, which Yijing described later became the first learner of Sanskrit for the Chinese monks and was widely disseminated up to the modern time in Japan.[32] The eighteen chapters, which is a complete set of consonant-vowel combination, was described in detail and copied out in its entirety in Zhiguang 智廣's *Xitanziji* 悉曇字記 (c. eighth century CE).[33] For over a millennium, the XTZ was tirelessly copied by the Buddhist monks in Japan as not only exercises of Sanskrit orthography, but also as a Buddhist practice and even calligraphy on its own right.[34]

Like the Indians, the Chinese considered the Sanskrit alphabet not only as a linguistic tool, but also the embodiment of an esoteric body of knowledge, as in the case of the exegetical *dhāraṇī*. In the Hōryūji 法隆寺 manuscript (c. sixth century CE), the *varṇamālā* was placed underneath the *uṣṇīṣavijayadhāraṇī*, preceded by the auspicious "*siddham*" just as Yijing described (figure 14.4).

While the exact purpose of the *varṇamālā* in this particular instance has not been clarified with satisfaction, its function is unlikely to be merely linguistic. Furthermore, there are evidences which suggest that the Sanskrit alphabet, as well as the XTZ, were chanted as a mantra.[35] While such act might have struck the more learned Buddhists as ludicrous, as a child singing the alphabet song of "ABC" might to the modern listeners, it was apparently performed in all earnestness. Possibly in response to such doubt, Kūkai explained in an early ninth century commentary:

> Question: The Siddham alphabet is studied by all the children of the [mundane] world. How is it different from the [Supramundane] Teaching of the Mantras? Answer: The "Siddham Chapter" now studied in the world was originally taught by the Tathāgata and was disseminated to the [mundane] world through the continuous lineage of Brahma and so on. Although one may say that the apparent functions are identical, one does not necessarily know the nature of the *akṣara* and the meaning of the *akṣara*, that is, the True Meaning. Thus, those who are conversant only in the four mundane kinds of language do not obtain the Mantra of such Meaning. All words without understanding of the True Meaning are words of falsehood. Words of falsehood lead to the four kinds of verbal karma, which are the causes of misery of the three wretched paths [of transmigration]. If one knows the True Meanings [of the alphabet], all sins would be expiated and all knowledge may be obtained. Just like poison, the effect of knowing and not knowing [of the True Meaning] is immediately recognized.—*Himitsu mandara jūjū shinron,* fascicle ten.

> 問：悉曇字母者世間童子皆悉誦習，與此眞言教何別？答：今世間所誦習悉曇章者，本是如來所説，梵王等轉轉傳受流布世間。雖云同用，然未曾識字相字義眞實之句。是故但詮世間四種言語，不得如義之眞言。不知義語皆是妄語，妄語則長四種口業，爲三途苦因。若知眞實義則滅一切罪，得一切智。譬如毒藥，知與不知，損益立驗。《祕密曼荼羅十住心論卷第十》[36]

But what exactly is this "True Meaning?" In explaining what the "Teaching of Mantra" is, Kūkai wrote:

> What is the Teaching of Mantra? It is to take the *akṣara*-s such as *ka kha ga gha ṅa . . . śa ṣa sa ha* as the basis (*benmu*, lit. "original mother"). For each [consonantal] *akṣara*, there are twelve derived *akṣara*-s (through combination with the twelve vowels). With each of these twelve as the basis, there are additional *akṣara*-s with single, double, triple and quadruple conjuncts, resulting in over ten thousand [composite *akṣara*-s]. Each of this *akṣara-mukham* contains immeasurable and boundless meanings of exoteric and esoteric teachings. Each sound (*sheng*), each *akṣara* (*zi*) and each "real representation" (*shixiang*) permeates the *Dharmadhātu*. [The *akṣara*-s are] the *samādhi-mukhāni*, the *dhāraṇī-mukhāni* of all the venerable [Buddhas]. According to the capacity of the sentient beings, [these *akṣara*-s] reveal the exoteric and esoteric teachings.—*ibid.*

云何眞言教法？謂 ka kha ga gha ṅa乃至śa ṣa sa ha等字爲本母。各各字有十二轉生字。此各各十二爲本，有一合二合三合四合等增加字，都計餘一萬。此一一字門具無量無邊顯密教義。一一聲一一字一一實相周遍法界。爲一切諸尊三摩地門陀羅尼門，隨衆生機根量，開示顯教密教。《祕密曼荼羅十住心論》[37]

From the hermeneutic writing of Kūkai we can see how the pedagogical "Siddham Chapters" merged with the religious mnemonics "Doors of letters" to form an esoteric worldview in the mind of certain East Asian Buddhists. While there is no evidence that such view was ever envisioned in India, the idea continued to gain momentum in East Asia. It evolved eventually into a mystical doctrine which combined sound, form, and meaning of the religious alphabet, a notion that became central in East Asian Esoteric Buddhism, and is arguably conceptually larger than its Indian counterpart which combined only sound (*vāc*) and meaning (*artha*). The sinicization of "Buddhist Sanskrit" in East Asia may be witnessed in other forms as well. In the case of the East Asian *maṇḍala*-s, Sanskrit seed-letters (*bīja*) representing various Buddhist deities were featured arguably more visually than aurally; in other forms of epigraphy and sūtra-copying, Siddham letters came to be written vertically following the Chinese tradition. As we shall see, more extreme forms of sinicization emerged as the Chinese continued to develop larger and more inclusive concepts to subsume their Indian antecedents.

3.3 Master Pu'an's Mantra[38]

An example of the sinicization of the Sanskrit alphabet may be seen in a Chinese Buddhist mantra known as the Mantra of Pu'an or *Pu'anzhou* 普庵咒 (PAZ). The mantra is essentially a Chinese Buddhist liturgical work consisting of an opening and closing in Chinese, and a sinicized Sanskrit mantra of 558 syllables in the middle, attributed to Pu'an (1115–1169 CE), a Chan patriarch celebrated for his supernatural powers.[39] The mantra has circulated widely both within and without the Buddhist milieu from the late sixteenth century onward. The earliest specimen is its canonic version titled *Pu'an zushi shenzhou* 普庵祖師神咒, found in the "mantra section" 咒類 of the *Zhujing risong jiyao* 諸經日誦集要 (1600 CE), a Chan liturgical anthology found in the Ming dynasty *Jiaxing* Canon 嘉興藏 (figure 14.5).[40]

The same mantra is also found in an independent anthology known as the *Chanmenrisong* 禪門日誦, a collection dated early eighteenth century which became widely circulated throughout China up to the twentieth

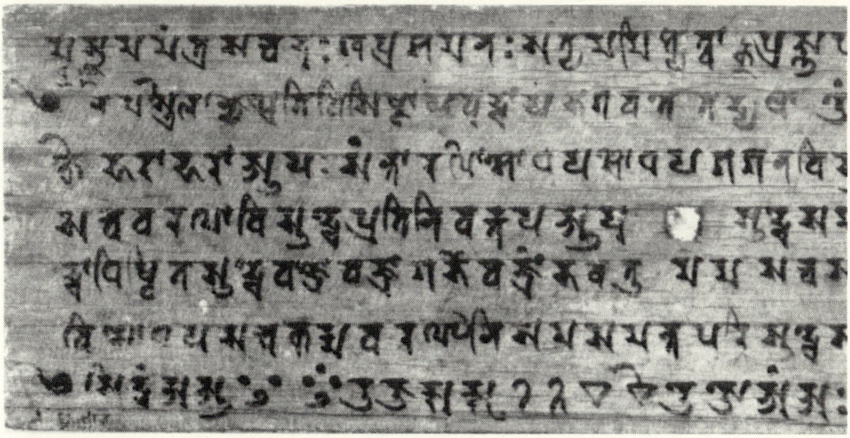

Figure 14.4. Earliest record of "Siddham letters" from Hōryūji manuscript (sixth century?). From the bottom row: siddhaṃ *a ā i ī u ū ṛ ṝ ḷ ḹ e ai o au aṃ aḥ*. The line continues with the consonant syllables *ka kha ga gha ṅa . . . śa ṣa sa ha llaṃ (kṣa)*. Source: Tokyo National Museum Collection (Bonji I:2).

century. The mantra was alternately titled in the latter *Pu'an dade chanshi shitanzhang shenzhou* 普庵大德禪師釋談章神咒. The term *shitanzhang* is merely a phonetic variation of *Xitanzhang*, which points to its affinity to the phonetic work XTZ.

The Mantra of Pu'an, as anyone with a fair acquaintance of sinicized Sanskrit could tell, consists of neither meaningful Sanskrit words nor a correct rendition of the *varṇamālā*. Thus Van Gulik remarked,

> among the better known qin tunes there is one entitled *Shih-t'an* "Buddhist Words," which is nothing but a Mantrayanic magic formula, a *dhāraṇī* . . . The words are also given, for the greater part in transcribed bastard Sanskrit, the usual language of *dhāraṇī* . . . (Van Gulik 1956: 51)

Although Van Gulik recognized the corrupted nature of the *dhāraṇī*, he did not recognize any explicit connection between the PAZ and the XTZ despite what the alternate title of the PAZ suggests. If we compare the first motif and the second motif starting from *ka* (迦) of the two works, the relation between the two becomes immediately apparent (tables 14.2, 14.3).[41] While there are certain curious variations yet to be accounted for, the organization of the twenty-five consonants and the vowel permutation on consonants clearly follow that of their Indian, and ultimately the Vedic, precedents as we have seen earlier (§2.1).[42]

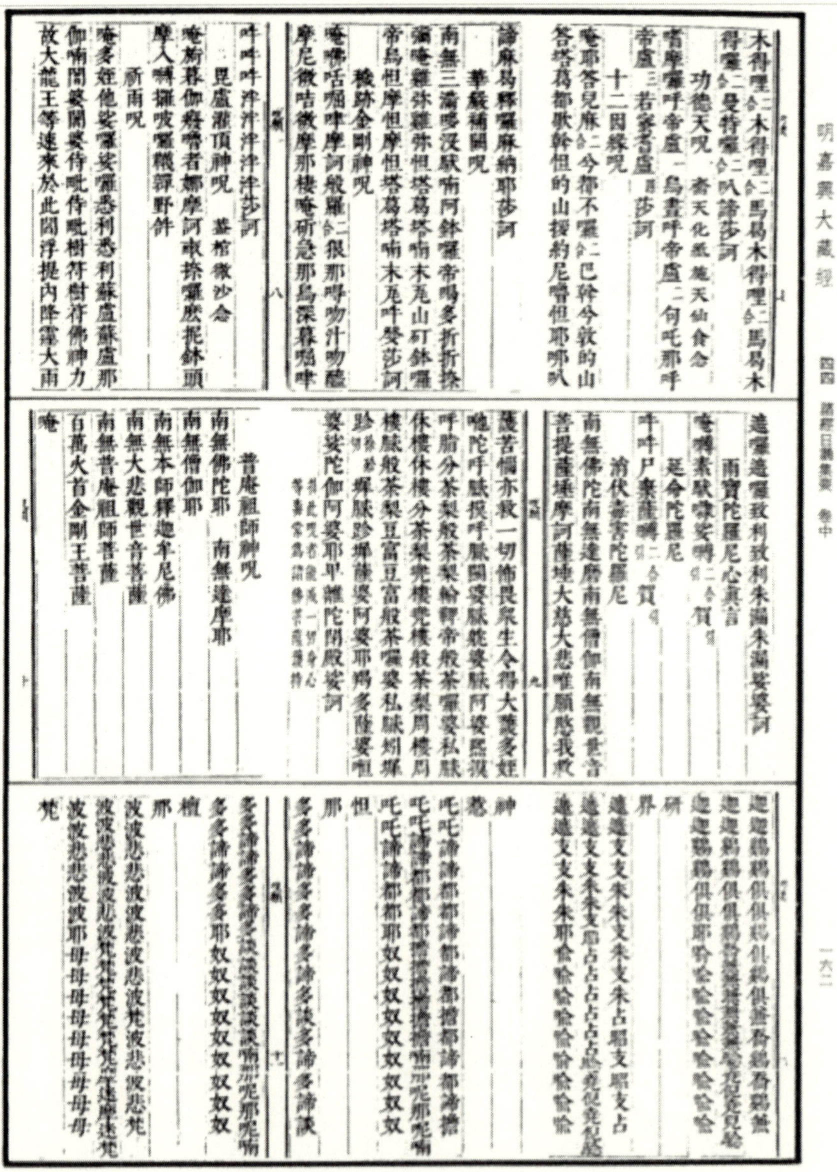
明嘉興大藏經　四四　諸經日誦集要　卷中　一六二

普庵祖師神咒

南無佛陀耶　南無達摩耶

南無僧伽耶

南無本師釋迦牟尼佛

南無大悲觀世音菩薩

南無普庵祖師菩薩

百萬火首金剛王菩薩

Figure 14.5. **"Master Pu'an's Mantra" in Ming Canon (c. sixteenth century). Source: Jiaxingzang 19.44.162b–163c.**

Table 14.2. 25 Plosive & Nasal Consonants

PAZ	迦	迦	迦	研	界	遮	遮	遮	神	惹	吒	吒	吒	怛	那	多	多	多	檀	那	波	波	波	梵	摩
	kya	kya	kya	yān	nyaḥ	ścya	ścya	ścya	śen	chye	ṭa	ṭa	ṭa	dan	ṇu	tu	tu	tu	dhan	nu	pa	pa	pa	van	mu
XTZ	迦	佉	伽	恆	誐	遮	車	闍	饍	若	吒	他	荼	袒	拏	多	他	陀	禪	那	波	頗	婆	渀	麼
	ka	kha	ga	gha	ṅa	ca	cha	ja	jha	ña	ṭa	ṭha	ḍa	ḍha	ṇa	ta	tha	da	dha	na	pa	pha	ba	bha	ma

Table 14.3. Vowel Permutation on *ka*

PAZ	迦	迦	雞	雞	俱	俱	雞	俱	雞	俱	兼	喬	雞	喬	雞	兼
	kya	kya	kye	kye	kyo	kyo	kye	kyo	kye	kyo	kyaṃ	kyao	kye	kyao	kye	kyaṃ
XTZ	迦	迦上	枳	雞引	句	句引	計	蓋	句引	啗	佽	迦				
	ka	kā	ki	kī	ku	kū	ke	kai	ko	kau	kaṃ	kaḥ				

4.0 CORRUPTION OR INDIGENIZATION?

Despite the corruption, the structure of the PAZ shows its author's awareness of the internal organization of the Sanskrit alphabet.[43] It is most likely that before the PAZ was canonized in its corrupted form, somewhere along the oral transmission of this XTZ-based mantra, the linguistic understanding of the XTZ was compromised by the artistic interpolation of the transmitters—that is, by making repetitions and different types of variations to impress upon the listeners a more acoustically convincing form and hence a larger structure.[44]

Another curious development of the PAZ is found in Zhao Yiguang's 趙宧光 (1559–1629 CE) study of the PAZ in his *Xitanjingzhuan* 悉曇經傳 (1611 CE).[45]

Although the author was familiar with the XTZ, he did not connect it with the corrupted PAZ. Instead, he went on to reconstruct its Sanskrit form by transcribing the Chinese pronunciation of the PAZ in *rañjana* script. In other words, Zhao considered the PAZ an efficacious mantra when uttered by a Chinese.[46] The Sanskrit transcription served not only to persuade the readers of the authenticity of the mantra, but also preserved the historical Chinese pronunciation of the mantra.

Through the examination of the evolution of the PAZ, certain strands of the Chinese ideas concerning Sanskrit may be identified. The Chinese were first and foremost fascinated by the alphabetical writing system of Sanskrit. Despite attempts to understand the phonetic principles which underlie the Indian language, the Chinese were generally more interested in the concept of Sanskrit sounds rather than the sounds themselves, which led to the blatant corruption and sinicization. If such trajectory were to be followed, the Sanskrit sounds themselves could have been altogether discarded, leaving behind the mere idea of a mysterious yet spiritually potent language. This turns out to be the case for certain musical renditions of the PAZ, many of which survive as *guqin* tablatures without the mantric text which (d)evolved from the original texted version.[47]

While the idea of a Sanskrit mantra without the mantra might seem preposterous, it attests to what the Chinese must have imagined to be the essence of a sacred, magical language known as Sanskrit. In a way, it was the logical conclusion of what a truly esoteric language should be—a pure sonic experience beyond language, that is, the Brāhma Sound, or *fanyin* 梵音, analogous to certain recurring themes in Chinese philosophy, namely the Daoist "nameless name" and the "inaudible sound."

To sum, the sinicization of Sanskrit mantras may be seen as an example of cultural appropriation which accounts for their living though "corrupted" presence in Chinese Buddhism.[48] Their evolution follows the trajectory of the Chinese's pursuit of the transcendent and the beyond.

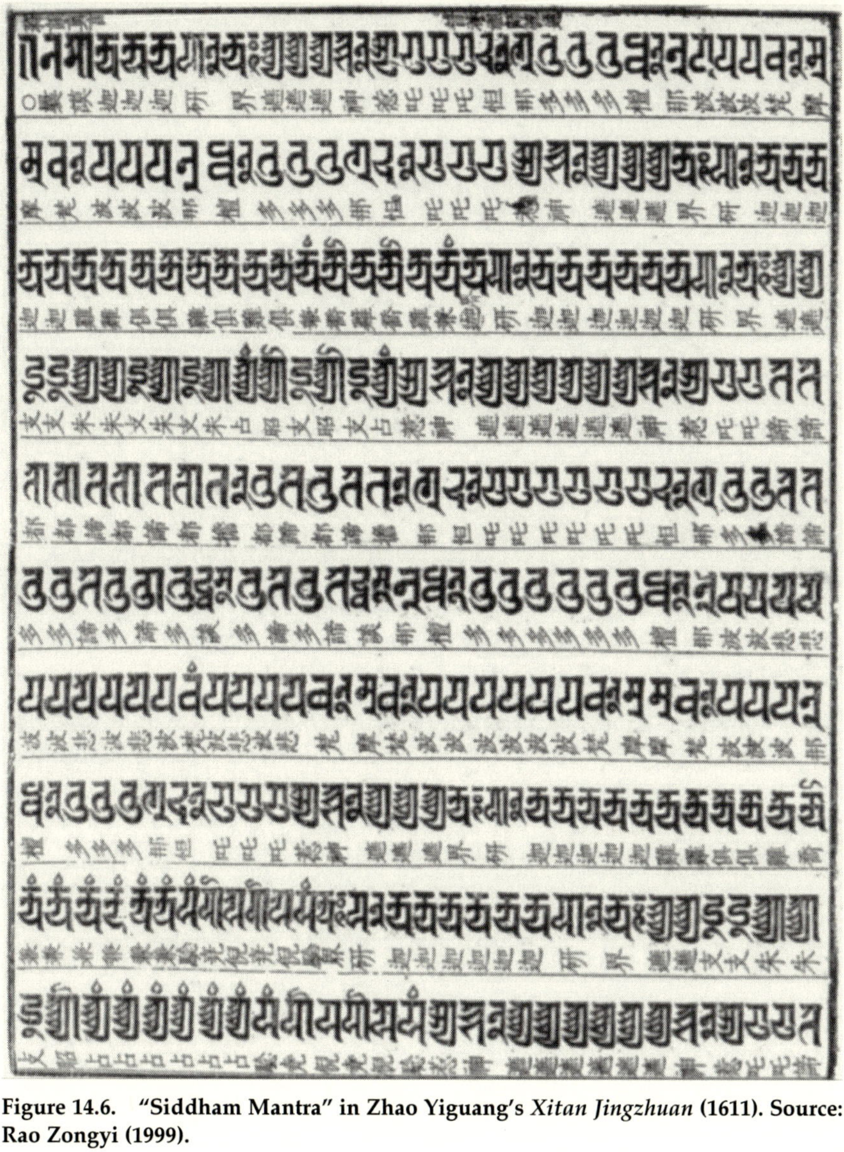

Figure 14.6. "Siddham Mantra" in Zhao Yiguang's *Xitan Jingzhuan* (1611). Source: Rao Zongyi (1999).

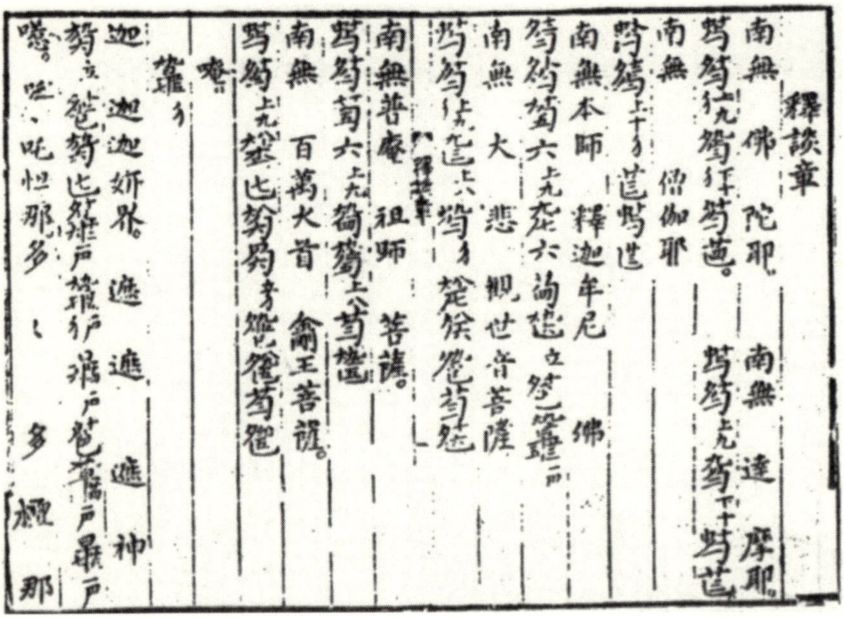

Figure 14.7. Guqin tablature "Xitan zhang" in Sanjiao tongsheng (1592). Source: *Qinxuejicheng* 6.110.

The ways these mantras were adopted by the East Asian Buddhists are of methodological interest as the absorption of sinicized Sanskrit mantras into Chinese Buddhism points to the larger questions of how the sinicization of Buddhism might have taken place and what the driving mechanisms and parameters could have been.

ABBREVIATIONS

PAZ	Pu'anzhou 普庵咒
HYDCD	Hanyu dacidian 漢語大辭典
J	Jiaqingzang 嘉慶藏
T	Taishō shinshū daizōkyō 大正新脩大蔵経
XTZ	Xitanzhang 悉曇章

NOTES

1. Staal 1986: 8.
2. For an overview of the Sanskrit writing systems, see Diringer 1948: 301ff, Salomon 1998: 7–41.

3. By Indic languages I mean here not only Sanskrit, but also other Prakrits such as Pāli and Gandhārī, which preceded Sanskrit as far as the textual history of Buddhist texts are concerned, as well as other Central Asian languages (*huyu* 胡語) spoken along the Silk Road. For discussions on the Buddha's language policy, in particular, his admonition against his words being turned into *chandas* ("metrical Sanskrit") (*Cullavagga* V.33.1), and the subsequent rise of Sanskrit as a lingua franca within the Buddhist community, see Lamotte 1988: 646; Ji 1982: 402–438, 1985: 74.

4. For a general discussion on the influence Sanskrit phonetics and alphabet have on various indigenous cultures and languages across Asia, see Staal 2006.

5. Staal 1986: 23–4, Salomon 1998: 8.

6. The origin of Brahmī had been widely debated by scholars. Most scholars favor Bühler's view that the Brahmī script was derived from a semitic prototype of which Aramaic is one of the most likely candidates (Salomon 1998: 13, 29–30). In terms of epigraphical evidences, Brahmī first appeared in Mauryan inscriptions of the third century BCE.

7. *Taittirīya-prātiśākhya* 1: 1–14; 2: 4–39 (Whitney ed.). Another *akṣarasamāmnāya* which is less well known but nonetheless important for the Indian linguists is the so-called *Śivasūtra* attributed to Pāṇini. According to some, the economical construction of this *akṣarasamāmnāya* reflects Pāṇinian grammar (Staal 1962, Kiparsky 1991).

8. The "Florence Fragment," a palm leaf folio with Sanskrit alphabet written in old Sinhalese script on both sides, dated possibly no earlier than the twelfth century on orthographical ground showed both parts of the *varṇamālā* as well as the *ṣoḍaśākṣarī* (permutation of a consonant with sixteen vowels including the four liquids). Unlike other folios in the same batch known as "Nahman II," the characters are unusually large and somewhat clumsily written. They were furthermore incised without charcoal, which suggests the fragment likely to be an exercise by a novice. Other exercises such as the *dvādaśākṣarī* (permutation with twelve vowels) and *varṇaparicaya* (or *phalaka* according to Bühler, compound consonants with vocalic combinations) are practiced for various middle Indian dialects in India (Bühler 1898: 29–30, 120–1; Chaudhuri 2011: 60).

9. Bühler 1898: 31–2. The pillar bases of the cloistered walk in Mahābodhi Gaya were thought to have been marked with eleven vowels followed by consonantal syllables starting with *ka*. Also the *ṣoḍaśākṣarī* or letters in permutation with sixteen vowels was known to have been used for the traditional pagination of palm leave folios (Godakumbura 1980: L–LI).

10. The word "*dhāraṇī*," from $\sqrt{}$*dhṛ* ("to hold"), has the connotation of memory in the sense of mental retention, hence mnemonic.

11. While the opposite is conceivable as suggested by some scholars, the idea of an alphabet created for an unattested collection of Buddhist terms is problematic (Salomon 1990: 256).

12. The Sanskrit phrasing is somewhat clumsy as typical of the *Prajñāpāramitā*. My rendering follows largely Kumārajīva's translation T(223)8.256a, supplemented by Conze's English translation (1975: 160). Salomon translated *mukha* as "head," taken with the following genitive, which seems to me unlikely since

mukha was highlighted earlier as a technique (*dhāraṇīmukham, akṣaramukham*), synonymous with *akṣarapraveśa* (Salomon 1990: 256).

13. *Pañcaviṃśatisāhasrikā Prajñāpāramitā*. Dutt 1934, 212; Kimura 1986–2009, 1–2: 85–7.

14. The *Arapacana* of forty-two letters, known as *dvācatvāriṃśad-akṣarāṇi*, containing compound consonants such as *stha, śva, sta, jña, sma, hva* not found in the *varṇamālā*, is found in some of the earliest Mahāyāna sūtras such as the *Lalitavistara* and the *Pañcaviṃśati-prajnāpāramitā*. Epigraphical evidences suggest that this alphabet with unusual order had close connection with the Gandhārī language and the Kharoṣṭhī script (Brough 1977: 94, Salomon 1990: 256).

15. While I make no attempt to date Indic Mahāyāna texts based on their Chinese translation, the Gandhārī connection of the *Arapacana* (second century CE) corroborates with the early dating of the Chinese translations of the *Arapacana* (third century CE). See §3.1.

16. List of works containing such use of the alphabet (Tokunaga 1990: 62): Dakṣiṇamūrti's *Uddharaṇa-Kośa* (chap. 5), the *Rāmapūrvatāpanīya Upaniṣad*, the *Agni Purāṇa* (chap. 348) and Bhāskararāya's *Varivasyā Rahasya*.

17. *Jayākhyasaṃhitā* 6.40cd–42cd. From Tokunaga 1990: 27.

18. Two types of such deities are distinguished in the Śaiva tradition: *Śabdaraśibhairava* and *Mālinī*. Vasudeva 2007: 517–519, 536.

19. Zhou 2002:183–185.

20. *Xianshu pin* 現書品. T(186)3.498c. Curiously this text "translated" the *Arapacana* alphabet instead of transcribing it phonetically.

21. *Guan pin* 觀品. T(222)8.195c–196b.

22. *Rulaixing pin* 如來性品. T(374)12.412c–414b.

23. *Zimu pin* 字母品. T(468)14.498a–b.

24. Thus Kumārajīva in his *Dazhidulun* 大智度論 suggested that the forty-two letters of *Arapacana* were the basis of all (Sanskrit) words, without any mention of the *varṇamālā*. T(1509)408b. Centuries later, in one of Kūkai 空海's tantric commentaries, the idea that the *Arapacana* was derived from the *varṇamālā* was mentioned. T(2425)77.362b. How widespread this belief was is however unknown.

25. Thus in various Chinese Buddhist exegeses, *shengming* 聲明 (*Śabdavigyā*, Sanskrit phonetics) was often described as *xiaowu* 小悟 or "minor enlightenment."

26. The *Arapacana* is also known in China as *huayan zimu* 華嚴字母 or "Avataṃsaka alphabet." Its popularity is likely due to the popularity of the *Avataṃsaka* itself in China. The text described the *Arapacana* as a "Dharma gate of Wise Letter," *zhizi famen* 智字法門, through which one may enter into the immeasurable gate of *Prajñāpāramitā*. T(293)10.805a. For discussion of the *Arapacana* liturgical tradition, see Zhou 2004: 33–53. Ironically, there is no known liturgical tradition developed around the *varṇamālā*, except the *Pu'an zhou* or the Mantra of Master Pu'an (§3.3).

27. The earliest Chinese reference to a text with the term "*xitan*" 悉曇 (transcription of *siddham* or *siddhām*) included in its title is found in Dao'an 道安's "Catalogue of texts of unknown translators" 失譯經録 (late fourth century CE), where a certain text titled *Xitanmu* 悉曇慕 (presumably another variant transcription of *siddham*) of two fascicles was mentioned. T(2145)55.18b. Fei Zhangfang 費長房 in his *Lidai Sanbao ji* 歷代三寶記 also mentioned a text of the same title but of

only one fascicle, included under the category of "Catalogue of Hīnayāna sūtras of unknown translators" 小乘修多羅失譯録. T(2034)49.118b. For discussion on the transmission of the XTZ in China, see Rao 1993: 143, Zhou 2000: 90, 94–95. As for the Indian sources for *Siddham[ātṛkā]* as a script, see Salomon 1990: 39.

28. *Xiaoxue* 小學 in Han Periods refers to the study of Chinese characters as children's first subject of study. Later on from Sui onward it covered also lexical and phonetic studies (HYDCD).

29. According to Takakusu's counting, only 6613 *akṣara*-s, while the text itself (Japanese version) says 16550 (Takakusu 1896: 171 fn.3). The *śloka* is not to be taken literally to mean "verse," but rather just a convenient unit of thirty-two *akṣara*-s as it was explained in the text (10000 / 32 ≃ 300).

30. Cf. English translation and annotations by Takakusu 1896: 169–172. Takakusu was among the first modern scholars to identify Yijing's description with the XTZ extant in Japan.

31. T(2125)54.228b.

32. Although there are various Dunhuang fragments bearing titles of XTZ, the transmission of XTZ appears to have ceased in Mainland China after Tang. The tradition continued in Japan where it was further developed alongside with the phonetic studies of the Japanese language (Tan 2009: 141).

33. T(2132)54.1186. The manuscript was brought by Kūkai from China to Japan in 806 CE and widely circulated in Japan.

34. Siddhm (Sanskrit) writing has a wide application in various tantric rituals in Japan. For samples of the XTZ extant in Japan, see *Bonji* I: 344–7, also.

35. S1344《通韻》：或作吳地而唱經，復似婆羅門而誦咒. Despite the somewhat problematic attribution of the text to Kumārajīva, the liturgical tradition of XTZ is well attested by a number of Dunhuang fragments. *See Rao 1990: 46*; Hirata 1994: 53; Wang 1992: 71–75; Mak 2013.

36. T(2425)77.362b.

37. T(2425)77.362a. The edition includes the vowels "*a ā*" before *ka kha ga gha ṅa*.

38. Some preliminary attempts to examine the source of the mantra have been made (Picard 1990 and the unpublished thesis of Chen Songxian 陈松宪). For a discussion on the textual history of the mantra, see Mak 2013.

39. The earliest biography of Pu'an extant is found in the *Fozu tongji* 佛祖統紀 of Zhipan 志槃. T49(2035)435c. Similar account with greater detail is found in the *Fozu lidai tongzai* 佛祖歷代通載 of Nianchang 念常. T49(2036)691b. While Pu'an was associated with supernatural experiences with the *Avataṃsaka*, magical healing and possibly writing as well in one biographical account (T(2036)49.691b), there has not been any explicit mention of the mantra in any of the biographies.

40. J19.B44.162b. Apparently, there was at least one attempt to remove this mantra from the canonic liturgy (J32.B277.565a), which was apparently a failed one as the mantra survived in the canon extant.

41. It is remarkable that Zhao Yiguang and Van Gulik, both scholars of Sanskrit phonetics and authors of works on Siddham, treated the PAZ as an independent creation. François Picard, a French musicologist, was the first modern scholar to point out the connection between the two (Picard 1990, 1991).

42. The Chinese transcription of the fourth *akṣara* of each series has a characteristic nasal ending which suggests a curious connection with Dharmarakṣa's trans-

lation of the *Mahāparinirvāṇa* (T374) (Mak 2013). The influence Dharmarakṣa's translation had on the Chinese dissemination of "Siddham studies" has been noted (Rao 1993: 146, 208).

43. Most remarkably, an adhoc sequence of *pa-ta-ṭa-ca-ka* 波多吒遮迦 toward the end of the PAZ, which represents the retrograde of the unvoiced, unaspirated series.

44. In the second motif (table 14.3), the structure appears to be deliberately altered and its form can only be meaningfully explained when juxtaposed against the XTZ. The loss of distinction between long and short vowel as well as the overall corruption suggest that the purpose of the PAZ was not to inform the listeners about Sanskrit phonetics. Rather, the PAZ was a work inspired by the XTZ and artistically manipulated to appeal to the Chinese audience who neither knew much nor were concerned with the Sanskrit linguistic science. Beside the audible structure, the concern for a visible structure is demonstrated by the acrostic arrangement of the PAZ in its canonic version (figure 14.5), resembling the traditional Chinese *huiwen* 回文.

45. Rao 1999.

46. This is not surprising since the efficacy of the sinicized mantra, as practiced by Chinese Buddhists, has been widely attested up to the modern time. See for example popular lay Buddhist master Nan Huaijin's description of the "efficacy" of the PAZ under the chapter titled "Miraculous effects of sound on the body" (Nan 1993: 301).

47. The musical version of the PAZ was dated roughly the same time as the earliest canonical version extant. In Qu Ruji's 瞿汝稷 *Zhiyuelu* 《指月錄》 (1595), the musical transformation of the mantra was described (肅之呪世間盛傳，至被管弦). There was also a curious anecdote noted by a Jesuit missionary about Emperor Kangxi playing the PAZ, allegedly a "Taoist work," on a harpsichord (Melvin and Cai 2004: 65–66). The mantra, both in its canonical and musical versions, has been a favorite subject-matter for novelists from late Ming up to modern time, starting from Luo Maodeng 羅懋登's *Sanbao taijian xiyang ji* 《三寶太監西洋記》 (1597) and Wu Chichang 吳熾昌's *Kechuang Xianhua* 《客窗閑話》 (1839) to contemporary works such as *Jin Yong* 金庸's *Xiao'ao jianghu* 《笑傲江湖》 (1967–1969).

48. The latest example would be the so-called "Sanskrit songs" of the Mainland Chinese singer Sa Dingding 薩頂頂 who has allegedly self-learned Sanskrit and Tibetan. Her work *Wanwusheng* 萬物生, though utterly incomprehensible in any known language of humankind, is in fact a sinicization of the Tibetan version of the *Vajrasattvamantra* or the so-called hundred-syllable mantra, which was originally composed in Sanskrit.

BIBLIOGRAPHY

Bonji kichō shiryō shūsei 『梵字貴重資料集成』. 1980. Two Vols. Tōkyō: Tōkyō Bijutsu 東京 美術.

Brough, John. 1977. "The 'arapacana' Syllabary in the Old 'Lalita-vistara.'" *Bulletin of the School of Oriental and African Studies* 40 (1): 85–95.

Bühler, Georg. 1898. *On the Origin of the Indian Brahma Alphabet.* Strassburg: K. J. Trübner.

Chaudhuri, Saroj Kumar. 2011. *Sanskrit in China and Japan.* Delhi: Aditya Prakashan.

Conze, Edward. 1975. The Large Sutra on Perfect Wisdom, with the Divisions of the Abhisamayalankara. Berkeley: University of California Press.

Diringer, David. 1948. *The Alphabet: A Key to the History of Mankind.* New York: Philosophical Library.

Dutt, Nalinaksha. 1934. *Pañcaviṃśatisāhasrikāprajñāpāramitāsūtra.* London: Luzac.

Godakumbura, 1980. *Catalogue of Ceylonese Manuscripts.* Edited by Kaare Grønbech. Catalogue of Oriental Manuscripts, Xylographs etc. in Danish Collections. Vol.1. Copenhagen: The Royal Library.

Hirata Shōji 平田昌司. 1994. 『謝靈運「十四音訓叙」の系譜』. In *Chūkoku goshi-no shiryō to hōhō* 『中國語史の資料と方法』. 京都: 京都大學人文科學研究所.

Ji Xianlin 季羡林.1982. *Yindu gudai yuyan lunji* 《印度古代语言论集》. Beijing: Zhongguo kexue chubanshe 中国科学出版社.

——. 1985. *Yuanshi fojiao de yuyan wenti* 《原始佛教的语言问题》. Beijing: Zhongguo kexue chubanshe.

Kimura, Takayasu. 1986–2009. *Pañcaviṃśatisāhasrikā Prajāpāramitā I-VIII.* Tokyo: Sankibo Busshorin.

Kiparsky, Paul. 1991. "Economy and the Construction of the Śivasūtras." In *Pāṇinian studies: Professor S. D. Joshi felicitation volume.* Michigan: Center for South and Southeast Asian Studies, University of Michigan.

Lamotte, Étienne. Webb-Boin, Sara (trans.). 1988. *History of Indian Buddhism: From the Origins to the Saka Era.* Louvain-la-Neuve: Université catholique de Louvain, Institut Orientaliste.

Lin Guangming 林光明. 2004. *Lanzhati fanzi rumen* 蘭扎體梵字入門. Taipei: Jiafeng 嘉豐.

Mabuchi Kazuo 馬渕和夫. 2006. *Shittanshō-no kenkyū* 『悉曇章の研究. Tōkyō: Bensei Shuppan 勉誠出版.

Mak, Bill M. 麦文彪. 2013. "Bukkyo-mantora-no ichirei—*Pu'anzhou*-ni okeru shittan jibo-ni tsuite." 「仏教マントラの中国化の一例—普庵咒における悉曇字母について」. *Tōhō gakuhō*『東方學報』京都88冊.

Melvin, Sheila and Jindong Cai. 2004. *Rhapsody in Red.* New York: Algora.

Nan Huaijin 南懷瑾. 1993. *Daojia mizong yu dongfang shenmixue* 《道家密宗與東方神秘學》. 1995 reprint. 11th edition. Taipei: Lao gu wen hua 老古文化.

Picard, François. 1990. L'harmonie universelle : Les avatars du syllabaire sanskrit dans la musique bouddhique chinoise. Thèse de doctorat, Université Paris I.

——. 1991. "Pu'an Zhou: The Musical Avatars of a Buddhist Spell." *Chime. Journal of the European Foundation for Chinese Music Research* 3: 32–37.

Rao Zongyi [Jao Tsong-yi] 饒宗頤. 1990. *Zhongyin wenhua guanxishi lunji—yuwenpian.* Hong Kong *shitanxue xulun*: 《中印文化關係史論集 語文篇 –悉曇學緒論》. Chinese University Zhongguo wenhua yanjiusuo 香港中文大學中國文化研究所.

——. 1993. *Fanxueji* 《梵學集》. Shanghai: Shanghai guji chubanshe 上海古籍出版社.

——. 1999. *Zhao Yiguang ji qi xitanjingzhuan* 《趙宧光及其〈悉曇經傳〉》. Taipei: Xinwenfeng 新文豐.

Salomon, Richard. 1990. "New Evidence for a Gāndhārī Origin of the arapacana Syllabary." *Journal of the American Oriental Society* 110 (2): 255–273.

———. 1998. *Indian Epigraphy: A Guide to the Study of Inscriptions in Sanskrit, Prakrit, and the other Indo-Aryan Languages*. New York: Oxford University Press.

Staal, Fritz. 1962. "A Method of Linguistic Description: the Order of Consonants according to Pāṇini." *Language* 38:1–10.

———. 1986. *The Fidelity of Oral Tradition and the Origins of Science*. Amsterdam: North-Holland.

———. 2006. "The Sound Pattern of Sanskrit in Asia: An Unheralded Contribution by Indian Brahmans and Buddhist Monks." *Sanskrit Studies Central Journal, Journal of the Sanskrit Studies Centre, Silpakorn University* 2:193–200.

Takakusu, Junjirō. 1896. *A Record of the Buddhist Religion as practised in India and the Malay Archipelago*. Oxford: Clarendon Press.

Tan Shibao 譚世保. 2009. *Shitanxue yu hanzi yinxue xinlun* 悉曇學與漢字音學新論. Beijing: Zhonghua shuju 中華書局.

Tokunaga, Muneo. 1990. "Names of the Alphabets in some Pañcarātra Saṁhitās." In *Ajia-ni okeru bunkakōryū-to gengōsesshoku-no kenkyū* アジアにおける文化交流と言語接触 の研究. 21–64.

Van Gulik, R. H. 1956. *Siddham*. Nagpur: International Academy of Indian Culture.

Vasudeva, Somadeva. 2007. "Synaesthetic Iconography: 1. the Nādiphāntakrama." In *Mélanges tantriques à la mémoire d'Hélène Brunner. Tantric studies in memory of Helene Brunner*. Pondicherry: Institut français de Pondicherry. 517–550.

Wang Bangwei 王邦維. 1992. "鳩摩羅什《通韻》考疑暨敦煌寫本S.1344號相關問題." *Zhongguo wenhua*《中國文化》7: 71–75.

———. 1999. "四十二字門考論." *Zhonghua foxue xuebao*《中華佛學學報》12: 17–24.

Whitney, William Dwight. 1871. The Tâittirîya-Prâtiçâkhya, with its Commentary, the Tribhâshyaratna: Text, Translation, and Notes. New Haven: American Oriental Society.

Zha Fuxi 查阜西 (ed.). *Qinxuejicheng* 《琴學集成》. 1963–1982. Vols. 1–16. Beijing: Zhonghua shuju.

Zhou Guangrong 周广荣. 2000. "Tangdai xitanzhang chuanben jishu" 唐代〈悉昙章〉传本辑 述. *Wenxian jikan*《文献季刊》4: 90–100.

———. 2002. "Xitanxue xulun." 悉曇學敘論. *Pumen xuebao*《普門學報》9:183–212.

———. 2004. *Fanyu xitanzhang zai zhongguo de chuanbo yu yingxiang*《梵语〈悉昙章〉在 中国的传播与影响》. Beijing: Zongjiao wenhua chubanshe 宗教文化出版社.

15

Mixed up on "Matching Terms" (*geyi*)

Confusions in Cross-Cultural Translation

John M. Thompson

Many aspects of the transmission of Buddhism to China are unclear, particularly during the "Period of Disunity" (220–581 CE), when "China" was a patchwork of small states rather than a united political entity.[1] One of the most vexing topics in this area is *geyi* 格義 (Jpn *kakugi*), a technique for rendering Buddhist terms into Chinese. While obviously a means for bridging Indian and Chinese cultures, much about *geyi* remains mysterious. Scholars agree that *geyi* enjoyed a brief heyday only to be abandoned as the Chinese became more familiar with Buddhism, but beyond that there is no consensus. Thus *geyi* exemplifies the problems that arise when interpreting across cultural, historical and religious boundaries.

In this chapter I try to bring some clarity to the subject of *geyi*, starting with translation problems facing Buddhists in China during the early middle ages. After this I turn to *geyi* itself, focusing on what the term means, what modern scholars claim it is, and what early Chinese Buddhists say about it. Not surprisingly, I have found that *geyi* is difficult to define, that modern scholars are divided over what it entailed, and that early Buddhist historians are unclear as well. By highlighting such disagreements, we can see how differing assumptions hinder our understanding of an important issue in Chinese Buddhism. Twentieth-century historian of Chinese thought Tang Yongtang (1951, 276–286) describes *geyi* as a "method of synthesizing Indian Buddhism and Chinese Philosophy," implying that *geyi* aims at fusing two distinct worldviews. In light of this, I suggest that Hans-Georg Gadamer's work in hermeneutics can help us more fully appreciate *geyi*'s role in the transmission of Buddhism to China.

ORIGINS OF *GEYI*

Since Buddhism includes a multitude of technical terms (e.g., *dharma, skandha*), translation is a perennial problem. Of course translation has always been permitted in Buddhism and in early sources Śakyamuni authorizes his disciples to teach the Dharma in whatever language was necessary. Translation probably posed few problems while Buddhism remained within the greater Brahmanic cultural sphere (modern India, Pakistan, Nepal, etc.) or as it expanded into Central Asia, an area heavily influenced by Indic culture. However, translation was a major obstacle when Buddhism entered China, since most Buddhist texts (both oral and written) were in Indic languages whose structures differ radically from Chinese.[2]

Buddhist missionaries such as An Shigao 安世高 (second century CE) and Zhi Qian 支謙 (third century), as well as their Chinese converts, devised various ways of dealing with these linguistic problems: paraphrasing, literal renderings, even phonetic transliteration.[3] At the same time some early Chinese converts composed apologetic treatises (e.g., the *Mouzi* 牟子) to counter opposition to their new faith (Dutt 1966, 135–136).[4] *Geyi* first appears during this time as a method to explain Buddhism in native Chinese categories. By the late fourth century, however, scholar-monks such as Daoan 道安 (312–385) were critically re-appraising such practices, thereby anticipating the more mature understanding of Buddhism which developed in the fifth and sixth centuries (Link 1958, 1–2; Robinson 1967, 77; Zücker 1959, 203).

EXAMINING *GEYI*

Three approaches immediately suggested themselves in my examination of *geyi*: terminological, critical, and sinological. The terminological approach focuses on the term *geyi* and seeks to derive an adequate translation and/or definition. The critical method involves analyzing the works of scholars of Buddhism and Chinese traditions who discuss *geyi*. The sinological approach involves investigating Chinese sources. I chose to combine all three approaches to shed as much light as possible on this vexing term.

Problems of definition

An obvious first step in investigating *geyi* is to come up with a working definition, yet this is difficult since various scholars of Buddhism do not agree. Paul Demieville (1973), for example, defines *geyi* as "analyzing the meaning" [lit. "*scruter le sens*"], while Arthur Wright (1959, 37) calls it "matching concepts." Tang (1951, 278), by contrast, defines *geyi* as "(the method or scheme of) matching ideas (or terms) or 'equation of ideas.'" Kenneth Ch'en (1964, 68) terms *geyi* "the method of matching the meaning," while Charles Prebish (1993, 161) defines it as "stretch the meaning," and "matching concepts." All of these definitions point to some sort of "matching" or "equating" between Buddhism and Chinese traditions but beyond this observation, they are not very informative. Indeed, they may contradict each other in certain respects since it is unclear whether we are dealing with "meanings" (a matter of semantics), "concepts" (which could involve cognitive issues), actual terms (linguistics), or all three.

Chinese (and Japanese) dictionaries offer little help here. The term "*geyi*" is a compound of two separate words: *ge* 格, "to reach, to come or go to, to investigate" as well as "rule, pattern," and *yi* 義, "meaning, purport" or "morality, righteousness." None of the generalized dictionaries I consulted (Matthews, Giles, Kenkyūsha, Nelson, Spahn, and Hadamitzky, the *Zhongwen Dacidian* 中文大辭典), though, have entries for "*geyi*." Buddhist dictionaries are not much help either. Of the seven that I consulted (Daito Shuppanshu's *Japanese-English Buddhist Dictionary*, Hisao Ingaki's *Dictionary of Japanese Buddhist Terms*, Charles Scribner's Sons *A Dictionary of Buddhism*, the Nichiren Shoshū International Center's *A Dictionary of Buddhist Terms and Concepts*, W. E. Soothill's *A Dictionary of Chinese Buddhist Terms*, Charles Prebish's *Historical Dictionary of Buddhism*, and the *Sōgō Bukkyō Daijiten* 總合佛教大辭典) only two (Prebish and the *Sōgō Bukkyō*) have anything on "*geyi*." Both entries describe *geyi* as a means of conveying Buddhist meaning through Daoist terms employed in the early phases of Buddhism's entry into China, and that eventually Chinese Buddhists became aware of *geyi*'s shortcomings.

Scholarly views of *geyi*

While the terminological approach provides a basic sense of *geyi* and ties it to a specific time period it gives few details. Another approach is to examine scholarship on *geyi* itself. Unfortunately, most scholars of Chinese Buddhism disagree over what *geyi* is.

By and large, scholarly views of *geyi* can be sorted into two general camps. The most prevalent view holds that *geyi* involves selecting

Chinese (usually Daoist or "Neo-Daoist"[5]) terms as equivalents for Sanskrit terms. For example, the Sanskrit *śūnyatā* ("emptiness") would be rendered as *wu* 無 ("non-being," the primordial state of the cosmos). Accordingly, this "majority view" presupposes that practitioners of *geyi* assumed structural parallels between Buddhism and Daoism. Paul Demieville (1973, 26), Feng Youlan (Fung Yu-lan 1953, 241–243), Arthur Link (1958, 1–2), Wing-tsit Chan (1963, 336), Lao Siguang (1971, 251), Daisaku Ikeda (1986, 57–59), Zenryū Tsukamoto (1985, vol. 1, 299ff), Whalen Lai (1979), W. Pachow (1980, 132, 150), John Snelling (1991, 126), Ito Takatoshi (1992, 57), and Julia Ching (1993, 127) all hold the "majority view" to varying degrees. Kenneth Ch'en (1964, 68) puts the "majority view" best when he writes:

> Since the Buddhists of this period [third through fourth centuries] were familiar with the external or Taoist literature, it is not surprising to find them having recourse to Taoist texts for words and phrases to use in their translations. This practice of the Buddhists of searching through Chinese literature, mainly Taoist, for expressions to explain their own ideas is known as *ke-yi* [sic], or the method of matching the meaning. This method was used especially by the translators of the *Prajñā* sutras for the purpose of making Buddhist thought more easily understood by the Chinese.

Most proponents of the "majority view" maintain that *geyi* was abandoned as Buddhism grew and more texts were translated but disagree over the figures associated with the practice. Ch'en (1964, 69) notes the scholar-monks Zhu Faya 竺法雅 and Kang Falang 康法朗 (both fourth century) but cites Huiyuan 慧遠 (334–416), the most famous Chinese monk of the era, as *geyi*'s foremost practitioner, while Snelling (1991, 126) cites Sengzhao 僧肇 (374–414), author of several treatises, as his primary example. Proponents of the "majority view" also differ over who is responsible for *geyi*'s abandonment, with some naming Daoan and others singling out Kumārajīva (344–413), who translated Mahāyāna texts during the Eastern Jin dynasty (317–420).[6]

According to the "majority view," then, *geyi* has several defining features:

1. It is a technique devised by Chinese to express the Dharma in Chinese cultural categories.
2. It involves using *Daoist* terminology to explain Buddhist concepts.
3. It is especially associated with translators and propagators of Mahāyāna (*Prajñā*) texts.
4. It should be viewed in a negative fashion (most scholars espousing the "majority view" regard *geyi* as distorting Buddhist ideas).
5. Chinese Buddhists abandoned it when they realized its limitations.

The second or "minority view" of *geyi* is more complex. In this view, *geyi* involved pairing numbered technical terms (*shi shu* 事數) from Buddhist texts (e.g., the five *skandhas*, the twelve *āyatanas*) (Liu 1976, 130) with more familiar numbered categories from Chinese texts. Thus, the four *mahābhūtas* ("great elements") might be paired with the *wu xing* 五行 ("five phases"), or the five precepts would be paired with the *wu chang* 五常 ("five constant Confucian virtues"). Such pairing is common in Han-era writings, as, for example, in the *Chunqiu fanlun* 春秋繁露 ("Luxuriant Gems of the Spring and Autumn Annals") by the great synthesizer Dong Zhongshu 董仲舒 (179–104 BCE).[7] In the "minority view," *geyi* is just an instance where scholar-monks employed correlations to help their Chinese audience comprehend the numerical lists found in Buddhist texts.

Only a few scholars (see Tang 1951, 276–286; Wright 1959, 37–38; Zurcher 1959, 12, 184, 187) hold the "minority view," and even they disagree over how long *geyi* was used. Wright (1959, 37), for instance, believes that *geyi* enjoyed its heyday during the second and third centuries while both Tang (1951, 279–280) and Zurcher (1959, 184) confine *geyi* to the fourth century. According to the "minority view," *geyi* was abandoned because it was "contrary to reason,"[8] as the resulting pairings were based on numerical correspondence rather than substantive equivalences.

Summing up, then, according to scholars who uphold the "minority view":

1. *Geyi* was a technique based on specific, well-known precedents in Chinese scholarship.
2. It was a rather limited technique addressed to an elite, learned audience.
3. It functioned as an aid in explaining certain very technical terms in Buddhist texts, with an aim towards demonstrating how Buddhism harmonized with Chinese thought.
4. While *geyi* involves Chinese sources that we might classify as Daoist, it also draws on Confucian sources, or even sources that do not fit neatly into such categories.
5. It was based on very superficial resemblances, and was soon recognized as such.

Interestingly, Sukmar Dutt espouses a view of *geyi* midway between the two previous views. Dutt notes that Chinese translations regularly used both Confucian and Daoist terms for Buddhist concepts, but *geyi* was a systematic technique for doing so. According to Dutt (1966, 134–135), *geyi* was a matching of Buddhist concepts with Confucian and Daoist ones (basically the "majority view") but in particular involved collating categories from Chinese texts alongside of seemingly analogous Buddhist doctrinal categories (the "minority view").

Geyi as described in Buddhist texts

The critical approach to *geyi* has yielded some information, revealing two general ideas of *geyi*, each of which has been espoused by noted scholars. Is there a way of deciding between these alternatives? One solution is to turn to Chinese Buddhist sources but this approach is hampered by the fact that the term *geyi* rarely appears in Buddhist texts. I have found only six passages in the *Taishō shinshū daizōkyō* 大正新修大藏經 version of the Buddhist canon where the term occurs: three times in the *Gaosengzhuan* 高僧傳 ("Biographies of Eminent Monks"), twice in the *Chu sanzangji ji* 出三藏記集 ("Collected records on the production of the *Tripiṭaka*"), and once in the *Zhongguan lunsu* 中觀論疏 ("Commentary on the Middle Treatise").[9] Since these passages are short I translate them in full.

1. Passages from the *Gaosengzhuan*
   a. From the biography of Zhu Faya:
   At that time Faya's followers were versed in worldly literature but were not yet skilled in Buddhist principles. [Fa]ya, then, along with Kang Falang and a few others, took the *shi shu* from the *sūtras* and paired them with the "outer books." They thus made examples to foster explanations, calling it "*geyi*." At this point Pifou, Tanxiang and others also used *geyi* to teach their disciples (T.2059: 347a19–22).
   b. From the biography of the scholar-monk Sengguang 僧光:
   [Dao]an said, "The old method of *geyi* widely diverges from Buddhist principles." [Seng] Guang replied, "For the time being we should aim at easy analysis. How can we judge the rightness or wrongness of former masters?" [Dao]an answered, "In proclaiming the principles and teachings we should make them satisfactory. In striving to [beat the] drum of Dharma, who [really] goes first or follows after?" (T.2059: 355a25–27)
   c. From Kumārajīva's biography:
   Of itself the Great Dharma began to be carried East during the Han's brilliance. Down through the Wei and Jin dynasties *sūtras* and *śāstras* gradually increased, and yet of monks who came from India, many regarded the literary [method] of *geyi* as obstructing [true understanding] (T.2059: 332a27–28).

2. Passages from the *Chu sanzangji ji*
   a. From the preface to the *Vimalakīrtinirdeśasūtra Commentary* by Sengrui 僧叡:
   At the close of the Han to the beginning of the Wei . . . the worthies who sought the essence of Buddhist ideas began to have fixed places to lecture. They expanded [their lectures] with *geyi* and distorted them with matching explanations (T.2145: 41a10–12).[10]
   b. From Sengrui's *Yuyilun* 喻義論 ("Treatise instructing on Rightness"):
   The wind of Wisdom has blown the Dharma's words eastward, causing the chants to flow. Even so, the *geyi* method of explaining distorted and perverted the fundamental [message]. [Thus,] the Six Houses are one-sided and do not approach the doctrine of the emptiness of the nature [of things] (T.2145: 59a1–3).[11]
3. Passage from the *Zhongguan lunsu*:[12]
   Master Seng says, "Before Kumārajīva caused the chants to flow, the *geyi* method of explaining distorted and perverted the fundamental [message]. [Thus,] the Six Houses are one-sided and do not approach the doctrine of the emptiness of the nature [of things]." Both the *Middle Treatise* and the *Hundred Treatise* had not yet reached here, and so there was no penetrating understanding [of the Dharma] (T.1824: 4c10–12).[13]

The six passages from the *Taishō* are sketchy when it comes to *geyi*, and in one case (the passage from the *Zhongguan lunsu*) merely quote an earlier source. Still, we can use them to pick out key features of geyi according to medieval Chinese Buddhists:

1. It (*geyi*) was associated with a certain group of monks in the fourth century.
2. It was used to provide examples for explaining Buddhist ideas to a Chinese audience.
3. It involved "outer books," that is, non-Buddhist texts.
4. It entailed some sort of "pairing" of Buddhist concepts with more familiar Chinese ones.
5. It specifically concerned certain "numerical categories" (*shi shu*) from the *sūtras*.
6. Over time it was recognized as hindering the grasp of Buddhist ideas and was abandoned.

It is difficult to construct a theory on *geyi* based on these points but it appears that the more sweeping claims by advocates of the "majority view" cannot be supported by Chinese sources.

Of course there are problems with using this approach to investigate *geyi*. While we might assume that the "original" texts would give us the best understanding we should note that all three of these sources were written after the time *geyi* flourished: Huijiao wrote the *Gaosengzhuan* in 530; Sengyou compiled the *Chu sangzangji ji* in 515–518; Jizang wrote his *Zhongguan lunsu* in the late sixth to early seventh century. Thus over a century had elapsed between *geyi*'s heyday and when our earliest sources were written—long enough for information to be forgotten and key sources to be lost.

Furthermore, there are conflicting notions among these Chinese sources. For instance, they differ on the time frame—did *geyi* begin to be used in the late Han and continue to the early Wei (first to sixth century), or was it only used during the fourth century? Moreover, not every Chinese source describes *geyi* as distorting. The description in Zhu Faya's biography presents *geyi* in neutral terms, while Sengrui's reference in his *Vimalakīrti* preface is, strictly speaking, neutral as well (he reserves his criticism for "matching explanations," which may be a separate practice).

ASSESSING THE VIEWS

All three approaches we have explored have revealed confusion about what *geyi* is but none of them have been fully satisfactory. Nonetheless, taken together they do shed some light on *geyi* and provide a basis for evaluating previous scholarly views. To begin with, the fact that only six passages in the *Taishō* even mention *geyi* argues against it being a widespread technique. Instead, it would seem to have been highly specialized. *Prima facie* this contradicts the "majority view," which considers *geyi* to be the widely practiced method of rendering Buddhist concepts in Daoist terms. Moreover, the six passages from the *Taishō* are so sketchy that any full theory of *geyi* will have to draw on other evidence. Going further, the Chinese sources also speak of *geyi* as a method of explaining specific sorts of passages from the *sūtras* for the benefit of people unfamiliar with Buddhism but none of them speak of it as a method for translating.

The Chinese sources are unclear on the exact time when *geyi* flourished but in some cases do associate the practice with specific monks: Zhu Faya (who may have devised the method), Kang Falang, Pifou, Tanxiang, Daoan, Sengguang, and Sengrui. What's more interesting is that all of these men spent most of their careers in the same geographic region and were connected by lineage. Zhu Faya, Kang Falang, and Daoan were disciples of Fotudeng 佛圖登 (d. 349), a Central Asian missionary whose legendary occult powers led to his becoming "court chaplain" during the Later Zhao dynasty.[14] Sengrui was Daoan's disciple, and Sengguang was either Daoan's disciple or a junior colleague. Pifou and Tanxiang most likely were junior colleagues of Zhu Faya and Kang Fanglang (Tang 1951, 277, 279, 284–285). None of these sources mention other Chinese monks of the period such as Huiyuan. Kumārajīva does figure briefly in one passage but to mark the boundary between the *geyi* and post-*geyi* periods.

We can glean another clue to help us understand *geyi* from the life and work of one of the monks listed above, Daoan, a crucial figure in the transmission of Buddhism to China.[15] He studied all Chinese Buddhist texts, compiling several catalogues, and spent his last years in Chang'an, heading up the official translation bureau. Daoan was renowned for his knowledge of Chinese learning, and probably had the best grasp of Buddhism among all the Chinese *saṅgha*. It is significant, then, that he is the only figure associated with *geyi* who specifically criticizes the technique as distorting Buddhism; if there were anyone familiar with issues in rendering the Dharma into Chinese, it would be Daoan. However, throughout his own work he regularly mixes Daoist and Buddhist terms and was even the nominal "founder" the *Benwu zong* 本無宗 ("School of Original Non-Being"), one of the six "*prajñā* schools" that explained Buddhist teachings through "Neo-Daoist" philosophical terminology. Once more, this casts doubt on the "majority view" that *geyi* involved translating Buddhist concepts through Daoist terms.

Another interesting point is that our sources do not specify what sorts of Chinese texts were used in *geyi*. Only in the passage from Zhu Faya's biography do we have reference to a category of non-Buddhist texts: "outer books" (*wai shu* 外書). By contrast two passages specify that the Buddhist texts used in *geyi* are "the *sūtras*" (*jing* 經) (T.2059: 347a19–22) or "the *sūtras* and *śāstras*" (*jing lun* 經論) (T.2059: 332a27–28). What texts qualify as *wai shu*? Certainly by the Tang dynasty *wai shu* includes *all* non-Buddhist writings,[16] a grouping that makes sense from a Buddhist standpoint. After all, the crucial distinction is between texts promulgating Dharma and those that do not; any differences within the "outer books" would be of little importance to Buddhist writers. In addition, Huijiao, author of the *Gaosengzhuan*, uses *wai* when referring to the Chinese learning that scholar-monks were versed in before becoming schooled in Buddhist thought (Tang 1951, 277). Perhaps *wai shu* is a generic label for *all* native Chinese writings, be they Confucian, Daoist, or whatever.

A final point to consider is whether learned *Buddhists* in fourth century China viewed Buddhism as a form of Daoism. While *geyi* was a technique for bridging Buddhist and native Chinese philosophies, the example of Daoan casts doubt on the notion that by his day Chinese Buddhists were so overwhelmed by apparent resemblances between Buddhism and Daoism as to assume deep similarity between them. This assumption of near identity was common during the Latter Han, when the *hua hu* 化胡 ("conversion of the barbarians") theory was in vogue,[17] but by the fourth century scholar-monks realized Buddhism was *not* a form of Daoism. Indeed, the whole premise behind the invention of *geyi* was that Buddhism was something different. To be sure both Feng Youlan and Ch'en quote two fifth century Chinese writers—Liu Qiu 劉虯 (438–495) and Fan Ye 范曄 (398–445)—who *do* seem to consider Buddhism and Daoism as essentially the same, but neither thinker was well versed in either tradition.[18] *Geyi*, then, was not a way for Chinese scholars to understand Buddhism so much as a way for learned Chinese Buddhists to lead non-specialists to a greater understanding.

Considering the evidence, then, the "majority view" of *geyi* cannot be correct while the "minority view" is plausible. According to the "minority view," *geyi* was a particular method of explaining certain aspects of Buddhism used by a small circle of Chinese scholar-monks in the fourth century. However, was *geyi* abandoned by the fifth century, as most scholars (be they proponents of the "majority" or "minority" views) maintain? It is difficult to answer this question definitively, but we do have the example of Guifeng Zongmi 圭峯宗密 (780–841), the Chan/Huayan Buddhist patriarch. Zongmi was also a scholar of native Chinese traditions, and was deeply imbued with the Confucian concern for educating people. In his *Yuanren lun* 原人論 ("Inquiry into the Origin of Humanity"), a primer on the origins of the human race, Zongmi consistently relies on the technique of *geyi* without actually naming it. Thus while Takatoshi overstates the case when he claims that all Chinese Buddhism is *geyi* (Takatoshi 1992, 57), his implying that Chinese scholars (or at least some of them) did not give up the practice is correct.

THE PURPOSE OF *GEYI* AND WHY IS IT IMPORTANT: A HERMENEUTICAL SUGGESTION

As we have seen, there are various issues surrounding *geyi* and it may be impossible to resolve them all. Nonetheless, based on our investigations both the "majority view" and the "minority view" espoused by modern scholars are problematic, although the latter makes more sense. However, I suggest approaching *geyi* from another disciplinary perspective that provides a better understanding and takes into account *geyi*'s larger historical-cultural setting.

To do so I begin with my own definition of *geyi*. My first clue for formulating a definition comes from another compound term from the same period, *gewu* 格五 (lit. "reach five"), a game much like checkers that was played by the gentry class (Liu 1976, 390). *Gewu* shares the same initial component with *geyi*: *ge*, meaning, "to reach." Using this information and drawing on the definitions provided by various Buddhist dictionaries as well as definitions from Ch'en ("the method of matching the meaning") and Tang ("the method or scheme of matching ideas or terms, or 'equation of ideas'"), I define *geyi* as "reaching for the meaning." Not only does this phrase reflect the literal meaning of the *geyi*'s component terms, it also captures the synthesizing dimension that seems so central to *geyi* itself. *Geyi*, whatever else it is, aims at bringing elements of different cultural systems (Chinese and Buddhist) together by reaching for some common meaning. *Geyi* is a striving for cross-cultural understanding, which places it within the field of Hermeneutics, the study of interpretation. In particular I think that the work of Hans-Georg Gadamer, perhaps the most influential theorist of interpretation, sheds a positive light on *geyi* and helps us see it as part of the process of Buddhism's sinification.

As he notes in *Truth and Method*, Gadamer (1994, 476, 483) views human understanding as rooted in a people's "historically effected consciousness" derived from their particular cultural heritage. Thus, understanding, for Gadamer, is the creative, historically situated human consciousness coming to know itself and its world. Rather than approaching any situation with a *tabula rasa*, we are informed by certain enabling prejudices by which we understand the world, and it is through these that we encounter that which is initially "other" and expand our worldview.

Gadamer, however, is not proposing mere recapitulation or blind obedience to authority. His ideal is a "hermeneutical understanding" which seeks to be transparent to its own basis and procedures. Following Edmund Husserl, Gadamer (1994, 302) considers our understanding to be like a delimited area of vision, a "horizon" or openness to the world. Tradition provides us access to the world and this includes the many other horizons available through other traditions; tradition allows "us" to interact with "others." Through such interactions we strive for a "fusion of horizons" in which our understanding joins with the other's and thus is transformed and expanded. This "fusion" can come about only through critical interplay in which we come to understand the "other" and achieve new awareness of our own prejudices (Gadamer 1994, 306). Hermeneutical understanding is therapeutic in that it helps us see our limits and go beyond them.

Distance is crucial in the fusion of horizons, for it is through the distance between a text and ourselves that the initial differences assert themselves. Only by carefully facing difference can we check our pre-set conceptions. "The important thing is to be aware of one's own bias, so that the text can present itself in all its otherness and thus assert its own truth against one's own fore-meanings" (Gadamer 1994, 269). By being aware of the text's initial "otherness" we can then approach it and engage with it. Note that this distance can be temporal, cultural or both, but it is always the starting point of any hermeneutic encounter and must be bridged if understanding is to occur. The text, after all, "calls to us" across the distance and it is this call to which our understanding responds (Gadamer 1994, 311). Yet Gadamer (1994, 297) seems to deny that we must bridge over an "abyss," for we are connected to the text through tradition. For Gadamer, to encounter a text is to already be in a relationship of understanding with it. Hermeneutic interpretation is a matter of deepening that relationship. We must come close yet allow the "other" to be itself, reminding ourselves constantly that it is always distant in some respects.

Applying Gadamer's philosophical hermeneutics provides crucial insights into *geyi.* As Gadamer argues, our ways of understanding are rooted in our own socio-cultural situation. We are informed by our cultural conditioning and it is only with great effort and risk that we can move beyond our original horizons. Buddhism's entry into China provides a large-scale illustration of this process. Despite problems with the Chinese texts we have examined, they reveal Chinese thinkers pushing against the confines of their conceptual categories, reaching toward the meaning of the Dharma as proclaimed by missionaries and in translated texts. They did so on the basis of their Confucian-Daoist heritage, and continued to work toward further understanding through more study and their own writings. As Wright (1948, 40) observes, *geyi* "contributed to the understanding of Buddhism among the educated Chinese and was a step forward in the long process of the sinicization of Buddhism."

To expand on this point, we need to recall that there is ample precedent for *geyi* in Han dynasty scholarship as, for instance, in the numerical pairing used by Dong Zhongshu in correlating aspects of humanity with the cosmos. In fact, one of the first Buddhist missionaries to China, An Shigao, sought to render the complex Abhidharma texts with their various numerical categories (e.g., six *āyatana*) into Chinese (*liu ru* 六入) using the same sort of numerical matching (Zurcher 1959, 30–34). Thus, *geyi* is just an extension of a known method to a new subject. Indeed, the process of correlation here is informed by "enabling prejudices" on the part of Chinese intellectuals (e.g., that the cosmos is an interrelated whole whose individual parts complement each other) that serve as inroads for further understanding. This, or course, is merely an early point in a process leading gradually to a "fusion of horizons" such as we see in the rise of fully Chinese schools of Buddhism such as Tiantai and Huayan.

Tang's analysis of early Chinese Buddhism also helps us make sense of this view of *geyi.* He notes that fourth century scholar-monks came to their own understanding of the Dharma through *geyi* but went beyond it as they became more immersed in Buddhist literature (Tang 1951). While somewhat speculative, Tang's work also explains the case of Daoan, whom as we have seen, was critical of *geyi* as time went on and he gained a deeper understanding of the Dharma. More to the point, this view also fits with what some of the Chinese texts themselves say, that *geyi* was a method designed for teaching aspects of Buddhism to Chinese intellectuals unfamiliar with the Dharma. It was essentially a heuristic technique, and one that those more versed in Buddhist teachings rightly understood as limited, and hence went on to discard.

Interestingly this view of *geyi* deeply resonates with aspects of the *xuanxue* philosophy that dominated the Chinese intellectual world in the third and fourth centuries. *Xuanxue* thinkers time and again emphasize that words and symbols are limited; they "fix" (*ding* 定) the mind to specific, definite things but the "mystery of mysteries" embraces *all* things and is undefinable. It can be named provisionally by words such as "Dao" or "great" (Zurcher 1959, 89), yet when we get the meaning, as Zhuangzi says, words should be forgotten (Palmer 1996, 242). This understanding of the limits of language coincides with Buddhist views as well, most notably as expressed in the parable of the raft—when one "gets" the meaning, one should discard the language that led to such realization. In this case, *geyi* would be among the initial ways by which Chinese intellectuals learned Dharma only to be discarded once they attained deeper knowledge and *geyi* had served its purpose.

CONCLUSION: A POSITIVE VIEW OF *GEYI*

As I have argued, most issues surrounding the definition and function of *geyi* are the result of misunderstanding. Why should this matter? Isn't this in the end a minor tempest in the Chinese Buddhist teapot? To a degree, yes, however there are important reasons for this extended discussion. First, this discussion underscores the fact that scholarship, be it in Buddhism or any field, is a communal activity marked by disagreement and discontinuity. Secondly, the confusion concerning *geyi* points to problems in Buddhist and Chinese studies, specifically, Indocentric and Sinocentric presumptions about what "Buddhism" and "Daoism" are, and a failure to appreciate the complex interpretive process initiated by the coming of Buddhism on Chinese soil. At the very least, we need greater awareness of such matters and endeavor to pass beyond them.

In addition I would like to address the disparagement of *geyi* that is common among those who discuss it, particularly those who harp upon its distorting effects. In fact, as we have seen, even those people involved in the spread of Buddhism in China during fourth and fifth centuries speak of *geyi*'s limits. Such remarks, however, miss the point. Based upon what I have determined, *geyi* was a technique to aid an educated Chinese audience with little knowledge of the Dharma to a basic grasp of Buddhist doctrine and practice. It was never intended to be the means for arriving at the definitive meaning of Dharma. Drawing a parallel to early Christianity, *geyi* might initially appear to be "pouring new wine into old wineskins" (Matthew 9: 17), but on closer inspection seems more analogous to Paul's missionary work with the church at Corinth, whom Paul describes as "infants in Christ" to be fed with milk, not solid food (1 Corinthians 3: 1–2). Overlooking the heuristic purpose of *geyi* marks a failure to grasp the enormity of the task facing the early Chinese *saṅgha*. To attempt to grasp the intricacies of Buddhism through a hodge-podge of texts (often clumsily translated) on the basis of their classical heritage and in the case of several scholar-monks, *teach* it to others required a tremendous effort on the part of the Chinese. In fact, Daoan should be commended for his insights, since he was an early advocate of *geyi* yet after years of study came to see its limitations.

Finally, we should note that contemporary Buddhological and Sinological scholarship are generally speaking secular endeavors, and perhaps encourage scholars to read their secular assumptions back into earlier historical periods. Once more, this is a highly problematic assumption. In a traditional Chinese and/or Buddhist setting, learning always entails self-transformation, not just intellectual (or narrowly "academic") enrichment. *Geyi* would thus have had a *religious* role in Chinese history, drawing Chinese thinkers into a more profound level of Buddhist understanding and practice. It deserves our respect.

NOTES

1. In his classic study of this era, Zurcher (1959, 18) remarks on the "curious fact" that "no period has been studied more thoroughly than the one about which almost nothing can be known."

2. On the difficulties involved in translating the *Tripiṭaka* into Chinese see Lancaster 1977, 145–151.

3. The latter, which uses Chinese words to approximate the sound of Indic terms, was likely the first of these "methods" (it is common in An Shigao's translations of *dhyāna* texts) and continued to be used for centuries. The Kuchean translator Kumārajīva, for instance, uses it for some terms (e.g., *puti* 菩提 for "*bodhi*").

4. The *Mouzi* is collected in the *Hongmingji* 弘明集 ("Collected Essays on Buddhism"), T.2102, compiled by the scholar-monk Sengyou 僧祐 (ca. 515).

5. That is *xuanxue* 玄學 ("dark learning"), the Chinese intellectual movement of the third to fifth centuries focusing on metaphysical speculation based on the "Three Mysteries" (*Yijing, Daode jing, Zhuangzi*), and that played an important role in the adoption of Buddhism among educated Chinese.

6. Those favoring Daoan include Link 1958, 43–45; Ch'en 1964, 96; Prebish 1993, 161. Those stressing the role of Kumārajīva include Lai 1979, 238; Ikeda 1986, 57; Ching 1993, 127.

7. Chan 1963, 281–282. The "five viscera" are the heart, liver, stomach, lungs, and kidneys.

8. *yu li duo yuan* 於理多遠. Attributed to Daoan, this quote comes from the biography of the scholar-monk Sengguang as found in the *Gaosengzhuan* 高僧傳 ("Biographies of Eminent Monks"), T.2059: 355a25.

9. The *Gaosengzhuan* was compiled by Huijiao 慧皎 (497–554); the *Chu sanzangji ji* was written by Sengyou 僧祐 (435–518); the *Zhongguan lunsu* was written by Jizang 吉藏 (549–623).

10. Sengrui (352–436) was a disciple of both Daoan and Kumārajīva.

11. The "Six Houses" were a group of early Chinese Mahāyāna "schools."

12. Quoting the above passage.

13. The *Middle Treatise* (*Zhonglun* 中論, *Mūlamadhyamakakārikā*) and the *Hundred Treatise* (*Bailun* 百論, *Śataśāstra*) are two of the main texts of the *Sanlun zong* 三論宗 ("Three Treatise School"), the Chinese version of the Indian *Mādhyamika* School.

14. Fotudeng's biography from the *Gaosengzhuan* is translated in Wright 1948.

15. For an overview of his accomplishments see Thompson 2003.

16. For one example see the Guifeng Zongmi's *Yuanren lun* 原人論. For an English translation see Gregory 1995, 68–69.

17. The *hua hu* theory is based on legends concerning Laozi. Essentially the idea is that after writing the *Daodejing* and vanishing into the wilderness, Laozi made his way to India where he "became" the Buddha and promulgated a simplified version of his teachings suited to the "barbarians." For details see Zurcher 1959, 37, 77, 280, and 288ff.

18. Feng 1953, 240 and Ch'en 1964, 64. Ch'en, in fact, merely quotes Feng's citations. Interestingly, even some modern scholars do not always clearly distinguish between Buddhist and Daoist teachings. See, for example, Wu 1991, 42.

BIBLIOGRAPHY

Chan, Wing-tsit. 1963. *A Sourcebook in Chinese Philosophy*. Princeton: Princeton University Press.

Ch'en, Kenneth K. S. 1964. *Buddhism in China: A Historical Survey*. Princeton: Princeton University Press.

Ching, Julia. 1993. *Chinese Religions*. Maryknoll, NY: Orbis Books.

Demieville, Paul. 1973. "La Penetration du Bouddhisme dans la tradition philosophique Chinoise." In *Choix D'Etudes Bouddhiques (1929–1970), par Paul Demieville* (Leiden: E. J. Brill), 241–260.

Dutt, Sukmar. 1966. *Buddhism in East Asia: An Outline of Buddhism in the History and Culture of the Peoples of East Asia*. Delhi: Indian Council for Cultural Relations.

Feng, Youlan (Fung Yu-lan). 1953. *A History of Chinese Philosophy. Volume II: The Period of Classical Learning (from the Second Century B.C. to the Twentieth Century A.D.)*, translated by Derk Bodde. Princeton: Princeton University Press.

Gadamer, Hans-Georg. 1994. *Truth and Method*, 2nd revised ed., translated and revised by Joel Weinsheimer and Donald G. Marshall. New York: The Continuum Publishing Company.

Gregory, Peter N. 1995. *Inquiry into the Origin of Humanity: an Annotated Translation of Tsung-mi's Yuan jen lun with a Modern Commentary*. Honolulu: The Kuroda Institute, University of Hawaii Press.

Ikeda, Daiseku. 1986. *The Flower of Chinese Buddhism*, translated by Burton Watson. New York and Tokyo: Weatherhill, Inc.

Lai, Whalen. 1979. "Limits and Failure of *Ko-I* (Concept Matching) Buddhism." *History of Religions* 18: 238–257.

Lancaster, Lewis R. 1977. "The Editing of Buddhist Texts." In *Buddhist Thought and Asian Civilizations: Essays in Honor of Herbert V. Guenther on His Sixtieth Birthday*, edited by Leslie S. Kawamura and Keith Scott (Emeryville: Dharma Publishing), 145–151.

Lao Siguang 勞思光. 1971. *Zhongguo zhexue shi* 中國哲學史. Vol 2. Hong Kong: Xianggang zhongwen daxue Chongji xueyuan.

Link, Arthur. 1958. "Biography of Shih Tao-an." *T'oung Pao* 46: 1–48.

Liu I-Ch'ing. 1976. *Shih-shuo Hsin-yu: A New Account of Tales of the World*, translated by Richard B. Mather. Minneapolis: University of Minnesota Press.

Pachow, W. 1980. *Chinese Buddhism: Aspects of Interaction and Reinterpretation*. Washington, D.C: University Press of America.

Palmer, Martin, trans. 1996. *The Book of Chuang Tzu*. London and New York: Arkana, Penguin Books, Ltd.

Prebish, Charles S. 1993. *Historical Dictionary of Buddhism*. Metchen: The Scarecrow Press.

Robinson, Richard H. 1967. *Early Mādhyamika in India and China*. Madison: The University of Wisconsin Press.

Snelling, John. 1991. *The Buddhist Handbook: a Complete Guide to Buddhist Schools, Teaching, Practice and History*. Rochester, VT: Inner Traditions International, Ltd.

Takatoshi, Ito. 1992. *Critical Studies on Chinese Buddhism*. Tokyo: Daizo Shuppan.

Tang, Yongtong. 1951. "On 'Ko-yi,' the Earliest Method by Which Indian Buddhism and Chinese Thought Were Synthesized." In *Radhakrishnan: Comparative Studies in Philosophy Presented in honour of his Sixtieth Birthday* (London: George Allen and Unwin Ltd.), 276–286.

Thompson, John M. 2003. "Philosopher as Exemplar: Daoan's Dao." *Religion East & West* 3: 59–77.

Tsukamoto, Zenryū. 1985. *A History of Early Chinese Buddhism: from its Introduction to the Death of Hui-yuan*, translated by Leon Hurvitz. Vols. 1–2. Tokyo, New York and San Francisco: Kodansha International Ltd.

Wright, Arthur F. 1948. "Fo-t'u-teng, A Biography." *Harvard Journal of Asiatic Studies* 11: 321–371.

———. 1959. *Buddhism in Chinese History*. Stanford, CA: Stanford University Press.

Wu, Yao-Yu. 1991. *The Taoist Tradition in Chinese Thought*, translated by Laurence G. Thompson and edited by Gary Seaman. Los Angeles: Ethnographics Press, University of Southern California.

Zurcher, Erik. 1959. *The Buddhist Conquest of China: The Spread and Adaptation of Buddhism in Early Medieval China*. Leiden: E. J. Brill.

16

The Ludic Quality of Life

A Comparison of the Caitanaya-caritāmṛta *and the* Zhuangzi

Carl Olson

During the course of a human life, it is not unusual for a person to turn to play as a form of relaxation, an escape from personal problems, and the world of work. Thus, the embracing of play is not confined to a person's childhood, but it rather extends throughout an individual's life and even into old age to some degree. In the West, the notion of play, a neglected aspect of life, achieved attention with the publication of *Homo Ludens: A Study of the Play Element in Culture* by Johan Huizinga in 1955. In this book, he identified several characteristics of play: (1) a voluntary activity that suggests freedom; (2) stands opposed to real life and gives participants an opportunity to leave the world of work and enter a realm of pretending and fun; (3) it is a disinterested, temporary activity that operates as an interlude in our lives, while also being an integral part of life that enhances one's existence; (4) it is performed within particular limits of space and time; (5) however temporary and limited, play creates order that brings participants under its spell by captivating and enchanting them with its rhythmical and harmonious natures; (6) play is risky and uncertain and thus results in a tension; (7) it eliminates doubt with its binding rules for participants; (8) it is secret in the sense that it is for a participant and not others. Huizinga concludes that without the element of play a civilization cannot endure or exist. Long before Huizinga's book was published, the importance of play was stressed by Indian and Chinese cultures in a Hindu devotional text, the *Caitanaya-caritāmṛta*, and by a Daoist text, the *Zhuangzi*. The former text uses the notion of play prominently as a central theme, whereas the latter uses play in more subtle ways.

Within the context of devotional forms of Hinduism, work is considered a human shortcoming because an ability to play is more comparable to being divine. In other words, the ability to enter into play spontaneously is believed to be characteristic of divine nature. To be characterized as a playful deity means that such a being does not need or desire anything because such a being is complete. Although many Hindu deities exhibit playfulness, Kṛṣṇa is the divine player par excellence, and serves as the paradigm for the life of Caitanya, a Bengali saint and incarnation of the god according to followers.

The hagiographical *Caitanya-caritāmṛta* (hereafter cited CC) composed by Kṛṣṇadāsa Kavirāja (1517 to ca. 1615–1620) is partly modeled on the life of the deity Kṛṣṇa with each part of the text divided into different forms of play (*līlā*): (1) *ādi-līlā* (chapters 1–17); (2) *madhya-līlā* (chapters 1–25); (3) *antya-līlā* (chapters 1–20).[1] The initial division focuses on Caitanya's early life including his becoming a renouncer (*sannyāsin*). Covering his life at the city of Puri, the *madhya-līlā* also includes his pilgrimages to southern India and north to Vṛndāvana and numerous theological reflections and interpretations. Dealing with Caitanya's later life, the *antya-līlā* section also stresses the frequent attacks of madness upon the holy man. From an overall perspective, Kavirāja is not writing a historical account of a saint's life, but he is rather creating a hagiography that also interprets the meaning of the saint's life through the theological insights of the six Gosvāmīs, especially Rūpa and Jīva whose voices can be heard in the text. With the teachings of the Gosvāmīs placed into his mouth, Caitanya represents a divine incarnation, functioning as a vehicle for the spread and validation of their teachings. In his portrayal of the saint, Kavirāja is particularly concerned to understand the meaning of the play (*līlā*) of Caitanya.

While Kavirāja's hagiography was being created and before it gained wide acceptance among the devotional followers of the saint, the composer accomplished two things: he hierarchized prominent aspects of Gosvāmī thought and reorganized Caitanya's hagiographical tradition to reflect a theology that reflected his personal thinking. This double compositional event implies that the textual narrative communicates simultaneously both the voices of the author and of the individual speaking within the text. Citing Mikhail Bakhtin and his notion of double-voiced discourse, Stewart observes, "From this perspective, the author's voice passed through other voices and in either direct or indirect discourse; it is not just a report, but the words are being infused with the author's narrative purpose" (Stewart 2010, 191). This procedure is intended to be used to interpret the meaning of Caitanya's life lived on the paradigm of divine play depicted by Kavirāja by carefully crafting a textual structure that synthesized theological insights with aesthetic sensibilities.

A careful study of the hagiographical text enables Stewart to identify and isolate three accomplishments: theoretical, social, and ritual. Stewart elaborates that "The *Caitanya-caritāmṛta* rectified the theories of divinity and hierarchized them according to form; socially it accounted for each group of devotees, while placing each definitively in the final structure of community; ritually the Caitanya codified practices, ranked according to end and efficacy; and finally, it established a proper textual authority" (Stewart 2010, 269). As the text became accepted overtime as the authoritative account of the saint's life and the foundational document for the community of devotees, a remarkable event occurred that can be summarized simply as the text becoming a teacher (*guru*) for the community (Stewart 2010, 306).

Unlike this Hindu devotional work, the *Zhuangzi* is a Chinese Daoist classic in which the theme of play is a pivotal notion in a more methodological sense. This Chinese text is named for a sage who is the central figure of the text, and is reputed to have lived during the reigns of King Hui of Liang (370–319 BCE) and King Xuan of Qi (319–309 BCE). According to Sima Qian's *Record of the Historian*, Master Zhuang's given name was Zhou, living contemporarily with Mengzi, an idealistic Confucian thinker. The *Zhuangzi* was eventually edited by Guo Xiang (d. 312 CE), a Chinese scholar. This revised text contains 33 chapters, although an older and larger text of 52 chapters has been lost. There are three major sections of the current text: the inner chapters (1–7), outer chapters (8–22, c. 180 BCE), and the mixed chapters (23–33, c. 25 BCE). The text demonstrates a variety of literary styles with the inner chapters representing the oldest material, which probably dates these chapters to the sage's teaching as a member of the Jixia Academy (c. 330–301 BCE) (Kohn 2009, 40–41; Littlejohn 2009, 25–42; Graham 1982).

Even though the *Zhuangzi* and the *Caitanya-caritāmṛta* are far removed from each other historically, philosophically, and culturally, they both share a common interest in the notion of play. And it is precisely the notion of play in each text that this essay proposes to examine and compare. In this respect, the proposed topic for this cross-cultural dialogue is intended to break-out of the pattern of doing such comparative philosophy using an East-West mode of comparison, suggesting the fruitfulness of cross-cultural dialogues between eastern cultures.[2]

NATURE OF PLAY

The transformative character of history suggests for Zhuangzi that apparent opposites, such as life and death, preservation and loss, failure and success, poverty and wealth, worthiness and unworthiness, hunger and thirst, and cold and heat, are merely the playful alternations of the world (Watson 1968, 293). These alternations of worldly existence also suggest that similar to life, play manifests a to-and-fro movement that is not related to any goal that would bring it to an end. In contrast, Caitanya's debate with a learned *paṇḍita* goes back and forth until the thinker's defeat and surrender to the devotional leader (CC 1.16.26–102). Zhuangzi's notion of play is comparatively more open-ended, whereas Caitanya's playful exchange with a learned individual comes to a conclusion in this particular case. In addition, there is no external goal of the movement because play simply renews itself in constant repetition.[3] The repetitive nature of play for Caitanya is evident in the recitation of mantras (sacred formulas) especially the Kṛṣṇa mantra, *dharma* (law) of the present evil, degenerate Kali age, that possesses the power to save a person from the world, consisting of the repetition of the god's name (CC 1.7.71–72). In addition, Caitanya's life is modeled on the following: games of continuous hide and seek with his deity. To give one example, Caitanya thinks that he sees Kṛṣṇa under an *aśoka* tree, and goes running and laughing toward the vision. Suddenly, Kṛṣṇa disappears. But Caitanya finds Kṛṣṇa again only to lose him again. At the point of despair, Caitanya faints and falls to the ground. Even though Kṛṣṇa had disappeared, the garden is permeated by his perfume. Upon smelling the perfume, Caitanya becomes unconscious and then mad as the scent enters his nostrils (CC 3.19.80–84). These various cross-cultural examples suggest that play represents a predominance of a movement of renewal and repetition in both the *Caitanya-caritāmṛta* and the *Zhuangzi*.

Within this to-and-fro movement, Zhuangzi supports, for instance, a reversal of feelings associated with life and death, which is illustrated by the sage with the narrative about Master Yu, a diseased, deformed, and dying old man:

> He was asked whether or not he despised his lot in life. He replied: "Why no, what would I resent? If the process continues, perhaps in time (the Creator will) transform my left arm into a rooster. In that case I'll keep watch on the night. Or perhaps in time he'll transform my right arm into a crossbow pellet and I'll shoot down an owl for roasting. Or perhaps in time he'll transform my buttocks into cartwheels. Then, with my spirit for a horse, I'll climb up and go for a ride. What need will I ever have for a carriage again?" (Watson 1968, 84)

This story of transformation suggests a philosophy of change in which things are comprehended as forever in a process of transformation. However, things do not change for some end or goal, suggesting that there is no purpose in the Daoist universe because things simply spontaneously occur in a regular fashion. Nonetheless, it is important for humans to know the laws of change in order to adapt to them. Since the laws of change (an alternation of the flow of *yin* and *yang* for example) cannot be altered, it is just best to submit and adapt oneself to them. There is also an important role for change in Kavirāja's text represented by love, a phenomenon that grows continuously: "The *prema* of Rādhā is all pervasive and eternal; though there is no room for growth, still it grows greater with every moment" (CC 1.4.111). Caitanya admits that he is continually overwhelmed by the love (*prema*) of Rādhā, primary *gopī* lover of Kṛṣṇa. It is this overflowing love that transforms Caitanya into a madman. This over abundant love (*prema*) is differentiated from *kāma,* an egoistic useful desire that pleases oneself, whereas *prema* is egoless, involves continual excitement, and is done for god's sake (CC 1.4.164). This scenario enables us to see that spiritual transformation is central to Caitanya's and Zhuangzi's lives and messages, and the two respective texts that are the focus of this essay invite a self-transformation in the reader. This process of spiritual transformation is available to everyone in both texts (Allinson 1989, 24).

The themes of renewal and repetition are also evident in the hagiography of Caitanya. The giving of food as the gift of *prasāda* (literally meaning grace and giving of gracious offerings to a deity) is a common repetitive Hindu religious activity, representing additionally accepting the gracious food leftovers of the deity being worshiped. On one occasion, Caitanya distributed *prasāda* to others who were astonished by its sweetness and fragrance. Caitanya said that the various material things associated with it were a world apart because the *prasāda* has been touched by the lips of Kṛṣṇa, which transforms the material elements of the gift (CC 3.16.98–105). Besides the repetitive nature of the gift of food, Caitanya and his followers are often depicted dancing and singing. Kavirāja traces this play of dance to love: "*Prema* causes Kṛṣṇa to dance, it causes the *bhakta* to dance, and itself dances—these three dance in one place at once" (CC 4.18.17–18).

In addition to themes of renewal and repetition, the biography of Caitanya embodies the spirit of transformation as in the narrative about a prostitute and Haridāsa. According to the story, Caitanya's follower Haridāsa, an ascetic, lived alone in the forest doing *kīrtana* (singing the praises of Kṛṣṇa) night and day. He was adored and worshiped by the local people, a situation despised by the jealous ruler Rāmacandra Khān. This impious ruler devised a plan to subvert the spirituality of Haridāsa by having a beautiful prostitute seduce him. An especially young and comely prostitute boldly announced that in three days she would sexually unite with the ascetic when he could then be seized by the king's henchmen for being a fraud. After arriving at the dwelling of the ascetic, the prostitute removed her clothing and offered herself to him in a melodious and flattering voice. Haridāsa promised her that he would grant her wish when he finished reciting the names of Kṛṣṇa and ordered her to sit and listen to the recitation of *nāma-saṃkīrtana* (repeated singing of the names of god). When morning arrived the prostitute excused herself and reported to the ruler, informing him that she would unite with the ascetic the next day. The following day met with an identical result. On the third day, Haridāsa claimed that the recitation would surely end. While the pious ascetic continued to recite into the evening, the mind of the prostitute was transformed; she fell at the feet of the ascetic, and divulged the sinister plot of the ruler. After repenting over her sinful life, the ascetic instructed her how to save herself. After shaving her head and becoming an ascetic, she proceeded to become a locally renowned Vaiṣṇava (CC 3.3.91–134). It is the repetitive action of the sagacious male ascetic that transforms and renews the salacious life of the prostitute.

EXPERIENCE OF PLAY

To be serious when engaged in play renders play wholly play. Those individuals who do not take the game seriously tend to be a spoil sport. Even though a participant enters freely into play, it is important that all participants maintain seriousness with respect to their effort and interrelationship to others. Caitanya's seriousness about his devotion to Kṛṣṇa drives him mad at times. During the night, Caitanya wanders away, for example, and he is found by followers lying on the ground. The followers are joyful at finding him, but their initial reaction turns to concern after they see his condition:

> Prabhu was lying on the ground, five or six hands long; his body was unconscious, and there was no breath in his nostrils. His arms and legs were each three hands long; the joints of his bones were separated, and over the joints there was only skin. His arms and legs and neck and hips—all the joints of his body were separated and spread out. The joints had become long, and covered only with skin, and when they saw Prabhu, all were greatly distressed. There was foam and spittle on his mouth, and his eyes rolled up into his head, and when they saw this, the breath left the bodies of all the *bhaktas*. (CC 3.14.57–67)

Caitanya's followers revive him by loudly reciting Kṛṣṇa's name in his ear, and the saint eventually responds by shouting "Hari bol!" and arises from the ground. When he regains his consciousness his body resumed its normal shape. For Zhuangzi, it is not a matter of seriousness or frivolity; it is more important to adapt to change and go with it, although how the Daoist sage adapts to change is grounded in seriousness (Watson 1968, 88–89).

From the Daoist perspective, play can be serious and non-serious. This implies that play is not against frolic because they are equally ways of being enchanted. "Seriousness keeps frolic from going flippant, and frolic keeps seriousness ever free and unstuck" (Wu 1990, 111). By combining seriousness and its opposite, play becomes fun. In fact, seriousness and non-seriousness need each other because they make genuine life a way of play.

By entering into a play, a person takes a risk, an attractive feature of the activity, because the outcome is not predetermined and remains uncertain. By taking the risk invited by play, the player risks being injured or losing, if it is a game with mutually accepted rules. Caitanya's great risk is to become separated (*viraha*) from Kṛṣṇa.[4] The mechanism of love in separation operates in the following way: "Separation prolongs desire, whereas gratification ends it" (Haberman 1988, 29). When this separation occurs Caitanya becomes sorrowful, anguished, and mentally and emotionally deranged (CC 3.6.4–6). In fact, Caitanya's separation from Kṛṣṇa drives him mad and motivates dangerous impulsive behavior. His madness dramatically affects his behavior as evident in the story about him being in a state of *prema* aboard a boat with some followers. When he sees the waters of the Yamunā River he gives a shout and leaps into the river. His frightened disciples pull him out, get him on board the boat again, and Caitanya begins to dance on the boat's deck (CC 2.19.69–73). According to Rūpa Gosvāmī, Caitanya's symptoms of madness are manifested in features that are characteristic of play, such as laughing, dancing, singing, running aimlessly, shouting, and performing strange forms of behavior that are contrary to social norms (*Bhaktirasāmṛtasindhu* 2.4.80; see Haberman 2003).

The participant also makes a decision whether or not to engage in play, and enjoys the freedom offered by such a decision. But this decision is limited by time, place, and human feelings. Any decision to engage in play is not limited by a participant's imagination because any activity can be a form of play or transformed into play. Thus even work can become a form of play as evident from American popular culture in the Disney cartoon "Snow White" when the Seven Dwarfs sing "whistle while you work" and enter into work in the spirit of play.

Zhuangzi applies these insights about the nature of play into lessons concerning dealing with a ruler as the figure Yan He advises:

> In your actions it is best to follow along with him, and in your mind it is best to harmonize with him . . . If he wants to be a child, be a child with him. If

> he wants to follow erratic ways, follow erratic ways with him. If he wants to be reckless, be reckless with him. (Watson 1968, 62)

This advice for placating a ruler suggests that play is not necessarily a useful activity, but this is acceptable because what is essentially useless is useful in the long term. The case of the ruler invites the Daoist to enter into a playful game with the intent of harmonizing the participants. In the *Caitanya-caritāmṛta,* Caitanya makes a playful decision to possess the body of the pious Nakula, a *brahmacārī.* Similar to the mad behavior of Caitanya, Nakula emulated the saint by becoming mad, laughing, weeping, dancing, and singing. The text attributes Nakula's tears, trembling, stupefaction, and sweating as devotional *sāttvika* signs (CC 3.2.15–21). This scenario demonstrates Caitanya playing through the body of a pious follower instead of Kṛṣṇa playing through his body, suggesting the incarnational status of Caitanya.

Zhuangzi discusses the usefulness of the useless by highlighting, for instance, gnarled, bumpy, rotten trees with poisonous leaves that are unfit for building anything. Since such trees are fundamentally useless, they are not harvested by foresters and used by builders, transforming their uselessness into something useful in the sense that their uselessness allows them to grow tall and live long (Watson 1968, 62). Although play possesses physical and mental benefits for participants that suggest usefulness, it is a useless activity from Zhuangzi's perspective because it is not for the sake of something else, but is only useful for itself, which ultimately gives it an advantage over things and actions (Wu 1990, 382).

Besides the experience of the useless nature of play, there is a lightness associated with it that suggests its effortless character in the sense that play happens by itself. Zhuangzi does not mean to suggest that there is absolutely no effort exerted by participants. What he does want to stress is that there is an ease of play that suggests the absence of strain, which implies that play is a form of relaxation and an opportunity to relieve tension. The spirit of this aspect of play is expressed when Zhuangzi instructs us to live a "free and easy wandering" style of life. Zhuangzi elaborates on this style of life by stating, "It is easy to keep from walking; the hard thing is to walk without touching the ground" (Watson 1968, 58). Zhuangzi also refers to those with the ability to shift back and forth between various perspectives and opinions without friction of conflict or emotional upset.

Within the life of Caitanya, the spirit of uselessness is evident in *kīrtana* (singing the praises of god), a performance that possesses no purpose beyond itself because it is pure play. It represents an opportunity for devotees to imitate the *gopīs* of the *Bhāgavata-purāṇa* as they sing the praises of Kṛṣṇa. According to Kavirāja's interpretation, *kīrtana* accomplishes two desirable outcomes: it destroys meaninglessness and evil (CC 3.20.9–10). *Kīrtana* does not have anything in common with work, a form of human shortcoming. The overall significance of *kīrtana* needs to be understood in the context of the totality of play because there is no end to the play (*līlā*) of Caitanya (CC 3.20.71).[5]

When engaged in play the participant loses oneself in the activity. This absorption could extent to losing self-consciousness or being aware about being engaged in a specific activity. The absorptive nature of play finds a parallel with Zhuangzi's discussion of meditative techniques such as breathing and entering trance states: "Fish thrive in water, man thrives in the way . . . the fish forget each other in the rivers and lakes, and men forget each other in the arts of the Way" (Watson 1968, 87).

There are numerous incidents when Caitanya is completely absorbed in play and is oblivious to what is occurring around him in the ordinary world. Caitanya hears, for example, a *devadāsī* (temple consort) singing from the *Gītagovinda*, an erotic poem about the love dalliances of Kṛṣṇa and Rādhā, composed by Jayadeva in 1170. From a distance, Caitanya could not know whether a man or a woman was singing; so, he ran, completely absorbed, to meet the singer. His path was lined with *sija* trees that pricked him as he ran in an absorbed condition. Govinda, a disciple of the saint, caught him by the arm and informed him that a woman was singing. The saint thanked Govinda for saving him from touching a woman and violating his renouncer status (CC 3.13.77–84).

Taking into consideration numerous examples from the hagiography of Caitanya, play, a human capacity, is subjunctive ('as if') and replaces the indicative mood (normally used by writers to express facts, opinions, or questions). By using the subjunctive mood, a person is able to articulate dissimilar ways of classifying reality and to develop a view of another possible reality. Moreover, the subjunctive indicates the creative potential of play. It is also dangerous in a dissident sense "Because of its subjunctiveness play by nature is subversive" (Droogers 2006, 83). Zhuangzi helps us grasp the subjunctive nature of play when he refers to the cicada and little dove, comparing their feeble attempts to fly with that of the mighty Peng with his massive size and wings that resemble clouds (Watson 1968, 29–30).

THE NATURALNESS OF PLAY

According to Zhuangzi, the play of human beings is a natural process, which suggests that the player is a part of nature. By becoming aware of this, a person gains a pure self-realization. This does not mean that Zhuangzi thinks that there is primacy of consciousness over play. In fact, play is independent of the consciousness of those who play. Moreover, it is even irrelevant whether or not a subject plays because it is the game that is played, rendering play predominant over the consciousness of the player and making all playing a being played. This scenario suggests that play is limited to representing itself and its mode of being is self-representation, making play a simple totality. Kavirāja grasps the totality of play differently than Zhuangzi by envisioning the world floating in an ocean of Caitanya's play (CC 2.17.219).

The totality and naturalness of play is illustrated by the activity of Cook Ding in the *Zhuangzi* as he carves an ox. While engaged in carving the carcass of the ox, Cook Ding is so absorbed in his activity that he keeps rhythm as he slices, coordinating his activity with a harmonious rhythm (Watson 1968, 50–51). Since play (carving) takes precedence over his own consciousness, this anecdote indicates a lack of subjectivism on the part of the cook. Being absorbed in himself, the cook forgets his self, but his self also "grows into itself" (Wu 1990, 382).

The naturalness of play in the life of Caitanya is evident by the *jala-līlā* of Jagannāth when the icon of the deity is placed on a boat to play in the water. During this event, *bhaktas* perform *kīrtana*, weep with love (*prema*), play instruments, sing, and dance. These activities represent praising the water-play of the deity. With other *bhaktas*, Caitanya descended into the water to frolic (CC 3.10.30–49). Water plays a central role in another narrative when Caitanya perceives the sea, mistakes it for the Yamunā River, and jumps into the water where he faints and becomes consciously oblivious to his situation. Caitanya both sank and floated on the water at times, reminiscent of Kṛṣṇa playing with the *gopī*s in the water (CC 3.18.24–27).

From Caitanya's perspective, there is nothing wrong with living life on the model of the *rāsa-līlā* (circle dance), which was originally performed by the *gopī*s with Kṛṣṇa in the forest. A feature that suggests its attraction for Caitanya is its effortless nature. The disciple Sanātana, for example, holds the feet of the saint and humbly entreats him, clenching grass in his teeth, confessing to his low birth and worthlessness, and thanking the saint for rescuing him (CC 2.20.92–95). This is a good example of a disciple going beyond emulating the behavior of *gopī*s and imitating a cow, animal lovers of Kṛṣṇa.

An ordinary occurrence can be lived on the paradigm of the *gopī*s behavior with Kṛṣṇa. According to Kavirāja's text, at the end of the rainy season, devotees journey to visit Caitanya. In spite of orders to remain at Gauḍīya, they went to see him anyway with the disciple Nityānanda going in a state of *prema* (ecstatic love) to visit his master. Kavirāja explains, "For the sign of deep love is this—that one does not obey injunctions; so he broke the command in order to be with him. It was during *rāsa*, when [Kṛṣṇa] orders the *gopī*s to go home, they disobeyed his order and stayed with him" (CC 3.10.2–6). Within the context of the world of play, injunctions of any kind do not hinder or deter anyone.

The image of the *rāsa-līlā* (circle dance) sometimes appears in dreams to Caitanya. Kavirāja describes a dream by stating that Kṛṣṇa appeared beautiful in the *tribhaṅga* pose (three bends appearing at the head, torso, and legs), his flute to his lips, wearing yellow garments, and garlands of forest flowers. In this position, the *gopīs* were dancing around Kṛṣṇa in a circle and in the center of the circle danced Rādhā. After awakening from his dream and realizing his experience was a dream, Caitanya was very sad and disappointed (CC 3.14.15–19). Caitanya's disenchantment does not compare to the reaction of Zhuangzi after he awoke from the butterfly dream, questioning what is real or unreal, although Kavirāja is convinced that *gopī-bhāva* (emotion) is a power that the mind cannot grasp. He writes, "They were not seeking their own happiness, but even so their happiness increased. This is a paradox. But there is a solution to this paradox in that the happiness of the *gopīs* lay in the completion of the happiness of Kṛṣṇa" (CC 1.4.159–60).

PLAY AND TRANSFORMATION

From Zhuangzi's perspective, everything is in a constant state of transformation. Because things do not change for some end or goal, there is no purpose in the universe, but things rather occur spontaneously in a regular fashion. This law of change, an alternation of the flow of *yin* and *yang*, cannot be altered, which implies that it is best for a person to adjust and ultimately to adapt to it. Thereby, a person merges with the ever evolving transformations and attains unity with the whole.

The law of change and transformation is illustrated by Zhuangzi with the vivid, playful image of metamorphosis associated with the life of a butterfly:

> Once Chuang Chou dreamt he was a butterfly, a butterfly flitting and fluttering around, happy with himself and doing as he pleased. He didn't know he was Chuang Chou. Suddenly he woke up and there he was, solid and unmistakable Chuang Chou. But he didn't know if he was Chuang Chou who had dreamt he was a butterfly, or a butterfly dreaming he was Chuang Chou. Between Chuang Chou and a butterfly there must be some distinction! This is called the Transformation of Things. (Watson 1963, 49)

The butterfly, a transient creature, gives rise to an image of metamorphosis, suggesting a transformation from inferior to superior, from old to new, from lowly to high, from crawling to flying, or from less developed to more developed condition. By shedding the skin of its chrysalis, the butterfly, a symbol of beauty and its birth, illustrates that transformation takes place when the old gives way to the new, representing an internal change. Even though the butterfly is a transient creature, it is a carefree, ludic creature whose playfulness is a direct result of its transformation. Despite its brief lifespan, the butterfly is playful, reflecting "the result of the transformation" (Allinson 1989, 76).

In the dream of the butterfly, Zhuangzi playfully indicates a change in the level of the subject's consciousness. By inviting a reader to reflect on the dream of the butterfly, Zhuangzi gains knowledge that awakens him and releases him from the tyranny of obsession with objective realism. This scenario suggests that Zhuangzi uses such an awareness to awaken himself from ignorance. By awakening from ignorance, a subject is free to enter a meandering and blithe journey within the flux of ontological transformation.

According to Kavirāja's hagiographical account of playful transformation, a fisherman captured a corpse that he originally thought was a huge fish. After its spirit entered his heart, the fisherman trembled in fear, wept, and his voice was choked, whereas the misidentified body either groaned or remained totally unconscious at other times. The fisherman thought that a *bhūta* (ghost of the dead) had seized him, and he was determined to get it exorcise by a magician. By means of a mantra, Svarūpa Gosvāmī exorcised the fisherman and slapped his head three times. After placating the man, Svarūpa informed him that the corpse was not a ghost but rather Caitanya under the control of *prema*. Due to the distorted body, the fisherman could not accept the fact that the falsely assumed corpse was Caitanya. In reply, Svarūpa attributed his transformed body to the power of love (CC 3.18.44–67). The transformative power of love extends to nature. According to Kavirāja, when Caitanya instructs tigers and deer in the forest to recite the name of Kṛṣṇa they begin to dance, shout, weep, embrace, and kiss each other. Birds are similarly influenced and creepers on trees suddenly blossom. All the creatures of nature are drunk on love (*prema*) grounded in the name of Kṛṣṇa (CC 2.17.37–43). In this scenario, nature is transformed into a paradise on earth in which mortal enemies live in peace. The transformative power of Kṛṣṇa's name extends to social relationships because it can raise lower caste members (CC 2.19.67).

According to Zhuangzi, within the flux of constant transformation, it is not wise to act on inflexible principles, fixed preconceptions, and forcing one's will against the spontaneous course of things. When acting on inflexible principles, a subject is apt to tenaciously cling to one's position even when the situation changes because one insists on the absolute validity of one's position against conflicting assertions. It is wiser to cease to distinguish between one thing and other. Zhuangzi ridicules this type of rationalist position by indicating that inflexible people are like displeased monkeys when told, for instance, that they can have three rations of acorns in the morning and four at night, but become pleased when told that they can receive four in the morning and three at night (Watson 1968, 39–40). Zhuangzi refers to such an inflexible position as the "contrived this" (*wei-shi* 為是), whereas a preferable position is called the "adaptive this" (*yin-shi* 因是), which suggests adopting a position that allows one to change with changes in situations. This means to adapt to circumstances without imposing fixed principles on them. Zhuangzi's Daoist way is to make relative judgments according to changing situations. This involves not distinguishing between alternatives. When used by the same person "this" and "that" are indexicals that change as the speaker's position changes. These context-dependent terms of language suggests that Zhuangzi's insight "is that all language is indexical," a position that allows him to call attention to the pluralistic and pragmatic character of language (Hansen 1992, 282). With the whole of one's being, it is preferable to be flexible and non-committal towards one thing or another and simply react to a changing situation from one moment to the next without concern for order.

If Zhuangzi does not adhere to fixed principles that hinder play, Caitanya's position is grounded in Kṛṣṇa, who is full of *prema* (love) and *līlā* (play), his only *dharma* (CC 1.5.25; 1.4.21). The earthly play of the two deities, Rādhā and Kṛṣṇa, is modeled on its heavenly Vṛndāvana where play is eternal. As Dimock writes, this scenario has important implications, because "any given moment of the *līlā,* including the moment of union, is a capsule of eternity" (Dimock 1966, 139). Kṛṣṇa, paradigmatic player, became incarnated as Caitanya in order to experience the *rasa* of Rādhā, called *hlādinī śakti* (power of bliss).[6] Therefore, in the body of Caitanya, Kṛṣṇa and Rādhā unite to experience bliss (CC 1.4.49–53).[7] This theological scenario bears a resemblance to the flow and alternation of *yin* and *yang* in Daoist philosophy and emphasis on the importance of the feminine role on the path to liberation.

CONCLUDING REMARKS

By comparing a Daoist text with a Gauḍīya Vaiṣṇava text, this essay has been engaged in a back-and-forth movement characteristic of play. Even with their very different philosophical presuppositions about reality (e.g., Dao versus a personal deity), means of liberation (e.g., becoming one with the Dao or surrendering to a theistic/androgynous deity), or different experience (cognitive awareness versus devotional emotionalism), we have discovered remarkably similar positions on the phenomenon of play. The incongruity of this essay reflects its topic. Instead of attempting to reconcile the incongruity, this essay has attempted to oscillate between play and non-play and to allow the irreconcilable philosophical positions to remain.

By allowing oscillation rather than synthesis to occur, we overcome any inducement or proclivity toward philosophical reductionism between, for instance, the outsider (current writer) and insiders (subjects being compared). By accepting the play of Zhaungzi and Caitanya, it is imaginatively possible to accept two diverse ways of classifying reality. Being playful with the notion of play, the interpretive outsider enters into the playful experience of the insider other. It is also possible for methodological play to enable an outsider to playfully engage the insider without having to bracket-out their conception of reality and experience. This approach enables the outsider to have an inter-subjective grasp and appreciation of the philosophy being considered. The outsider plays with the insiders in an attempt to achieve understanding and dialogical respect without converting to the reality espoused by the others.

This chapter implies that play possesses a liminal nature, which invites inversion, experimentation, and a new mode of thinking. The liminality of play also generates an inner dialogue in the mind of the outsider as viewpoints are compared and contrasted. This is an internal dialogue that allows the outsider to simultaneously embrace opposites such as normal and abnormal.

If this hermeneutical dialogue accomplishes anything, it is that play suggests that humans are more than rational creatures. The hagiography of Caitanya and the philosophy of Zhuangzi enable us to see that play has an irrational quality and is not the exact opposite of seriousness. We have also seen that play is intimately connected to the comic, even though a subsidiary of play which is beyond foolishness. Moreover, play is not antithetical to wisdom and folly because play subsumes and transcends both of these opposites. The common message of Caitanya and Zhuangzi is the following: keep playing and laughing.

NOTES

1. I have used a recent translation of the text by Dimock (1999). I cite the text in the body of the chapter as CC.

2. I have addressed the issue of cross-cultural dialogue in the two following books: Olson 2000, 18–22; Olson 2002, 2–10.

3. The definition of play used for this essay is dependent on the following authors: Huizinga 1955; Caillois 1961; Cox 1969; Droogers et. al. 2006; Coomaraswamy 1941; Hawley 1983; Kinsley 1975; Kinsley 1972; Östör 1980; Haberman 1994; Wu 1982; Wu 1990.

4. The theme of *viraha* (separation) is developed at length by Hardy 1993.

5. Haberman (1988, 37) contends that Rūpa Gosvāmin extends aesthetic experience to all life, making the world a stage upon which humans are actors in a playful drama.

6. In his *Bhaktirasāmṛtasindhu* 3.3.85 (see Haberman 2003), Rūpa Gosvāmin defines *rasa* in the following way: "Rasa is judged to be that which passes beyond the course of contemplation (*bhāvanā*) and becomes an experience of abundant amazement that is relished intensely in a heart illuminated by purity."

7. De (1961) suggests that the notion of a double incarnation originates in writers of lyric poems (*padas*) and later developed by Kavirāja.

BIBLIOGRAPHY

Allinson, Robert E. 1989. *Chuang-Tzu for Spiritual Transformation: An Analysis of the Inner Chapters*. Albany: State University of New York Press.

Caillois, Roger. 1961. *Man, Play, and Games*, trans. Meyer Barash. New York: The Free Press.

Coomaraswamy, Ananda K. 1941. "Līlā." *Journal of the American Oriental Society* 61: 98–101.

Cox, Harvey. 1969. *The Feast of Fools: A Theological Essay of Festivity and Fantasy*. Cambridge: Harvard University Press.

De, Sushil Kumar. 1961. *The Early History of the Vaiṣṇava Faith and Movement in Bengal*. Calcutta: Firma K. L. Mukhopadhyay.

Dimock, Edward C. 1966. *The Place of the Hidden Moon: Erotic Mysticism in the Vaiṣṇava-Sahajiyā Cult of Bengal*. Chicago and London: University of Chicago Press.

———, trans. 1999. *Caitanya Caritāmṛta of Kṛṣṇadāsa Kavirāja*, edited by Tony K. Stewart. Cambridge, MA: Harvard University Press.

Droogers, André, et. al. 2006. *Playful Religion: Challenges for the Study of Religion*. Delft, The Netherlands: Eburon Academic Publishers.

Graham, A. C. 1982. *Chuang-tzu: Textual Notes to a Partial Translation*. London: SOAS, University of London.

Haberman, David L. 1988. *Acting as a Way of Salvation: A Study of Rāgānugā Bhakti Sādhana*. New York: Oxford University Press.

———. 1994. *Journey through the Twelve Forests: An Encounter with Krishna*. New York, Oxford: Oxford University Press.

———, trans. 2003. *The Bhaktirasāmṛtasindhu of Rūpa Gosvāmin*. New Delhi: Indira Gandhi National Centre for the Arts.

Hansen, Chad. 1992. *A Daoist Theory of Chinese Thought: A Philosophical Interpretation*. New York and Oxford: Oxford University Press.

Hardy, Friedhelm. 1993. *Viraha-Bhakti: The Early History of Kṛṣṇa Devotion in South India*. Delhi: Oxford University Press.

Hawley, John Stratton. 1983. *At Play with Krishna: Pilgrimage Dramas from Brindavan*. Princeton: Princeton University Press.

Huizinga, Johan. 1955. *Homo Ludens: A Study of the Play-Element in Culture*. Boston: Beacon Press.

Kinsley, David R. 1972. "Without Kṛṣṇa There Is No Song." *History of Religions* 12.2: 149–180.
——. 1975. *The Sword and the Flute: Kālī and Kṛṣṇa, Dark Visions of the Terrible and Sublime in Hindu Mythology*. Berkeley: University of California Press.
Kohn, Livia. 2009. *Introducing Daoism*. London and New York: Routledge.
Littlejohn, Ronnie L. 2009. *Daoism: An Introduction*. London and New York: I. B. Tauris.
Olson, Carl. 2000. *Zen and the Art of Postmodern Philosophy: Two Paths of Liberation from the Representational Mode of Thinking*. Albany, NY: State University of New York Press.
——. 2002. *Indian Philosophers and Postmodern Thinkers: Dialogues on the Margins of Culture*. New Delhi: Oxford University Press.
Östör, Ákos. 1980. *The Play of the Gods*. Chicago and London: University of Chicago Press.
Stewart, Tony K. 2010. *The Final Word: The Caitanya Caritāmṛta and the Grammar of Religious Tradition*. New York, Oxford: Oxford University Press.
Watson, Burton, trans. 1968. *The Complete Chuang Tzu*. New York and London: Columbia University Press.
Wu, Kuang-ming. 1982. *Chuang Tzu: World Philosopher at Play*. New York: Crossroad Publishing Company and Scholars Press.
——. 1990. *The Butterfly as Companion: Meditations on the First Three Chapters of the Chuang Tzu*. Albany, NY: University of New York Press.

17

The Poet and the Historian

Criticism of the Modern Age by Rabindranath Tagore and Qian Mu

Gad C. Isay

Rabindranath Tagore (1861–1941) and Qian Mu 錢穆 (1895–1990) were erudite scholars, remarkably aware of the challenges of modern change to their respective traditions, the Indian and the Chinese. Concerned as they were for the values of traditional culture they cared also about the fate of humanity and the world. Indeed, their writings about the modern age are distinguished for the way they reconciled patriotic sentiments with universalistic concerns. They were not of the same nation or generation although they were contemporaries, but they shared a humanist vision of the modern age that would de-center what they both recognized as a Western modernity (Webb 2008, 202)[1].

This chapter is confined to Tagore's two volumes of collected essays, *Creative Unity* and *Towards Universal Man*, and Qian's *Quiet Thoughts at the Lake*, that are representative of their ideas on the modern age (Qian 2001; Tagore 1922, 1961). These sources were self-consciously written in a nonsystematic style. Inspired by their ideas, the present study arranges them in an analytic order. Due to considerations of space this chapter leaves out the question of intellectual relations between the two.[2] The discussion moves between Tagore and Qian in accordance with the following three themes: the first section asks how they explain the cultural difference between India and China, on the one hand, and the West, on the other. The second discusses how a major characteristic of both Indian and Chinese culture—according to their view—the non-dichotomous perspective—converts the above mentioned differentiation into a qualitative cultural advantage possessed by the East. The third section then studies their criticism of the modern age.

TRACING CULTURAL DIFFERENCES TO ENVIRONMENTAL CONDITIONS

In their discussions of how to explain the cultural difference between India, in the case of Tagore, and China, in the case of Qian, from the so-called "West," both draw on environmental conditions and, especially in the case of the latter, on economic and social consequences of these conditions.[3] Hereafter, this pattern is referred to as the "environmental principle." Indeed, Tagore applies this principle to differentiate between cultures in general and not only those of the West and the East. Around 1922 he recalled a recent voyage to Europe when he sailed Northward across the Red Sea. On the left he saw the "gleaming sands of Egypt" and on the right the "red and barren rocks of Arabia." Associating his impressions of the landscape with cultural observations he commented that in the ancient culture of Egypt, the people avoided "the barrier of alienation" between themselves and other areas (Tagore 1922, 64). In Arabia, on the other hand, "man felt himself isolated in his hostile and bare surroundings" (Tagore 1922, 64). Tagore further concluded that the former assumed the spirit of harmony whereas the latter assumed the spirit of conquest (Tagore 1922, 64).[4]

The environmental principle, applies also in Tagore's differentiation between the West and the East. Positing those he calls "the Northmen of Europe" as the other of the Indian people, he associates the former's distinctive character with the nature of the sea. "The history of the Northmen of Europe is resonant with the music of the sea" (Tagore 1922, 46). "That sea," to him, "is not merely topographical in its significance, but represents certain ideals of life which still guide the history and inspire the creations of that race" (Tagore 1922, 46). From the various images suggested by the sea Tagore highlights what he considers as the tension along the shore between the water on the one hand, and the land and the people who live there, on the other. He further portrays the sea as a representation of an aspect of danger and as a barrier which apparently is in constant conflict with the shore and the people who live by it. To the Northerners of Europe the sea presented the challenge of untamed nature. Confronted with this challenge they developed "the spirit of fight. . . . They find delight in turning by force the antagonism of circumstances into obedience" (Tagore 1922, 46–47).

Unlike the Northerners of Europe, the men of Northern India posses the mind that favors unity rather than difference and tension:

> In the level tracts of Northern India men found no barrier between their lives and the grand life that permeates the universe (Tagore 1922, 47). . . . They could not think of other surroundings as separate or inimical. So the view of

> the truth, which these men found, did not make manifest the difference, but rather the unity of all things. (Tagore 1922, 46–47)

The environment has a major role in Qian's cultural differentiation as well. To him, the dissimilarities between Westerners and Chinese derive from fundamental differences in their natural environments and the resulting processes of production and commerce. The desert vagabonds and the seafarers in the Middle East and in Europe lived on trade, and their intensive life routines forced them to adopt a pattern of taking initiatives. Consequently, according to Qian, certain mental approaches developed. In the agricultural society of the Chinese plateaus, the affairs of life were slower, and there the call for taking initiatives was relatively reduced. Hence, the Chinese people developed what he calls a relaxed mentality. Humanity and peace prevailed over power and struggle (Qian 2001, 128).

> In China, environmental conditions, climate and natural resources, living conditions, and economic circumstances, tended to promote unity. Accordingly, the view of the world and the view of history encouraged the causes of humanism and peace. In the West, environmental conditions, climate and natural resources, living conditions, and economic circumstances, tended to promote separation. Accordingly, their view of the world and their view of history encouraged the use of power and struggle. (Qian 2001, 58)

Consequently, conditions in ancient China, on the one hand, did not call for much initiative, and, on the other hand, created a sense of unity and the attributes that Qian specified as humanism and conciliation.

Both Tagore and Qian ascribe to the culture of the West a tendency to create boundaries that separate the people from their surroundings and from each other.[5] The former discusses the people of the West in terms such as "antagonism of circumstances," "separate or inimical," and "difference." Inversely he associates the people of India with "unity." The latter posits "separation" against "unity." Then they associate these tendencies with cultural mentalities such as "the spirit of fight [conquest]," and "the use of power and struggle," as defining characteristics of the West. At the same time, "the level tracts of Northern India" and the Chinese environment, promoted a sense of "unity" and the spirit of harmony.

THE VIRTUES OF THE NON-DICHOTOMOUS PERSPECTIVE

Significantly, both Tagore and Qian assume a non-dichotomous approach that assigns a dichotomous approach to their cultural other. Contrastive environmental conditions in the West and unitary environmental conditions, in India, according to the former, and in China, according to the latter, correspond to the tendency in the West to dichotomize and to Indian and Chinese non-dichotomous perspectives.[6] Both avoid testing their assumption with regard to the environmental principle and its relation to specific cultural orientation in either their Chinese or Indian neighbors.[7] Indeed, the association between environmental conditions and cultural orientations says more about Tagore and Qian's internal motives for making comparative assumptions than about the accuracy of a state of affairs in fact.

To Tagore, a dichotomist perspective defines the people of the West:

> Truth appears to them [Europe's northerners] in their aspect of dualism, the perpetual conflict of good and evil, which has no reconciliation, which can only end in victory or defeat. (Tagore 1922, 47)

Antagonism of circumstances is apparently reflected in the people's thinking categories as seen in their differentiations between nature and themselves, evil and good, defeat and victory.

In another essay, "The Religion of the Poet," Tagore observes how in Western dramas Nature appears in her own right and only occasionally peeps out (Tagore 1922, 51). He uses William Shakespeare to illustrate "man's struggle with Nature and his longing to sever connection with Nature.[8] In Indian drama, on the other hand, "the hermitage shines out, in all our ancient literature, as the place where the chasm between man and the rest of creation has been bridged" (Tagore 1922, 50). The merits of the non-dichotomous perspective are obvious: "Not that India denied the superiority of man, but the test of that superiority lay, according to her [India], in the comprehensiveness of sympathy, not in the aloofness of absolute distinction" (Tagore 1922, 62).

Qian associates the dichotomist view with monotheist ideas about creation. To him, the major difference in the cultural orientations that developed in China and in the West can be traced to the tendency of the latter to use dichotomies and the tendency of the former to avoid dichotomizations. The following summarizes Qian's argument about the concept of Creation and the distinctive character of Chinese culture:

> The Chinese . . . held that the myriad things in the universe are one happening (*shi* 事), with no beginning and no conclusion, just one happening. What did they mean by "happening?" Chinese thought used for that purpose the word "motion" (*dong* 動). The myriad things in the universe . . . are nothing but motion. This motion could be portrayed as change (*yi* 易). Change is transformation in motion (*bianhua* 變化). As far as visible events and appearances are concerned, the myriad things, from beginning to end, are nothing but transformations in motion (*biandong* 變動), nothing but changes, [and] these transformations in motion harbor a dynamic (*youwei* 有爲). But this dynamic does not require anything to cause it (*wei er wei* 為而為), hence

> there was no necessity to articulate the idea of creation by God (*Shangdi* 上帝). Moreover, these transformations in motion apparently are not for any purpose (*wu suo wei er wei* 無所為而為). Therefore, Chinese thought disregards the question of the purpose (*mudi* 目的) of the world, the hope for the End of Days (*zhongji xiangwang* 終極嚮往), and the wish for attaining the final rest (*zhongji guisu* 終極歸宿). The argument goes that the beginning of the world is one motion, and the conclusion is, equally, the same one motion. This motion was also called change. These motions and changes are but one phenomenon. [Whether] there is or there is not an underlying original substance (*benti* 本體), this question did not occur to the Chinese (Qian 2001, 38–39).

According to Qian, Chinese thinkers view the divine, (*shen* 神)[9] and the human as one and the same sphere that is immanent and transcendent and has no other sphere beyond it.[10] To him, this view is characteristic of what essentially is Chinese in Chinese culture.

Both scholars' non-dichotomous approach is best tested in their evaluations of the doctrine that originated in India and eventually disseminated in China—Buddhism. In his essay "An Indian Folk Religion" Tagore contends with views of Western scholars who, according to his account, accuse Buddhism of overemphasizing moral concerns while neglecting the continuity of human life. In his words: ". . . coldly leading to the path of extinction." This argument possibly refers to the obstinate path that leads the Buddhist monk to the highest goal, that is, to cease transmigration by union with emptiness. Tagore thinks that these scholars are misled by an inaccurate image of the personality of the Buddha. He concedes that an element of infinity pervades the Buddhist doctrine, but an activist facet is rather emphasized: "The personality which stirs the human heart to its immense depth, leading it to impossible deeds of heroism, must in that process reveal to men the infinite which is in all humanity" (Tagore 1922, 69–71). Thereafter the course of his argument shifts to the Buddhist Mahāyana school, according to which the Buddha in his personality introduced "the utmost sacrifice of love."

> True emancipation from suffering, which is the inalienable condition of the limited life of the self, can never be attained by fleeing from it, but rather by changing its value in the realm of truth—the truth of the higher life of love. (Tagore 1922, 69–71)

Qian's discussion of Buddhism differentiates between the Indian and the Chinese versions of the doctrine and now history rather than environment is the determinative factor. "History," he says, "is different in different places and so is the life of men." Accordingly, "Confucius could not have been born in India and neither could the Buddha been born in China" (Qian 2001, 108). Qian's references to Indian Buddhism seem to resemble Tagore's "Western scholars." Indian Buddhists, who are pessimist and tragic, he argues, seek to leave the world (Qian 2001, 152). Elsewhere he elaborates on other differences between Confucians and Buddhists and, respectively, Chinese and Indians, stating that whereas Confucians prefer experience over assumption, Buddhists revert from experience to the pure and direct observation (Qian 2001, 82).

Yet there are common denominators as well, and, in accordance with Tagore, Qian associates these with the Mahāyana school. Just as Confucians say that everyone can become a Yao and a Shun,[11] Buddhists declare that everyone can become a Buddha. Furthermore, unlike monotheists, Confucians and Buddhists avoid godliness and advocate sageliness (Qian 1995).[12] This view is consistent with the non-dichotomous perspective, and, indeed, he insists, though somewhat problematically coalescing time and space, that the sagely era is different from the godly state (Qian 2001, 74–75). Again, like Tagore, Qian highlights the bodhisattva ideal, but unlike the former he stresses the Chinese role in the development of Buddhist this-worldliness (this-worldliness being synonymous with non-dochotomous perspectives and, inversely, other-worldliness being synonymous with dichotomist perspectives):

> When the Buddhist doctrine arrived in China it shed the idea of the liberation from this world. The idea of the bodhisattva accorded the social sageliness of the Chinese. . . . in China Buddhists sought a new sage [different from the one sought in India], one who leaves traces in the human realm, and this is the Sinification of the Buddhist doctrine (Qian 2001, 76).

To be sure, Qian does not claim Chinese origination of the idea of this-worldliness. He rather argues that the idea was prioritized by the Chinese to an extent unmatched by other cultures, the Indian culture included. Accordingly, while Tagore associates the non-dichotomous perspective as a virtue, mainly of Indian culture, and the dichotomous perspective as a source of cultural flaws, Qian, in addition, discusses the dichotomous and non-dochotomous distinction as a theoretical issue in its own right. This observation allows a glimpse into the different styles of the two scholars. Indeed, a reading of the sources examined in this chapter reveals that the former is impressionist in his style and strong on the aesthetic side, while the latter's arguments are explanatorily articulated. It is with this observation in mind that the title of this essay refers to Tagore as poet and Qian as historian.

CRITICISM OF THE MODERN AGE

The dichotomous and non-dichotomous differentiation permeates Tagore and Qian's criticism of Western modernity. Both avoid a definition of modernity but agree that the modern process is a development of recent centuries. Their idea of the modern is associated with the advancement of science, with the quest for wealth and power, crisis in religion, and the general acceleration in the pace of life (Qian 2001, 86–87).[13]

A major target of criticism is the quest for wealth and power and in several cases the tendency to associate aspects of this quest with religious patterns. Tagore singles out "money"—along with science, nationalism (Tagore 1922, 120),[14] and other forces, not mentioned by name—as having "some semblance of religion." Using terms that have medical and military associations, Tagore associates the "last fatal stages of decease [suffered by humanity in the modern age]" with the invasion of the "influence of money" into both the intelligence (brain) and the emotions (heart) of the body of humanity. The discussion of the "fatal influence of money" consists of the following five features: (1) its methods, which are softly sheathed like the claws of a tiger's paw; (2) its massacres, which are invincible but attack the very roots of life. (3) "Its plunder is ruthless behind a scientific system of screens, which have the formal appearance of being open and responsible for inquiries." (4) "By withstanding its stains it keeps its respectability unblemished." (5) "It makes a liberal use of falsehood in diplomacy, only feeling embarrassed when its evidence is disclosed by others of the trade." Furthermore, "An unscrupulous system of propaganda paves the way for widespread misrepresentation" (Tagore 1922, 121). A major characteristic of the fatal influence of money is the unseen quality of its activity / the way it avoids having its true nature exposed.

In yet another place Tagore observes how in the modern age the pursuit of power has become more comfortable due to man's "art of mitigating the obstructive forces that come from the higher region of his humanity." He refers to the "cult of power" and "idolatry of money" as, "in a great measure," a reversion to primitive barbarism, and adds that "barbarism is the simplicity of a superficial life. It may be bewildering in its surface adornments and complexities, but it lacks the ideal to impart to it the depth of moral responsibility" (Tagore 1922, 120–121).

The differentiation between the superficial life that appears on the surface and the truth of the experience recurs in Tagore's discussion of freedom. Alluding to the people of the West he argues how "They are flattered into believing that they are free, and they have the sovereign power in their hands." "But this power is robbed by hosts of self-seekers." What is enjoyed by the mob-mind, he writes, is merely "an apparent liberty," while "true freedom is curtailed on every side" (Tagore 1922, 134).[15]

Qian generally agrees with Tagore's criticism of facets of the modern process. The latter's differentiation between the surface and the deeper level, and between the apparent and the true, converges with the former's argument about the modern tendency to prioritize appearance (*yingxiang* 影像) over actuality (*shizhi* 實質). The difference being that Qian specifically associates this argument with the non-dochotomous perspective. He raises the temporal distinction between the future on the one hand, and the present and the past, on the other, too. In the case of his criticism of the modern age, both distinctions involve the prioritizing of former over latter. But what is the actuality of human life?

Tagore's answer to this question emphasizes spirituality:

> For, after all, man is a spiritual being, and not a mere living money-bag jumping from profit to profit, and breaking the backbone of human races in its financial leapfrog. (Tagore 1922, 107)

The two quotes that follow reveal his idea of what spirituality consists of:

> Men spend an immense amount of their time and resources . . . to prove that they are not a mere living catalogue of endless wants [that the instruments of our necessity assert that we must have food, shelter, clothes, comforts and convenience]; that there is in them an ideal of perfection, a sense of unity, which is a harmony between parts and a harmony with surroundings. (Tagore 1922, 4)

And,

> Our society exists to remind us, through its various voices, that the ultimate truth in man is not in his intellect or his possessions; it is in his illumination of mind, in his extension of sympathy across all barriers of caste and colour; in his recognition of the world, not merely as a storehouse of power, but as habitation of man's spirit, with its eternal music of beauty and its inner light of the divine presence. (Tagore 1922, 27)

Tagore's idea of a harmonious integration of the person with the whole is suggestive of major Confucian concerns that Qian firmly supported.

According to Qian, an understanding of the actuality of human life requires what he calls, a real purpose: "Without a purpose progress becomes wasted effort. Life without purpose is not real. Logically, progress is conditioned by the existence of a purpose" (Qian 2001, 113). Two pages later he writes that the human mind seeks both a purpose and content (Qian 2001, 115). What is that purpose? What is that content? The possibilities are various. "When art is the purpose, art is the authentic manifestation of life (*shengming zhi zhenshi* 生命之真實). When science is the purpose, science is the authentic manifestation of life" (Qian 2001, 113). As these examples demonstrate, Qian's foremost concern is neither with art nor with science. No matter what a person does, it must be a reflection of his innermost being, of his authentic self. All doing, therefore, presupposes honesty and integrity (Qian 2001, ch.21–22).

Qian declares that concern with mental and spiritual growth leads to the sense of contentment (*manzu* 滿足) which is the original and true purpose of cultural life. Culture, however, still contains remnants of earlier ways of life, when man was not yet fully human and survival was his major purpose. Unfortunately, the advanced purpose of contentment is contested by the earlier, less mature purpose, and is not necessarily triumphant. Man's advance toward contentment involved the realization of his power (*qiangli* 强力) of life,[16] which stimulated in him a sense of a celebration of life (*shengming zhi xiyue* 生命之喜悅) (Qian 2001, 114). Contentment was thus overshadowed by the sense of power. Whereas a person's original purpose was a search for contentment, in time, power—which originally served merely as a means—moved from the margins to the center of his attention and preoccupied him to the neglect of everything else.

When Qian writes "a celebration of life," we may assume this is a synonym for fetish, that for Freud was the worship of the superficial substitute in place of the real, and which, etymologically and practically, similarly refers to a sort of a celebration.[17] According to him, in modern times, the actual and real, the sense of contentment was gradually replaced by the outward appearance, the search for representations of progress by means of concrete and material achievements. The replacement or appearance was moreover celebrated as if it were the actual and the real. The distinction between the actual and appearance is based on realizing which of these belongs more directly to the human experience of life. According to Qian:

> [T]he celebration of life cannot take the place of contentment in life. Contentment is the actual (*shizhi* 實質), the celebration its outward appearance (*yingxiang* 影像). When contentment is realized, then the celebration of life is realized. But we should not confuse celebration with contentment. Unfortunately, the person who mistakenly substitutes the actual with its appearance, his life is no more than the search for power (Qian 2001, 114).

Hanging on to an aggressive mode of life, modern man repeats the pattern that characterized him at the immature stage of life. Recalling Tagore's earlier observations about "primitive barbarism," we observe yet another convergence in the two scholars' critical ideas about the modern age.

In Qian's discussion the point of how power is subsumed to life is made still clearer. According to him, power is mistaken for life itself, when in effect power is one thing and life another. To live, power is needed, but it must not become an end (Qian 2001, 114). The process of development that is modeled on the search for power and the forward striving pattern, diverted man from both the content and the purpose of life, and caused him to embark on a path of wasted effort: "Erroneously identifying power as life, man deviated from the straight path and [instead] considered wasted effort an attainment" (Qian 2001, 113).

Another convergence in the two scholars' critical ideas about the modern age becomes apparent in their claims that associate the increase in the pursuit of power with humanity's cultivated ignorance of higher values and ideals. The bad choice follows apparent goods that in actuality are of a low nature. In other words, the influence of money is fatal because it misleads humanity to seek the lower rather than the higher goal.

The tragic consequences of this pattern suggest yet another convergence. Mistaking power for life represents, according to Qian, a tragedy. In modern life man shifted attention from his own capacity to a celebration of his power. "Human beings long to experience authentic life, but they are captured by the image of the celebration of power (*qiangli zhi xiyue* 强力之喜悦)" (Qian 2001, 115). The tragedy of modern life consists in the gap between sincere human intentions and persistently pursuing, and falsely celebrating, a wrong path.

Tagore, too, and much earlier, accentuates [modern] man's tragic self-deception, seen in the way he is mislead to choose a path that leads to his own diminution:

> In fact, man has been able to make his pursuit of power easier today by his art of mitigating the obstructive forces that come from the higher region of his humanity. (Tagore 1922, 121)

CONCLUDING REMARKS

Both Tagore and Qian explain cultural differences between, respectively, India and China, on the one hand, and the West, on the other, as outcomes of environmental conditions, or what is called above, the environmental principle. Qian's differentiation between Indian and Chinese Buddhists that draws on a historic explanation introduces an exception that puts the whole environmental principle argument in doubt. Nonetheless, both assign a non-dichotomous perspective and, equally, this-worldliness, to their own culture and a dichotomous perspective and other-worldliness to the culture of the West and, respectively, to the modern age. Again, it is Qian who insists that this-worldliness is fundamental more to the Chinese than to the Indians. Their discussions of the modern age put forward the goals of spirituality, aesthetic qualities, in Tagore's case, and authenticity in Qian's. Both also agree on the purpose of humanist integration. In their criticism of what they identify as the quest for wealth and power both differentiated between the outside appearance and a "true" internal content of this quest. Both also associate the tendency to prioritize the former with deterioration to primitive patterns of living. Both, too, associate that fallacious priority with the tragic and self deceptive course of the modern age.

While both scholars do not oppose modern change, and their critical ideas are meant as contributions to that process, neither conceals his disappointment with regard to modern characteristics of the culture of the West. Tagore mentions the disappointment of "[P]eople in the East," and assigns the following question to their thoughts: "Is this frightfully overgrown power really great? It can bruise us from without, but can it add to our wealth of spirit? It can sign peace treaties, but can it give peace?" (Tagore 1922, 107) Writing in 1948, Qian, too, points to the cultural weakness of the West. Alluding to events associated with World War II he observes that the call to assist the Westerners who go in what he calls "the useless and meaningless road," is obvious (Qian 2001, 8).[18]

To be sure, the sense of disappointment with the culture of the West suggested to both, as it did to others, the essential importance of involving Indian and Chinese patterns and ideas in modern change. Tagore writes that "In the midst of much that is discouraging in the present state of the world, there is one symptom of vital importance. Asia is awakening" (Tagore 1922, 169). Similarly, writing in 1951, Qian expresses his firm optimistic confidence with regard to the future of China (Qian 2005). Probably recalling WWI Tagore admits that the world of his time is offered to the West but, "She will destroy it, if she does not use it for a great creation of man." A simplistic material—spiritual differentiation, not to say dichotomy, directs his view of who is to contribute what and the order of priority. Science is needed, and yet, the creative genius is in man's spiritual ideal (Tagore 1922, 99). Qian adopts a similar stance when he concludes his *HSXSL* with the following:

> Today in China the Western natural sciences are thriving, but the most urgent task in front of us is to exhaust that which has been ours for a long time and to establish a spiritual [humanist] science. For we cannot overlook our obligation to repay the people of the West with a present in return (Qian 2001, 152).

We need to consider, however, that in his view about how to affect change, Qian followed the pattern of self-cultivation or human attainment exemplified in the classical Confucian (*Rujia* 儒家) text of the *Daxue* (大學, *The Great Learning*). There, the process involves eight levels, beginning with the individual person and proceeding to the broader interpersonal frame of the family and on to the realms of the kingdom and the world.[19] The idea is that a certain degree of agreement needs to be reached among transmitters of the Way (*Dao*) before their contribution extends within the intellectual scene and then further to the West and all over the world. Accordingly, Qian viewed the reform of China as a precondition for the reform of the world. The same principle applies in Tagore's writings when he calls on the Indian people to build up their own before they "are in a position to face other world cultures, or co-operate with them" (Tagore 1961, 220).

How shall we evaluate Tagore and Qian's criticism of the modern age? Recently, Adam K. Webb observed:

> In any case, the countermodern moment did fail. The forces of modernity, whether liberal or socialist in flavor, continued gaining ground, especially after the dust from World War II had settled. The régimes that emerged in Pakistan, India, and China by midcentury affirmed their independence from the West but committed to playing much the same game. If anything, those régimes stepped up the assault on the high-culture traditions that had inspired Iqbal, Tagore, and Liang. The social changes of the last few decades have made the whole outlook of these thinkers seem quaint and quixotic. The social base for such critiques of modernity has also largely vanished with broader shifts in the composition of educated strata. Cultural leveling and a concentration of power in the technocracy have proceeded apace. (Webb 2008, 211)

Indeed, there can never be a return to the days of the twentieth century, but the synthesis of the non-dichotomous view, the pursuit of the spiritual, and the way Tagore and Qian reconciled patriotism and universalism, are relevant today as they were when the two scholars first promoted them. From my point of view, claims for values never fail. In the short run they may be overshadowed by contemporary concerns, but in the long run they do have their impact. Viewed from a broader, process perspective, "countermodern" scholars such as Tagore and Qian were a necessary step along the way of confronting modernity and modern change.

NOTES

1. Recently, Webb (2008, 202) observed that scholars such as Tagore, and Qian's contemporary and friend, Liang Shuming (1893–1988), in their writings addressed "what they saw as a soulless global social order, in the name of higher spiritual and cultural principles."

2. Suffice it to say that relations were one sided as Qian was familiar with Tagore's ideas. When Tagore lectured in Shanghai in April and May 1924, Qian was teaching in the nearby 3rd Normal School of Jiangsu Province and it is possible that he attended some of Tagore's lectures. For Tagore's lecture tour of China see Das 2005. Qian mentions Tagore (Taige'er 太戈爾) in his writings and in 1975 he reviewed the Chinese translation of the latter's *Nationalism*.

3. The association of environment and culture can be traced to G. W. F. Hegel (1770–1831).

4. Tagore carefully adds: "And both of these have their truth and purpose in human existence."

5. Both referred to their own nationality (that is Indian or Chinese) but also to the people of Asia (in Qian's case, *dongfangren* 東方人). They differed in that Tagore used "Asian" much more than Qian. See the discussion of their views on "how to affect change" in the concluding remarks.

6. Tagore compares India with the West just as Qian concerns himself with comparing China and the West. Both, however, sporadically refer to their nationalities as representative of the East.

7. Qian invoked "history" to distinguish Chinese Buddhism from its Indian sources. See discussion below.

8. But Tagore (1922, 60–61) also expresses his reservation with regard to Shakespeare: "I hope it is needless for me to say that these observations . . . show in his works the gulf between Nature and human nature owing to the tradition of his race and time."

9. In chapter 17 of the *HSXSL shen* 神 is identified as non-human, transcendent, absolute, all encompassing, and as creator of all beings and things. Since the traditional Chinese view is above all non-anthropomorphic, *shen* is translated as the divine rather than God.

10. A critical examination will show that exceptions to this view were heard both in China and in the West. See Yu 1987, 12.

11. Yao and Shun are two legendary rulers exemplified as model personalities in the Chinese tradition.

12. Qian (1995) presents a concise discussion of Buddhism and its affinities with Chinese thought.

13. Tagore's agreement with these attributes of the modern is demonstrated in the following.

14. There he refers to "nation" as "[the] worship and the idealizing of organized selfishness."

15. For Qian on freedom see Isay 2009, 425–437, esp. 433.

16. The use of the term "power" reminds one of Nietzsche's Will to Power.

17. Fetish, originally a theological term referred to a confusion of substituting the end with the means, or, for instance, God with His material images. With Marx and Freud this term became part of the criticism of modernity in the West.

18. Like Tagore, Qian in several places refers to "the people of the East" (*dongfangren* 東方人). See one case in Qian 2001, 107.

19. The terminology used here draws heavily on Plaks 2003, see especially page 58.

BIBLIOGRAPHY

Das, Sisir Kumar. 2005. "The Controversial Guest; Tagore in China." In *India and China in the Colonial World*, edited by Thampi Madhavi (Delhi: Social Science Press), 85–125.

Isay, Gad C. 2009. "A Humanist Synthesis of Memory, Language, and Emotions; A Philosophical Reading of Qian Mu's *Quiet Thoughts at the Lake*." *Dao: A Journal of Comparative Philosophy* 8.4: 425–437.

Plaks, Andrew H. trans. and annotator. 2003. *Ta Hsüeh and Chung Yung (The Highest Order of Cultivation and On the Practice of the Mean)*. London: Penguin Books.

Qian Mu 錢穆. 1995. *Zhongguo Sixiangshi* 中國思想史 (*A history of Chinese thought*). Taipei: Xuesheng shuju.

———. 2001. *Hushang Xiansilu* 湖上閒思綠 (*Quiet thoughts at the lake*). Taipei: Lantai Chubanshe.

———.2005. "Zhongguo wenhua yu guoyun" 中國文化與國運 (Chinese culture and the fate of the nation). *Sixiang yu Geming* 思想與革命 1 (Jan. 1951). In Han Fuzhi 韓復智, *Qian Mu Xiansheng Xueshu Nianpu* 錢穆先生學術年譜 (*A chronological record of Qian Mu's writings*), vol. 4. Taipei: Wunan tushu Chuban Gongsi.

Tagore, Rabindranath. 1917. *Nationalism*. New York: MacMillan.

———. 1922. *Creative Unity*. New York: MacMillan.

———. 1961. *Towards Universal Man*. New York: Asia Publishing House.

Webb, Adam K., 2008. "The Countermodern Moment: A World-Historical Perspective on the Thought of Rabindranath Tagore, Muhammad Iqbal, and Liang Shuming." *Journal of World History* 19.2: 189–212.

Yu Yingshi 余英時. 1987. *Zhongguo Sixiang Chuantong de Xiandai Quanshi* 中國思想傳統的 現代詮釋 (*A Modern Interpretation of Traditional Chinese Thought*). Taipei: Lianjing.

Index

About the Contributors

Friederike Assandri has studied sinology and indology at the University of Heidelberg. She is a research associate at the Center for East Asian Studies, the University of Heidelberg, and at the Center for the Study of Chinese Characters, East China Normal University, Shanghai. Her research focuses on the interaction of Buddhism and Daoism in early medieval China.

Joshua Capitanio is assistant professor of religious studies at the University of the West in Rosemead, CA. His research focuses on the connections between Buddhism and Daoism in medieval China.

Tim Connolly is associate professor of philosophy at East Stroudsburg University, PA. His research interests include ancient Greek philosophy, early Confucianism, and comparative philosophy. His essays have appeared in the *Journal of Chinese Philosophy, Dao: A Journal of Comparative Philosophy,* and *Teaching Philosophy*. His book *Doing Philosophy Comparatively* is forthcoming in 2014.

Nicholas F. Gier is professor emeritus of philosophy at the University of Idaho. He has written three books on comparative philosophy and religion: *Wittgenstein and Phenomneology* (1980); *Spiritual Titanism* (2000); and *The Virtue of Non-Violence: From Gautama to Gandhi* (2004). He is currently writing a book on "The Origins of Religious Violence: An Asian Perspective."

Yong Huang is professor of philosophy at the Chinese University of Hong Kong. He is the editor of *Dao: A Journal of Comparative Philosophy* and *Dao Companions to Chinese Philosophy*. His research interests include ethics, political philosophy, and Chinese and comparative philosophy. He is the author of seven books (three in Chinese, four in English) and about sixty articles each in Chinese and English.

Gad C. Isay is chair of the Department of East Asian Studies in Telhai College. His areas of study include East-West intellectual relations, Chinese intellectual history, and questions of memory and religiosity. He has published several articles on Qian Mu's thought, and recently published *The View of Life in Modern Chinese Thought* (2013).

Ram Nath Jha holds a PhD in Sanskrit, and is assistant professor at the Special Centre for Sanskrit Studies, Jawaharlal Nehru University, New Delhi. He specializes in Vedānta, Sāṃkhya-Yoga, Navyanyāya and comparative philosophy. He is the author of *A Reader in Indian Philosophy: Sāṃkhyadarśana* (English and Hindi).

Sophia Katz holds a PhD in East Asian studies from the Hebrew University of Jerusalem (2009). Her academic interests include different aspects of Chinese intellectual history, philosophy, literature, and religion. Her research is focused on Song-Ming Confucian thought, with an emphasis on religious and theological dimensions of Confucianism.

Livia Kohn is professor emerita of religion and East Asian studies at Boston University. The author or editor of over thirty books as well as numerous articles and reviews, her specialty is the study of the Daoist religion and Chinese longevity practices. She has served on numerous committees and editorial boards, and organized a series of major international conferences on Daoism. She now lives in Florida, serves as the executive editor of the *Journal of Daoist Studies*, and runs various workshops and conferences.

Bill M. Mak completed his linguistic training at McGill University and received his PhD from Peking University, specializing in Sanskrit and Buddhist literature. Subsequently, he had conducted Buddhological and Indological research at the Asien-Afrika-Institut, Hamburg University, and Kyoto University. Currently, he is visiting assistant professor at the University of Hong Kong. His academic interests include Sanskrit linguistics, Buddhist philology, and Indian astronomy (*jyotiṣa*).

Alexus McLeod is assistant professor of philosophy at the University of Dayton, OH. His main areas of specialization are early Chinese philosophy (pre-Qin through Eastern Han), ethics, and comparative philosophy, but he is also working in areas such as Indian philosophy (especially Vedānta and early Buddhism) and metaphysics.

Carl Olson is professor of religious studies at Allegheny College, PA. Besides numerous essays in journals, books and encyclopedias, his latest books include the following: *The Many Colors of Hinduism: A Thematic-Historical Introduction* (2007); *Celibacy and Religious Traditions* (2007); *Historical Dictionary of Buddhism* (2009); *Religious Studies: The Key Concepts* (2011); and *The Allure of Decadent Thinking: Religious Studies and the Challenge of Postmodernism* (2013).

Ithamar Theodor is a scholar of Hinduism. A graduate of the Theology Faculty, University of Oxford, and a life member of Clare Hall, University of Cambridge, he is lecturer at the University of Haifa and adjunct assistant professor at the Chinese University of Hong Kong. His publications include the award winning book *Exploring the* Bhagavad Gītā*: Philosophy, Structure and Meaning* (2010).

John M. Thompson is associate professor of philosophy and religious studies at Christopher Newport University, VA. He has broad interests in Asian cultures and religions, and has authored *Understanding Prajñā: Sengzhao's 'Wild Words' and the Search for Wisdom* (2008), and *Buddhism*, Volume Three in the *Student's Guide to World Religions*, edited by Lee Bailey (2006).

Guang Xing received his PhD from School of Oriental and African Studies, the University of London. He is assistant professor at the Centre of Buddhist Studies, the University of Hong Kong. His publications include *The Concept of the Buddha: Its Evolution from Early Buddhism to the Trikāya Theory* (2005) and *The Historical Buddha* (2005). He is currently working on two monographs: "Filial Piety in Chinese Buddhism" and "Buddhism and Chinese Culture."

Zhihua Yao is associate professor of philosophy at the Chinese University of Hong Kong. His research interests cover Buddhist philosophy, Indian philosophy, and philosophy of religion. His publications include *The Buddhist Theory of Self-Cognition* (2005) and various journal articles in *Journal of Indian Philosophy, Philosophy East and West, Journal of Chinese Philosophy, Journal of Buddhist Studies*, and *Comparative Philosophy*.

Wei Zhang is professor of philosophy at University of South Florida, Tampa, FL. Her present research includes the translation and critical study of the "Seven Chapters of the Inner Classic," the classical medical canon of the traditional Chinese medicine, forthcoming. She has written two books on continental and comparative philosophy.